Earl
Hooker

Sebastian Danchin

University Press of Mississippi
Jackson

Earl Hooker

BLUES MASTER

www.upress.state.ms.us

Copyright © 2001 by Sebastian Danchin
All rights reserved
Manufactured in the United States of America

09 08 07 06 05 04 03 02 01   4 3 2 1
♾

Library of Congress Cataloging-in-Publication Data
Danchin, Sebastian.
Earl Hooker, blues master / Sebastian Danchin.
p.   cm.—(American made music series)
Includes bibliographical references (p.), discography (p.), and index.
ISBN 1-57806-306-X (cloth : alk. paper)—
ISBN 1-57806-307-8 (paper : alk. paper)
1. Hooker, Earl, 1929–1970. 2. Blues musicians—United States—
Bibliography. I. Title. II. Series.
ML419.H65 D36   2001
787.87'1643'092—dc21
[B]   00-044913

British Library Cataloging-in-Publication Data available

In memory of my mentor, Sim Copans;
my friend, Bernard Nicod;
and my brother, Hilaire

Contents

Acknowledgments

For their continuing help throughout this project, I would like to express my sincere gratitude to the late Georges Adins; Murray Allen, Universal Recording Corporation; Jean-Pierre Arniac; Paul Asbell; Ben H. Ashley; Cary Baker; Alan Balfour; Ralph Bass; Bruce Bastin; the Blues Archive at Oxford, Mississippi; Fritz Svacina and the late Franziska Svacina at *Blues Life*; Howard Colson and Neil Gillis at BMI; Bruce Bromberg; Alfred E. Buscher, Warden, Vandalia Correctional Center; Sid Graves and Margaret Littlepage, Carnegie Public Library and Delta Blues Museum in Clarksdale, Mississippi; Emmanuel Choisnel; Madelaine Cooke; Bill Daniels; Jimmy Dawkins; Jim DeKoster; Jacques Demêtre; Burrell Denton; the late Jean-Paul Dethorey; Willie Dixon; Les Fancourt; Suzanne Flandreau-Steele; Arvel A. and Johnny D. Furr, Tribune Show Print; Galen Gart, Big Nickel Publications; Steve Gronda; D. T. Hargraves Jr. and his wife, Roseann; Gérard Herzhaft; Norbert Hess; Cilla Huggins; Michel Huth; Judy Pennel and Michael Baker, Jackson/Madison County Library, Jackson, Tennessee; the late Carl Jones; Keri Leigh; Willy Leiser;

Phyllis J. Lilley, Public Library, Belle Glade, Florida; Tommy Löfgren, *Jefferson* magazine; Peter B. Lowry; Fritz Marschall; Edward Michel; Kurt Mohr; Deborah Anna Beroff, Museum of the Great Plains, Lawton, Oklahoma; the late Jack Myers; Little Bobby Neely; Paul Oliver; Jim O'Neal; Johnny Otis; Sonny & Pepina Payne; Jacques Périn, *Soul Bag* magazine; Powerhouse Pete; Sam Phillips; Bob Pruter; Juhani Ritvanen; Michel Rose; Michel Ruppli; Robert Sacré; John A. Singleton; Neil Slaven; the late Franz Renard Smith; Arbee Stidham; Chris Strachwitz; Bez Turner; Claude Van Raefelgem; Amy Van Singel; Professor Douglas L. Wilson, Seymour Library, Knox College, Illinois.

My thanks also go to Hooker's friends and associates, in Chicago and elsewhere, for their generous sharing of memories.

For their hospitality and warmth through the years, I wish to thank Steve Berger; Milton and Pat Campbell; Bruce Iglauer; Jim & Nancy Kirchstein; Jane "Charly" Kolokathis; Snapper Mitchum; Bertha Nickerson-Chism; and Bert "Top Hat" Robinson.

A special mention should be made of Craig Gill (senior editor), Anne Stascavage, Walter Biggins, and Steven Yates at the University Press of Mississippi; of John Kane, for his fine and patient copyediting; and of David Evans, my editor, who must have used up a couple of red-ink pens correcting my bad punctuation; on a more serious level, his interest and knowledge on the subject have been a source of enlightenment.

But most of all, I feel indebted to my dear friend Dick Shurman for his unfailing support and encouragement, as he unhesitatingly took time and pains to answer never-ending lists of questions, providing me with tapes of rare recordings whenever necessary, and believing in this book from the start. None of this would have been possible without him.

—S. D.

Introduction

As it clearly comes back to my mind, the scene could be taken from Frederick Wiseman's *Public Housing*, a fine documentary on everyday life on Chicago's South Side: the building at 5127 South Prairie Avenue, two blocks west of Washington Park, once was the home of an affluent WASP family before this area—one of the most fashionable in the city at the end of the nineteenth century—progressively merged into Chicago's Black Belt during the twenties. On this late September afternoon of 1978, walking past a glass door next to the mail boxes at the bottom of the stairs, I ascend to the second floor, the sound of my climb muffled by worn-out carpeting. At the landing, the door on my right is fort-knoxed by not one but two iron grids like the ones generally used to safeguard storefronts. I start wondering if I'll manage to get my hand through to knock on the door when I see a doorbell. A buzz, silence, the sound of shuffling feet, more silence, and a voice through the door: "Who is that?" "Mrs. Hooker? . . . I called you up on the phone yesterday. I wanted to talk about your son, Earl Hooker." Without a word, the voice unlocks the door, pulling it open about an inch, and I can see two eyes scrutinizing me.

In the padded silence of this quiet residential building, I can hear children laughing outside on their way back from school, the only way for me to know that time hasn't stopped completely. The eyes brush me over a couple of times; whatever they spied must have been reassuring enough, for they widen into a face as the door opens halfway and the voice asks me to wait. Removing the three heavy padlocks that fasten the irons bars and sliding both grids to the side takes about a minute, and I am invited to come in with a warm smile. A couple more minutes to put everything back in place and lock the door, and my dignified, smiling hostess is leading me to a stuffy living room. Judging from the pictures and posters of Earl Hooker everywhere in sight, I know I have come to the right address. "So you're the man from overseas," Mrs. Hooker says appreciatively. "But you're almost a boy! And you seem to know so much about my Earl. . . . It's so nice of you to come and visit me, but you got to tell me this. Why is it you wanna write a book about my boy?"

Of course, I expected Mrs. Hooker's query. Indeed why would a twenty-one-year-old Frenchman want to write the life story of such an obscure Chicago artist? Hooker's status as a musician's musician surely isn't enough to account for my interest in him, although his playing struck me quite early as virtuosic and moving. My earliest memory of Hooker's music goes back to 1969, when I heard played on the radio the "Wah Wah Blues" he recorded for Arhoolie, before the announcer said it was the latest record by Earl Hooker, "the man who invented the wah-wah pedal." During the years that followed, I made it a point to acquire all of the albums of this amazing guitar wizard at the same time as my knowledge of the blues became more consistent. Listening to records and reading the works of pioneers such as Paul Oliver, Sam Charters, and David Evans soon wasn't enough, and in the fall of 1975 I became friends with Eddie Boyd, an expatriate bluesman living in Finland.

Boyd told me quite a bit about his past, the Delta, and the Chicago scene—all things quite abstract to me at the time—and Earl Hooker's name, always related to colorful anecdotes, cropped up frequently in the conversation. At Boyd's instance, I made the trip to the Windy City the following year, becoming acquainted with several of his friends, Willie Dixon, Jump Jackson, and Jimmy Conley among others. Earl clearly was not the only character the various people I met talked about, yet six years after his death he seemed to be very much present in the collective memory of the Chicago blues milieu.

The impression was confirmed in 1977 when I started traveling (and playing) with Son Seals and his band, which included A. C. Reed at the time. Earl's example was used so often in relation to subjects essential to blues musicians—remembering life on the road, telling tall tales, making fun of others and having fun with women, or simply playing the guitar—that I became somehow convinced that Hooker was the epitome of the modern itinerant bluesman. Given the extent of his reputation and influence, Hooker could truly be considered a "ghetto hero," and as such, his life story deserved telling. It was my intention to spend some time in the American blues world, and researching every phase of his eventful existence would provide me with a unique way to familiarize myself with this milieu, describing in the process a widely romanticized but globally unknown musical and cultural "underground."

When Mrs. Hooker asked why I had in mind to write a book about her son, she should have asked me *how* I intended to do it. After several months of active research into the literature, I knew that if Hooker's name was sometimes mentioned in the scant blues press available at the time (*Living Blues* in the United States, *Blues Unlimited* in Great Britain, *Jefferson* in Scandinavia, *Soul Bag* in France), in a handful of album liner notes and in even rarer book releases, Earl had died without being properly interviewed. His entire life story would thus have to be reconstructed through an "oral history" methodology already used by previous writers for prewar artists such as Peetie Wheatstraw and Tommy Johnson. In these pioneering biographies, the songs recorded by these early blues artists had been quite helpful because they gave useful indications as to the musicians' vision of the world, but no help of this sort could be expected in the case of Hooker, who was essentially an instrumentalist. As for Chris Albertson and his excellent biography of Bessie Smith, his work had undeniably been made easier by the fact that his subject was a widely recognized "star," a status Earl never achieved by far. To complicate matters even more, Hooker had never stopped traveling throughout the United States ever since his teens, and potential informants were scattered around the country.

Being a musician allowed me to overcome these obstacles as it gave me access to information only an "insider"— "one of the family," as Junior Wells once told me—could hope to get. Strangely enough, the fact that I was a foreigner proved helpful since I didn't belong to any known category of the American society and was myself a "minority"; unlike Caucasian Americans with an interest in blues music, most of whom drove back to their suburban homes or North Side apartments when ghetto clubs closed their doors, I was living on the South Side with friends such as Little Milton and Pat Campbell, bassist Snapper Mitchum or drummer Top Hat Robinson, staying at one point at the infamous housing projects, the Robert Taylor Homes. In very little time, my face became familiar to people like Junior Wells, Big Moose Walker, or Andrew Odom, whose never-ending stories about Hooker eventually provided me with a wealth of questions when formal interviews were set up. As a general rule, having had the occasion to question many artists formally at the end of a concert or in hotel rooms, I can say it makes a lot of difference when interviewer and interviewee are frequent collaborators whose conversations happen to be recorded at leisure.

After months of active guitar playing and concomitant researching, Earl Hooker's story began to shape up, much in the way a photographic print slowly becomes visible in the developing tray. Born in Mississippi in 1929 and raised in the black ghetto of Chicago where his parents settled in 1930, he became from the late forties the most creative and virtuosic electric blues guitarist of his generation. A favorite of black club and neighborhood bar audiences in the Midwest and a seasoned entertainer in the rural states of the Deep South, Hooker spent more than twenty-five years of his short existence burning up U.S. highways, making brilliant appearances wherever he played, yet choosing never to settle down in a lasting way.

Afflicted with tuberculosis from a very early age, he died in 1970 on the verge of major success and international recognition. Until the preceding year, Earl's music had been available exclusively on singles marketed by small independent labels; if his production was not scant, the limited distribution of his records made them available only to ghetto dwellers and southern black populations. The situation changed in the last few months of his life, when Earl's following expanded dramatically as a result of the growing interest of young Whites in blues, and the related blues album boom.

His death brought an end to his waxing popularity, and soon, only his peers remained to tell about his talent. Listening to them, I noted contradictions and inconsistencies at times that I decided to expose as such every time they couldn't be accounted for. Dates especially were a problem, most people having a fluctuating memory when it comes to specific years or months; in such cases, I would use my judgment, cross-checking events ("was that before or after the assassination of Dr. King?") and making deductions.

The unveiled respect that Hooker's virtuosity never failed to arouse in the most noted representatives of his musical genre accounts for the laudatory comments that never failed to come up when Earl's name was mentioned. According to Dick Shurman—a respected producer and critic—Hooker was constantly used as an example even during his lifetime. As an illustration, Shurman described the typical way harmonicist-singer Big John Wrencher, on his way to record for producer George Paulus during the summer of 1969, eulogized Hooker: "When Paulus and I picked up Wrencher to do his album for Barrelhouse, Wrencher says, 'Last night, I saw the greatest slide player of all times. Guess who it was?' I said, 'Earl Hooker,' and he said, 'Yeah, that's him.' That was such a typical thing; everybody was just like that about him. He was very respected by his peers."

The tendency of witnesses to make lavish use of superlatives when describing Hooker's musical creativity turned out to be a major inconvenience, for I couldn't run the risk of breeding the skepticism of readers; at the same time, downplaying spontaneous comments was often difficult if I didn't want to betray reality. Such was the case with vocalist Lee "Shot" Williams—a Hooker alumnus who made his singing debuts in Earl's band of 1962—when he recalled the way B. B. King once gave in publicly to Hooker's unmatched talent: "He was between T-Bone [Walker, and] B. B. [King], but really and truthfully, you wanna hear the truth? And it's bad to say this. Earl would outplay those people. We went to see B. B. in Gary [Indiana], me and Earl Hooker. B. B. said, 'Ladies and Gentlemen, my friend Earl Hooker's in the house.' They said, 'Bring him up!' B. B. said, 'No way,' he said, "cause this man, I can't hold up to this man.' I'm serious, this man could play a guitar like you never heard before."

Lee "Shot" Williams's testimony, in its apparent excessiveness, could pass for highly exaggerated if B. B. King himself hadn't confirmed it recurrently. In an interview published by *Guitar Player* magazine in 1975, King even placed Hooker at the top of his personal list of favorite guitarists: "To me he is the greatest. He always KNEW exactly what he was doing. For instance, take a truck driver (I used to drive trucks, too)—you tell him to park next to the curb,

and he knows exactly where to put the rig. That's how Earl Hooker played. . . .
Robert Nighthawk was Earl's teacher. . . . I was influenced somewhat by
Robert, but only by his slide work. Earl Hooker, though, could get me both
ways."[1] When time came to put pen to paper in the mid-eighties after ten years
of research, the portrait of Earl Hooker drawn here was patched together from
oral elements for the most part collected directly from Earl's peers, friends, and
relatives. Unless otherwise noted, all quotations in this book are taken from interviews I conducted from 1975, the complete list of which appears at the beginning of the bibliography. Clearly, my intention was to give an account of the
everyday life of a cultural milieu through the existence of one of its prominent
members, someone who could be regarded as emblematic of the characteristic
traits of his community. Sociologist Charles Keil, one of the first who foresaw
the close relationship binding popular African American culture to its musicians, wrote in 1966: "On the basis of my own limited research into lower-class
life, I would [suggest] that the hustler . . . and the entertainer are ideal types
representing two important value orientations for the lower-class Negro and
need not be distinguished from the lower class as a whole. Both the hustler and
the entertainer are seen as men who are clever and talented enough to be fi-
nancially well off without working. . . . If we are ever to understand what urban
Negro culture is all about, we had best view entertainers and hustlers as culture
heroes—integral parts of the whole—rather than as deviants or shadow figures."[2]

According to Keil's recommendations, I have tried to document the culture
of the ghetto through the example of a central character—such as it is retained
in the collective memory of his environment—thus describing the cultural experience on which is based the more or less spontaneous elaboration of vocal
blues. In this respect, the choice of Earl Hooker was a relevant one; insofar as
Hooker never was a lyric writer and consistently showed disinterest in his vocal repertoire, there was no risk of studying his perception of ghetto life
through his texts. More than a singer, Hooker was a brilliant guitarist who crystallized in his person the unstable existence of a road-addicted urban bluesman:
in the same way he dominated his fellow bluesmen with an unequaled instrumental virtuosity, Hooker brought to a paroxysm the qualities and defects of
his peers.

Earl Hooker's life may tell us a lot about his milieu; it also tells us a great deal about the blues. Being involved in a central moment of the history of that music—specifically the development of electric ensemble blues in the South and in Chicago in the two decades following World War II—the main aspects of this historical phase are presented here. As I gave an in-depth picture of the lifestyle of a characteristic itinerant musician, I tried to account for the social and psychological forces that shaped the lives and careers of most blues artists of Hooker's era.

The reader may now start reading this biography, knowing that it should be apprehended in the historical context of Hooker's music, cultural environment, and time. The late Junior Wells, Earl's childhood friend, will introduce this story with both dignity and emotion by saying, "Earl, as far as I'm concerned, as long as his music is alive, he is alive, and it's an honor to even speak about him because he was such a tremendous guitar player. Earl Hooker was one of the greatest guitar players that I ever heard in my life. He made a lot of guitar players sit down, he made a lot of guitar players listen to him, he made a lot of guitar players understand what it meant to have soul for what you wanna do. As of today, you got a lot of good and great guitar players, but I would like for everyone to know about a young man, he couldn't read, he couldn't write, but his music says it all."

—*Sebastian Danchin*

Earl Hooker

The Early Years

(1929–1946)

The life of Earl Hooker—like that of many mythical figures—
is filled with the historical inconsistencies that both plague
the historian and help build up true legends. In Hooker's case,
problems start early with the very date and location of his birth.
Hooker himself claimed to various inquirers (including Arhoolie
Records producer Chris Strachwitz, blues historian Paul Oliver,
and nurse Wilma Hart at Chicago's Municipal Sanitarium, where
he died) that he was born in Clarksdale, Mississippi, on January
15, 1930, a statement that has never been challenged since. The
guitarist's grave marker, however, cites his year of birth as 1929, a
date supported by his obituary, which gave the location as Quitman County, a rural area neighboring the eastern border of
Clarksdale's Coahoma County. Confronted with a difficulty of
that sort, a biographer's most reliable source of information would
no doubt be a birth certificate; unfortunately, it was impossible to
trace one for Hooker in Mississippi, confirming Chris Albertson's
opinion when he wrote in his fine biography of Bessie Smith,

"Southern bureaucracy made little distinction between its black population and its dogs; such official records as a birth certificate were not always considered necessary."[1]

This cannot be simply viewed as a romantic exaggeration; in the very year Earl was born, sociologist Charles S. Johnson was making a survey of 612 African American families in a rural Alabama county, and he wrote in his subsequent study, *Shadow of the Plantation*, "The county health officer [does not] know what proportion of the total [number of births] was registered. There is some evidence that the number of Negro births registered is less than the actual number of births."[2] In the absence of official documents, Earl's own mother, Mary Blair Hooker, was the most likely informant, and she vividly recalled giving birth to her eldest son on January 15, 1929. In order to test her memory, she was asked similar questions (including the birth date of her daughter Christine, for whom a birth certificate was found in Chicago) and she systematically provided the right answers, tending to indicate that her memory could be trusted.

Whereas Earl's mother certainly remembered the circumstances of his coming into the world better than he did, the fact that Hooker chose to give 1930 as his date of birth is indeed surprising. In the blues community, musicians sometimes try to pass themselves off as younger than they actually are as a kind of ostentatious mannerism, but had this been so in Hooker's case, it would have made more sense to opt for a later date. Considering his rather eccentric and carefree nature, a likely explanation would be that a round figure like thirty simply appealed to him for purely arithmetic reasons when it came to figuring his own age. In much the same way, citing Clarksdale (the main cotton center in the northern part of the Delta) as his place of birth might have been a way for Earl to place himself on the map when he reconstructed his life story for interviewers. At any rate, official records did exist at this time, but the Clarksdale city directories list no Hooker until 1936, and the 1920 U.S. census cites only one black Hooker family (George, wife Gussie, and daughter Carrie) living in Coahoma County; on the contrary, the same census listing for Quitman County shows that Earl Hooker (Earl's father), age twelve, was the fourth of eight children born to Mary and Jefferson Hooker, a tenant farmer.

By the end of the decade, Earl Sr. was old enough to start his own family, and he married a sixteen-year-old neighbor named Mary Blair, who soon gave him a son, as she recalls: "In my family, it was eighteen of us. We got preachers, all of 'em is preachers. I was livin' on a farm then where my parents were raisin' cotton, outside of Clarksdale; it was a great big place in Quitman County, Mississippi, a few miles away from Clarksdale in the country. Earl was born exactly the fifteenth of January, 1929. I called him Earl Zebedee Hooker." Earl shared his date of birth with civil rights leader Martin Luther King Jr., born on the very same Tuesday of January 1929 in Atlanta, Georgia, less than four hundred miles east of Quitman County.

Unlike King, whose family belonged to the urban black bourgeoisie—W. E. B. Du Bois's celebrated "talented tenth"—Earl belonged to the South's rural lumpenproletariat. His very early days were spent on the farm tended by the Blair family in the vicinity of Vance, in the heart of the Delta. This area had—and still boasts—a large black population, most of which was scattered around small rural towns that hardly numbered more than a hundred souls. Only three centers in the Delta held larger populations—Greenville, Greenwood, and Clarksdale, the latter being the smallest of the three with some 10,000 citizens, but also the closest to the Blairs' farm. Earl's maternal grandfather was a sharecropper on one of the cotton plantations to be found all around the Mississippi Delta, working under what the Georgia Baptist Convention labeled "debt-slavery" shortly after World War I.[3] Sharecroppers then lived with their families in rough wooden shacks along dusty roads under a harsh, paternalistic system that had undergone few changes since the Civil War and the emancipation of black field hands. Against the loan of a shotgun house and several acres of land, the sharecropper was contracted to a landowner for whom he grew and picked cotton. At the end of the growing season, the crop was divided between them, and deductions were made for cash advances and "furnishings"; when the accounts were settled, many cotton-raising families ended up in debt, thus becoming chained to "the man" and having to start over again the following year.

"There was nothing unusual about 1929; it was an ordinary year," writes Lerone Bennett Jr. in *Before the Mayflower*. "Babies were born and old men died. Funeral services for John Lisle, a Civil War veteran, were held at Charles Jackson's funeral home on the South Side of Chicago. . . . In October there was a new Louis Armstrong record, 'When You're Smiling.' The Gay Crowd let their hair down at a series of parties celebrating the October 26 football game between Tuskegee and Wilberforce. That same weekend the Harlem night club season went into high gear with the opening of the new revue at Smalls Paradise. Sunday came and Monday and Tuesday—and the bubble burst with the collapse of the stock market."[4] In the perspective of time, 1929 stands out in the eventful period that bridged the two world wars mainly because of the financial crash that rocked Wall Street on that black October Thursday. But the economy of the rural mid-South had not waited for that final blow to collapse; ever since the end of the Great War, prices had consistently slumped, reaching an all-time low in the last year of the decade. Due to the increasing competition of artificial fibers, the value of King Cotton dwindled, and farmers saw their incomes slump by over 30 percent between 1919 and 1929. As a consequence, the migratory movements that developed during the teens were growing more important each year. Between 1916 and 1940, it is estimated that more than two million African Americans left Dixie to settle in large northern industrial cities like Detroit, Cincinnati, Pittsburgh or Chicago. In the latter, the black population more than doubled during the decade, from 109,458 in 1920 to 233,903 ten years later. For the year 1930 only, 80,000 black migrants decided to leave the southern states in the hope of finding more lucrative jobs in the north. Among the black families that deserted Mississippi and rolled up the Illinois Central railroad line into Chicago's imposing Central Station that year were the Hookers. Probably because the prospect of becoming another dirt-poor tenant farmer didn't appeal to Earl Sr., Earl's parents decided not to stay on the plantation, possibly coaxed by the engaging descriptions of the life in the North that could be found in Robert Abbott's *Chicago Defender*.

Earl J. and Mary Hooker first arrived in Chicago by themselves, temporarily leaving one-year-old Earl with the Blairs in Mississippi because they realized that it would be more difficult for them to settle there with a baby. Within a few weeks, they had found a place to stay on the West Side, quickly learning about bustling city life, high rents, and Chicago's terribly cold winters. "When we started out we lived on the West Side, 1037 West 14th Street!" Mary Hooker says. "I was so upset about this house, you see. It was somethin' I didn't like. I don't think it was right. You'd be surprised. . . . But I stayed at 1037 West 14th Street for quite a long time."

Those who are familiar with Chicago's layout know that the city's black districts are mostly concentrated today on the West and South Sides, two clearly distinct areas offering their own particular features, and both of which have enhanced their own specific brand of blues music. Although Earl Hooker was later to become somewhat more of a South Side man, his first few years in Chicago were spent in Jewtown, a part of the near West Side extending from Halsted in the east to Sangamon and Morgan in the west, along Maxwell and 14th Streets.

Throughout the Depression, a constant stream of black families filtered into the old West Side ghetto to escape the high rents of the tiny "kitchenette" apartments found in the South Side black belt. Recent migrants from the southern states often made it their first stop when they came to town. More sophisticated black Chicagoans generally looked down on the West Side, where Italians, Mexicans, and poorer Jews dwelled along with Blacks in dilapidated buildings. There the educational level of the black population was the lowest. In the West Side of the Depression years, most African American families either found their income through WPA programs or received direct relief from the city. At the intersection of 12th and Halsted Streets, close to the Hookers' home, one could find the West Side "slave market," an infamous street corner where a large number of black women congregated every morning, hiring themselves out as domestics by the day to the highest bidder, waiting for affluent white housewives to drive by in their limousines.

Jewtown was a harsh neighborhood, yet an animated one. This was especially true during the weekend. Whereas the ground-floor stores of most of the brick-and-frame buildings bordering Maxwell Street—a busy east–west thoroughfare—operated in a normal way during the week, on Sundays the sidewalks of Jewtown would gradually fill up with stands and pushcarts as the street suddenly turned into something like an oriental bazaar. The Maxwell Street Market—as it was known to all until it was the victim of urban renewal in the 1990s—was launched by Jewish immigrants at the end of the nineteenth century. On Sundays, everything could be peddled and bought at the market, from southern spices and country goods noisily advertised by strong-voiced criers to stolen watches, firearms, and narcotics pushed by furtive dealers. Blues music brought a colored touch to Maxwell Street Market's loud atmosphere. Jewtown sidewalks were the main source of musical activity for newly arrived southerners, and a rather lucrative one indeed, according to the statement of slide guitarist Hound Dog Taylor, who started performing there on a regular basis upon his arrival in the Windy City in 1940: "You used to get out on Maxwell Street on a Sunday morning and pick you out a good spot, babe. Dammit, we'd make more money than I ever looked at. Sometimes a hundred dollars, a hundred twenty dollars. Put you out a tub, you know, and put a pasteboard in there, like a newspaper. When somebody throw a quarter or a nickel in there, can't no-body hear it. Otherwise, somebody come by, take the tub and cut out. I'm telling you, Jewtown was jumpin' like a champ, jumpin' like mad on Sunday morning."[5]

The neighborhood around Maxwell Street also stood out as the roughest area in town, according to police statistics. As such, "Bloody Maxwell" cer-tainly was not to the liking of Mrs. Hooker. After a few months, her mother had come up from Mississippi with young Earl, and Mary Hooker had imagined living with her family in a more appropriate setting. Yet the housing shortage was such that Earl's parents couldn't afford to move to more comfortable prem-ises, and the Hookers' grim financial reality did not improve for the better with the arrival during the Depression of Christine Hooker, nicknamed Earline, who was born at the Cook County Hospital on Friday March 23, 1934, at 4:25 in the afternoon: "See, I had four children with my husband, two boys and two girls, and Earl was the oldest one. Earline was the next one. Then I had another girl, but of course she is dead. You see, two of my children's dead."[6]

The promising prospects that led the Hookers to settle in Chicago four years earlier had finally given place to disillusion; unemployment was soaring, and it was common knowledge in the ghetto that Blacks were the last hired and the first fired. For want of a paying job, Mary Hooker tended to domestic chores, and the city records show that her husband—like one out of every four black males in the nation at the time—was on relief when Earl's sister was born. Things brightened up when the Hookers left their dilapidated 14th Street apartment toward the mid-thirties to move to a more acceptable building lo-cated in the heart of the South Side, in the basement of 3139 South Park Boulevard, a busy thoroughfare later renamed Martin Luther King Jr. Drive.

According to an often verified cliché, the musical sensitivity of black chil-dren is usually aroused in church, but it wasn't the case with Earl. His mother was more interested in the Saturday nightclub scene than in the Sunday morn-ing worship service, and it seems that he was exposed to secular music quite early, since both his parents were capable dancers. His father also displayed some proficiency on several musical instruments, and Earl listened extensively to music at home from a very early age. Another influential factor might be the presence in the family of John Lee Hooker, who went on to become a world-famous bluesman and the living symbol of guitar boogie music. "Johnny Lee Hooker, that's our cousin, so Earl had known him since he was very young. He met him in Chicago," Mrs. Hooker says. "He's some relation to us on my husband's side." Mary and John Lee Hooker could not be more specific as to the nature of the latter's kinship with Earl Sr., and the Mississippi census data were of no help in this respect. In any case, John Lee was about ten years older than Earl,[7] and he was raised on a farm between Clarksdale and Vance before making the move up north in the late thirties. Established in Cincinnati at first, he probably met his young cousin around that time when he visited his relatives in Chicago.

By the time Earl turned ten in 1939, his father realized that Chicago was not the northern paradise he had dreamed of, and he left a wife and two young children in the Windy City before eventually winding up in Kansas City, where the Hookers had relatives. "After that I never married no more, although I could have remarried, you know, a couple times. My husband is dead now. He's been dead about five years. I didn't know that he was dead myself, and I just got the news in Arkansas," Mrs. Hooker said in 1978. Approximately around the time his parents separated, Earl decided to take up an instrument and fixed his choice upon the guitar, a popular instrument he had seen both his father and his cousin John Lee use. The purchase of a guitar was no small investment for a humble home like the Hookers', and Earl ordered his first instrument from the Sears and Roebuck Company, with a one-dollar down payment and fifty-cent weekly installments.

Earl was going to school then, attending successively Douglass Elementary School, at 3200 South Calumet—one short block west of his mother's South Park apartment—and Doolittle School, located at 535 East 35th Street, just east of Park. Both were overcrowded institutions mainly staffed by white teachers, most of whom resented being assigned to black schools. At the time, the limited number of schools in Chicago's South Side compelled principals to set up two shifts in order to satisfy local needs—one from eight until noon, and a second until four. Compared to the educational facilities available to black children in the South, Douglass and Doolittle were heavens, but teachers were too busy taking care of studious pupils to give proper attention to someone like

Earl, who proved refractory to all forms of training; his capacities for reading and writing actually were the only learning he derived from his school days. His interest for music was growing as fast as his strong distaste for education, and most of his time was spent with other boys who could play the guitar like him: his best childhood friend Vincent Duling as well as young Ellas McDaniel, another guitarist and singer who later became known as Bo Diddley, a nickname earned as a child. Another Doolittle Elementary student that Earl probably ran into at one time or another was future gospel, soul, and pop star Sam Cooke.

With Vincent and Bo in tow, Earl would often skip school to hang out with street gangs in the vicinity of 35th Street, to the despair of Mrs. Hooker, who tried her best at providing her son with a decent education: "Douglass School, it was a school for bad boys, 'cause I had a pretty rough time with him in school. He just didn't want to go to stay in that school; it was just that music! I went to see the teachers there, and they said, 'Mother, there's some good in that boy, that boy's got all kinds of talents.' But he just wouldn't learn, wouldn't do nothin' but that music, it kept me so worried."

Singer and harmonica player Billy Boy Arnold, who later became friends with Earl and Bo Diddley, makes a good description of those days: "I know Hooker used to play around 31st on the streets and Bo Diddley played around the streets so they knew each other. Hooker told me once how he used to skip school. His mother'd think that he'd be going to school, but he'd be hiding in the closet with his guitar, and when she came home in the evening, he'd still be in the closet playing his guitar." "He spent a lot of time doing that," Dick Shurman, a friend of Hooker's in the latter years, confirms. "They say his mother had to pass his food into the closet 'cause he'd stay there all day. I guess he'd do that just for privacy, just a place to go to and keep others out of, just you and the guitar against the world, I can see that." Hooker playing the guitar in a closet, filling it up with sound, possibly for acoustic reasons. Hooker and his guitar against the world, a pattern that would more or less remain the same until the end.

Earl's best friend, Vincent Duling, was slightly younger than he was, being born in Chicago on September 2, 1931. By 1942 Earl and Vincent were proficient enough on their instruments to play for tips on the streets, and they rode the public transportation across town every weekend to perform at the

Maxwell Street Market in Jewtown. Bo Diddley sometimes joined them on the sidewalks of 31st or 35th Streets—two busy east–west South Side thorough-fares—unless they met at 4746 Langley Avenue, where Bo lived at the time. Soon Bo had his own street corner outfit that he called the Hipsters before changing to the even hipper Langley Avenue Jive Cats: "Earl Hooker was the one that got me interested in playin' on the street corners with a band, because he had one an' I saw they were makin' all these nice coins, so I said: 'Hey!' Earl and me, we was in the same classroom at school. I used to hang around Earl a lot. We ditched school together, we'd get caught by the truant officer."[8]

Earl Hooker and his friends practically lived on the streets, playing music, busting windows, and drinking cheap wine. On the streets, Earl met most of his childhood chums, some of whom later became musical associates or partners on a professional level, like guitar player Louis Myers who was to remain one of his closest friends until the end: "Now how I met Earl Hooker it was like in a little gang fight. . . . And I know Hooker he was running around with a little street gang then, and I never did know he played guitar, they jumped us one time on 35th Street and the next time I saw Hooker, he was on the street play-ing guitar. And now he could play, he was around my age bracket. . . . When I saw him that kinda made me wanna come on out and play on the street too, but I never did 'cause see I was always shut in by my peoples or the religion on my auntie's side. . . . Wasn't no use, my auntie didn't allow me to play . . . in the house so I quit and picked it back up especially when I saw Hooker. . . . Hooker was a terrible young guitar player."[9]

For street-smart ghetto boys like Earl Hooker, Vincent Duling, Bo Diddley, or Louis Myers, music was an essential component of their lives. It was present on the sidewalks; in the neighborhood bars and taverns in front of which they sometimes hung around for hours, trying to sneak in; and, of course, in church, a source of inspiration that proved widely influential in the case of Bo Diddley. By the time they reached their teens, they had all resolved to become profes-sional musicians, a decision they stuck to. While Bo Diddley later grew into a member of a black rock 'n' roll triumvirate alongside Little Richard and Chuck Berry, Louis Myers achieved international fame as leader of a widely acclaimed Chicago blues unit known as the Aces. Only Vincent Duling remained in rel-ative obscurity, although his instrumental virtuosity earned him the respect and admiration of many of his peers; after working quite extensively on the

Chicago scene, Duling crisscrossed the southern states during the fifties with the outfit of multi-instrumentalist Dennis Binder—even making a handful of recordings for the Memphis-based Sun company—before he eventually settled in Oklahoma with Binder.

A factor of importance was the tremendous influence records and radio stations had on the black community. Even the poorest homes proudly exhibited a radio and a phonograph, as Drake and Cayton show in their sociological study of black Chicago, Black Metropolis, where they give the following description of a typical West Side home in the mid-forties: "The furnishings of this home are those of very poor people, but everything is clean and in order. The only new article in the living-room is a modern portable Zenith radio. Other furnishings include a large old-fashioned stove, a day-bed, three chairs, a trunk with a clean towel spread over it, a Victrola [phonograph], and a table."[10]

The blues were Earl Hooker's own favorites from the very beginning. By the time he took up the guitar, country-tinged blues sounds were becoming outdated as electrically amplified instruments gradually replaced acoustic ones. One of the very first blues guitar players to start using an electric instrument was Texas-born Aaron "T-Bone" Walker, who settled in California in the mid-thirties, where he perfected his style at about the same time as jazz guitar pioneers Eddie Durham and Charlie Christian. For a few months in 1942, T-Bone Walker had his name up in lights at the front of Chicago's Rhumboogie Club, a Garfield Boulevard venue. Managed by Charlie Glenn with financial backing provided by heavyweight champion Joe Louis, the Rhumboogie featured Walker's show for a three-month run. Walker was an immediate hit with Chicago club-goers, who lined the sidewalks of Garfield Boulevard night after night to catch one of his flamboyant shows and see him doing splits without missing a lick, playing the guitar behind his head or picking it with his teeth. At the end of his nightly set at the Rhumboogie, T-Bone rarely failed to make the rounds of after-hours spots on the South and West Sides, sitting in with local musicians, paying special attention to his younger fans, so that he had a considerable impact on upcoming blues guitarists, as Billy Boy Arnold explains: "Hooker really liked T-Bone 'cause T-Bone was the top guitar player before B. B. King was on the scene. So Hooker being a guitar player and playing in that style, he listened to T-Bone."

The new dimension T-Bone Walker introduced into his playing, the genuinely modern aspect of his swing-influenced blues records, appealed to Hooker more than anything else. Walker's style actually helped shape Earl's guitar playing in more than one respect. Even in the latter part of his life, Hooker showed a great debt to T-Bone in the intricate chordwork he showcased in his playing and in the jazzy way he would sometimes run the blues scales, but a more obvious and direct influence can be traced in Hooker's stage dynamics; Earl, in the purest T-Bone-style, would play his guitar behind his neck or pick it with his teeth, putting on the type of show his Texas master was well known for.

The influence of T-Bone apparently stopped there, for Earl never tried to emulate the mellow singing style of his idol, nor did he seem to have a strong inclination for singing as a general rule. This may seem strange, since Earl's favorite musical idiom, the blues, is an essentially vocal genre, but the young boy's lack of interest for singing can easily be accounted for; Earl was afflicted by birth with a speech impediment that somehow cooled off his interest in singing. The problem itself may have had its origin in the Hooker family, as Earl's cousin, John Lee Hooker, also suffered from a pronounced tendency to stammer. Although worthy vocalists, including John Lee Hooker himself or harmonica wizard John Lee "Sonny Boy" Williamson, overcame their handicap and made successful careers, Earl's stutter enhanced his need to express himself through his instrument. "Oh yeah! He stuttered! They say he used to stutter real bad when he was a kid," Kansas City Red, a drummer and singer who was a close Hooker associate in the late forties and early fifties, recounts. "But it look like to me he would stutter more when he's gettin' funny or somethin', you know, then he always put that 'M-m-m-man,' just like that." Characteristically, Earl started playing with his stutter quite early, calling his friends and associates according to a recurrent pattern. In addition to the quite common "man," Earl constantly addressed women with stammered "g-g-grandma" while his fellow men would indifferently be "g-g-grandpa," "b-b-bossman," or "c-c-cousin."

Other than blues, Earl was particularly keen on country music, the hillbilly style of southern Whites. Chicago became a major center for country music quite early, due to its recording activity and the popularity of WLS station's *National Barn Dance*, broadcast regularly since 1924. One of Earl's favorite radio shows was the one hosted on WLS by country music star Gene Autry, who moved to Hollywood in the mid-thirties to make a brilliant career on the screen as a popular "singing cowboy." Since radio stations were owned exclusively by white operators in the United States until the end of the forties, the tastes of white listeners always prevailed, and programs aimed at the black audience were only allowed very restricted airplay, as Jimmy Johnson, a Mississippi blues singer and guitarist, explains: "I guess I grew up on country & western, 'cause that's all you would hear on the radio. When I was a kid growing up, I can't remember exactly if it was every day through the week or just one day, but it was fifteen minutes, there would be a blues program come on. But now the rest of it was C&W all over the radio."[11]

The fact that black people can easily relate to hillbilly music is quite natural, considering that blues and country music are two sides of the same regional cultural coin. The constant musical exchanges that took place between Blacks and poor Whites in the South illustrate the strong musical bonds that linked both communities, explaining that the very essence of black music can be traced in the playing of the white country artists Earl Hooker admired: Ernest Tubb, Red Foley, Bob Wills, Hank Williams, Merle Travis, and above all Roy Rogers and Gene Autry, whom Hooker later recalled watching as a youth.

There are even stories in Chicago that Earl's first fan was no less than Gene Autry himself. "Louis Myers told me that when Hooker was something like eight years old, that he was already well known, and that Gene Autry went to Hooker's mother and asked her if he could take Hooker and like sort of adopt him, teach him how to play guitar and use him on the show, but Mrs. Hooker wouldn't let him take her kid away from her, which is possible, because I do know that he was well known pretty young," says Dick Shurman. "Who knows?" Shurman adds laconically. Regardless of the fact that this anecdote is most certainly apocryphal, since Autry left Chicago around 1934, it clearly shows the legends Earl generated throughout his life.

Biographical notes printed on the covers of several of Hooker's albums[12] mention that Earl was formally taught at the Lyon & Healy School of Music in Chicago. These allegations were strongly denied by all of Hooker's friends. Hooker himself gloried in his lack of musical education, and his associates confirmed that he couldn't read notes and picked up by ear the guitar parts he would hear on records or the radio. Earl was a self-taught musician, but he benefitted nevertheless from the expert advice of a limited number of people who helped him when he first started out, showing him licks and teaching him basic guitar chords. Among such informal teachers were the Blevins brothers, whom Earl met as he was playing on the sidewalks and street corners around 35th Street.

Leo and Kinky Blevins were slightly older than Earl, and it was Leo who seems to have taught Earl much of the chording technique he himself inherited from T-Bone Walker at the time of his 1942 stint at the Rhumboogie. In her fine biography of the great Texas guitarist, Helen Oakley Dance writes that "Leo Blevins was a teenage guitarist who never let T-Bone out of his sight except at night when he fronted a small group of schoolmates who carried their horns over to Maxwell Street looking for a place to stay. T-Bone never acted big-time, especially with kids, and not being secretive the way musicians are, he let Leo in on some of his tricks. At the Rhumboogie, he sneaked the boys into his dressing room so they could hear the band stretch out."[13]

The confidence Walker placed in Leo Blevins was not betrayed, as the young man eventually turned into a much sought-after session man whose inspired playing was featured on various recordings by tenor saxophonist Tom Archia, vocalist Andrew Tibbs, or great bebop sax man Gene Ammons. Along with brother Kinky, Leo Blevins acquired a fine reputation in jazz-blues combos on the Chicago club scene of the forties and fifties before he eventually moved west to California toward the mid-sixties. Leo occasionally returned to the Windy City on various occasions, such as the time in the late seventies when he performed at Roberts' 500 Room with singer Jimmy Witherspoon.

Mrs. Hooker clearly remembered Kinky Blevins as one of her son's friends, also recalling that the young Muddy Waters, who made the move to the Windy City from Mississippi during the war and who would later grow into the patriarch of postwar Chicago blues, also gave Earl informal guitar lessons: "Muddy Waters learned him quite a bit when he was very young, 'cause they used to hang around a lot together." Earl apparently kept fond memories of those days, according to his friend Billy Boy Arnold: "Hooker must have been fifteen, sixteen or something, and he was already playing good, because Earl Hooker told me that Muddy Waters used to come to his house and ask his mother could he play with him in the clubs, and his mother said, 'Okay,' as long as Muddy was looking after him."

15   *The Early Years (1929–1946)*

It was not in the clubs but on the sidewalks of Bronzeville—as the South Side ghetto was known then—that Earl Hooker met his mentor and main source of influence, Robert Nighthawk. A mythical figure and a living personification of rambling Mississippi Delta musicians, Nighthawk was born Robert Lee McCollum in the town of Helena, Arkansas, in 1909, twenty years before Earl. McCollum apparently had no intention of becoming a guitarist as a youth; a competent harmonica player, he only took up the guitar in his early twenties after meeting a Mississippi player named Houston Stackhouse, who gave him friendly guitar lessons. Turning his newly acquired proficiency to account, McCollum wandered through the southern states, traveling from Arkansas to Mississippi, Tennessee, and Florida. He was eventually compelled to leave the South after running into some trouble there, and he moved north to St. Louis. It is likely that Missouri was not safe enough, however, for he finally wound up in Chicago, where he changed identity to evade legal authorities, assuming his mother's maiden name and becoming known as Robert Lee McCoy. Under his matronymic, he recorded several sides for the RCA-Victor subsidiary label Bluebird and gained some renown with a song called "Prowling Nighthawk," waxed in 1937.

As he went on with his peregrinations, Robert realized that people remembered his song better than they did his name, and he started calling himself Robert "Nighthawk," using this new surname as a visiting card from then on. After the outbreak of World War II, Robert Nighthawk decided to move back to the South and established himself in his hometown of Helena, Arkansas, where he played the bars and gambling joints, advertising his band through various radio broadcasts sponsored by Helena commercial companies. Whenever his longing for the road got the better of him, Nighthawk worked his way up to Chicago and played around the city for a while before he decided that the climate was much warmer and nicer in Arkansas.

It was during one of Nighthawk's trips to the Windy City that Earl Hooker met him for the first time in the early forties. "Thirty-fifth Street, that's the street where he met Robert Nighthawk," Earl's mother stated when Nighthawk's name was mentioned. "Now Earl was already playin' some before, he learned by hisself, but Robert taught him. And he used to go with Robert Nighthawk to play too." Nighthawk had more bearing on the Chicago blues scene than has often been thought, notably because he was one of the first in

Chicago to switch to electric guitar in the early forties, following the example set earlier by T-Bone Walker, Memphis Minnie, Big Bill Broonzy, Tampa Red, and the very versatile George Barnes.

Even though he originally started out in the thirties with a straight acoustic instrument, Nighthawk had perfected an electric slide guitar style that strongly bore his stamp by the time he met Earl Hooker. Slide guitar, or bottleneck style, calls for the use of specific open tunings; instead of using his bare fingers, the guitarist slides a cut-off bottleneck or steel tube across the strings of his instrument, in Hawaiian fashion. Nighthawk's own slide technique, inspired to a large extent by that of a widely influential Chicago musician, Tampa Red, was rather unique because of its truly amazing clearness and smoothness; instead of sliding his bottleneck across the width of the guitar neck like most country players, Nighthawk played single-note staccato runs; combined with the novelty of his electrically amplified guitar styling, it gave him a tremendously appealing and blue sound that was widely imitated by Delta-born players, including Muddy Waters and Elmore James.

Yet it was Earl who became Robert Nighthawk's best imitator, no doubt because he was taught by the master himself. Nighthawk, a rarely smiling and taciturn person, took a liking for Earl and painstakingly showed his young student runs on the fretboard of the guitar, teaching him how to play in "E Natural" (open E), "D Natural" (open D) and Spanish (open G) tunings, slowly shaping up Earl's super-light guitar touch. Nighthawk's influence didn't stop there, for he also trained the young man vocally. Like Earl in this respect, Nighthawk did not have a great voice as such, but he used it with taste, and it suited perfectly the slow blues he sang in a deep, solemn, heavy and almost gloomy way. Nighthawk apparently ended up bequeathing Earl more than his musical ability, for Hooker also inherited some of Nighthawk's traits of character, acquiring the restlessness and carefree ways of his mentor.

Earl's highly unstable nature emerged early in his life, and he frequently ran away from home, leaving his mother and sister behind worrying; it was not without a certain amount of retrospective fear and emotion that Earl's mother recalled the most spectacular escapade of her son, who broke away from home for nearly two years when he was thirteen and stayed in Arkansas with white people who had given him shelter: "One day the bad boy just ran off, he just thought that he was a man. I went to every house on Michigan [Avenue],

17   *The Early Years (1929–1946)*

called the police and everythin'. Then after a couple of years I heard someone say that he'd seen him down in Arkansas. Then I went to Arkansas and he was stayin' there with some hillbillies on a boat. He tried to hide 'cause he thought that I was gonna whoop him, see. And I whooped him. I don't know who slipped him out. I believe Robert Nighthawk would have asked me before. I don't know whether he went alone and I don't know how he went, he never told me yet how he got over there.

"After that, I couldn't tell you how many times he went away. Like I went to this house in Florida and this woman had bought my boy amplifiers, and she had bought him guitars, and she had bought him everythin'; I never was so mad in my life! I said, 'What is this all about?!' so she said, 'You're Earl Hooker's mother?' and I said, 'Yes, I'm Earl Hooker's mother,' she said, 'I thought Earl didn't have no Mama!' I never was so mad in my life. He had told the woman his mother was dead. I couldn't blame the woman, 'cause you never know what kinda lie the boy told her. He was just like that."

Earl's recurrent trips away from home inevitably led him to the southern states and more specifically to the Delta, where he could feed his restless desire to play music. The Delta was familiar ground for Hooker, who still numbered quite a few relatives in the Clarksdale area, some of whom could provide him with food and shelter in case of need. Although her son's conduct certainly was not to Mrs. Hooker's liking, experience taught her to accept it, since nothing could contain Earl's love for the guitar.

The only thing that compelled the teenager to come home was the illness that plagued most of his life and that was to lead to his early demise. It isn't known precisely when Earl became afflicted with tuberculosis, but his earliest associates remember him being sick from a very young age. It is likely that he caught TB early, particularly since the ghetto slum apartments where the Hooker family spent their first few years in Chicago were especially unhealthy. Dampness, want of proper food and heat, and the utter lack of hygiene in Chicago's dilapidated tenements possibly took their toll then. A U.S. Public Health Report published in 1944 shows that for the period 1939–41 the tuberculosis death rate for Blacks in Chicago was more than five times that of Whites,[14] a situation that lasted into the sixties. But Hooker could also have caught TB during one of his Delta escapades, since the problem was just as crucial in the South. In 1938, the National Anti-Tuberculosis Association even produced a short film titled *Let My People Live* in which black movie star Rex Ingram sensitized African Americans to the ravages of the disease in rural communities.

Despite the fact that Earl's condition did not become critical until the mid-fifties, it drove him to the hospital at regular intervals. One of his very first so-called professional engagements was brought to an abrupt end that way after young Hooker spent several months touring Mississippi joints with the Lee Kizart band. "That's a long time ago, 'round about '43 if I'm not wrong in that," pianist Joe Willie "Pinetop" Perkins remembers. "Yeah, Earl used to play with us, me and some other boys down in Mississippi, a little place out there called Tutwiler. He's around thirteen years old then. He was livin' up here in Chicago, but he had some peoples in the South, and he'd come down to visit them. And so we got together and made a little band up, and me and him and Lee Kizart played a long while together. Where we played, they didn't know how old he was. All they wanted to do was hear the music, and he really could play it. He was active. He'd jump around like with his guitar behind his back, doing turn-flips and stuff; he learned that fast, that little. He just picked it up, he's gifted, he was the baddest guitar player around Chicago. So after a while his mother came down and got him, because he had taken sick, and she had to put him in a hospital, he had TB. And then he stayed there for a while, and he'd run off and come back, and he used to come out and tell the boys, 'I'm well, I'm ready to play, now!' Then after a while he'd get sick and had to go back."

In between hospital stays and trips to the Delta, Earl spent most of his time playing on the streets and trying to hustle club engagements in Chicago. It was around that time that he met young Amos Wells Blakemore, just arrived from Memphis, Tennessee, with his mother. The future Junior Wells already had a good voice, and he was blowing a cheap harmonica well enough to gather forces with Hooker, starting a long friendship that was to last over several decades. From their initial encounter, Hooker's strong charisma impressed Junior, who recalled years later the self-assurance and determination that guided Earl's career from the very start: "I met Earl Hooker way back years ago in the forties. And he had an old piano player called A. C., so Earl told A. C., he say—you know how he stuttered and things like that—he say, 'I-I-I-I want you to hear Junior, 'cause Junior and me we gonna make a lot of money.' You could feel what he had inside of him. He didn't wanna just be a person that just

19   *The Early Years (1929–1946)*

played in Chicago, he wanted to be like the other big artisses that was playin' around the country and things like this. Now this is what he was pushin'. He's always been an ambitious person, you know what I mean. He told us, he say, 'Well, we gonna make some big money.' So here we go, out on the road, followin' him, little biddy things, runnin' away from school and everythin', doin' our thing."

Since his street friends were too young to take to the road seriously on a lasting basis, Hooker devised other ways of keeping his street band busy around the Chicago area. On week days, streetcars provided them with a lucrative way of performing their music away from windswept sidewalks. "At that time, I was about ten years old," Junior Wells reminisces. "We'd be standin' on the corner, the police would ask us, say, 'What you all waitin' on?' and Hooker say, 'W-w-we on our w-w-w-way to school!' At that time, they had streetcars in Chicago, and we used to be standin' on the corner, cold, nose runnin' and everythin', waitin' on the streetcar to come along. We used to get on one streetcar and ride it to the end of the line, collectin' money with the hat. Ride that one to the end, get off, get on another line, ride it 'til the end, all across Chicago, and we was makin' pretty good money. I was dancin', and we had another boy—I can't remember his name right now . . . Rob! And he used to play, not a bass but it was a washtub with a rope and a mop handle. And then we did some things on the West Side in Jewtown, and at that time, so many peoples was comin' over to shop and everythin' like that, and we used to knock down about $350 on Sundays. We's makin' far much more than an average musician at that time was makin' playin' in a club; he go to the regular gig, and the regular gig is payin' only $8. And so we was doin' real good."

In addition to money, the market area made it possible for youngsters like Earl or Junior to make friends. On the teeming sidewalks of Maxwell and 14th Streets, they met musicians such as Floyd Jones, Otis "Big Smokey" Smothers and his brother Abe, Homer Wilson, or John Brim—who remained a close friend of Earl's over the year and who also sang for nickels and dimes on every market day. During the week, Hooker hustled jobs whenever he could, especially in the vicinity of 35th Street, where he knew just about everyone. One of his first jobs saw him playing his guitar with a piano player (possibly the A. C. mentioned by Junior Wells) and Vincent Duling on a flat-bed truck, advertising a local vegetable dealer named Red. It was also during the war years that

Earl got to know the owners of a large hotel located on Michigan Avenue, who took a liking for him: "They were the nicest peoples I ever met in my life," Mrs. Hooker says. "This white fellow had a colored boy working in the hotel, it was right around 33rd and Michigan, and he brought Earl to the hotel and that's probably how it happened. He gave Earl that nice guitar and a violin. They didn't have no children; they just about adopted him. Earl was playin' in the streets, and this man, he went with Earl on the streets. Just to be more with Earl." This story, as well as the fact that he could run away from home and find foster parents and a shelter with extravagant ease, tend to show that, regardless of his unruliness, Earl Hooker was an engaging, attractive, and extrovert teenager whose strong charisma appealed to the people he met. These characteristics were also noted by those who knew the man Earl grew into; Dick Shurman and producer Ed Michel both described him as an incredibly gentle, warm, and physically harmless, though highly unpredictable, adult.

Earl tried to find good-paying jobs at night in taverns and neighborhood clubs as soon as he looked old enough to be admitted there, and he eventually wound up on the North Side at one point with guitarist Lee Cooper, a man who established a reputation for himself in the forties and fifties when he played and recorded with the likes of Eddie Boyd of "Five Long Years" fame and harmonicists Big Walter Horton and John Lee "Sonny Boy" Williamson. In order to get more work, Earl Hooker used to hang around the places where older and more established bluesmen performed. In spite of his young age, his boldness and natural talent often made it possible for him to sit in with some of the local celebrities, including saxophonist J. T. Brown, pianists Sunnyland Slim and Big Maceo, or Big Bill Broonzy, a virtuosic guitarist with an impressive number of recordings to his credit.

Another early acquaintance was Arbee Stidham, an upcoming singer who made it to the top in 1948 with "My Heart Belongs to You," a recording waxed for the RCA-Victor company. "The first time I met Hooker," Stidham reports, "it was a place on 47th Street and Indiana. J. T. Brown was playin' in there at that particular time, and we went in there one night. Hooker wasn't playing but he got up and played with J. T. Brown. When he came down I introduced myself to him, and we talked. And then the next time I saw him was in Evanston, Illinois, he was playing at a club out there—uh, I'm trying to think of the guy's name . . . Pete Hines! From then on, we kind of would bump into one another, every time we got a chance. He kind of hung around Bill [Broonzy] and Sunnyland Slim, and that's how I would get to see him."

Stidham rapidly struck up a friendship with his young fellow musician, and the two men grew more intimate when Stidham decided to take up the guitar: "My wife wanted me to start playing a guitar, so I bought one. So then [Big] Maceo told me, he say, 'I'll tell you what,' he said. 'You're runnin' around with Hooker all the time. Now that's somebody who could tell you something.' So between Bill [Broonzy] and Hooker, I started to learn. Hooker would teach me the single-string thing, because he was a wizard at that. He would stop by every once in a while and give me pointers."

Another Chicago blues celebrity was John Lee "Sonny Boy" Williamson. A singer and harmonica player originally from Jackson, Tennessee, Williamson made Chicago his home after the worst of the Depression, eventually growing into one of the most popular bluesmen of his day, recording some 120 sides for RCA-Victor/Bluebird between 1937 and 1947. Sonny Boy was a very moving and persuasive singer afflicted with a slight speech impediment that he used to good effect and that conferred on his singing an irresistible appeal. But more than a vocalist, Sonny Boy was a powerfully inventive instrumentalist who took the harmonica to a higher plane, making people take it seriously. In his hands, this tiny toy stopped providing an unobtrusive accompaniment to the guitar to become a soloing instrument.

Sonny Boy lived on the South Side, about two short blocks west of the Hookers' South Park home, and his house at 3226 Giles Street was constantly crowded with neighborhood children and fellow-musicians who stopped by for a chat and a drink. Sonny Boy was aware of Earl's musical potential, and they would sometimes get together at Sonny Boy's house. One day that he was going to Tennessee on a tour, Sonny Boy offered to take Earl and his friend Vincent Duling with him, Earl later told Billy Boy Arnold: "See, Hooker lived right around the corner from Sonny Boy, and him and Vincent went to Jackson, Tennessee, with Sonny Boy. They were kids, they must have been fifteen, sixteen or something, you know, young kids. Hooker said, 'Damn! that Sonny Boy, man, that cat blew, man!' See, I had a picture of Sonny Boy and I showed him the picture. I said, 'Who's that?' This was in the sixties when he was playin' at Theresa's [Tavern]. I just wanted to see if he remembered. He said, 'That's

Sonny Boy!' He said, 'Yeah, man, he took us down South. We used to go to his house all the time and play with him!'"

The end of the war brought deep changes in Chicago, and Earl decided to leave the city for the Delta in 1946. With the progressive mechanization of cotton culture, new waves of black migrants flocked to Bronzeville every day, hoping to find a better life there. At the same time, the soldiers who had served their country during the war were returning home from the Pacific and European battlefields, and this double phenomenon made it harder for everyone to find a decent job in the city, including musicians. Small independent recording companies had not emerged yet to question the supremacy of majors, and the Chicago club world was still almost exclusively dominated by the main recording artists of A&R man Lester Melrose, who exerted his pressure on the local scene for Columbia and RCA-Victor.

Another immediate consequence of harsh competition and population increase was the development of criminality, as Earl's neighborhood was becoming more violent with time. "At the time," Billy Boy Arnold reports, "that neighborhood was a very rough neighborhood. Some of the roughest people lived around 31st and 26th Street and this is where all the blues people lived. You get south of 47th Street, you hear jazz on the radios and jukeboxes, but north of 47th Street on down to 29th, 26th, 22nd, this is where the blues people lived."[15] By the time Earl started to establish his reputation throughout the southern states, his thirty-four-year-old friend Sonny Boy Williamson was dead, murdered one night in June 1948 on his way home from the Plantation Club at 328 East 31st Street, where he had performed that night, killed by a man who stabbed him in the head with an icepick.

On the Road

(1946–1953)

The immediate postwar years saw Earl Hooker setting off on his own more and more often, his erratic peregrinations bringing him back to Chicago and his mother's apartment at 3139 South Park at regular intervals. As restless as he was, Hooker was not very particular about the route he took, but the road almost inevitably led him to the southern states, more especially to his native Delta, which he reached after playing his way down through southern Illinois and Missouri. Earl was always at home in the Delta, where he was familiar with the members of the local blues community.

He was particularly keen on playing with Robert Nighthawk, the man who had taught him much of his technique. Nighthawk was staying at 308½ Franklin Street in the Mississippi River town of Helena, Arkansas, when Earl joined him in the mid-forties. After the war, Helena was as good for blues performers as any town in the Delta. Seventy percent of its ten thousand inhabitants were Blacks, originally from the rural areas of the Delta, who knew there was more money to be made on the levees unloading barges, in Helena's cotton industrial complex and railroad yards, or nearby in the West Helena Chrysler plant than in the fields. While Helena was situated at a strategic point on the Mississippi River some sixty miles south of Memphis—unchallenged capital of the Deep South—the town of Clarksdale, another thriving Delta center, was almost directly across the river less than thirty miles away in Mississippi. Helena's and West Helena's throbbing nightlife took place in black juke joints scattered all over town, where locals could gamble and drink at will to the sound of small Delta blues combos after a hard week's work.

"The town was loaded with musicians," rambling bluesman Johnny Shines says, describing Helena's rough nightlife at the time. "And lots of places to play there, too. Juke joints, I guess you'd call them. . . . Now, a juke joint is a place where people go to play cards, gamble, drink, and so on. So far as serving drinks like you would in a bar or tavern, no, it wasn't like that. Beer was served in cups; whiskey you had to drink out of the bottle. You didn't have no glasses to drink the whiskey out of, so you drank it from the bottle or you used your beer cup, and they were tin cans usually. See, they couldn't use mugs in there because the people would commit mayhem, tear people's head up with those mugs. Rough places they were. When you were playing in a place like that, you just sit there on the floor in a cane-bottomed chair, just rear back and cut loose. There were no microphones or PA setups there; you just sing out loud as you can."[1]

Besides its pulsating joints, Helena's main claim to fame from a musical standpoint was the exceedingly popular *King Biscuit Time* show, broadcast daily on KFFA radio from 1941. This program, sponsored by the Interstate Grocer Company, maker of King Biscuit Flour, featured the harmonica acrobatics of Rice Miller, an enigmatic singer also known as "Sonny Boy Williamson #2"— the number 2 being added later by blues historians in order distinguish him from John Lee Williamson, the other "Sonny Boy," whom Hooker knew in Chicago. KFFA was white owned, and most of its programs were intended for Delta "hillbillies," but a restricted share of its airplay was aimed at the black audience, accounting for its popularity with local Blacks. After the war, as radio station owners realized that the colored population largely outnumbered its white counterpart in most Delta towns, a larger portion of broadcasting time was progressively devoted to this widely unexplored commercial market. The trend was initiated by a handful of pioneers like the Interstate Grocer Company when they appointed Rice "Sonny Boy Williamson" Miller host and star attraction on *King Biscuit Time* in November 1941, only days before Pearl Harbor, inspired by the example of W. Lee "Pappy" O'Daniel, maker of Light Crust Flour and sponsor of a popular western swing program, whose broadcast eventually propelled him to the Texas state governorship.

Sonny Payne, original KFFA staff announcer on *King Biscuit Time*, relates the program's genesis. "Actually, Sonny Boy came in looking for a job. He wanted to play on the radio, and he talked to my boss, Sam Anderson. My boss called Max Moore over at Interstate and says, 'We got a couple of boys over here, they're wanting to play on the radio, will you sponsor 'em?' and Sam and Max got together, decided, 'Hey! Here's an opportunity to sell flour for you, Max, and an opportunity for KFFA to have blues, since this is the Delta.' This was a chance for us to have a blues band, which no one else had. Back then, for the most part it was the Artie Shaw, Glenn Miller type music, and then once a day we would have the blues."

King Biscuit Time's tremendous popularity was not merely due to its pioneer position. Rice Miller's charisma, weird personality, and powerfully inventive harmonica playing as well as his choice of accompanists contributed to the program's fame. Sonny Boy initially started the show in the company of guitarist Robert Jr. Lockwood before he was led to increase his backing unit, spurred on by the enthusiastic reaction of black listeners. Over the years, the King Biscuit Boys comprised at one time or another James "Peck" Curtis on drums, Earl's friend Joe Willie "Pinetop" Perkins and Robert "Dudlow" Taylor on piano, as well as a string of guitar players who followed the example originally set by Lockwood: Robert Nighthawk, his mentor Houston Stackhouse, Joe Willie Wilkins, Sammy Lawhorn, and Earl Hooker, among others. The show was broadcast live every day in the week from 12:15 to 12:30 out of KFFA's precarious studios at 123 York Street in crumbling downtown Helena premises. "The buildin' was rotten," KFFA announcer Sonny Payne reminisces with a smile. "The floors were so squeaky that you can almost fall through them. Especially when Dudlow, the piano man, got on 'em. You got about 280 pounds or maybe 300 pounds of solid blubber, and—well, in fact he did fall through one of the floors!"

In between improvised blues offerings, Sonny Boy's King Biscuit Boys advertised King Biscuit Flour exclusively until 1947, when the Interstate Grocer

Company, in the light of the tremendous success encountered by its program, launched its new Sonny Boy cornmeal packaged in bags boasting a naive drawing of a smiling Rice "Sonny Boy" Miller, sitting on a giant corn ear and cupping a harmonica in one of his huge hands. In addition to the live blues music featured on his program five times a week, Interstate Grocer president Max Moore rapidly set up a sophisticated promotional policy. On a simple request, fans received a special King Biscuit envelope with detailed *King Biscuit Time* schedules and current pictures of Sonny Boy and band taken by Helena photographer Ivey Gladin. Moore went one step further when he had the King Biscuit Boys travel and perform around the Delta on their days off, advertising Interstate products, Sonny Payne remembers: "They made personal appearances over in Mississippi, these towns around, for Interstate Grocer, promotioning Sonny Boy Meal and King Biscuit Flour. In the wintertime they would go by bus, and in the summertime on a flatbed truck. That was their stage. They would pull up in front of a grocery store; there was nothin' to plug in, but they would draw good crowds, you better believe it!"

Forming a direct contrast with Max Moore's elaborate advertising policy, *King Biscuit Time* radiated a sense of informality that gave it a very special appeal. "A typical Monday," Sonny Payne adds, "to start the day off right after a drunken weekend by these guys, would be to come up the steps about two minutes before time to go on. And then sometimes we had to delay it five minutes to get 'em on, because they would still have cobwebs in their minds. A lot of the times, they weren't even prepared, they didn't have their schedule of songs to go on, and we would have to coax 'em like children. Dudlow might show up one day, and if he didn't they'd find somebody else, but for the most part we didn't care as long as they played their tunes and went on the air; people loved 'em."

The immediate success met by *King Biscuit Time* incited other local flour companies to sponsor similar programs in an attempt to challenge their lucky competitor. By the time the war was over, KFFA in Helena and WROX in Clarksdale were putting on the air several flour shows, all of which featured blues music, by far the favorite of cornmeal-buying black households. And while Robert Jr. Lockwood moved on from King Biscuit to Mother's Best Flour, Robert Nighthawk plugged Star Bright Flour, sometimes backed by guitarist Joe Willie Wilkins or pianist Pinetop Perkins.

27 *On the Road (1946–1953)*

The King Biscuit Boys were only getting paid a dollar a day for their fifteen-minute slot, but the program helped spread Rice Miller's reputation far beyond the Delta. On the strength of his name, Sonny Boy decided to leave Arkansas after the war and moved north to Chicago and Detroit, where he stayed until 1948, when he abruptly returned to the KFFA studios one morning, confident that he would always be welcome on his show. When he did not work with Robert Nighthawk's band, Earl Hooker performed on various occasions with Miller over the air on *King Biscuit Time*, although the young guitar player was more often hired by the King Biscuit Boys when they played at night in the small Delta juke joints. It was on one such trip that Hooker met drummer Arthur Lee Stevenson.

Stevenson, like Earl in this respect, acquired his initial musical experience in the band of Robert Nighthawk, who soon started calling him "Kansas City Red" because when on stage Stevenson never failed to sing "Kansas City," a popular ditty. Hooker and Red would later become close associates, and they ran into each other one night in a country juke house a few miles east of Clarksdale in Quitman County. "I met Hooker in a place called Horace Broomfield's out from Marks, Mississippi," Red remembers. "It was just a juke house. Horace Broomfield was kind of a well-off guy. He was a farmer, the share croppin' deal. Cotton be picked and everythin', and he made his money out of the juke house on Friday, Saturday nights. Pinetop [Perkins] played for him too, and that's where I met Hooker at. In fact, he was with this band called the King Biscuit Boys. James Peck Curtis, I believe Dudlow [Taylor] was on the piano, and Sonny Boy Williamson was on the harmonica."

Between gigs with Miller's King Biscuit Boys Hooker resumed his position as guitarist with Robert Nighthawk. Together they roamed the southern states, making frequent incursions south into Louisiana or north into Missouri and southern Illinois. One of their favorite stopovers in the Delta was the country town of Tutwiler, situated sixteen miles southeast of Clarksdale and only six miles from Earl's birthplace, where they usually teamed up with local pianist Lee Kizart. Earl had known Kizart since the early forties, when they played weekend dances around the area together with Pinetop Perkins. In Tutwiler Nighthawk and Hooker ran into Kansas City Red, whose drumming and vocal qualities got him hired on the spot. This marked the start of a long association between Earl and Red, who stuck together through thick and thin until the mid-fifties. Due to Nighthawk's unpredictable nature, Earl and Red soon learned how to work by themselves. Many times they woke up in the morning only to find that their bandleader had vanished. On such occasions, an additional guitar player was welcome, and they usually called upon the talent of Lee Kizart's son Willie, who inherited a large part of his guitar technique from Earl.

By 1947 Hooker and Red followed Nighthawk to Clarksdale, where they started doing radio broadcasts for various sponsors on WROX, a radio station that broadcast locally since 1939. Nighthawk and his men, including a young pianist named Ernest Lane, were paid close to nothing when they broadcast over WROX, but their show was the best way to advertise the band, and they never failed to announce on the air the location of their next few engagements. Several nights a week, and more especially on weekends, Nighthawk would take his outfit to the tiny country juke houses and larger dance halls to be found in large number around Clarksdale. The crowds that they drew because of their radio appearances allowed them to ask for more money. Or if they played "for the door," the night's pay was directly related to the number of people who left a small fee at the door to get in.

At the time, Clarksdale was seething with excitement; if the Depression had taken its toll before the war, it enjoyed an unprecedented economic boom in the late forties, leading to a population increase for the decade that reached 35 percent in 1950, or 16,539. Life in Clarksdale was centered on a tight network of business streets boasting local bank buildings, a post office, and a library in addition to a rich variety of stores and restaurants. As always in the Delta, Blacks lived apart from the Whites, across the railroad tracks. Clarksdale's black section numbered various joints and cafés, including the Green Spot and the ones owned by the parents of saxophonist Raymond Hill: "We had what they used to call juke houses here. A big house and you just set it up, take everything out of this large house and set it up just like a club—call them juke houses. Well, by my father and my mother running one, I was small, but they used to bring in these little blues bands. Sonny Boy, Robert Nighthawk, used to have Pinetop [Perkins] all the time, used to have him at the place. . . . The entertainment was mostly blues all the time. Most times when Robert [Nighthawk] would come, he would come with just the drums and guitar, that's all he would have."[2]

When they were not playing the Clarksdale joints, Nighthawk and band traveled extensively through the Delta, picking out a different place every night. Marks, Lambert, Vance, Tutwiler, Drew, Ruleville, Parchman, Lula, Leland, Greenville, and Greenwood were playing spots, whereas Arkansas on the other side of the river provided them with additional opportunities to gain a faithful following. Until July 1961, when a bridge finally opened just a few miles south of Helena, the only way across the river was to take one of two ferryboats, the *City of Helena* or the smaller *Belle of Chester*, and it was often a time race coming back from an engagement and catching the last night ferry. One of the ferry pilots then was Floyd Jenkins, whose son Harold obviously benefitted from the presence around the Delta of blues musicians, as he later reached fame in the field of country music under the name Conway Twitty. The scope of Earl's ambition equaled his talent. By the time he turned twenty in early 1949, he realized that he didn't have much of a future performing for local crowds in small Delta towns, and he decided to try his luck in the Delta's main musical center, Memphis, Tennessee, seventy-five miles up Highway 61 north of Clarksdale. Since the 1850s and the cotton and timber boom, Memphis had grown into the commercial capital of the Delta. Until the Second World War, the city was better known for its jug bands and medicine shows or the more sophisticated pre-jazz blues of W. C. (William Christopher) Handy, who was held in high favor by Memphians early in the century. Even though rambling Delta blues musicians and barrelhouse pianists regularly passed through town during the twenties and thirties, African Americans from the Delta, attracted by the numerous jobs they were offered in the city, started moving to Memphis in large numbers after Pearl Harbor. Thanks to these newly urbanized Blacks, a new brand of blues developed that sounded more modern and polished than its overamplified country counterpart. The new Memphis sound, as it smoothly incorporated the brassy sophistication of big bands, fit in well with Earl's musical ambitions.

Another factor of importance was the presence in Memphis of WDIA, the first black-oriented station in the South. Because it gave exposure to young upcoming talents, WDIA contributed to a large extent to the development of a more urbane Memphis blues. By 1949 the WDIA offices at 2074 Union Avenue were somewhat of a meeting place for blues artists whose home grounds had so far been restricted to the lively Beale Street clubs and theaters that hosted the likes of Riley B. King (later known as B. B. King), Johnny Ace, Rufus Thomas, and Earl Forrest, to cite a few. The black theater tradition on Beale Street went back to the Lincoln, the first to be founded with black capital, and this precursor had been followed by a string of others, including the Grand Theater, later renamed the New Daisy. In the early postwar period, the best known of Beale Street theaters was the Palace, duly considered the finest black entertainment venue in the South. The Palace had originally been built by Antonio Barrasso, son of a rich Neapolitan immigrant and brother of Fred Barrasso, the man who planted the seed for the main southern vaudeville organization of the 1920s, The Theater Owners Booking Association, when he launched his Tri-State Circuit in 1910. In segregated times, the white public was not admitted to the Palace except on special occasions, and the theater was famous during the thirties for its weekly talent shows emceed by radio announcer Nat D. Williams, usually referred to as "Professor" due to his position as a high school teacher.

When Earl Hooker arrived in Memphis in 1949 in hopes of winning some recognition, things did not look as bright and easy as they had seemed from Clarksdale. The Memphis music scene was concentrated in the hands of local artists who shared between them radio appearances, talent shows, and club gigs. Memphis was swarming at that time with musicians whose ambitions were similar to Earl's, partly accounting for the limited amount of space left for obscure Delta musicians like him. His sojourn in Memphis was not totally fruitless, however; on the strength of his dynamic stage act, Earl hustled a few dates in the blues taverns of West Memphis, a musically active town located in Arkansas across the Mississippi River from Memphis. But in the end, the search for properly paid engagements inevitably brought starving talents back to Beale Street and its various clubs and theaters.

"When I first came to Memphis, Beale Street was very active then," B. B. King reports. "Many little clubs on Beale Street. So with music goin' on all up and down the street on the weekend, like Friday night, Saturdays, Saturday nights, you could find some of the best players, even guys with names would come, and out to the park, and listen to people play. At that time, there was three theaters, movie picture theaters, and two of them used to have amateur shows. The one where it had amateur shows every Tuesday or Wednesday night was the Palace Theater. So all of the amateur musicians used to come in there, whatever they played, because if you're able to go on the stage, you would get a dollar, and if you won, you got five dollars, and everybody tried to go. Including myself, many times. Well, you found a lot of folk guitar players like [Frank] Stokes; Bukka White, my cousin; Robert Nighthawk, many of the guitar players. Earl Hooker and all of us would go through there, even after I made records, I still would go there sometimes."

Like Earl Hooker, B. B. King was rebuffed by the fact that he was not as well accepted in Memphis as he was in the Delta. But when King persevered, eventually getting a daily show on WDIA, Hooker resumed his chaotic trips throughout the southern states, opting for the immediate success encountered with rural audiences. The most positive aspect of this initial trip to Memphis was that Hooker made several good friends there, some of whom became celebrated blues artists in their own right, including Herman "Little Junior" Parker, a gifted young harmonica player and singer who owed part of his instrumental proficiency to Rice Miller; Bobby "Blue" Bland, a gospel-influenced vocalist from Rosemark, Tennessee; and Rosco Gordon, a teenage piano wonder.

Earl Hooker enjoyed nothing better than the independence of being on the road with his own ensemble. The two musicians he used most often were drummer Kansas City Red and pianist Ernest Lane. In addition to Helena and Clarksdale, the Hooker trio discovered early another blues heaven in the town of Cairo, Illinois, which became their home base from 1949. For rural Blacks who left the South heading north, Cairo, situated midway between the Delta and Chicago, was where the North began; as such it was a symbol of freedom. "They had a black curtain on the bus—white folks in front, us in back. They took it down in Cairo,"[3] a former plantation worker once recalled to *National Geographic* writer Charles E. Cobb Jr. Located at the confluence of the Ohio and Mississippi Rivers at the southern tongue of the state of Illinois, Cairo lies in the same floodplain as the Delta, in an area that has long been known as "Egypt." The levee around Cairo completely encircles it, and during great floods the city is temporarily isolated. During the first half of the nineteenth century, speculators rushed to acquire title to this rich land, convinced that the nation's greatest metropolis would soon arise on this site. This was a time when much of the enthusiasm for western settlement was based on expectations about founding great cities. While St. Louis grew to enjoy a future foreseen for similar reasons, Cairo failed to develop into a major urban center—much to the despair of the many English investors who were the victims of the Cairo

City and Canal Company in the late 1830s, and whose plight Charles Dickens described in *Martin Chuzzlewit*.

In the late 1940s, with a mere five thousand souls, Cairo remained half the size of comparable centers like Helena in Arkansas, but it had an important African American community for a number of reasons. Before the Civil War, Cairo had given fugitive slaves fleeing the South through the Underground Railroad their first taste of freedom, and since the beginning of the Great Migration it had been a natural stop on the way to Chicago, Indianapolis, or Detroit. The city Charles Dickens had most unkindly depicted a century earlier in his *American Notes*[4] as "a dismal swamp . . . teeming . . . with rank unwholesome vegetation, in whose baleful shade the wretched wanderers who are tempted hither, droop, and die, and lay their bones; . . . a hot bed of disease, an ugly sepulchre, a grave uncheered by any gleam of promise: a place without one single quality, in earth or air or water, to commend it," now boasted an intense musical activity; it stood within reach of Paducah, a larger town in Kentucky that traditionally welcomed blues musicians from the Delta, while southern Missouri and its thriving nightlife were found directly across the Mississippi River toward the west.

Cairo's strategic position made it a meeting point for several of Earl's Delta musician friends, including Houston Stackhouse—who remembered seeing Rice Miller there for the first time—or Pinetop Perkins, who settled in Cairo around 1949, shortly before Hooker's arrival, and who shared his time between his day job at a local radiator shop and weekend dates with his own ensemble. "It's a small town, it ain't too big, but it was a lot of music in there," Pinetop Perkins confirms. "A whole lot of black people. See, it's where the two rivers come together; there was barges comin' there, and they kept workin' on the barges and stuff, and people'd come and spend their money in town." Cairo's blues past was nothing recent in fact, as Cannon's Jug Stompers's "Cairo Rag" and Henry Spaulding's "Cairo Blues," respectively waxed in 1928 and 1929, clearly show.

Hooker and Red were already familiar with the Cairo club scene, to which they had been introduced by Robert Nighthawk. With pianist Ernest Lane in tow, they moved there in 1949 and used it as their regular base for two years. Very few bluesmen actually lived in Cairo. Keyboard specialist Jimmy Smith sometimes visited his aunt, who ran an undertaking business there, and legend

goes that he eventually adopted the organ after playing at her request for fu-
nerals; but other than Pinetop Perkins and until pianist Eddie Snow's In The
Groove Boys moved to Cairo in 1951, Hooker and band were the sole permanent representatives of the blues tradition locally, explaining the tremendous
success they obtained from the start. "Peoples would come there from out of
Missouri, Kentucky, anywhere else," Kansas City Red reports. "They kept us
workin' seven nights and seven days practically. Cairo was a good-time place,
that was one of the best. Helena, Arkansas, used to be a good swingin' place,
and Cairo was just about like that. Well, then practically every corner was a
club, and everythin' was lively."

"It was some more [bands] there," Pinetop Perkins adds, "but it was a jazz
band; they called the boy Horace, he played piano, and another boy played
drums with him, George Morris. He's a good jazz drummer, he here in Chicago
now. So Hooker came to Cairo around that time and told us he was well, which
he wasn't. 'Well, I'm well, now,' he said." The tuberculosis that plagued
Hooker's health from the very beginning seemed to have abated. Apart from
older acquaintances like Perkins who were aware of the young man's condition,
more recent associates never suspected a thing until years later, as Earl took
care not to display any symptom of a highly contagious sickness which might
have killed the enthusiasm of his entourage. "Well, he didn't show signs of
bein' sick down there," Kansas City Red categorically states.

Outside music, Earl and his band did not really care about anything. When
they weren't on stage, they flirted with local females and swallowed large quantities of alcohol during their long working hours. Earl regarded personal health
problems with deliberate coolness, as his intrinsic laxity urged him never to acknowledge any symptom likely to hinder the course of his career. Yet, he
needed all of his energy to provide thrilling entertainment to Cairo tavern
crowds all through the week, first at the Palms Hotel.

"We played at the Palms Hotel, 34th and Commercial. That hotel is all de-
molished now. I go through there every so often, take a ride and look around
and everything is different now," Kansas City Red recounted thirty years later
with a touch of nostalgia. "But the Palms Hotel was real nice; it had a bar in the
front, a lounge in the back. It was owned by Earl Palms, that was his name. So
he got in bad health and he lost one of his legs, so he sold it to a guy by the
name of Memphis. He had a big nightclub up in Mound City, they called it the

Silver Slipper or somethin' like that. He was a nice guy, Memphis. He was one of them big-time gamblers; I don't know how, he couldn't see good. He was pretty wealthy, you know, so me and Earl Hooker and Ernest Lane and this boy Homer, he liked us."

Hooker and band also performed in the rougher bars of the omnipotent Wade Brothers, who reigned supreme over the local black club world. "Sam Wade, George Wade, Ed Wade, it was a lot of 'em there," guitarist Son Seals, who played in Cairo on various occasions in the sixties, remembers. "They wasn't white, but they was mixed all up. They looked Spanish, they had real curly hair and shit. They had two or three joints, man." "They had several clubs, one on 13th Street and one on 29th Street," Kansas City Red confirms. "The one on 13th and Poplar was somethin' like a hangout joint for guys. They didn't do no gamblin' in there. All they did was dance and drink and have a good time, when they wasn't fightin'. It was a rough place, yeah. Just one of 'em old honky-tonk places, you know. Open twenty-four hours, cheap booze, and some of the guys mostly slept there. Places never did close, especially this one on 13th, 'cause we would start before the sun go down, and the sun'd be up when we out.

"The man even built a hotel for us right behind the place. It wasn't no great big place, but we didn't have to pay no rent, nothin' like that. Food, we didn't have to buy no food. All we had to do was keep our clothes clean and work. And a little money on the side. We'd make a hundred and some dollars a week, nothin' big, but then we would go out of town somewhere we can pick up a few hundred dollars apiece. . . ."

Hooker, Red, and Lane got on well together. The mere fact that Earl did not get rid of his sidemen during their long stay in Cairo gives ample proof of the feeling of mutual understanding that prevailed in the band. When the presence of another guitarist was requested, Hooker used Homer Wilson, a musician he had picked up on the sidewalks of Chicago's Maxwell Street. Wilson usually played in the band of Earl's friend John Brim in the Windy City, but Hooker used him when Homer stopped over in Cairo on his way to his hometown located near Hopkinsville, Kentucky.

More than another guitarist, Hooker needed a talented vocalist to round off his blues crew. In addition to Red, whose singing repertoire was ample enough to grant the requests of most patrons, Earl would use his old friend Pinetop Perkins, who spent his spare time on stage on the weekend unless Hooker came back from one of his regular out-of-town trips with a good singer. Soul star Bobby "Blue" Bland for one has kept fond memories of his singing stints under Hooker's auspices in Cairo. Regardless of the quality of his singers, Hooker was an outstanding showman, and he had no trouble getting the attention of the public, according to Kansas City Red: "You heard of Les Paul, he was a madman? Earl Hooker was like that. He was a monster. Earl Hooker was puttin' the guitar behind his back, pickin' it with his teeth, with his feet! That's where all these guys got that stuff from, Earl Hooker. At that time, I could walk the bar and play my drums, and Ernest Lane'd be on top of one of them big pianos, playin' it backward, and all that kinda stuff. But we all got it 'cause Earl Hooker started us all to clownin'. We really didn't need but three pieces. And when I got with Hooker, then I had the freedom to do all of that stuff, you know. He wanted everyone to go for hisself." His capacity at getting the very best out of his musicians was one of Earl's most precious qualities. Although he would not use sidemen unless they were up to par, even average players would go beyond their limits under his direction.

Actually, there were two separate sides to Hooker's deep-rooted sense of showmanship, the first having to do with his uncanny way of playing his instrument. "Anythin' he could do to put on a good show, Hooker did it, no matter what it was," pianist Big Moose Walker insists. "I've seen him turn a flip with the guitar, landin' on his feet. Played with his teeth good. Behind his neck, he got that from T-Bone [Walker]. We had somethin' like a show, I'd pick him up, you know, I's big and stout, so I put Hooker up on my shoulders, and he'd play the guitar, and walk all around in the house with him playin' the guitar."

In addition to the action he could do with his instrument, Hooker rapidly understood there were technical ways of turning his playing to account. He realized that electrified amplification could provide any imaginative player with a whole new range of sonorities and possibilities; this awareness only bore fully ripe fruits later on in his career, but early tricks included playing with two amplifiers at the same time, thus creating a premature form of stereophony; using the tone control knob on his instrument to obtain voice-like wah-wah effects as he played; or performing with a hundred-foot-long guitar cord that allowed him to walk from one end of a club to the other while his accompanying musicians backed his playing from the stage.

The unusual flamboyance of Hooker's performances, fully enlivened by the incredible number of tricks he pulled from his bag, could only enhance the reputation and popularity of his band not only in the immediate vicinity of Cairo but in neighboring towns and villages as well. To that extent, the geographical position of Cairo was strategic, with a large number of small clubs and road-houses found within close reach: in addition to Paducah, a lively Kentucky river town straight east of Cairo, the southern part of the state of Missouri, which lay right across the Mississippi River, was teeming with country towns that eagerly welcomed traveling musicians. Earl's favorite hangout there was the club owned by Walter Taylor in the town of Lilbourn, just off of Highway 61, in the heart of New Madrid County. From Charleston to Caruthersville, from the Illinois border to the Missouri–Arkansas state line, almost every place was a possible stop for the Hooker outfit. Earl, Red, and Ernest Lane took every available opportunity to go back on the road for a few days, sometimes a few weeks, to draw a deep breath of fresh air before they returned to their Cairo digs.

"I had a car for a while, a Lincoln, in Cairo," Red says. "Then I bought a old Chevy, and Ernest Lane bought a car, that was two cars, then. We would travel in that wherever we wanted to go. In Future City, in another place called Monkey's Eyebrow—that's well out in the country—Mound City, and a little old place they called Mounds. Those were the majors, and then we played all in Missouri, Sikeston, and another one, Hayti. We had all of that sewed up in there. Paducah, we played a place they called Foot's, and quite a few places in Tennessee. Then Hooker would always come to Chicago and stay with his mother, and then he'd come back. And if he stayed too long, we'd send for him to come on back."

It was on the occasion of such a visit to his mother that Earl met one of his closest associates. Earl Hooker was riding on a train, heading for southern Illinois on his way back from the Windy City, when a young fellow traveler saw his guitar case and decided to talk to him. The young man, a dark-skinned steelworker named Aaron Corthen, was on his way to Mounds, a small Illinois town just north of Cairo, where most of his relatives resided at the time.

Corthen, better know today under the name of A. C. Reed, was born in southern Missouri's Wardell in 1926, and he made the move to Chicago as a teenager where a war job in an iron foundry prevented him from being drafted.

His true interest lay well beyond the army-truck assembly lines and whatever savings he had after purchasing a secondhand saxophone in a Chicago pawnshop were spent in music lessons. Aaron Corthen was drawn to the sound of big bands like Erskine Hawkins's or Duke Ellington's, but he was flattered to be offered to sit in with Hooker's band at the time of their initial encounter. A few weeks later, Earl and A. C. ran into each other again. "When he come to Chicago, I run up on him," Corthen says. "We's all around on 31st Street, and I started to takin' my horn around playin' with him and he started comin' back gettin' me for jobs. When I first started goin' on the road with him, we'd go down South all the time playin'. At first, I would work, but we'd go out on weekends, like Missouri, southern Illinois. And durin' a couple years, it musta been somethin' like '49 or '50, I was out of a job, and we traveled all the time. We played in Tupelo, Mississippi, with Hooker; I played in a lot of places with Hooker."

Earl Hooker and A. C. Reed would play and travel more extensively together during the following years, but their collaboration was suddenly brought to a stop after Earl's uncanny knack of "borrowing" the musical equipment of others without asking for prior permission sent him right into the arms of the law. Although their complicity was never established, Ernest Lane and Kansas City Red were forced to share Hooker's plight.

Hooker's eccentric manners developed quite early, for piano man Pinetop Perkins remembers the first time he and fellow band members caught young Hooker red-handed: "When he was thirteen, down South, he stole one of Lee Kizart's guitars, and we caught up with him and got it back, and he asked Lee did he want to charge him, police charge, so we said, 'No, we just want the guitar, we'll just let it go.'" This bad habit, far from abating with time, soon took such proportions that it alienated Earl from a large number of people. It took a charitable musician like Houston Stackhouse, appointed guitarist with the King Biscuit Boys then, to put up with the young man's wild personality. "Robert [Nighthawk]'d say Earl's fingers got to stickin' to stuff when he'd go into stores, you know; he had to let him slide," Stackhouse later recalled. "Robert say he didn't want that, 'cause it could get them all put in jail like that. So when he come over to Helena and went to stayin' with me, I found out his hands would stick by him taking my amplifier! I was gone and had the house locked up, and he broke in there and got my amplifier, and taken my pickup out of my guitar, and brought it off somewhere. Sold it. But he musta couldn't sell the pickup, and he went back and broke back into my house and put that back in the guitar. I just happened to come in the next morning, I was just lookin' around, I said, 'Well, my old guitar ain't got no pickup in it. I will just pick it up and sound off on it.' Then when I looked, there's the pickup. And I looked at that thing, I said, 'Now what the—that scoundrel—done been back here and put the pickup,' and I went to lookin' around for the amplifier, I didn't see it. So when he show up I got at him about the amplifier. 'Oh, I'm shipping it back, it'll be back in a day or two.' That amplifier ain't got back yet!

"Yeah, that boy was terrible. I started to jump on him, but I got to thinkin' I gotta son that mighta been a year or two older than he was, and I said, 'Well, I won't do that,' I just talked to him. Told him don't do that, that was wrong. He said, 'Well, I ain't gonna do it no more.'"⁵

Earl obviously did not pay close attention to Stackhouse's wise advice, because his "sticky fingers" had him, Kansas City Red, and Ernest Lane arrested during the early summer of 1950, and they spent six months in the Illinois State Correctional Center at Vandalia. Johnny "Big Moose" Walker, a broad man with broad shoulders and a broad smile then known as "Cochise" because he was part Indian, tells the story the way he heard it from Hooker himself: "What happened, the owner of the place, he was testin' the mike, 'One, two— one, two.' But he don't hear nothin'. He looked in the hook-up, the stand was still sittin' up like that, but the hook-up didn't have nothin' inside! Hooker had taken the speakers out of the box! [Hooker] was on the bus on the way back, so the owner called the highway patrol, and they had to take him off the bus, so they sent him to Vandalia for six months, him and Ernest Lane, a beautiful piano player who used to play with Ike Turner, too."

Earl Hooker was playing locally around Cairo at the time of the incident; in spite of the connections they had in the black community there, Hooker and his bandmates were hurriedly locked up before they could leave town. Contrary to Moose Walker's magnified version, Earl's arrest took place at the Palms Hotel. The account of the event given by Kansas City Red, who shared time in jail with Hooker and Lane although he was clearly innocent, speaks volumes for the haste with which African Americans were imprisoned. On Tuesday, July 18, 1950, Hooker, Lane, and Red were hurried to the Illinois State Farm at Vandalia, some 150 miles straight north of Cairo on Route 51, where they served a six-month sentence on a "charge of vagrancy originated in the city of Cairo, Alexander County, Illinois," according to Illinois Department of Corrections files. In various states, especially in the South, local government had enacted laws in the wake of the Civil War with the clear intention of limiting the freedom of Blacks. Among such laws were so-called vagrancy acts, which allowed any representative of the law to arrest African Americans arbitrarily, a practice that lasted well into the 1950s.

Regardless of such iniquitous methods, the most frustrating aspect of this grim experience for both Red and Lane was their complete ignorance of the true motive for their incarceration, as Earl Hooker was careful enough not to straighten things out in an attempt to escape their wrath. "Yeah, I really didn't know the reason of it, I found out a little later," Red chortles. "Hooker stole the speaker from this guy. It wasn't in the Wade's Club, this is another club on 23rd Street. It was a little fancy club, and me and Hooker and Ernest Lane played there. Hooker had somebody to take his stuff out to the car, and his guitar, but he didn't put his guitar in his case. So maybe this is how he got the speakers into the case. He's pretty slick, off of that. Next thing I know, they come to the hotel and arrested all three of us and they didn't tell us anythin'. We all had a gun apiece. They taken away all the guns, and they locked us up. We called our friend Memphis to come and get us out. Now we hadn't had no court, no kinda trial. Before Memphis could come down, they throwed us in the car and take us to Vandalia. Didn't nobody tell us until after we done got out of it, about the speakers. I had done served the time, I say, 'Well, I'm out, now,' I couldn't get mad, you know."

Although located in Illinois, the Vandalia correctional center was similar to the state farms found in the South. Sleeping and dining premises were comparable to those found in a traditional prison, but working hours were spent out in the country, where convicts performed various tasks in the fields. Located on Route 51 a few miles off of the northern limits of Vandalia—a rural town about the size of Cairo—the Illinois State Farm housed a majority of minor offenders. As such, the overall atmosphere which reigned there was nothing as harsh as that of a penitentiary, and Hooker, Red, and Lane did not suffer beyond measure from their inglorious stay at Vandalia. "You weren't fenced then, but you were locked up in the dormitory and all," Red says. "Vandalia was a pretty large place, they had roughly about ten dormitories. The building was a big brick building, beautiful, it was clean. It was just the idea you'd be locked up at night, 'cause after me and Earl Hooker got there for a while, they found out we was musicians. When they comin' in for dinner, they had a little band that was playin' mostly the sad stuff, and me and Earl Hooker and Ernest Lane, we got up there, and they had an electric guitar, and we started playin' this hard stuff, and half of the guys stopped eatin' and listened at this. The warden was a pretty nice guy, and he would bring his family, and he'd sit up in the back and listen to us play, and after then, they started givin' parties, barn dances and things, it was a lot of fun. They dress us up in white, black shoes, black bow-tie, then we had it made pretty good. We ate with the guards, so we weren't eatin' the bad stuff no more, we didn't have to work no more then." For obscure reasons, Lane benefitted from "preferential" treatment and was released on December 6, 1950, while Hooker and Red—listed respectively as Zebdee (sic) Hooker and Arthur Lee Stevenson on State Farm records—were discharged on Thursday, January 4, 1951. Undaunted, they headed back for Cairo as spirited as ever.

Neither Ernest Lane nor Kansas City Red had much to gain from this experience, but it could have proved beneficial at least to Hooker; in fact, it only incited him to be more cautious in the future. With time, Earl was to perfect a technique that enabled him to steal the latest musical equipment at Chicago's largest retail music store, Lyon & Healy, located on Wabash in the heart of the Loop. "All the musicians knowed how he'd get his stuff," Red confirms. "He come up once with a brand-new set of drums, and he didn't pay a quarter for 'em! The way I heard it—now I ain't never been with him when he was stealin' that—but that boy told me this; him and Earl went down there, and he say he'd be talkin' to one guy, and he switched over talkin' to another one tellin' this one guy he was interested in somethin' else, and while he got this other guy's attention, the other boy put the stuff in the car."

It did not take the Hooker band much time to resume their former position as the leading blues outfit on the Cairo scene. They didn't try to hustle another engagement at the 23rd Street club where Earl had made himself unwelcome, but the town offered many more opportunities, including the set of nightspots operated by the Wade brothers. In between Cairo gigs and out-of-town performances in the immediate vicinity, Earl Hooker still found the time to make occasional forays into the Delta, unless he decided to head north for Chicago, where he visited his mother.

At the time of a trip to the Windy City, Earl was introduced to a man who could well have transformed the course of his career if bad luck had not stepped in. With the deep changes that were taking place in the field of black music in the postwar years, small independent record firms were emerging in an attempt to fill in the gap left by the gradual disengagement of the majors. Among the shrewdest representatives of the new "indies" were Leonard and Phil Chess, two Jewish brothers of Polish origin whose financial interest in the black Chicago club scene led them to record some of the entertainers they hired in their venues. In the spring of 1947 they founded the Aristocrat label, essentially devoted to brassy big bands and sophisticated jazz trios.

By 1951 Aristocrat had been replaced by the Chess and Checker labels that featured the heavily amplified Delta blues made famous by Muddy Waters. In addition to Muddy, the Chess brothers were showing interest in Robert Nighthawk as well as in piano players Sunnyland Slim and "Little" Johnny Jones. It is quite possible that it was Jones, a friend of Earl's approximately of the same age, who introduced him to Leonard Chess. Chess took an immediate notice of Earl's potential, especially as an instrumentalist; following a rapid audition, Hooker asked for enough time to round up his men, and a session was set up for a few weeks later. Earl was excited at the prospect of cutting a record, and he had no difficulty convincing his associates to leave the Cairo scene and move on to bigger things in Chicago.

Hooker was going to be the victim of his own success when Big Jim Wade, his current employer who feared his exceedingly popular house band might never return from Chicago, decided to keep the Hooker band from deserting Cairo. According to Kansas City Red, "They locked us up a second time; they say we broke a contract. At that time, I couldn't sign my name, and I don't think Hooker could sign his, so we didn't have no contract. Big Jim Wade was the guy that was the cause of that 'cause he didn't want us to leave because we was bringin' in peoples from different states and cities, so he had us locked up. We tried to slip away, but they pulled us off the bus in Cairo. We was locked up two weeks at the city jail, right across from the courthouse, and we had to agree that we would play for 'em before they get us out of there."

Jim Wade apparently underestimated Hooker's craving for freedom. After spending a few additional weeks confined to the Cairo night underworld, Hooker and friends pretended that they had an audition in Paducah. Instead of getting on the bus to Kentucky, they grabbed their instruments and took the first Greyhound to Chicago.

Forming a sharp contrast with their glorious arrival on the Cairo scene several months earlier, their escape from a town that loved them all too well was definitely a lackluster one for Earl and band. Kansas City Red and Ernest Lane prudently decided to avoid Cairo during the years that followed, but Hooker could not check his desire to visit his old stomping grounds. Even though he never fully reintegrated into the Cairo scene after 1951, the course of his road travels would regularly take him to southern Illinois until way into the sixties, when social and cultural metamorphoses gradually dimmed the flame that once animated the town's musical life. By 1963 the blues had given way to Black pride in Cairo, and local African Americans staged sit-ins in local restaurants and recreational facilities in an attempt at fighting de facto segregation. Never one to commit himself outside the scope of music, Hooker no longer belonged there.

Earl had better incentives than Red or Lane for venturing back into Wade-controlled territory. The presence in Cairo of Sadie, a girl he had met several months before his departure, must have been compelling enough, for after spending some time in Chicago he headed back for Cairo to join her. There is no telling what the reaction of Jim Wade was when he found himself face to face with the man who had challenged his authority shortly before; it may be assumed that Jim Wade made the best of the situation, since he immediately gave Earl a job at one of his clubs. After a while Earl finally brought his girl-friend to the Windy City, where she moved in with him at Mrs. Hooker's South Side home, much to the dislike of Mary Hooker, whose over-possessive attitude toward her son was legendary among Earl's friends. Rather than stay in an inhospitable environment, Sadie rapidly gained her independence after she found a steady occupation as barmaid at Chuck's Corner, later renamed the Globetrotter's Lounge, a West Side bar located at the intersection of Damen and Madison Avenues, where Earl often performed. "That's where she worked at all the time, 'cause Hooker would come by and see her when he was in town," Kansas City Red says. "He had a kid by her or somethin', I don't know was it one or two."

Upon his return to Chicago after his long spell in Cairo, Earl Hooker played around the city quite a bit. One of his main hangouts then was the city of

Chicago Heights. This industrial urban center of forty thousand, located twenty-five miles south of the Chicago Loop, numbered a respectable amount of bars and taverns where the working-class population of "the Heights" could be entertained. Among other locations, rhythm & blues players found regular jobs at the Cut Rate Lounge at the corner of 15th and Wentworth, at the Sunset Lounge on 16th Street, or at Cole's Quality Lounge situated on 14th Street, but the Black & Tan, at the corner of 17th and Hanover, across the street from the busy railyard, featured the best live music in town. Hooker often took his band there, sometimes using his sister Earline on saxophone.

One of Earl's fans was fourteen-year-old Andrew Brown, a native of Jackson, Mississippi, who lived with his mother in the Heights. It was not there, however, but in southern Illinois that Brown first met Hooker, on the occasion of an overnight stop in Cairo on his way back from a vacation in Mississippi. Young Andrew was underage at the time and as such was not allowed inside clubs; yet his overpowering interest in the music and his burly stature were his passport to the inside of the Wade's Club. He later remembered vividly his first impressions upon hearing Earl Hooker: "When I was thirteen years old, I weighed 170 pounds and had a moustache. I can remember this real good. 'That's All Right.' I heard [Hooker] play it in Cairo, Illinois, in 1950. It was a little club called Wade's Club. I heard him play that tune with a slide, and that's when I knew that it wasn't nobody in the world could play a slide like that. Because he could actually make a guitar talk. I believe he influenced me more than anybody, because the things he would do with a guitar was awful strange, and as a kid I wanted to get the sound that he got. Because like B. B. King had a certain sound, T-Bone Walker had a certain sound, Lowell Fulson had a certain sound . . . but Earl Hooker had everybody's sound, and HIS sound. So he was altogether like the boss of the guitar as far as I was concerned."[6]

Brown, upon hearing that his idol was playing at the Black & Tan several months after their initial meeting, invited him over to his house. Earl gave the teenager a few tips on the guitar, teaching him useful chords and showing him how to set the knobs on his guitar amplifier, advising his young pupil to use a plain (unwound) G string when playing blues. It was not uncommon for young fans to come to Hooker for advice, as they found it less intimidating to speak to someone who looked almost as young as they did than to approach older and more solemn musicians.

Earl not only provided help very readily; he even let beginners sit in with his band when the occasion arose. Herb Turner and Ronald "Bobby Little" Bluster who also lived in the Heights, were approximately Andrew's age and they would hang outside the Black & Tan every time a Chicago band played there to grab with their eyes and ears as much as they could whenever the door opened or closed. Herb Turner remembers: "Chicago Heights was a southern town, meaning it had a great migration from the South. This town had more factories than any other town this size in the country. Inland Steel, American Brake Shoe, DeSoto, you name 'em, it's here. Lots of workers, and a lot of clubs, and a lot of blues, and a lot of money. The first time I saw Hooker, it was at the Black & Tan. I guess I was about thirteen, fourteen at the time. Every week it was a different band, Muddy Waters, Howlin' Wolf, Jimmy Reed, Earl Hooker. And so I listened outside the door, and you know I was just completely interested in music. But see, Bobby [Little] is about the same age I am, we grew up together, we hung out in the taverns, but he could play drums so he could get in and I couldn't. Hooker would let him sit in on drums."

Earl Hooker's main source of work when he left Chicago remained the club scene of the southern states. Although he spent most of his time around Cairo from 1949, he never stopped making occasional forays into Mississippi or Arkansas, either with his own outfit or as a guest with various Delta combos. The King Biscuit Boys in particular would usually hire him for their daily KFFA radio show whenever he came through Helena, especially after *King Biscuit Time*'s star, harmonicist Rice Miller, left Helena in the late forties, heading for West Memphis with guitarist Joe Willie Wilkins in tow.

Following Miller's departure, the remaining King Biscuit Boys, including drummer James Peck Curtis and pianist Dudlow Taylor, made it their business to take over the program. As a replacement for Wilkins, they hired Houston Stackhouse, a fine singer and slide guitar virtuoso to whom Robert Nighthawk owed a large share of his technique. Earl's own participation in the Delta's most popular blues show reached a climax in the spring of 1949 when he appeared with Curtis and Taylor on the 2,000th broadcast of *King Biscuit Time*. A commemorative photograph taken on this glorious occasion shows a twenty-year-old Hooker proudly picking an acoustic guitar with a pickup added for amplification, whereas a short article in the *Chicago Defender* described the event: "Earl Zebedee Hooker, self-taught guitarist and son of Mrs. Mary Hooker of 3361 Giles Ave., has been going great guns on the station KFFA's *King Biscuit Time*, beaming in the Helena, Arkansas area. *King Biscuit Time* recently completed its 2000th broadcast over station KFFA. Young Earl has been with the group about 6 months."[7]

During part of 1951 and most of 1952, after his progressive withdrawal from the Cairo scene, Earl spent most of his time in the Delta, where he resumed his spot with the King Biscuit Boys. As a regular member of the band, he took part with Stackhouse, Curtis, and Dudlow Taylor in the Monday-through-Friday fifteen-minute program, advertising King Biscuit Flour and Sonny Boy Corn Meal, while weekend nights were devoted to club work throughout the Delta. "Earl come over to Helena and went to playin' with us," Houston Stackhouse later recalled. "He stayed around us two years over there playin' with me and Dudlow and Peck, there was just four of us then. He played with us 'cause I was playin' guitar on the program then, and so he came and went to playin' guitar on the program. There was two guitars. That was *King Biscuit Time*."[8]

In addition to their daily engagements over KFFA radio, 1360 on the AM dial, the King Biscuit Boys played every Saturday morning on the flatbed truck of the Interstate Grocer Company, singing and advertising their sponsor's products in front of country grocery stores and gas stations. Cashing in on their tremendous following around the Delta, the King Biscuit Boys drew most of their income from the unbridled performances they gave on weekend nights in the large dance halls and teeming juke houses encountered in Mississippi or Arkansas. "You usually played in the little towns, like Indianola, for instance, where I grew up. They had a place there called Jones' Night Spot," blues star B. B. King, whose outfit roamed the same circuit as that of the King Biscuit Boys, explains. "If you played Arkansas, then you had a place called Slackbritches in Birdsong, or Hick's Corner. Each one of these places was a little nightclub. The place would hold maybe a hundred people, a hundred and fifty at the most, and they'd usually have one little room for gamblin', and all of the swingin' people would have fun dancin' and playin' music in the big room. They'd have food, music, boys and girls, young people and old people, it was a lot of fun."

Although he never missed a King Biscuit broadcast, Stackhouse had to stay in Helena during the week due to his professional obligations, and he could only work out-of-town gigs with his bandmates on Saturdays and Sundays. Hooker's association with Houston Stackhouse was highly beneficial, for it enabled him to perfect his technical proficiency; the presence of accomplished guitarists like Joe Willie Wilkins or Boyd Gilmore also proved helpful to a large extent. By the time Earl came back from Cairo and started playing with the King Biscuit Boys on a regular basis, he had definitely earned the reputation of best guitar player around, quite an honor considering his age and the fact that Delta instrumentalists were not known to be mediocre players.

"Bottleneck?" says Joe Willie Wilkins, former King Biscuit Boy and a fine guitarist in his own right who taught Earl a few licks when the teenager visited the Delta in the mid-forties. "That's the reason I left mine alone, 'cause Robert Nighthawk, that Earl Hooker, and that Stackhouse—well, when you get to them fellows, it wasn't no more bottleneckin'. 'Cause they was all of it. Yeah. So when I was around those fellows I kept mine in my pocket."[9] In the space of a few years, the worthy student had transcended his masters: "Joe Willie and them helped him," Stackhouse states, "but Earl Hooker was the best to my idea. . . . He used to could play all kinda guitar. He started to usin' the slide, I reckon, after Robert [Nighthawk] learned him how to play a guitar. So he started foolin' with the slide, around there with us. He got bad with the thing, too!"[10]

By the second half of 1952, Earl Hooker decided to free himself from the *King Biscuit Time* routine, and he left on his own, picking up sidemen in the course of his travels. This period of his life was marked by his encounter with the most influential of modern blues guitarists, B. B. (for Blues Boy) King. Although Earl and King had often played the same country juke houses and nightclubs for several years, and even though Earl had visited the Beale Street theaters in Memphis where King and friends performed with regularity, the two men had never met. Yet B. B. King was aware of the King Biscuit Boys on account of their daily broadcast over KFFA, and Hooker had been exposed to King's work. With a national R&B hit to his credit since Christmas 1951 ("Three O'Clock Blues"), King was clearly on his way to stardom.

It was because they wished to see B. B. King perform that Earl and band, on their way back from the Delta, met him at the Club 61, a country joint sitting astride the Arkansas–Missouri state line. "I met him at a place called the State Line of Arkansas and Missouri, it used to be above Blytheville, Arkansas," B. B. King remembers. "He and his group was travelin', comin' from the South, goin' back to Chicago. So he stopped by with his group, and that night after we finished playin' the concert, he and I and the band, we played all night, we just sit and played. That was my first time meetin' him, and from then on, we was friends the rest of his life."

It seems that both men showed mutual respect for each other from the start. Until his death, Earl would never miss an opportunity to sit in with King, much to the delight of appreciative audiences. King on the other hand still expresses today his boundless admiration for his friend's stunning ability, and the crisp picture he draws of Hooker betrays the importance he attached to their friendship: "A quiet, a real nice man, a real gentleman. I never heard him swear. Most people swear, I do, a lot of people, but I never heard him swear. Never. He was interested in music, only. You could tell, because when he came on stage, playin'—I think it's kinda like me, I hear a lot of people that play so near like me today, I have to listen myself to see if it's me. But that's the same thing with Earl Hooker. When Earl Hooker started playin', I KNEW that was Earl Hooker. I don't care who else played, whether it was Robert Nighthawk, Bukka White, anybody, you knew it was Earl Hooker.

"And he was a good organizer," King goes on. "He had a good eyesight for people. He knew about talent, he had a good ear for it, which is only a few people I find today that have it. In other words, he could recognize talent right off. And he did a lot of other things."

Cashing in on his growing reputation, Earl conscientiously played the usual nightclub circuit. After visiting Cairo once again, where he picked up a young drummer named Billy Gayles, the one-nighter trail led Hooker to Clarksdale, where he became acquainted with a twenty-one-year-old disc jockey named Ike Turner. A native of Clarksdale, Turner started playing piano at a very early age after he heard pianist Pinetop Perkins on the King Biscuit radio show. When he met saxophonist Raymond Hill in a Clarksdale high school, Turner formed his own band, the Kings of Rhythm, and they gained popularity in the vicinity of Clarksdale with their sax-led type of jump blues. The Kings of Rhythm made their recording debut in Memphis, Tennessee, for producer Sam Phillips in early March of 1951, recording four songs that were then leased to the Chicago-based Chess label. A resulting single issued on Chess (number 1458) and credited to Jackie Brenston and His Delta Cats—Brenston was the current vocalist with the Kings of Rhythm—soon became famous after its A-side titled "Rocket 88" became Chess Records' first number-one hit record, topping *Billboard*'s national rhythm & blues charts in May of the same year and remaining charted for a straight seventeen-week period. On the strength of this success, Turner and his fellow Kings of Rhythm toured until money disputes led to the breakup of the band. Ike was then recruited as a talent scout by the Bihari brothers, owners of the Modern/RPM record complex in Los Angeles. This new function provided him with new openings, and he was regularly requested to back up the artists recorded by the Biharis, cutting several sides himself for RPM in April of 1952. It was around that time that Turner and Hooker met. Turner, a very powerful and fast boogie pianist, was strongly impressed with Earl's driving guitar picking and impeccable slide style, his freshness, and his profoundly modern dynamism. When Ike decided to take up the guitar himself because his current girlfriend already occupied the piano stool, he turned to Earl, Hooker's influence in his playing being traceable to this day.

That June, Earl went on the road with a new outfit that featured Ike Turner and his girlfriend Bonnie Turner as well as Johnny O'Neal—one of the original singers with Ike's teenage bands, freshly out of the outfit of popular blues shouter Tiny Bradshaw—who also acted as the band's drummer. They first traveled north to southern Illinois and the lively Cairo scene, where they picked up Pinetop Perkins, before they eventually ended up in Florida after working Mississippi and Louisiana joints and dance halls on the way.

Guitarist-singer "Little" Milton Campbell, who was then leading his own ensemble across the country, gives an accurate description of the usual circuit blues bands currently played at the time: "Turner, Hooker, we were all doing the same thing, especially in the South; I had a little band, and I was like traveling around through the states like Arkansas, Louisiana, Tennessee, Mississippi, even Alabama; we'd play in little places like that. Florida is a little farfetched in a sense, but it is a state that you can work in for three or four months. It's different in Mississippi, where you kinda run out of places, but Florida, especially in the wintertime, that's the time when they're harvesting the fruits. And back then times were real good, lots of money, everybody was working, and it's many towns that there was to work in. If you just got a chance to play there three or four times in the same town it would keep you there maybe for three months, or at least for the time of the harvest season. It starts some time around November, December, what have you, until March, three, four months of it anyway."

The local scene must have been quite appealing to Hooker and his men, for they burned up the Florida roads until the late fall, playing every little town they went through. "We stayed down there about six, eight months," piano man Pinetop Perkins recalls. "We's playin' around Sarasota, Fort Myers, Stuart, Homestead, Miami, Bradenton. We played there a while. At that particular time, we didn't have a bass player, and I was playin' drums behind Ike Turner's wife, and when we'd get ready to play the blues, then Johnny O'Neal would get on the drums, and I'd get to the piano, that's the way we had the thing goin'. When Bonnie would get to playin' piano—see, she played nice piano, she could read it—and I'd get over and play the drums, and Johnny would sing then. She sang too, she had a good voice. We had a good band too, piano, drums and guitar, that's all it was."

The band's favorite spot in Florida was the Sarasota/Bradenton/St. Petersburg triangle, south of Tampa Bay on the gulf of Mexico, an area boasting a very active musical life. In Bradenton they ran into a piano player and singer originally from Tarpon Springs, Florida, named Billy "The Kid" Emerson, who performed in local clubs at the instigation of a local promoter for whom Earl and band also played at regular intervals: "Earl Hooker, yeah, I met Earl Hooker in Bradenton. Now that was a blues player. Now you talking about a blues player! Earl Hooker was probably, was one of the most pronounced blues guitar players that ever lived. We was workin' for the same guy, Buddy May . . . which is a guy who really did a whole lot for me in music, you know. He was a promoter out of Bradenton."[11]

Everything went smoothly until Earl and Ike had a falling out over financial issues at Dennis Simpson's Bar in Sarasota, a recurring problem with Hooker, who ended up that time with the short end of the stick: "Earl Hooker was the one that carried me to Florida the first time we went down there with Bonnie. . . . He promised me one amount of money and then when I got down there he was gon' pay me another one. This was a fight between he and I, so then the club owner fired him and so Bonnie and I started to playing there."[12]

In spite of his trouble with the Turners, Earl found life in Florida exciting enough, and he decided to stay around with singer Johnny O'Neal while Ike, Bonnie, and Pinetop stayed in Sarasota, eventually playing their way back home. After putting together another small unit with Roosevelt Wardell on piano, Ed Wiley on saxophone, Robert Dixon on bass, and Will Cochran on drums, Hooker and O'Neal hustled regular engagements around the Tampa Bay at music spots such as the Palms' Club in Bradenton, the Drive In in Sarasota, the Manhattan, the Elks Club or the Roseland in St. Petersburg.

If Earl and Johnny O'Neal had started to build up a reputation in Florida, Wardell and more especially Wiley could hardly be regarded as newcomers on the scene, for they had been leading their own ensemble in the state for a while. Wiley was a talented artist in his own right; besides his work with former Kings of Rhythm vocalist Jackie Brenston, he had already made a handful of records since the beginning of the decade. In addition to his fine work as an accompanist to Texas artists like guitarist Smokey Hogg, pianist Willie Johnson, or vocalists King Tut and Teddy Reynolds, Ed Wiley was notorious for his own Sittin' In With release "Cry, Cry Baby," later covered by Hooker's longtime sidekick Johnny Big Moose Walker, which earned Wiley a fourth position on the national R&B charts in the spring of 1950.

The Hooker/O'Neal/Wiley combination was a potentially promising one, and it drew the attention of a talent scout for the Cincinnati-based King Recording Company who attended one of their tear-it-up performances at a Bradenton club. Johnny O'Neal was hardly an unknown at King Records; his stint with Tiny Bradshaw had enabled him to cut several tracks for the Ohio firm in January of 1951. This did not escape the King representative, who offered to record both Johnny and Earl on the spot. A total of eight numbers were recorded with the help of a portable machine right in the club, after the end of the last set, on Thursday night, November 26, 1952.

Following this hurried session, King decided to release two of O'Neal's sides; as for Earl's own King 4600, it included "Blue Guitar Blues" and "Race Track," whereas his remaining two titles mistakenly saw the light on John Lee Hooker's *Every One a Pearl* (King LP 727) later on in the decade. These sides are rather disappointing efforts as a whole, and they don't do justice to Hooker's potential. While "Blue Guitar Blues" and "Happy Blues"—both of which show the influence on Earl's playing of West Coast jazz-blues specialist Pee Wee Crayton—are rather dull blues instrumentals marred by Wardell's inadequate piano accompaniment, "Race Track" and "Shake 'Em Up" are faster guitar items that showcase Hooker's elaborate chordwork and jazzy picking on a tight foundation of piano flourishes contributed by Wardell.

Of the four tracks dedicated to O'Neal's singing, two have remained unissued to this day, including a version of "Whole Heap of Mama," a song the singer had already cut under the auspices of Ike Turner for the short-lived Blues & Rhythm enterprise ten months earlier under the pseudonym of Brother Bell. "So Many Hard Times" and "Johnny Feels the Blues," released on King 4599, give a fair idea of O'Neal's charisma as a vocalist; to a certain extent, this full-chested coupling makes up for the mediocrity of Earl's own offerings. Although the band suffers from an obvious lack of rehearsal, the degree of interplay between Hooker and O'Neal gives a much clearer picture of their talent. "So Many Hard Times," taken at a slow pace, provides Earl with ample opportunity to showcase his sensitivity as a blues instrumentalist, whereas the jazz-tinged "Johnny Feels the Blues," complete with an alert be-bop tenor sax solo contributed by Ed Wiley, features Earl's imaginative guitar support, every chorus being adorned with new chords and phrases. All in all, this improvised live session, Earl Hooker's initial contact with the world of recording, gave him an overall impression of informality that may well have influenced his vision of the recording industry, accounting for the thoughtless, easy-going attitude he adopted in the studio as a general rule from then on.

For Hooker, that episode was a mere digression in his daily routine, and the next few weeks found him back on the road with his band. By the beginning of 1953, Earl and Johnny O'Neal had decided to go separate ways, and the guitarist joined forces with a harmonica player named "Little" Sammy Davis. Originally from Winona in the Mississippi hills, Davis had been living in Florida for some time, cutting logs and picking fruit in orange groves. After meeting Hooker when Ike and Bonnie Turner were still in Earl's band, he was flattered a few weeks later when the guitarist offered him a spot in his outfit, following O'Neal's departure. Hooker's inside connections with the club scene in Florida were many, and he was working seven nights a week when a second recording opportunity came his way. This time, the proposal came from a Bronx-born but Miami-based record distributor named Henry Stone. A shrewd business man with expert insight into the R&B market, Stone decided to diversify his trade in the early fifties by launching his own Crystal Recording Company, joining efforts with Andy Razaf, a pioneer jazz writer made famous by his collaboration with Fats Waller, and incidentally a grand-nephew of Queen Ranavalona III of Madagascar. After opening a studio in downtown Miami, Stone concentrated on local talent and started releasing his productions on the Rockin' and Glory labels, the first being devoted to blues and country music, while Glory boasted a gospel catalog.

After hearing Hooker and Davis in Bradenton one night, Stone approached them and made a recording offer. "I was the first distributor around," Stone later reminisced. "Like I had to make a living. That's how I got into distributing and hustling records. That meant daily bread for my family. I always recorded on the side, because I felt a big distribution down here. I needed a place to record. I've always had a studio in my hip pocket. Originally Rockin' was Ray Charles. He was doing a little blind-man thing. I got the word on him. He was giggin' around. Later I did Earl Hooker."[13] "I liked the way he played guitar."[14]

Stone's record business was quite new when Hooker walked into his studio in 1953; the first few Rockin' sessions had taken place in October 1952, when Stone recorded Ray Charles (freshly back from the West Coast, where he had achieved success at the head of the Maxin Trio), the blues sounds of W. C. Baker, and the Leroy Lang Orchestra. Another set of recordings the following January involved Leslie Louis (supposedly Memphian one-man-band Joe Hill Louis) and Manzy Harris as well as former Hooker pianist Roosevelt Wardell accompanied by Ed Wiley and his orchestra, but Stone was ready for more studio work. By the spring of that year, a relationship was established with Syd Nathan of King Records in Cincinnati, who eventually purchased the Rockin' masters during the following summer after Stone temporarily went out of business; on the strength of this new deal, Stone worked harder than ever on the recording side of his business all through the month of April at the precise time Hooker and Davis met him.

Within days of their initial encounter with Henry Stone, Earl Hooker and Sammy Davis, taking the band's drummer Tony with them, made the 220-mile trip from Bradenton and wound up at Stone's Crystal Clear Studios at 505 West Flagler in downtown Miami. This only Rockin' session was a rather productive one, as Stone recorded ten titles altogether. Sam Davis's singing was featured on the first four, while Hooker authored the next six numbers. This session was far more rewarding than the under-rehearsed King event of the preceding fall, as it gave a clear vision of Hooker's versatility and proficiency at a time when his idiosyncratic style was progressively shaping up. Listening to those sides today, you can hear Earl grow from a gifted traditional guitarist into an inventive and fully creative artist.

Despite the large amount of talent displayed by Hooker during the whole session, Stone seemed more satisfied with Davis's material, and he released it in its entirety on two 78s (Rockin' 512 and Rockin' 519), credited to Little Sam Davis. Davis's output no doubt pleased Syd Nathan as well, for the harmonicist's second coupling was soon reissued on the King-owned DeLuxe label that Nathan decided to reactivate after he leased the Rockin' masters from Stone in August 1953. Davis, if not a major instrumentalist, displays both conviction and versatility in these recordings although his music is quite derivative. Expressing himself in a wide variety of styles, Davis's recorded repertoire includes an R&B effort strongly rooted in the New Orleans tradition aptly titled "Goin' to New Orleans" alongside a slow, rustic Delta item called "Goin' Home to Mother" that showcases his pleasant singing and fine harp blowing, duly complemented by Earl's progressive picking and chording.

"She's So Good to Me" is a straight copy of Chicagoan Little Walter's "Sad Hours," which had run high in *Billboard*'s R&B charts all through December 1952 and January 1953; it gave Hooker an occasion to re-create the guitar parts initially contributed on Walter's original by his childhood friend Louis Myers. That left "1958 Blues" as the most exciting number recorded by Davis that day; this fast tune—showing the extent of Little Sammy's debt to the playing of John Lee "Sonny Boy" Williamson (Sonny Boy Williamson #1), whose mumbled singing style also proved influential here—was a superb variation on the traditional "Rollin' and Tumblin'" Delta theme. Its inspired lyrics, enlightened by Hooker's razor-edged, driving guitar lines, certainly point to Sammy Davis as a promising writer and competent harmonicist.

In contrast with Davis' offerings, only two of Hooker's own sides were considered worthy of a spring 1953 release on Rockin', probably because Hooker chose to stay on a strict diet of guitar instrumentals. In addition to a version of Pee Wee Crayton's "After Hours" and improvisations such as "Ride Hooker Ride" or "Alley Corn" that didn't see the light of day until 1998 on a Hot Records reissue album, Hooker's set also includes a fine vocal attempt titled "Sweet Angel." Rockin' 78 number 513 coupled this single song with a guitar–drums duet of the sort Hooker seemed particularly fond of, titled "On the Hook." Aurally, this up-tempo number is a fine rework of the "Happy Blues" put on wax for the King label five months earlier. Hooker had apparently turned this short period to account, for the sloppy, under-rehearsed November tune had become by then a more inspired jumper boasting heavily amplified, almost distorted chordwork interspersed with swift single-note runs; the faked fade-out effect Earl uses to bring the tune to a close also stands as a proof to Hooker's sense of dynamics.

"Sweet Angel" is no less interesting, but the song already had a long history when Earl recorded it in 1953. It was penned in 1930 by one of the few non-vaudeville female blues singers of the prewar era, Lucille Bogan, who waxed her own "Black Angel Blues" for Brunswick in December of that year. Tampa Red, one of the most prolific blues recording artists of the twenties and thirties, then put on wax an influential rendition of the song for Vocalion on the very day of March 1934 when Earl's sister Christine was born, before re-recording the tune for the RCA-Victor label in 1950 as "Sweet Little Angel." Tampa Red, whose crystal-clear bottleneck sound was widely imitated by slide guitarists, had a determining influence on Earl's teacher, Robert Nighthawk, who in turn recorded the song on the Chess brothers' Aristocrat label on the occasion of a 1949 trip to Chicago. By the time B. B. King made a hit out of it with his own 1956 cover, the original "Black Angel Blues" had been revamped into a fully orchestrated "Sweet Little Angel," bereft of any color connotation, allowing it to become a classic many urban blues artists still keep in their bag of songs today.

It is hard to say whether Earl had heard Lucille Bogan's original; at any rate, his Rockin' version was patterned after Nighthawk's Aristocrat recording. As such, it is still very much rooted in the raw tradition of the Delta blues, with its over-amplified and distorted guitar and harmonica sounds. Earl cleverly alternates smooth and eerie slide passages with vocal lines, his slide work coming as an extension to his singing. Surprisingly enough for a man who distrusted his own singing enough to consistently carry a vocalist in his band, Hooker is endowed with a very nice, distinctive voice, which he uses here quite wittily. Listeners only need to listen to the first verse of the song to realize how persuasive a singer Hooker could be: "I got a sweet black angel / And I love the way she spreads her wings / When she spreads her wings over me / It brings joy and everything." Hooker stretches out the end of the third line, "over me-e-e-e-e-e," which lazily wraps itself, wing-like, around one's shoulders in a highly effective manner. Sammy Davis should also get credit for his drone-like

harmonica accompaniment, which blends perfectly with Hooker's performance. Although the latter's debt to Nighthawk was obvious on this early
recording, "Sweet Angel" isn't a mere copy but rather a tribute paid by a worthy pupil. Like any good student, Hooker had by now transcended his teacher,
coming up with an exciting Delta blues performance that deserves to be classi-
fied today as a true gem of the early postwar black American tradition.

The Memphis Scene

(1953)

A fter their Rockin' session at Henry Stone's Miami studios, Earl Hooker and his men went back on the road, spending the next few weeks in the Tampa Bay area, working the busy club scene around Sarasota and Bradenton. By the late spring of 1953, with the end of the fruit harvest season in Florida, Hooker worked his way back to Chicago to visit Mama, stopping over in Cairo, where he introduced Little Sammy Davis to Pinetop Perkins. Hooker hired and fired band members with monotonous regularity, however, and the new outfit he put together this time included his old associate from the Cairo days, pianist Ernest Lane, as well as a drummer known as Big Foot Frank. While working the usual circuit, Hooker and Lane ran into an old acquaintance, guitarist Boyd Gilmore, in Mississippi. Together they performed around the Tutwiler area before they ended up in Memphis that July, where at Ike Turner's prompting they recorded extended demo tapes for Sun label owner and manager Sam Phillips.

Sam C. Phillips, one of the most important figures of the rock 'n' roll era, is usually remembered as the one who discovered and launched the career of Elvis Presley, then an unknown white vocalist who made his first record at Phillips's studios in July of 1954, almost one year to the day after Hooker's own Sun session. Phillips should also be given credit for recording and releasing on his Sun label some of the finest country rock artists; the list of his protégés reads like a hall of fame, including the likes of Jerry Lee Lewis, Johnny Cash, Sonny Burgess, Roy Orbison, Conway Twitty, and Carl Perkins, among others.

Born in Alabama, Phillips moved to Memphis in 1945, doing engineering work for local radio stations. For him, black artists were providing Memphis with an original musical identity, one he thought stood a chance of success equal to that of the sounds emanating from more established musical centers like New Orleans or Chicago. "It seemed to me that the Negroes were the only ones who had any freshness left in their music," Phillips says, "and there was no place in the South they could go to record. The nearest place where they made so-called 'race records'—which was soon to be called 'rhythm & blues'—was Chicago, and most of them didn't have the money to make the trip to Chicago."[1] Phillips eventually decided to cash in on the lack of recording facilities in Memphis. In January 1950 he started his own "Memphis Recording and Sound Service" as a side occupation out of a small rectangular one-story building located in downtown Memphis at 706 Union Avenue, right at the slanted angle of Marshall Avenue. "My purpose was to simultaneously try to get acceptance for the artistry of black people, and hopefully then we would have more people that would get interested in black music. I was tryin' to get the foot in the door for the acceptance of black music, but I knew what it took to get it. I knew where I needed to break out first, and that would be the South, because they understood blues, they felt the blues. Because of the preponderance of Blacks in many states, you had a much better chance in the early days of gettin' it accepted in the South than you would in any other place in the nation.

"And I can tell you this. I knew what I was doin', because I had worked with the big bands and everythin', and put 'em on the CBS network every night, six nights a weeks, and this sorta thing, and that was a great era, but I felt that this void needed to be filled and so, when I went in, I didn't sit there with dollar marks in my eyes, you know, I didn't let that overwhelm me. I knew I had to have dollars to keep my doors open, but nonetheless, this is the way I worked with my artists."

Phillips was aware of the existence of ambitious small record company owners like Leonard and Phil Chess in Chicago and the Bihari brothers in Los Angeles, who were eager to work their way into the "race" market, given the declining interest of major firms for popular black music. Phillips's very first success stormed in during the spring of 1951, when he recorded Ike Turner's Kings of Rhythm, featuring vocalist Jackie Brenston. Brenston's "Rocket 88" had the effect of a bombshell for the Chess label to which it had been sold, providing the company with its first number-one hit on *Billboard*'s R&B charts. On the strength of this first achievement, Phillips went on producing a string of R&B records by B. B. King, Howlin' Wolf, and Rosco Gordon, which Chess in Illinois or Modern/RPM in California grabbed greedily.

As his recording experience grew, Phillips came to think that it might be more profitable for him to start his own record company. By then, he knew enough about production and the operation of an independent label to try his luck at it, and his next step was the foundation of the Sun label in the first few months of 1952.

Phillips soon discovered that most of the artists he had successfully recorded for others during his first years as a producer had now signed exclusive contracts with other record firms, but his knack at uncovering valuable talent proved useful once again. From 1952 until the advent of Presley and the development of a new policy, Phillips came up with a string of unknowns like "Little" Milton Campbell, Rufus Thomas, and Herman "Little Junior" Parker, all of whom were to have successful careers over the following decades. An enterprising company owner, Phillips was helped by Ike Turner, who was responsible for digging up many of the new artists featured on the Sun label in addition to leading his own Kings of Rhythm.

"There's been a lot of reports that Ike brought me all of my black artists, which is untrue," Phillips wishes to emphasize. "I'm not takin' anythin' away from Ike, 'cause Ike is a musical genius. Of course he brought a number of people in, but mainly I didn't depend on anyone to bird-dog, so to speak, artists for me because, believe me, after word got out and we did a few things and 'Rocket 88' broke—you have to keep in mind that at the time, it was known that I would record black people in the South, and they found out that I didn't charge them anythin' or that there was no hidden hooks somewhere down the line. The word spread pretty good."

Various opinions have been expressed as to the exact nature of the role played by Ike Turner; Little Milton for one will readily give Turner credit for most of what went on in the studio. "Sam Phillips was the guy that stood in the control booth and worked the tape recorder," says Milton, whose own recording career started in the Sun studios under Ike Turner's auspices. "Ike Turner was the man that took you in there. He'd carry his band in there. Ike was basically one of the major talent scouts in a sense. He always seemed to have inside connections with the people that had the record labels. He would scout the artists and take 'em to these different people and get you recorded, you know. And we didn't really worry about the business end of the thing, foolishly. We didn't really know, but the main thing we were interested in was getting a record recorded, and Ike was very instrumental in doing that." At any rate, it was in his capacity as talent scout that Ike Turner showed up at Phillips's Union Avenue studio on Wednesday, July 15, 1953 with Earl Hooker, Ernest Lane, and Boyd Gilmore.

The session went smoothly for Earl and Gilmore, who cut a handful of tracks featuring Ernest Lane's spirited piano accompaniment. As was usual when Phillips first brought musicians into the studio, this initial Sun session was pretty informal—he asked his artists to unwind in the studio while he engineered the session.

"We would go through what they had, and usually it was kinda like a baseball team that goes out and throws a few balls and hits a few fungoes, and plays around the field before the game's gonna start," Phillips recalls, describing the looseness that prevailed during such sessions while stressing the importance of professionalism. "So we got in, there was always a very relaxed atmosphere, but I was always very much to the point of business. I did not permit drinkin' on sessions. Occasionally I'd let 'em have a little wine, and this sort of thing; we'd take a break or somethin', but I never had anybody on a session that I recall that drank any to speak of. Which was important to me, because—not that I was against booze, 'cause I like to have a drink—but it was just that I wanted them to get that natural feel that they were welcome workin' with me; that it wasn't that everythin' was fine, and the next day, well, really, was I that welcome? Was this man that considerate? Was this man that capable? And this sort of thing.

"That was pretty important because I knew that to get things out of people, that, number one, I've always said, the patience is probably the single most important thing that I know when it comes to tryin' to recognize talent, and then try to utilize their intuitive powers of artistry. So that made it important that we had a good time, but we were very serious about it. Certainly they wanted to cut a hit record, and certainly I wanted 'em to, but I tried to get 'em to where I could tell of their natural instincts and their natural potential capabilities."

Phillips was a most careful and shrewd businessman; even when his ears convinced him that he was holding valuable recorded material, he would sometimes have it played tentatively over local radio stations before making up his mind to issue it on his Sun label, depending on the favorable response of listeners. For that reason, the term "audition" should be preferred to "session" when referring to the informal performance Hooker and Gilmore gave at Phillips's Union Avenue studio on that sweaty Wednesday of July.

Earl Hooker's music appealed to Phillips, for the audition went on longer than usual, Earl's guitar work being featured on most of the tracks recorded that day. Boyd Gilmore's contribution was much more discreet, as he merely stepped into the limelight to take over the vocal and guitar chores on "Believe I'll Settle Down" while Hooker remained in the background. This slow and solemn blues has an almost church-like atmosphere mostly due to the work of Ernest Lane, whose rolling piano basses make the band sound bigger than it actually was. But all in all, this was a disappointing track to Phillips, who knew right off that it could hardly stand comparison with the fine titles Gilmore had recorded for the Biharis one year earlier. For that reason, it remained unissued for nearly twenty-five years until British compilers finally decided to release it.

Hooker concentrated exclusively on his instrumental ability as usual, but his own efforts outshone Gilmore's by far. Recorded first was another rendering of one of his favorite themes; "The Drive"—a title given by compilers years later—was a new reading of the "Happy Blues"/"On the Hook" theme waxed for King and Rockin' respectively a few months earlier. This third version was a particularly fine one, with its spirited piano solo by Ernest Lane. Also taped then were a version of "Red River Valley" (a traditional folk song from the late nineteenth century), as well as a curious Tex-Mex guitar workout, "Mexicali Hip Shake."

Earl's finest side that day was an exciting cover version of Paul Williams's bestseller, "The Huckle-Buck," a hit that topped the black charts for a full fourteen weeks in 1949. Hooker's rendition of this jump blues classic, played in a very relaxed though musically tight manner, showcases his great chordwork and incredibly agile single-string runs in addition to a rocking boogie-oriented piano solo contributed by Lane. Earl, after executing the original theme with impeccable taste, moves through a set of variations before he deftly works his way back to the standard riff, bringing the song to a natural ending. Mention should also be made of Phillips's superlative engineering; the sound is surprisingly crisp and distinct, and it can still fill the listener with admiration today, considering the restricted technical resources then available in the small Memphis studio.

Because of the relatively large number of sides taped that day, Hooker succeeded in getting some financial compensation for his efforts, even though Phillips was not wont to paying auditioning artists. "We were not really paid," Little Milton remembers. "As I said, we were like ripped off in other words, but at that time we didn't know anybody and didn't really care; we just wanted a record out. You'd like sign a contract and [Phillips]'d buy all the rights and everything for a dollar, we discovered all this kinda stuff later on, you know. You'd go in and maybe he'd give you $50, $100, and you'd be in the studio all day, possibly half of the night, and that was basically it, you'd get half a cent royalty on that kinda stuff, you know, slavery, really."

If Phillips did not pay well the artists like Little Milton whose efforts he released on the Sun label, he certainly had no intention of giving Hooker and Gilmore much more than enough change to cover their expenses; and when Gilmore was royally handed $3 for gas and $4.74 for whiskey, Earl managed to get the lion's share as usual with a full $25 payment. But before Hooker and his team left that day, Phillips made sure that he knew where to get in touch with them in case of emergency; Gilmore indicated that he could be contacted at the Shurden Plantation in Drew, Mississippi, whereas Earl gave his mother's current address in Chicago before he added that he could also be found at De France's Barber Shop, at the corner of Poplar and Division Streets in Cairo, a sign which clearly pointed to the guitarist's continuing connection with the southern Illinois scene.

Indeed it was to Cairo, and more particularly to his old friend Pinetop Perkins, that Earl turned shortly after this first Sun audition, when Phillips asked him to tape additional material. None of the material taped in July ever saw the light on the Sun label, but Sam Phillips thought highly enough of Hooker's music to set up another session at his Union Avenue studio within a matter of weeks. "Well, I'll tell you," Pinetop Perkins explains, "I was livin' in Cairo at that particular time. And Hooker picked me up and we went to come to Memphis, and he said, 'Well, we gonna go over here and see can we do some recording.' So that's the way we got in with [Phillips]; Hooker, and I forget the drummer's name—let's see, I believe they called him Shorty, a little boy they called Shorty, that's who it was. I didn't get anythin' out of it, Earl might have gotten somethin', but I didn't. Sun's records, I think it was."

Shorty (real name Edward Lee Irvin) was no newcomer on the scene, since he had often worked with Hooker in the late forties when both men traveled with Robert Nighthawk. Shorty and Nighthawk were seen together so commonly, in fact, that Shorty was currently referred to as "Little Nighthawk" by other musicians; their longtime association was brought to a brutal end years later when Nighthawk's drummer jumped from a window one evening in Chicago and killed himself.

On the evening of Monday, August 10, 1953, Hooker with Shorty and Pinetop in tow entered the Union Avenue studio in Memphis, where he cut additional tapes under the direction of Sam Phillips. As opposed to Gilmore, who sang "I'm tired of runnin' around, I believe I'll settle down" a few weeks earlier, Earl Hooker claimed loud and strong in his only non-instrumental effort of the day that he was "goin' on down the line," not even bothering to turn back as his baby called his name. He sings the tune's jaunty lines at the top of his voice with the help of his fellow musicians, who back his vocals on a call-and-response pattern. Pinetop Perkins's boogie-woogie piano supports Earl's hot lead guitar superbly on this humorous "Going On Down the Line," a tune that incorporates all of the original elements that were to make rock 'n' roll music stand out shortly afterward.

The instrumental side of Earl's performance, though not as uniformly satisfactory as his sole vocal attempt, also displays both originality and drive. This is exemplified by "Earl's Boogie Woogie," a track enlightened by a rocking piano solo, reminiscent of the infectious "Guitar Boogie" waxed in 1947 by western swing guitarist Arthur Smith. "Guitar Rag" confirms Earl's interest in hillbilly music, a trait he shared with most black blues players. Little Milton, who learned his trade in the Delta in the early fifties, reports: "In the early part of my career, I also played some country & western. We'd play the black clubs on the weekends, but it wasn't really enough money being made to just survive about just working on the weekend, and we played some of the white clubs through the week. To tell you the truth, I think country & western is one of the most meaningful, realistic musics of today, that and blues and the gospel."

To that extent, Hooker's "Guitar Rag" is a fitting example of the close interaction that existed in the South between the black and white communities as far as music was concerned. This fine instrumental piece, recorded for the first time in 1923 by a black guitarist from Kentucky named Sylvester Weaver, remained part of the blues tradition until it inspired a white version waxed by Roy Harvey and Jess Johnston at the end of 1930. It was popularized in 1936 by Bob Wills and His Texas Playboys, whose western swing adaptation "Steel Guitar Rag," featuring the great solo work of steel guitar virtuoso Leon McAuliffe, was a national hit on the white market. As part of the country music repertoire, it influenced Hooker in his turn, who reintroduced it into black R&B in 1953. "Guitar Rag" actually was the first in a steady line of white country hits that Hooker recorded over the years, most of which were worthier efforts than this clumsy rendition marred by the inadequacy of Earl's back-up musicians.

The band was standing on more familiar ground for the session's final item, when Pinetop Perkins was given a chance to try his luck as a singer. A great boogie-woogie specialist, Perkins decided to contribute for the first time on tape a spirited version of his personal anthem, "Pinetop's Boogie Woogie," originally the work of Clarence "Pine Top" Smith, whose 1928 Vocalion recording officially introduced the term "boogie-woogie" into the English language, according to the *Oxford English Dictionary*. With this two-fisted piano performance, this second summer 1953 session brought Hooker's lightning association with Sam Phillips and the Sun label to a close. Phillips went on to bigger things with other artists, leaving Earl's demo material unissued until some twenty years later, when it cropped up on posthumous LP homage and compilation albums.

"Frankly, I think that Earl probably had as much potential as any of the artists that I recorded during that time," Sam Phillips admits. "Earl just did not get the opportunity that some of the others that I recorded did, and it certainly was not because of a lack of talent on his part, and I'm not being complimentary for complimentary sake. But it was a time thing. Now, I feel I could have taken Earl Hooker—in fact I know he could have been a tremendous hit. I don't know of anybody that plays the guitar better than Earl Hooker. I don't know of anybody that actually, in his way, could have been closer to a recognizable stylist, even when he sang, you know. He played the guitar with an awful lot of natural feel, and no doubt, had conditions been different—you gotta remember this was a rather hectic time for small operation, because you had to sell people psychologically.

"But it really is a shame that Earl never made it to the top. And I can assure you that I was totally aware of his talents but I had to put my priorities somewhere, with different artists, the ones I thought I could run with the soonest and get the most mileage out of. Not just to make money, but to get this whole era ingrained psychologically, so that people instinctively, if they heard it, they didn't care whether it was black or white, if it was in the groove, so to speak, that they wanted that record, because it had vitality, it had spontaneity. Being a small record company, I always definitely wanted to keep my number of releases to a minimum, and I had to keep my organization small because I had to do most of the work myself. I had rather do a little bit to the best of my ability than to try to be all things to everybody. So basically, that's the bottom line on what we did."

Inasmuch as they nicely complement Earl's earlier King and Rockin' Florida sessions, the Sun tapes stand today as a witness to Hooker's early musical style and formidable command of the guitar, showing that he was at the peak of his technical ability at the age of twenty-four. More than sheer inventiveness, his flowing improvisations display a crispness and genuine strength that his late recordings often lack, a fact that Hooker himself proudly confessed to in a rare interview with producer Chris Strachwitz in 1968: "Back in those days I was playing more guitar than I am now. I was younger and had more pep—I was playing better then—my fingers were much faster, and some of the music they are playing now—well, I was playing it back in 1949!"[2]

The fact that Hooker's initial recordings were made in Florida and then in Memphis is particularly significant, as it belies the current opinion that Earl was a typical representative of the Chicago style. Even though Hooker did use Chicago as a home base during most of his career, he unquestionably belonged to the early postwar tradition that combined rough Delta sounds with more modern, sophisticated overtones borrowed from the swing and jazz idioms, contributing in his modest way to the development of a specific Memphis R&B

sound. Unlike most Chicago guitarists of his generation, including Magic Sam, Jody Williams, Otis Rush, and Buddy Guy, Earl never became another imitator of the tremendously influential B. B. King, his own style schematically combining borrowings from Robert Nighthawk and T-Bone Walker. King and Hooker were aware of each other's existence in the early fifties, but they had both perfected their own stylings by the time they met in 1952 in Arkansas. If Earl discovered the records of French guitar wizard Django Reinhardt through B. B. King, the latter envied Hooker's eerie mastery of the slide, and he tried to imitate this sound by trilling his fingers on the strings of his instrument. "I tell you what Earl Hooker could do," Billy "The Kid" Emerson, another Sun artist, states with emphasis. "And as smart as B. B. King is, B. B. always learned from the other guy. Earl Hooker could play that slide. He mastered that. I don't think I've ever heard anybody could play slide like Earl Hooker. And B. B. wanted to learn that. But he's the first big hand shaker, he'd shake his hands to make the strings vibrate."[3]

B. B. King admired Earl's slide style so much in fact that he even tried at one point to convince Hooker to give him lessons. According to Andrew Odom, who was Hooker's favorite vocalist in the sixties, "Hooker was a guy like that. I remember the time that B. B. King offered him to pay him to teach him how to play the slide, and he told him, 'No, I don't teach nobody how to play my stuff, man.' That was at Kansas City Red's place on Madison and Loomis, B. B. King came by that night, and he axed Earl, say, 'Hey, man, why don't you teach me how to play the slide? I'll pay you a grand a week if you teach me.' 'Oh, no,' he said, 'Man, I-I-I-I c-c-can't t-t-teach you how to play my shit, man,' you know. And we had a little jam session that night."

Earl's main influence on the Delta scene was an indirect one. It is true that he left but a handful of unreleased Sun recordings, but his distinctive style could be heard in the playing of Ike Turner, largely patterned after Earl's, which was featured on many of the records that made the fame of postwar Delta blues. As a counterpart, the influence of Memphis on Hooker was a marked one in many respects, from a musical and personal standpoint. An example was the uncanny taste for eccentric clothing Earl derived from older and more established musicians, like saxophonist Adolph "Billy" Duncan, who rigged themselves out in the loud colored suits, shoes, and glittery accessories that could be seen in the windows of the Lansky Brothers' clothing store on Beale Street.

Musically speaking, the more sophisticated Delta sounds Hooker heard in Memphis had an effect not so much on his playing, which indelibly bore the stamp of Robert Nighthawk, as on his song repertoire. In addition to the instrumental renditions of Memphis R&B hits Earl regularly gave on stage, many of the songs he accepted to sing were drawn from the repertoires of artists he met around Memphis, including Little Milton, Bobby "Blue" Bland, Junior Parker, and Rosco Gordon. Earl's own recorded output bears witness to this: it includes several covers of Gordon's 1956 hit "The Chicken" and Parker's "How Long Can This Go On."

Earl seems to have borrowed even more from the repertoire of Ike Turner's Kings of Rhythm. When Turner left Memphis to settle in the St. Louis area, the close relationship he had with Hooker did not come to a close with this move North. The golden days of Memphis R&B carried all the more significance, as they did not last more than a decade. Sam Phillips, who had already played an essential role in the development of the postwar Memphis sound, was again at the source of the tremendous upheavals that impelled Ike Turner to take up a new home base. The discovery of Elvis Presley and the birth of white country rock music are well-known stories that need not be retold here; yet the advent of this overwhelming musical trend, despite the fact that it was deeply rooted in the blues—Mississippi-born Elvis Presley expressed his boundless admiration for B. B. King, Howlin' Wolf, and Earl Hooker, all of whom he met and heard in Memphis—rapidly eclipsed the R&B sounds from which it emerged, compelling many black musicians to seek refuge in larger northern urban centers. Change already was in the air when Ike Turner left the Deep South sometime in 1954.

Being one of the very first to make the move to St. Louis, Turner managed to drag along over the years most of the musicians who performed at one point or another with his Kings of Rhythm. A logical prolongation of the Memphis postwar tradition, the St. Louis/East St. Louis scene also stamped its mark on Hooker, who constantly stopped over in Missouri on his way South during most of the fifties and the first half of the sixties, more especially to hire St. Louis vocalists. Never at a loss for musical ideas as far as the guitar was concerned, Hooker usually tried to make up for his lack of vocal imagination by drawing his inspiration from the song bags of people like Clayton Love, whose "Do You Mean It" Earl covered several times over the years; Jackie Brenston, whose "Trouble Up the Road" theme generated Earl's 1969 "You Got to Lose;" or Billy Gayles, a powerful singer and drummer that Hooker featured on various occasions in his band after discovering him in Cairo, and whose "Do Right" directly inspired the fine "Don't Have to Worry" that gave its title to one of Earl's best albums in 1969.

The only guitarist to emerge from the Deep South and St. Louis scenes who impressed Hooker enough to inspire him instrumentally was Little Milton. Milton Campbell, a very sophisticated soul-blues giant who belies his nickname every inch, was born outside of Greenville, Mississippi, in 1934. Following quiet, though promising, recording debuts made under the auspices of Ike Turner for the Sun and Meteor labels in Memphis, and before he eventually reached international stardom with the Chess, Stax, and Malaco labels starting in 1965, Little Milton first achieved local fame in the St. Louis area thanks to his self-penned "I'm a Lonely Man," the initial hit release of his own Bobbin label. Milton's vocal prowess has too often enticed critics to overlook the originality of his guitar playing, but Hooker never made the mistake of holding him as just another B. B. King emulator; in addition to his instrumental renditions of Milton's Bobbin tunes, Earl added to his guitar playing licks borrowed from Milton, a favor he very seldom did any musician.

Hooker was not the type of person who could be satisfied with imitating others however; when he used elements sampled from the work of his peers, he managed to change them into highly personal and imaginative creations. With time and as his proficiency neared perfection, Earl would make fewer and fewer borrowings, but the roots of his distinctive styling would always betray the double influence of the Delta and St. Louis where he spent most of his formative years.

The Chicago Complex

(1953–1956)

But for a handful of sidemen who put up with his eccentric behavior and who didn't mind not sleeping in the same bed two
nights running, Earl Hooker never kept his musicians over any extended period of time. At the same time, Hooker was very particular about his associates, and he was not one to keep mediocre
musicians in his outfit, unhesitatingly firing the one who had hit
the wrong note at the wrong time. As a result, few over the
years—with the exception of Johnny Big Moose Walker—stayed
more with Hooker than "Pinetop" Perkins.

When Earl and Pinetop left the Memphis area in the late summer of 1953 after their Sun session, they ended up in Chicago.
Mrs. Hooker always greeted home her wandering son and his traveling partners, but there was no telling how long they would remain welcome. "Mary Hooker! She was mean, man!" Pinetop
Perkins insists. "It was three of us that was workin' with Hooker
for a while, we was stayin' there with her. When we'd have some
money we'd give it to her, but most of the time, we didn't have

nothin', and she put us out in the snow, man, so I went on and rented me a room like I had to get me some money."

Mrs. Hooker's unpredictable attitude must have been disheartening enough for Perkins, who soon left Chicago, moving back to Cairo and the southern Illinois scene. Earl decided to stick around the city, working the local club scene for a while. The early fall found him at the Black & Tan in Chicago Heights, where his friend and former jailmate Kansas City Red had been the house band drummer and leader for several months. Red's combo at the time included pianist Blind John Davis—a veteran bluesman whose rock-solid keyboard contributions had enlightened numerous ARC and Bluebird recording sessions of the late thirties and forties—as well as Jimmy Reed, a singer, guitarist, and harmonica player who was barely starting a prolific and successful career for the newly launched Vee-Jay label.

"I played in South Chicago; that's where I met Jimmy Reed at, South Chicago," Kansas City Red explains. "And from South Chicago, I went to the Heights. I went out to see Sunnyland Slim one Sunday evenin', he's playin' at this place, the Black & Tan, and this guy heard me play, and he wanted to hire me right then, you know. I said, 'No, you already got a band.' But Sunnyland then, he's playin' so many different places, he said, 'No, man, take this gig,' said, 'it'd be a good one for you.' So I started playin' out there. That was around the time Jimmy Reed recorded 'High and Lonesome,'[1] 'cause [Vee-Jay Records founder] Vivian Carter, she was tryin' to get me also to do recordings, I told her I didn't think I was good enough. Then Hooker came along, and we played all together about a month."

The night crowd at the Black & Tan was mostly local, but it also included Chicago musicians who spent an evening off there, hoping to sit in with the band. This is how Billy Boy Arnold, then an eighteen-year-old harmonica talent who was recording for the Cool label, remembers meeting Hooker: "I didn't know who Earl Hooker was, but I noticed that this guy was an unusual guitar player, he could really get down and play the melody and—I mean he was really outstanding. Memphis Slim was in the club that night. That was a gambling joint. And I asked Memphis Slim, I said, 'Who is the guy who's playing guitar?' And he said, 'That's Earl Hooker,' and that's the first time I saw him."

Hooker's urge to drift back on the road made him leave his engagement in the Heights to pursue his travels. Earl was in need of sidemen, and he somehow convinced Kansas City Red to put an end to his residency at the Black & Tan. With his current health problems, Hooker was keen on spending the winter months away from Chicago's bleak climate, but the Delta was not their destination this time; instead they headed toward Florida.

In addition to the mildness of its weather, Florida had always made Hooker welcome; after all, he had done his initial recordings there, and club work was abundant. This was true in the Tampa Bay area, but also in Pahokee, halfway between Tampa and Miami, where Earl had some personal connections and where the guitarist and his men wound up after an eventful trip recounted by Kansas City Red: "Hooker had this little old car, and it broke down somewhere in Tennessee, and we hadn't near got started to Florida! We had to sell that car to the junkyard. It was a fifty-some Plymouth, I believe it was. Then we set up the instruments at the bus station and played for peoples throwin' money in the hat. That's how we got money enough to go as far as Jackson, Florida.[2] Then he called this lady, somebody he knowed down there, some lady out of a little small town down there, right off from Pahokee, Florida. I can't think of the name of the little town, one of 'em little towns, no streets, nothin' but sand. She sent a car to pick us up, me and Earl, and John Hoffman. John Hoffman, well, he wasn't no musician. He was a big phony. He faked like he playin'. He supposed to been a bookin' manager too. He used to jive around with one of 'em big basses, you know. He couldn't do that, but the peoples couldn't hear it no way, 'cause me and Earl Hooker we'd be loud. It was just the three of us then."

Pahokee, the home of country music star Mel Tillis, sits on the southeastern side of Lake Okeechobee in swampy Seminole territory, the site of a memorable battle that saw American troops defeat Indian forces commanded by Alligator Sam Jones in 1837. The breathtaking landscapes of Lake Okeechobee—"river of grass" in the Seminole tongue—have been beautifully put to music by British composer Frederick Delius in his *Florida Suite*, but Hooker and band were not so much interested in the local sights as in the bars and taverns that catered to sugar cane cutters and vegetable pickers on the weekend. Within the next few days, Hooker hired a couple of musicians to round out his outfit, which he pompously named the All Stars or the Top Hats, depending on his mood, and they soon headlined at the Club Savoy, located between Pahokee and Belle Glade.

71   *The Chicago Complex (1953–1956)*

Throughout the crop-picking season in the Everglades, bustling centers like Belle Glade and Pahokee drew hordes of seasonal workers who traveled from as far as Georgia in order to pick up the change involved. "During the winter months tomatoes, green beans, peppers, and other vegetables are harvested, packed, and shipped, for the most part by black labor who dwell in long rows of shacks scattered along the streets under clumps of bright green banana trees, royal palms, and castor-bean plants," reads the *Florida* volume in the American Guide Series. "From Christmas until April, Pahokee is a 24 hour town; long trains of refrigerated cars roll out for northern markets day and night; the streets are noisy and crowded; bars, restaurants, and gambling places are seldom closed. . . . Itinerant pickers, both white and Negro, known as 'traveling hands,' swarm into this region at harvest time, occupying tents, rows of tumble-down cottages, and ramshackle boarding houses."[3]

Belle Glade's bustling nightlife was nothing new, either. Before the war, Harlem Renaissance novelist Zora Neale Hurston visited the town during the fruit season, and her recollections were published in her 1937 novel *Their Eyes Were Watching God*. "All night now the jooks clanged and clamored. Pianos living three lifetimes in one. Blues made and used on the spot. Dancing, fighting, singing, crying, laughing, winning and losing love every hour. Work all day for money, fight all night for love."[4] No wonder then that Hooker and his clan could make easy money entertaining transient bean and fruit pickers, eager to spend at night a strenuous day's income.

Hooker and Red had enough experience to entertain blues-hungry crowds by themselves, but the need for a skilled vocalist soon became acute, and a string of professional singers appeared at one time or another with the Hooker All Stars during the following months. Among these were John Gastin—a vocalist held in high esteem by his fellow band members, whose natural penchant for the bottle kept him from moving on to bigger things—as well as Earl's friend and recording mate Johnny O'Neal, who was currently going under the name of Scarface Johnny. Neither Gastin nor O'Neal were famous enough for Earl however, and the guitarist's uncanny need for "stars" urged him to take advantage of the naiveté of his audiences.

It was around that time that Hooker started featuring in his band singers that he passed off as national recording celebrities; in addition to the obscure Sonny Boy who impersonated Rice "Sonny Boy Williamson" Miller of *King*

Biscuit Time fame, the Hooker band boasted a harmonica player known as Little Walker. Capitalizing on the strong resemblance between Walker's stage name and that of Chess Records' Little Walter—whose latest releases "Blues with a Feeling" and "You're So Fine" were riding high on the national charts in early 1954—Hooker had no difficulty finding lucrative jobs in Florida nightspots, although such swindles were not to everybody's taste.

"I know Earl was mad about that," Kansas City Red reports. "See, he made money with 'em, usin' other peoples' names. It was supposed to have been Little Walker on the sign, but Hooker had it printed Little Walter, and peoples in Florida thought it was Little Walter. I don't know where Hooker found this boy at, but he was good, he knowed all of Little Walter's songs. He was terrific. Then the peoples hollerin' 'Little Walter!' you know, and we would ride through, and had these speakers on top of the car, go through these villages advertisin', man, the peoples just fallin'. But I didn't wanna be part of nothin' like that, that's one of the reasons I backed out. We could have get killed, like that, baitin' the peoples in and gettin' their money, and then it ain't the real guy."

Hooker's technique was rewarding to a certain extent, for he kept his band working seven days a week throughout Florida, using Pahokee as his home base, but his natural reluctance to pay his musicians accounted for the transience of his sidemen. Says Kansas City Red: "Him and John Hoffman got into it one night. I think Hooker was on dope too. I think he had a kick on the reefers. That particular night, he's gonna run off and leave John Hoffman. He had a old white Ford, and John Hoffman was hangin' on to the car. He was running round and round in the yard in circles, tryin' to hold on to it and grab Hooker. He never could get in there, but some kinda way he got Earl Hooker to stop, and they musta made up, and then they taken off! But I hadn't got my money."

Hooker's associates somehow found compensations that made up for their leader's behavior, and it wasn't rare for shorted sidemen to resume their seat in the band once tempers had cooled off. In addition to the fact that playing with an instrumentalist of Hooker's caliber was an experience in itself, Kansas City Red gives Hooker credit for coming up with the wildest and funniest ideas. The unforgettable memories he kept of his days in the Hooker outfit, after more than thirty years, clearly prove that people would tend to put up with Earl's bad side merely for the hilarious moments he would give them: "Hooker, he's a hell of a guitarist, to me one of the best, and he was just wild, and he's full of fun. I don't know whether you wanna hear this one, that really happened, in a little country place of Florida. We played there, we had Scarface [Johnny O'Neal], John Hoffman, Little Walker, and myself. Anyway, this little place had a little outhouse in the back; so Walker was collectin' money at the door, and Walker had been messin' with somebody's girl up in there, and this guy come to the door; and you see, about me playin' the drums, I saw a disturbance, and they got to fightin', and that made everybody in the house get to fightin'. Somebody got at Hooker, and Hooker broke out the back door, and the guy started chasin' Hooker round and round the buildin'. So pretty soon, Hooker spied this out-house, and he jumped for that, and he went down in that hole, and they had to go get him out of there! All this stuff was on him, couldn't nobody ride in the car with him, and we all had to hang on outside of the car. He was a mess! He jumped in there! And, boy, that was another laugh. We told him, we said, 'If you can jump in there,' we said, 'why don't you go down and jump in the lake and get some of that stuff off?' He said, 'No, man, I ain't goin' in there. It's too many alligators out there!' We had to ride all the way back to Pahokee. He was drivin', we all hangin' on top, anywhere we could.

"Another time, that'll show you how funny he is. We played at a Sunday matinée in that little club out there in Florida, and this woman had a monkey in the back. Hooker would go back there, messin' with this monkey, givin' him cigarettes, and the monkey burned hisself, you know. So this woman finally let him a-loose, Hooker went to go in the bathroom, and the monkey jumped down on his neck. Across the field, Earl who couldn't get rid of this monkey, and the monkey, you know, just grabbin' Hooker's shirt! Hooker come out, he couldn't talk, 'M-m-m-man, somebody b-b-b-better come and get this monkey off of me!' I would crack up. The man shouldn't have messed with that mon-key.

"We'd do some heck of a thing! Another boy too, he used to be with Earl, he's a good blues singer, he sang just like Muddy Waters, call him John Gastin, he died. Tellin' you what me and Earl used to do. John Gastin, he'd get drunk, and he wore his pants way up like this," Red continues, pulling his own trousers way up on his legs. "So we kept powder stuff in the car. We had a act, we go around sprinklin' powder on peoples' heads and all this stuff, you know, where we played at, and nobody get mad with us, they thought we's havin' fun. But this particular time, we had this powder, and we goes to the exhaust pipe, to get all the black stuff out of there and put it on [John Gastin]'s face, then we painted his mouth white. He couldn't feel it, he was drunk, you know. And then we got him up, 'bout time we got set up to start singin'. He didn't realize he had nothin' on him. He gets up on the bandstand and start singin', and the peoples just rollin', and he don't know what all these peoples laughin' about. He already was lookin' funny with these short pants on, and he thought they was gettin' a kick about him singin' or somethin', and we all was crackin' up too. Earl Hooker just lay down on the floor, he laughed until he couldn't catch his breath. So he finally made up his mind to tell him, he said, 'Man, why don't you go and take a look in the mirror.' He walks up to the bar and looks in the mirror, and he jumped, say, 'What's that?!?' We crackin', he say, 'No one told me,' he say, 'You all dirty cats, man.' We said, 'That's what gettin' drunk will get you to.' If I'd had a camera, I think I'd have had that picture today, 'cause he looked a mess, we had him fixed up good. That Earl Hooker boy was a monster, boy, he come on with some heck of ideas. That was in Florida, we had a lot of fun in Florida."

Although life on the road seemed exciting enough, few could get adjusted to the frantic pace of the Hooker band. After a collaboration of several months, both Kansas City Red and Little Walker decided to settle down for a while after being offered by owner Walter Glennon to take over the house at Pahokee's Club Savoy, while Hooker drifted on and worked his way out of Florida.

Back in Chicago, Earl set up another outfit within a matter of days. If upcoming instrumentalists sometimes drew his attention, Hooker favored familiar faces, like that of saxophonist Aaron Corthen. Since their initial meeting in southern Illinois, Hooker had often used him in his band. Corthen was a good singer in the Jimmy Reed mold, and the fact that he was unknown to club audiences incited Hooker to take advantage of this trait, billing Corthen as "Little Jimmy Reed." This strategy unquestionably bore fruit, for Corthen pursued his career as A. C. "Reed" from then on, claiming that he was Jimmy Reed's brother.

Besides A. C. Reed—whom Earl used with regularity until the saxophonist temporarily moved to Oklahoma during the second half of the fifties—another vocalist and saxophonist who also performed in the Hooker band was Jackie Brenston, a fine singer Earl had met in Clarksdale at the turn of the decade.

Brenston was still working the usual club circuit on the strength of "Rocket 88," his 1951 number-one hit with Ike Turner's Kings of Rhythm, when Hooker ran into him in Chicago in 1954, and they made regular club appearances there. "I never had a band in Chicago," Brenston said shortly before his death. "The only thing I had was pick-up musicians. I was in Earl Hooker's band at one time and he was in mine at another. We'd just hire one another. I played Silvio's and the Zanzibar. But most of the time I was in and out of Chicago. See, I didn't like the dog-eat-dog thing."[5]

The Chicago blues milieu of the mid-fifties was highly competitive, a situation that could make young artists like Hooker feel uncomfortable. The clubs were scattered over two separate areas corresponding to the West and South Sides of town, where most black families lived. West Side clubs and lounges were Hooker's favorite spots when he played around town, and he indiscriminately performed in taverns located on Roosevelt Road, Madison Street, or Lake Street, the main east–west thoroughfares running through that part of the city. One of his regular gigs there was Chuck's Corner, where vocalist Bobby "Blue" Bland clearly remembers getting his first job in Chicago through the efforts of Hooker, following Bland's discharge from the U.S. Army in 1955: "Earl Hooker . . . Magic Sam and all of us, we worked together at Chuck's place at Madison and Damen, on the West Side. Shit, I was just sittin' in for fifteen a night. Earl got me the gig."[6]

Earl's main reason for performing there at regular intervals was the presence behind the bar of his Cairo girlfriend and occasional concubine Sadie, with whom he shared his life on the occasion of episodic stays in the Windy City. Other West Side locations that welcomed Hooker included the Happy Home Lounge, the Garfield, and the Seeley Club, which later burned down, killing thirteen people. One of the most noted West Side venues was Silvio's, the friendly and informal atmosphere of which attracted confirmed talents like Delta slide expert Elmore James, or promising beginners like Billy Boy Arnold, and where Earl and Jackie Brenston succeeded in hustling engagements.

The South Side club scene was a fairly different one; it was home ground for name artists who had succeeded in gaining a local following through their recordings. Thus for relatively obscure figures like Hooker, jobs were harder to get at South Side lounges, so much so that Earl even developed some kind of a complex about it. The main Chicago blues rendezvous at the time was located on the corner of Langley Avenue at 708 East 47th Street, one of the South Side's pulsating arteries. As a tribute to its location, this club—once owned by Chess Records' Leonard Chess—was known to aficionados as the 708, and its owner exclusively booked reliable acts such as Muddy Waters, Little Walter, or later on in the fifties Billy Boy Arnold, who recalls, "When Earl'd come back to Chicago, he'd play in Chicago. There was a place down the street from the 708 called the 608. He'd play down there. He had a complex about the bigger clubs 'cause I was playing at the 708 Club and he came in and he asked me 'How did you get this gig? See if you can get me a gig here.' So he wasn't really known by the club owners in Chicago. And he heard one of my Vee-Jay records, and he asked me, he said, 'How did you make that record?' he said, 'How did you get with the company?' So he had a sort of complex against Chicago, and he wouldn't play in Chicago. He only started playing around Chicago in the sixties. Down in the early sixties he just like was in demand in Chicago.

"But he really had a complex against Chicago because when I first met him, he would be in town, and when he was in town that was just like some great gunfighter was in town. You know, the word, 'Earl Hooker's in town!' like if he was at a club. I remember Howlin' Wolf said, 'Yeah, Zeb Hooker is up there tonight,' and you know everybody would go to see him because he was quite a musician down here, 'cause he was so outstanding. But he never did try to play in Chicago. He didn't like to be around Chicago. He liked to be on the road; you see, down South it was really hipper than Chicago."

The fact that Hooker's reputation, unequaled at the level of his peers, had not reached the ears of club owners or record label owners clearly explains why he played the tiny, unpretentious West Side neighborhood bars and taverns rather than the larger clubs lining 43rd and 47th Streets when he came through town. At any rate, his favorite playing grounds remained the dusty roadside joints and halls scattered along the southern circuit, where he had developed a lasting following since the early postwar years. Hooker's own erratic behavior had much to do with the lack of recognition he was given by Chicagoans; patience was not one of his noted qualities, and Earl preferred the immediate success he met in rural areas to the more lasting fame he could easily have gained in his own hometown.

Much in the same way intense competition rebuffed him earlier in his career in Memphis, the presence in the Windy City of a large number of good musicians prevented him from reaching the stardom he craved. Earl was ready to make concessions in order to perform on the South Side nevertheless. His occasional presence in the Howlin' Wolf band, for instance, enabled him to appear in front of large audiences. Wolf, due to his popular recordings for the Chess company, had a reliable following in Chicago, and the addition to his band of a guitarist of Hooker's stamp was always greatly appreciated by club patrons. Yet, Earl's independent nature and obvious desire to lead his own ensemble finally brought an end to his collaboration with Howlin' Wolf, who ensured the services of guitarist Hubert Sumlin permanently from the mid-fifties onward.

During the fifties, the Hooker band found additional playing opportunities with the Monday morning shows that several South Side club managers organized at the instigation of Theresa Needham, who operated her own club, Theresa's Lounge, at 4801 South Indiana. The unusual hours of such gigs put off established blues players, but lesser-known figures like Hooker gladly accepted such morning engagements. "I lived right around the corner on 48th and Prairie, which was a block away," Hooker's friend, singer Arbee Stidham reports. "So anyway I met him one morning; he told me, 'Come on and go in here,' and I did. I went in and then we jammed around there. She'd cook food for the guys, and all of that stuff, Mama Theresa. And she would have what they call a breakfast dance, it musta been around ten or eleven o'clock, somethin' like that, in the morning. Mama Theresa had started the thing and the place was small, of course, but it would be just jam packed all the time. That was a meeting thing then, like any time that I wasn't on the road, on Monday morning if I didn't see Hooker through the week, I would see him for the breakfast dance, and then I would go in and jam then with Hooker and all of that bunch of guys. Then we started goin' to the Trocadero Lounge, which was right up the street at 47th, with [club owner] Banks. It was like we'd go from place to place then, get out at Mama's, then we'd be up at Banks's. I'd mostly sing, because you see, at the time, Hooker was one hell of a guitarist, and all I was doin' was stand-up singing."

Even when unexpected performances came his way—as was the case when Hooker's band, including sax man A. C. Reed, got an unhoped-for engagement at the club of a cab franchise owner, Herman Roberts, thanks to a cabdriver friend of his—Earl's patience wore thin before he could cash in on his success, and he inevitably went back on the road. "Hooker would come into Chicago to pick up musicians," singer Lee "Shot" Williams, who was part of Earl's outfit on various occasions in the sixties, confirms. "He might play a Thursday night or a Wednesday night, but weekends, he'd be gone. That's why a lot of club owners didn't wanna hire him. They wanted him, but they know he wasn't gonna be there on weekends. He wasn't gonna stay in Chicago; he'd be gone."

Hooker's tricks also put off many of his peers, who didn't trust him enough to work in his band. In this respect, the relation by pianist-writer Eddie Boyd of his initial contact with Hooker illustrates the way Earl progressively found himself excluded from the Chicago scene: "I first met him in 1954, I was playin' at the Ralph Club, at Leavitt and Madison Street in Chicago," Boyd, an established musician with several hit records to his credit, remembered. "And he and his mother, they came by there. He had on his army uniform. I don't think he had served no term in the army. They just had discovered that he had tuberculosis and discharged him on account of that illness.

"But Hooker was a good-lookin' little cat, and he had a beautiful personality. And his mother was really a nice-lookin' woman too, at that time. I think she introduced me to him, and he said he would like to jam a number with us, and that was the time when Lee Cooper was my guitar player. And Lee Cooper had got on that bend that carried him on out of the world. He had started drinkin', and half of the time he would be drunk, and I would have to go by his house and help him put on his clothes, and help him wash up, 'cause he done pissed in the bed and on hisself, and tryin' to sober him up and carry him to the job. And he'd be feelin' so bad 'til he had to try to kill that bad feelin' and get drunk again, and I was glad to see Earl Hooker, 'cause he asked me for a job. And that cat ain't never even played the first night with me! I had to play one night without a guitar player, because he's supposed to show up and—sheeeeet!—he ain't showed up yet! So I had to go back and work with Cooper again.

"But we never had a cross word about it, 'cause he was the type of guy that it would be hard for you to get mad with him anyway, because he always was just full of smiles all the time. But he sure was a jive-ass cat, man. He was one of the most undependable people I ever seen. After then, I never did trust him anymore. It wasn't because I didn't like his playin'. I *loved* it, but he was nobody to depend upon, he was a real character.

"Hooker could have a contract for three jobs, one in Gary and one in Chicago and, say, maybe one in Harvey or Robbins, and this is the first of the week. He'd get a deposit from them different cats, you know; he was so good, and they knowed if he played he was gonna pack the house. Hooker is a guy who, it wasn't just records that made him big, it was his personal appearances. And when that weekend come, that cat would be down in Catron, Missouri, or some place. I mean he was really a funny fellow. He was somebody that could do some of the wronger things. If it happened with somebody else, you would have got so angry with him, somebody might have wanna go upside the head for stickin' 'em up like that. This cat, man, he was one of the most jivingest cats you ever seen, and he kept workin' all the time."

Hooker regularly worked his way back to familiar locations. In addition to Florida and the Delta, he progressively carved his way through the states of the Deep South, developing an incredibly dense network of connections in cities like Mobile, Montgomery, and Birmingham in Alabama, and Atlanta and Augusta in Georgia. At the same time, Earl was always ready to explore new territories. This policy allowed him to extend his working zone to parts of Kansas, Oklahoma, and Texas as he realized that his popularity had a tendency to plummet whenever he made himself too common, and he went on to find new openings.

The year 1955 found him venturing on the Atlantic coast, eventually ending up in Virginia and Maryland with his favorite impersonator and harmonica player Little Walker. Also on that trip was Albert Nelson. Nelson's initial instrument was the drums, but Hooker preferred to use him as second guitarist with his band, especially as their chance encounter with Kansas City Red in a small Maryland community spared Hooker the trouble of finding an experienced drummer. Nelson and Red already knew each other from Gary, Indiana, where both had chopped their drumsticks for local combos earlier on in the decade. By the time they met again in Maryland, Nelson had changed his name to Albert King, claiming to be some kind of relation to B. B. King who enjoyed star status then. Considering Hooker's propensity for urging his sidemen to make such claims, he may have had something to do with Nelson's new stage identity. "After I done left this Club Savoy," Kansas City Red recalls, "after all this stuff I went through in Florida—you heard of a guy called B. B., this was kind of a cripple guy, he was a drummer, kinda heavy set. Anyway I met him down there in Florida, and he let me play the drums, you know, and I take over his little group. And he started bookin' us all up in Virginia and Ocean City, Maryland, and that's where I ran up on Hooker. Right out of Ocean City, another little town, Salisbury, Maryland, that's where it was. I believe he was somewhere in Virginia, then he had this gig in Salisbury, and that's where we got back together again. Walker would sing, Albert King would sing too; that's when Albert King was beginnin' to play a little guitar. He didn't have anythin' to do with B. B. King and that wasn't his real name. I think Hooker started that, 'cause like I said, he learned how to play that guitar messin' 'round with Hooker."

Earl Hooker did not keep this outfit longer than previous ones; after spending a few weeks in the vicinity of Ocean City, his distaste at sharing the band's profits led to a physical conflict with King. Hooker hardly stood an even chance with King and his 200 pounds of brawn, and he wisely chose to take French leave, while Albert King and Kansas City Red were left behind. "We didn't hang around there no more than about a month, I don't think," Red states, not without a touch of humor. "And Hooker and Albert got into it about some money, there in Ocean City. He was bad about that; he'd get that money and run in a minute. Albert hit him and knocked him out, and we stopped the fight, and Earl Hooker went and left all of us. We had a bookin' for a country club, and Earl Hooker didn't show, so me and Albert had to play it by ourself. Hooker had done left everybody. I never did have no hard feelings toward that, you know, 'cause we knowed enough to make some money; otherwise we'd have been messed. After me and Albert went to play that gig, we made enough money to go get that car. The car cost $900, and it was a Chrysler, and that's when we left there and came to Arkansas; Osceola, a club they called the T-99."

After deserting his fellow band members in Maryland, Earl Hooker drove back to the Delta, where he got in touch with former Kings of Rhythm bassist and pianist Johnny Big Moose Walker, currently in need of a job. Together, they took to the road, and the one-nighter trail led them straight west to California this time, with a sprinkling of engagements in Oklahoma and Texas on the way. A mainstay on the Los Angeles scene then was R&B pioneer Johnny Otis, a drummer of Greek origin who led an all-black swing band that played a repertoire of sophisticated ballads and big band blues to club audiences of all sorts in southern California. In addition to his work as a disc jockey for KFOX radio out of Long Beach, California, Johnny Otis launched his own Ultra label in the mid-fifties, the name of which he switched to Dig shortly afterward. Otis needed artists for his company, and he took advantage of the talent shows he set up wherever he played, primarily with the object of drawing capacity crowds, in order to scout around for talent.

It was on the occasion of such a show that Otis spotted a fine singer who introduced himself as Moose John, and that he featured on his second Ultra release, as he explains: "Back in the mid-fifties we played every Wednesday at a nightclub called the Harlem Hot Spot in San Pedro. San Pedro is twenty miles from L.A. It is part of L.A. inasmuch as it is situated in the waterfront right at the Los Angeles harbor. Full of sailors and hookers as you may imagine! Every Wednesday was Johnny Otis Talent Show Night. On other nights of the week we'd do the same at other clubs in the area. Thursday was the Night Life, Monday at the Rag Doll, Tuesday at the Rutland Inn. I don't remember where the hell Moose John was from or where he is now. He just showed up on the talent show one night at the Night Life and shortly thereafter we recorded him."[7]

Moose Walker was touring California with Hooker then, but money disputes arose between the two men, and Earl apparently did not stay long enough to take part in the session. He abruptly left Big Moose out in California where the latter found a job for several months with the Lowell Fulson Band, led by Choker Campbell, in order to make enough money to pay his way back South. In retrospect, Otis didn't try to hide his disappointment at having missed meeting Hooker when he declared in 1982, "If Earl Hooker was with Moose John on one of my talent shows, I don't recall it. That doesn't mean however, that it didn't happen. Isn't it too bad that things were so hectic then, that there is a possibility that I missed [a chance of] getting to know the great Earl Hooker?!!"

This trip to southern California took Hooker farther than he usually went when he traveled across the country, as he had never ventured further west than Texas or Oklahoma. In the latter state, one of Hooker's favorite hideouts was a town called Lawton, situated in the southwestern part of the state some thirty miles north of the Texas border. It was a town that Hooker had "discovered" through former Kings of Rhythm drummer Bob Prindell, whose father lived there. After a spell with Ike Turner's Kings Of Rhythm, Prindell had combined forces in Memphis with multi-instrumentalist Dennis Binder and Earl's childhood friend Vincent Duling—who had made the move South from Chicago in the very early fifties—and this trio had often been used as a back-up unit on recording sessions set up by Ike Turner. Binder eventually took his band north to Chicago late in 1954. It was not long before the Binder trio hit the blues trail again with the Dandeliers, a group featured on United/States Records. This tour took Binder, Duling, and Prindell to Texas, from where they headed for Lawton on a visit to Prindell's father. This short spell finally turned into an extended stay as they ended up settling there, establishing themselves as the main resident black band. Hooker, always on the watch for wide-open territories, soon found out about Lawton through Prindell, and he rapidly started using it as a regular base—especially after establishing a lasting relationship there with a girlfriend who gave him several children.

Lawton was a market town for the Fort Sill Military Reserve, the presence of which accounted for the large number of taverns and clubs that could be found in the downtown area, where visiting bands like Hooker's found steady work six nights a week. Lawton boasted a population of approximately 70,000 inhabitants, and its downtown black community was completed by a settlement located on the town's southern fringe. The presence of an Army base in Lawton is not the only explanation for the importance of its black population. In the first years of the twentieth century, when the black nationalist movement was in full swing, a man named Edwin P. McCabe campaigned for the establishment of an all-black state in Oklahoma. Even though McCabe's campaign eventually failed, more than two dozen all-black towns were founded in the Oklahoma Territory, accounting for the presence of many African Americans in that state.

On his way back from California, Hooker stayed in Chicago barely long enough to put a new outfit together, and he played a few jobs in the city before heading for Oklahoma. In the late fall of 1955, he brought singer-harmonicist Junior Wells and band to Lawton with him, and they stayed there for several weeks. Everything went fine until Hooker refused to give Wells whatever amount of money he had promised him; when Junior came back with his pistol and started shooting at Earl, both of them knew it was time to go back to Chicago, where they ended up around Christmas time. The Lawton club scene apparently had more appeal than Chicago's, at least in Hooker's view, for he soon found a replacement act for Junior Wells in the person of Billy Boy

Arnold, with whom he drove back to Oklahoma early in 1956, picking up Big Moose Walker—freshly back from his own California stint—at Ike Turner's Virginia Place home in East St. Louis on the way. Billy Boy's tale of this trip stands as an invaluable account, illustrating the type of life Hooker led when he was on the road, hiring and firing accompanists with truly astounding unconcern: "I was playing at a club called Mama's at 43rd and Oakenwald, and Earl Hooker had just come back to Chicago lookin' for a band to take with him to Oklahoma. See, Junior was down there the month before I went out there. What happened, he said Junior got homesick or something, he was walkin' around talkin' to hisself. So he needed another band, so he asked me, he said, 'Hey, you guys wanna come 'round to Oklahoma?' so I said 'Yeah.' He came around the club a couple of days, sat in with us, and then we went to Oklahoma with him. We stopped in St. Louis to pick up a piano player. Early January '56, a couple days after New Year's Eve. We stayed in St. Louis all day, buyin' tires for the car. So we went to East St. Louis and Hooker went inside of a house where a lot of musicians lived, maybe twenty musicians. He went in there and he came out with Big Moose Walker, that's the first time I ever met Moose, and we hit the road. We had a piano player!

"We was playin' at the Jive Club in Lawton, Oklahoma, it was at 29 C Street, the Jive Club. It was a big club there and Hooker went on real big there, he was really popular. I had Big Smokey Smothers on guitar, and Billy Davenport on drums, so we had three pieces and we stayed about a month—six nights a week. The money was good at the time, big money. We would play from around nine o'clock at night 'til about, I guess two in the morning, regular time. I was doin' shows like Hooker was playin'—he had a Les Paul gold Gibson, a old Les Paul; Muddy Waters had one too—and Big Moose was doin' a lot of singin' and I was the featured attraction, I'd come up and do several tunes. They had a hotel upstairs and this guy who owned the club named Syd, he'd let the musicians stay there, you didn't have to pay any rent."

At the time of his stay in Lawton, Billy Boy met musicians like Dennis Binder, Earl's childhood friend Vincent Duling, and saxophonist A. C. Reed, as well as several other Chicago sidemen who had originally made the trip from Illinois with Hooker before falling out with him over money issues, including guitarist Lee Cooper and a piano player named Cookie. Another musician of note who resided in Lawton was Walter Brown, former vocalist with the Jay

McShann band, who was currently running his own nightclub there before he died later on in 1956. "It was an Army base; you had people from all over the country, man, you know. That's why it was a good town for music," A. C. Reed, who was currently playing in the Binder outfit at the time, explains. "During the fifties then, see, this rock 'n' roll was gettin' a little stronger and the white people wanted the black music in their joints. We played white clubs, but Hooker played in the black club there in Lawton, the Jive Club. The Jive Club was the onliest black one. All the blacks, big bands come in there. Rosco Gordon, he played there a lot of times. See, they had a hotel upstairs. We was livin' upstairs, and the black club was downstairs."

In spite of the fond memories someone like Billy Boy Arnold may have kept of his stay in Oklahoma, the life there owed more to the American frontier of the turn of the century as it is pictured in Hollywood movies than to the peaceful cliché of the Midwest of the golden fifties: "It was a small town, but it was a nice town; we had a lot of fun there. See, it was a lot of soldiers there, and they had their wives from all over the country, and there was plenty of women. You got all the women you wanted, soldiers' wives. The soldiers had to be on the base, and they'd bring their wives there or their girlfriends, and at night they'd hear the bands. We had our pick of women, but they had so many guns, you know, that it was common to run into somebody who had one. Everybody in Lawton, Oklahoma, carried guns. There was always a shoot-out; it was just like the West. You could buy a gun like you could buy a candy bar or a pop. You were just walkin' in, you see; they had gun stores all over the place down the street, you'd just walk in and buy a gun.

"Every Saturday night, we used to go to a place called Dixie's Kitchen where we'd get out to eat, and that was a shoot-out. I was going there one night and I seen a guy shoot a couple of people, somebody got shot. Like I said, it was a soldier town, and it was dry. They had to bootleg whiskey from Texas. They had liquor stores just like service stations across the Texas line, and the people would go over there. The club owners'd bring cases of whiskey back, half-pints, the cheapest whiskey and gin you could get, and they'd bring it back to sell it about two dollars and a half a pint. You could buy beer, you know, but you got your whiskey under the table."

Besides their fellow citizens, the favorite prey of Lawtonites were the huge jackrabbits commonly found in this hilly part of southern Oklahoma. These apparently harmless creatures were a calamity for local farmers, so much so that rifle ammunition was dispensed gratis to those who wished to practice rabbit hunting. This was as good an opportunity as any for Hooker to trade his guitar for a rifle every now and then and make an easy score, by Junior Wells' recollections: "The police would give away bullets to the peoples who shot jackrabbits. And them rabbits was so big, man, Hooker'd say, 'Hey G-g-grandpa!' say, 'Them r-r-rabbits is like horses!' We had a lot of fun shootin' rabbits. Me and Hooker, we loved guns. Matter of fact, Mrs. Hooker gave me Hooker's guns after he died. Me and Hooker, we used to could light a match with a rifle! We were just hoodlums, you know what I mean. We'd see it on TV, cowboys carryin' guns and stuff, but we'd do it for real. We'd practice until we could do it."

After spending the first few weeks of 1956 in Oklahoma with Hooker, Billy Boy Arnold rushed back to Chicago with his band after he accidentally learned that his latest recording had been launched on the market, leaving Earl and Big Moose Walker in Lawton. Billy Boy's abrupt departure found Hooker looking for other band members, and he set up a new back-up unit with Lawton musicians. Although pianist Moose Walker occasionally slipped a song in during their nightly shows, the vocal side of the band's performances would have been inadequate but for the presence of a female singer Earl had sent for shortly before his harmonicist left Oklahoma. "What happened," Billy Boy relates, "Hooker told the club owner that his sister was a great singer. So the club owner got some placards made, it said EARLINE HOOKER, and everybody was very excited to see her. So she got to town, the club owner's wife owned a dress shop and gave her all kinds of nice dresses to wear on the stage, and she stayed down there. She was a great singer. She had a lot of feeling; she was on the singing like he was on the guitar. She wasn't no ordinary singer; she had a feeling that you don't hear. She could play harmonica, she could play so many instruments, piano, she could take any instrument and play on it."

Christine Hooker, Earl's only living sister, was five years his junior, but her resemblance with her brother was so striking that she and Earl claimed to whoever would listen that they were twins, a statement most people never questioned. Her mother had originally named her Christine, but she was currently known as "Earline" Hooker, or "Tiny," while her brother referred to her as "Grandma." With Mrs. Hooker, Earline was Earl's most avid fan, and the boundless admiration she showed for her brother's ability encouraged her to start a musical career on her own and take up several instruments. Her proficiency on harmonica, guitar, bass, organ, saxophone, and drums as well as her singing often came in handy for Earl, who regularly hired his sister in the fifties.

Earl and Earline would sometimes spend hours on end playing and jamming together, as Al Smith, then producer for the Vee-Jay and United/States recording companies, recalled shortly after Hooker's death: "Hooker also had a sister that was very talented. The three of us used to sit in my basement in the early days of VJ records at 5413 Drexel [Boulevard in Chicago] where VJ was doing all the records in the early stages of the company's development. We would play for hours at a time. Sometimes Hooker didn't even know what he was playing himself, the soul just rolled out of him."[8]

The exact amount of Earline Hooker's talent is a controversial issue. It is very difficult to determine today whether "Tiny" Hooker actually was the talented vocalist and instrumentalist Billy Boy Arnold claims she was. Other Hooker associates, including Big Moose Walker, have expressed opinions that do not precisely confirm the sayings of Earline's admirers. "She went on the road with us a lot of times. Earline played a little guitar, a little piano, a little drums, she just wasn't good on nothin', but just good enough to play," Moose Walker asserts, while several other former Hooker sidemen fall into line with Arnold's opinion. "Earline? She was a terrific musician," drummer Kansas City Red stresses. "She played all instruments, the harmonica, the drums, the guitar, the piano, and just like Hooker could, he could do all that, the violin, he played all of that stuff. Quite a few years back, they had it on the radio, they was tryin' to get in touch with her to do some recordings, I don't know if they ever did get her or not."

Recordings may indeed be a way of assessing Earline Hooker's talent, but on the strength of an audition tape made for Leonard Allen's United Record Company in the mid-fifties with Earl on guitar, Earline sounds like a rather bland and under-rehearsed vocalist as she gives forgettable renditions of Roy Brown's "Good Rockin' Tonight" and Bo Diddley's 1955 hit "I'm a Man." This impression will easily be confirmed by anyone who had the opportunity of hearing Earline when she occasionally sat in with South Side blues bands in the seventies. Those who knew Earl couldn't help being startled as she unexpectedly walked into a tavern at night. The masculine clothing and short hairstyle she wore would unavoidably give one the eerie impression that the specter of Earl

Hooker still haunted Chicago's South Side. "She looks so much like him that you just scared when you look at her," Moose Walker says. Earline underwent tragic changes after her brother and mother died. A chronic alcoholic, she roamed the dilapidated back alleys around 43rd and 47th Streets in Chicago for years, speaking in an incoherent manner to the passers-by she stopped on the streets, until she was found frozen to death in her South Side apartment at 4758 South Shields Avenue on January 9, 1995. At the time, this tragedy urged Chicago officials to call for gas shut-off reforms.[9]

Bob Koester, owner and manager of Delmark Records, one of Chicago's finest independent blues labels, was in the crowd at Theresa's Tavern on a hot summer night of 1978 when Earline Hooker shuffled in and instantly cooled off a quiet Blue Monday night atmosphere. "I don't know if she's retarded or what. You saw her last week grabbin' people's arms and so on? She's always been like that. A few years ago, Bill Kurtis of Channel 2, they have a show called *Two on 2*. I took Bill Kurtis down there. Well, Bill is a little bit too much of a jock for me but that's all, but I respect him a lot, and Grandma came along, Earline came along, and she was drooling, literally drooling on him, and he just about flipped out. I mean, here's a guy, Bill Kurtis is not just, you know, your 'pretty boy news announcer,' he went out to Vietnam, armpit of the world, doing stories and stuff, you know, but he couldn't handle it at all. Well, he did—said, 'I don't need that kinda stuff!' But my impression would be that she is retarded with an alcohol problem." Saxophonist A. C. Reed, who was standing at the bar that same Monday night at Theresa's, just said in an uncomfortable whisper, "She's the sister of that boy who played guitar, Earl Hooker. Pretty sad, uh?"

Singer Andrew Odom, who probably was Hooker's closest associate during the sixties, confirms that alcohol was partly responsible for Earline's rough ways: "Earline was just so mixed up. I guess she would drink a lot, but she was a good musician. She could play any damn thing up on that stage. That's the only thing [Hooker] hated about her because every time she'd wanna play, she'd be too high and he couldn't hardly get her off the stage. But other than that, he still loved his sister. He called her Grandma. 'Well, now, you know you can't do this, Grandma. You gotta get down, Grandma.' He would have a hell of a time to get Grandma off! The only person who could get her down was me. In fact, anytime she would get out on the street and the police would have a problem with her, her mother would call me, and I'd have to go get her because I'm the onliest one could go and get her and talk to her."

Earl Hooker lacked the patience to deal with his sister effectively. Mrs. Mary Hooker's son and daughter were obviously fond of each other, but they had a most unusual way of displaying their mutual love, as they constantly pursued never-ending arguments, especially when they traveled on the road together. "She's crazy," Big Moose Walker laughs, "Earline wasn't too good a friend of his. If she'd come in a place, she'd jump on him. I don't know; they couldn't stand one another, 'cause they'd start fightin' and he would put her out of the car and stuff on the highway. Yeah! So she was gettin' right in front of the car, and she lay down and she'd say, 'Run over me!,' and then she wouldn't move so we'd sit there all day. She's crazy! I mean she was just actin', not really, you know. She used to run me all the time, she's crazy, she'd say, 'Comin', Moose John?'"

If alcoholism obviously plagued Earline's health to a large extent, it was but an aggravating factor in relation to her mental problems, according to Bertha Nickerson. "She used to try to sing in the band, she could sing too. She could play some guitar, and she was good on drums." Bertha, who met Earline after she married Earl Hooker in the fall of 1963, explains. "But she was kinda spaced out. I don't know whether she had a problem or—you know, it's just some things happen to some people. But when she wasn't like that, she was just as good as she could be. Every once in a while, you could catch her when she wasn't strange. Like they put her in this place, somewhere like in some little town there. They put her in there for weeks and months at a time. When she'd get out, she'd be pretty well normal 'til she had to go back again. It had to be somethin' mental."

While Earline seemed to be the most unbalanced member of the Hooker family, her mother also suffered from slight mental disorders. In spite of the fact that Mary Hooker seemed to have a normal behavior most of the time, she was recurrently described as "weird" or "strange" by numerous friends of Hooker's, including Junior Wells, Dick Shurman, and Pinetop Perkins. In this respect, Kansas City Red's statements best describe the feeling of uneasiness experienced by those who were in close contact with the Hookers: "Earline, I always called her 'Screwball.' She was kinda, you know, crazy. Especially if she'd get a drink, she used to go out and stop the buses, and them things. She couldn't stand alcohol. And Mrs. Hooker, she was a mess! She was crazy, I don't know.

'Cause I stayed with 'em for about two weeks, and she got a little too rough on me, I had to get out of there. The daughter crazy and the mother's crazy. I said, 'This ain't no place for me.' She'd call us a bunch of bums. 'Why you comin' with these damn bums?! Get 'em outta here! Get 'em outta here!' Oh, yeah, she was mean. And when she would first meet you, she was just like an angel. She'd be so nice, she'd sit down and talk to you so nice. 'Earl Hooker,' she said, 'You have such nice friends . . . Get 'em outta here! Get 'em outta here!' all of a sudden like that. Earl wouldn't do nothin' but laugh at her, you know. He didn't pay her too much attention. But it made me kinda feel kinda embarrassed. And, boy, all of a sudden, she'd break out. Just like some sort of a click in her head, I don't know."

Considering the ominous antecedents noted in Earl's immediate family circle, one is entitled to wonder whether Hooker was himself mentally sound. While he could not be said to be deranged, his erratic behavior and unruly nature undoubtedly signaled a certain lack of balance. In the mouth of Kansas City Red, what was mental disorder in the case of Earline was mere whimsicality in that of her brother: "Well, he was a lot of fun. I can tell you the guy was a comedian, I'm tellin' you! That guy would keep you laughin'. See, when you hit that stage, you had a problem, 'cause he kept you laughin' around the clock. He would do some of the craziest things. You'd think Bob Hope is a nut, man, this guy was worse than Bob Hope! Oh man, he was somethin'. But it wasn't just stories, he'd do funny things. And I used to tell him that all the time. I said, 'Man, you should go to Hollywood!' He was a crackpot; he'd come out with a walk, I had never saw that walk. He put his foots some kinda way like this, you know, and go to jack-walkin' like this, and put his hat down, and start actin' goofy. That cat was somethin' else! I'll never forget, in Bradenton, Florida, we went to one of these second-handed stores where they sell old clothes, and old violins and stuff like that. He goes in and find one of these deep hats, and that long cloak they had, that's split behind. He grabbed this coat and he grabbed this violin, and pulled this hat way down on his head, you know, and he start playin' that thing and makin' faces, and, boy, everybody just cracked up with this guy. He was a nut! And I was rollin', I couldn't stop laughin'. He was just one of them guys, he'd go and see somethin' that looked funny; he had to do it.

"Same way in Cairo. The bread man couldn't deliver the bread to the restaurant, that man couldn't come in that place. He thought Hooker was stone nuts. He'd come in that door, he'd throw the bread and take off," Red chortles. "Well, everybody'd be crackin' up at the guy, until we finally caught him one mornin', and told him, 'The guy's like that, but he's not crazy,' you know. It was just in him, the way he wanted to have fun, but Mama, whoo! Mama Hooker, she was somethin' else! When Hooker said, 'I'm goin' home now,' I'd say, 'No, I'll stay up here. I ain't goin' by there, no!'"

The words "fun" and "amusement" invariably come up when his friends are asked to describe Hooker's character; Big Moose Walker, when interrogated on Earl's extravagance, merely confirmed the man's jocular nature. "No, he kept you laughin'. Then he wouldn't say nothin' but 'Y-y-y-you crazy, man. I don't know what to do about you.' Up and down the road he liked to joke, and keep you laughin', rather than go on and talk. Hooker would laugh all day long, but that would tickle me. And there was no way in the world you could beat him, you know. He'd bring up some parts or somethin' that you'd never heard."

Hooker's personality traits inevitably showed in his music, and the true charisma he displayed in his everyday life with his friends and associates accounted for the strong relation he had with audiences when he performed. His natural eccentricity urged him to come up on stage with a wide range of visual tricks intended to win the attention of his public, and his musical sentences were both flamboyant and imaginative due to his inventive nature. Earl's friend Dick Shurman probably described better than anyone Hooker's unusual shape of mind, accounting at the same time for the guitarist's weird manners and undeniable genius: "He definitely had personal charisma even though he wasn't that big of a dude. I mean, you would know when he was around. He was a good time guy as much as one can be, and he was a sociable guy. He had a thing in him, too. He raised hell every once in a while. Well, everybody is moody. You know, if you live in poverty and have to scuffle to make ends meet, you find out that you have your down periods. But both he and John Lee [Hooker], one thing about them is, some people's minds work in cycles, they go back to things. But both of those were like they're just on a line, they very seldom repeated themselves."

Upon her arrival in Lawton, Oklahoma, at the end of January 1956, Earline Hooker joined her brother's outfit as Billy Boy Arnold was getting ready to go back to Chicago. At the head of a new rhythm section, Hooker continued to give nightly performances at the Jive Club into the month of February, before he eventually drove back to Chicago. By the spring, Earl was back on the road, and he ended up in Missouri, where a lively blues scene was developing in the St. Louis area, more particularly with the arrival of Delta musicians who followed the example of Ike Turner. While in Missouri, Earl suffered a serious attack of tuberculosis, and he was rushed to a Chicago hospital through the efforts of his anxious mother.

Consumption came as a heavy handicap for someone as restless and unstable as Earl Hooker. The disease that plagued him from a very early age had never had any lasting influence on his everyday behavior until then, despite recurrent hospital stays for minor attacks, but the severity of this alert should have warned him against the inevitable consequences of his usual carelessness should he fail to undergo adequate treatment. Although his doctors advised him to rest as much as possible and move to a warmer part of the country, Earl refused to listen at first; somehow, he could not reason himself into spending less time on the road, since he thought that a sickness he had been living with for over fifteen years could hardly be that alarming. As his physical condition deteriorated with time, it eventually prevented him from working and traveling as much as he would have wanted to. The implications of Hooker's careless attitude were many, and further aggravations would later compel him to sit down when he performed and stop singing altogether, whereas frequent hospitalizations would force him to spend more of his time in Chicago later on in his life.

Zeb Hooker

(1956–1960)

As soon as he felt well enough to resume his wandering life, Earl Hooker left Chicago after several weeks of forced rest spent at home with his mother. At first he refused to listen to his attending physician, and despite his mother's recriminations he rapidly set up a new band, packed all the necessary equipment into his car, and headed for the Delta again. Whenever he visited the South, Hooker played the rough juke joints and cafés that provide live entertainment for the various rural communities located on both sides of the Mississippi River south of the St. Louis area. North of Memphis, he could often be found at various southern Missouri and northern Arkansas locations. These included Walter Taylor's in Lilbourn or the Club 61, located north of Blytheville at the Arkansas-Missouri state line, unless he appeared at one of the blues spots found in Osceola, Arkansas.

The blues scene in Missouri and Arkansas had apparently resisted changing trends more than its Mississippi counterpart, and an active musical current was running through Arkansas towns like

Forrest City, Pine Bluff, Hot Springs, and, more especially, Little Rock. In Forrest City, Earl found regular engagements at the White Swan, sometimes rounding off his outfit with Arkansas-born harmonica player Willie Cobbs, whom he had met in Chicago. As for the capital city of the state of Arkansas, Little Rock, it was the second major urban center in the mid-South. It attracted young country Blacks at a time when the mechanization of the cotton industry was taking its toll. In spite of the fact that most of the local players who had worked and recorded there during the early fifties were now gone, there were still many clubs in Little Rock or across the Arkansas River in North Little Rock where itinerant combos could build up a local following.

It was Osceola, Arkansas, a small town clinging to a Mississippi River bend forty miles north of Memphis on Highway 61, that Hooker visited most often. Osceola was highly popular with musicians, who knew that they could always find a gig at one of the town's many joints and cafés: the T-99, Distance's, Willie Bloom's, George York's, Bootleggers Alley, the Frisco Café, or the Morocco. In Osceola Hooker took a liking to a young drummer and guitarist named Frank "Son" Seals. Son's father, Jim Seals, was a gambler who supported his wife and fourteen children off the outcome from a little greasy-spoon café known as the Dipsy Doodle. Son was a mature teenager and a rough instrumentalist when he met Earl Hooker in the late fifties, and he was flattered to be offered a chance to sit in with his band.

"Well, Osceola is a pretty good-size town," Son Seals, today an established bandleader, explains. "It was a country town, but a lot of people. At that time, everybody didn't live right in the city limits, but I'd say the population should have been like then 'round about 20,000 people, see. That place, like that particular part of the country, was really mixed up, I mean, it was a lot of black people and a lot of white people. You'd see just about as many of one as you did the next. People lived out on farms and what-not, you know. All those people'd come to town on the weekends. If somebody was playin' some music, and they wanted to come to see him, they would all come to town, like especially on the weekend, 'cause T-99 would have some kinda live entertainment; they'd have a show every weekend."

Earl Hooker was not the only visiting bluesman in Osceola; musicians who came down from Cairo or up from the lower Delta played there regularly. Still, Osceola had a lively music scene of its own. In addition to Son Seals, vocalist

Jimmy Thomas and guitarist Walter Jefferson were leading their own ensembles around town, but the most popular local performer was Albert King, who had settled in Osceola in the mid-fifties with drummer Kansas City Red after falling out with Earl in Maryland. Up until the early sixties when he made the move to the St. Louis area, Albert King dominated the northern Arkansas scene, making new adepts everywhere he played.

"Albert King was livin' there," Son Seals, who professed for King a boundless admiration, explains. "And they all played together when Earl would come down. Robert Nighthawk, I guess he musta been livin' down there at that time, somewhere, because he played down there quite a bit. And of course my brother-in-law had a little band there of his own, a guy called Little Walter Jefferson. And another guy, Eddie Snow, he was out of Cairo, so he would come down and bring his group. And you had guys in that area, also like B. W. Morrison, whenever he wasn't all screwed up. He went to jail a couple times, shit, but when he was around, he had a good band. Pinetop [Perkins] was livin' around Cairo, so he would come down and fool around in Osceola a couple weeks or somethin' like that, and he'd go back to Cairo."

Using Cairo or southern Missouri as a home base, Earl Hooker set up a new outfit every summer. Driving along the Mississippi River, he played every roadside hall, country joint, or club he came across. Although his sidemen changed often, his bands included several mainstays, including pianist Johnny Big Moose Walker and a Cairo drummer named Bobby Joe Johnson who occasionally slipped in a song unless Hooker had picked up a vocalist in St. Louis on the way. During the week the Hooker band generally appeared in country juke houses, spending weekend nights in bigger towns. By Son Seals's recollections, "When he played Osceola, he'd play the T-99, the Frisco Café, there was one other place there around Luxora [Arkansas], he'd play up there. The T-99 would like to do Sunday night things with groups comin' through and stuff like that. So if he played in Osceola, he wouldn't just play there every other night or so, because he would do about three or four months in the South when he'd come down there, so he'd be done booked all down through Mississippi and Missouri. Now I would imagine that some of the places, that he probably did play two nights, like Friday and Saturday, but mostly it would be like one-nighters."

Over the same period of time, the place Earl would never fail to visit when he drove down from Chicago was St. Louis. More particularly, Hooker used as his base the three-story brick building Ike Turner had purchased on East St. Louis' Virginia Place in 1956—dubbed the House of Many Thrills by Ike because of the large number of females usually found there. Through Turner, Earl knew he could get together with the various R&B talents who worked on the bustling St. Louis/East St. Louis scene. Other than Ike, the most popular musician to emerge from the St. Louis scene was "Little" Milton Campbell, another Mississippian who had made promising recording debuts in Memphis for the Sun label at Turner's prompting. After spending most of his formative years in the Delta, Milton followed Turner's example and settled in East St. Louis, Illinois, some time in 1957. In the St. Louis area, Milton won the recognition of local R&B crowds who helped spread the word outside the restrained boundaries of local clubs, especially after Milton helped found the Bobbin label: "I lived in Mississippi; I never really lived in Memphis, and then I moved to East St. Louis, Illinois, where we got hooked up with Bobbin Records. Bob Lyons, he was the manager of the radio station KATZ, and him and Little Milton was the founders of Bobbin records. Mine, 'Lonely Man,' was the very first record that we did on the label. In fact, that was the birth of Bobbin Records. At that time, St. Louis was poppin'; it was great, you know. Ike [Turner] was like the big name. He was there first, and I came; then between the two of us we like had it sewed up. We were working twelve and fourteen gigs a week, believe it or not. We had so many gigs we had to give some to the other guys, people that wasn't really known too much then, like Albert King, Roosevelt Marks, and some of the local entertainers around there. Earl Hooker worked everywhere, all the time, man. We never worked together, we sat in several times. In fact, one of the last times I believe we sat in was around in East St. Louis," Little Milton remembers.

Things were truly thriving in the St. Louis area. By the late fifties the Missouri/Illinois scene, which had been dormant since the thirties, seemed like it was being reborn. As bandleaders emerged, new clubs opened their doors not only in St. Louis and East St. Louis but also in neighboring towns like Madison, Lovejoy, Eagle's Park, and Brooklyn on the Illinois side of the river. Illinois law was more liberal than that of Missouri, and nightclub patrons were known to flock across the bridge to the east side of the river. "St. Louis was a city like it closed real early," says singer Andrew B. B. Odom, who made his own singing debuts in the St. Louis scene of the late fifties. "After everything closed in St. Louis, everybody would go on the East Side, across the Mississippi, and go to a place called the Firework Station, also called Ned Love's, or to Slick's Lakeside Club, the Village Tavern, which was in Eagle's Park. Either that or they would go up in Venice, Illinois, to a place like Kingsbury Lounge. It used to be a big blues lounge where Ike Turner and Milton and [James] DeShay and Albert King and Benny Sharp would play. Clayton Love, and Jackie Brenston, and Billy Gayles, Tommy Hodge, and those guys. And then a place called Lovejoy, Illinois. We'd also go to one of the biggest clubs between Lovejoy and Brooklyn where they used to have Junior Parker; they would have Bobby Bland, Albert King; it was a big club down there. The last time I played there, they had Jimmy Reed upstairs, and we was downstairs."

Like Hooker, Ike Turner had the rather unpleasant habit of firing his back-up musicians almost as soon as he had hired them. Those who didn't keep enough cash to head back for the Delta where Ike had unearthed them in the first place were compelled to stay and hustle jobs locally. There seemed to be ample room for everyone, however, and artists like Johnny Twist and Albert King were glad to draw from this mine of local talent whenever they needed to strengthen their bands. At the same time, one of Ike Turner's most noteworthy qualities was his knack at discovering skilled vocalists. Over the years his out-fit featured on a regular basis the likes of Billy Gayles (whose drumming career Earl had launched in Cairo), Clayton Love, Jackie Brenston, Tommy Hodge, Jimmy Thomas, and Johnny O'Neal—one of the initial singers with the origi-nal Kings of Rhythm and the dynamic singer featured on Hooker's very first recordings in Florida.

When he was around St. Louis, Earl Hooker often worked with O'Neal, who was happy to welcome his flamboyant friend as a guest star attraction, Hooker's sensational playing never failing to draw large crowds. O'Neal himself was a powerful singer with a unique collection of stage names that went from his real identity, O'Neal Johnson, to more picturesque variations like Burntface Brother, Brother Bell, or Scarface Johnny. Other than Hooker, O'Neal's Hound Dogs also featured Earl's longtime friend Pinetop Perkins. After his recording session for Sam Phillips during the summer of 1953, Pinetop moved back to Cairo before pursuing the slow move north that would eventually take him to Chicago, reaching the St. Louis area during the second half of the fifties. According to him, it did not take long before O'Neal hired him in his band: "They called us Johnny O'Neal and the Hound Dogs. The drummer was 'Bad Boy'— Willie Simms—and Little Willie Kizart on the guitar, and Johnny Floyd Smith on the saxophone, and a boy called 'Ham,' I never did get his name, he played bass. Man, shoot! We had the best blues band in St. Louis, better than Ike Turner, man. We played all over the place. We had one place there on the Missouri side, we built that place up. It used to be on Goode and Easton, but it's Martin Luther King now and Goode. The Moonlight Inn. Hooker'd come by there sometime."

For Earl, the St. Louis/East St. Louis scene soon became the equivalent of a blues marketplace, teeming with clubs and swarming with musicians lining up for an opportunity to start traveling. One such aspiring candidate for the road was young vocalist Andrew Odom, who was currently learning his trade under the auspices of Johnny O'Neal. Odom, who later became a regular fixture in the Hooker band under the name of B. B. King Jr., recalls his first encounter with Hooker: "That was Hooker that really started callin' me B. B. King Jr. hisself. Back around in '57 or '58, I was with the Johnny O'Neal band then. Hooker had heard me sing because I was playin' over in a little place over on 14th and Kansas called Lorraine's Tavern, in East St. Louis. He tell me if I happen to come by over in St. Louis, he's playin' over there, and I finally stumbled on him. So he said, 'Well, stick around, I want you to sing. I'm gonna take intermission, and when I go back, I'm gonna call you back.' I said okay so after that, finally he axed me would I like to work with him. I say, 'Yeah, man,' 'cause I dug his guitar playin'. We played at the Moonlight Bar, at Goode and Easton, then we played at the Dynaflow Club on Glasgow and Cass. In fact, we played quite a few clubs in St. Louis with Earl Hooker, and then we played over in some places in East St. Louis." Although Odom played across the southern states with the Hooker band from then on, it was not until 1960 that the young vocalist settled in the Windy City, becoming one of Hooker's most faithful associates.

The implications of Hooker's developing tuberculosis were many; notably, it helped him overcome his Chicago complex as it kept him from traveling as much as he would have liked to. By the end of the fifties, Earl actually stayed around town over extended periods of time and regular appearances finally opened doors that had remained closed so far. Before the decade was over, most club owners in the Windy City were aware of his true potential both as a musician and crowd puller. With the development of a demand for Earl Hooker in Chicago, the scene there became more appealing to him because he was at last able to play bigger and better-known locations such as the 708 Club on the South Side, as Dick Shurman explains: "At that time the 708 was THE place for blues in Chicago and it had a window for passers-by to check out the music through. Usually a few people would look in, but Billy Boy Arnold told me that when Hooker played, the lure of his music was so strong that often thirty people or more would jam the sidewalk and occasionally back up traffic!"[1]

Around that time, on the occasion of a stay in the city, Hooker's path crossed that of his childhood friend Louis Myers. Since their early days together, Louis Myers had achieved relative fame as leader of a tight unit called the Aces that usually backed up harmonica genius Little Walter. On the strength of Walter's popular Checker recordings, Myers made extensive tours across the country but he usually worked on his own when he was in town. One day that Hooker was temporarily out of a band, Myers offered to gather forces, and they soon ferreted out club engagements in Chicago and in the neighboring industrial center of Gary, Indiana.

"Me, [drummer Fred] Below and [Otis Rush] had a band from about '56," Myers recalls. "[It] wasn't but us three playing together then we hired a cat from out of Mississippi named Willie D. Warren, playing guitar but he had it run down like a bass. . . . Then we hired a cat named Jerry, played horn, which was Below's friend. Jerry Gibson. And a cat started hanging around wanting to jam with us named Donald Hankins, big cat played baritone. . . . We went on the road down South and after we came back we hired Earl Hooker, that's around '56. We formed the biggest band in Chicago, we had the best band in Chicago. Sometimes other horn players come in and sit in because at that time me and Otis had the only horn band in Chicago. We'd look 'round, sometimes we'd have six or seven horns, cats just come in just wanna jam. We had a swinging band, played nine days a week in Chicago and you know there ain't but seven days a week. We played Sunday evening and night, Monday evening and night, we didn't hardly have time off."[2]

This large outfit was a rather unusual one for a Chicago blues band. Unlike the usual blues combos made up of a lead guitar player backed up by a drummer and another guitarist, this particular band included an electric bass player at a time when electric basses were still new. It was also most uncommon for a Chicago blues group to include several horn players who punctuated lead guitar phrases with raunchy riffs played in unison. Yet, there was hardly any room in the same band for two guitar players of the quality of Earl Hooker and Otis Rush—a superb upcoming guitarist with a highly emotional styling. Odie Payne Jr., who was drumming with the band then, remembers: "Earl Hooker, he had that double guitar, guitar and bass built in. He would play the bass and then sometimes he would sneak in a couple of licks while Otis Rush was playin'. Otis Rush would turn around there and look at him, and Hooker would look up in the air, you know, because he was a heck of a good guitar player. But he was uncontrollable in a way of speaking because the man was good."[3]

Even though Rush would sometimes concentrate on harmonica and leave guitar chores to Earl, the latter soon found out that the role of sideman didn't fit him, and he left his friends after a little while to set up his own big band, complete with two saxophonists. With this new group, Hooker performed in various clubs in the city, spending close to two months at the Happy Home Lounge located in the heart of the West Side on Madison Avenue. Hooker rapidly found out about the lack of flexibility of a seven-piece band however, and he promptly went back to his usual four-piece formula.

At the time of his stint with Louis Myers, Earl renewed his acquaintance with B. B. King, who was playing a series of club dates at Roberts' Show Lounge. This large black-owned club, situated on the South Side at 6622 South Park in a complex that also included a comfortable motel and several bars and restaurants, was one of Chicago's classier and smarter venues. Its owner, Herman Roberts, almost exclusively entrusted live entertainment to top jazz and R&B celebrities such as vocalists Dinah Washington, Sammy Davis Jr., Joe Williams, and swing master Louis Jordan. With national hit records like "Every Day I Have the Blues," "Ten Long Years," and "Crying Won't Help You" in 1956, B. B. King belonged to this exclusive milieu. Since their initial meeting in the very early fifties, Earl and King had built amicable relations based on mutual respect. B. B. King had lived through profound social and professional changes since his first hit had skyrocketed him to the forefront of show business in late 1951, but he had succeeded in remaining the genuinely gentle, modest individual that early friends remembered, and he invited Earl on stage when he saw him in the audience that night. In the room were several other well-known blues figures, including "Five Long Years" creator Eddie Boyd. B. B. King asked the club's photographer to take a commemorative picture and the reunion at his side of Hooker, Boyd, and Myers with the addition of B. B.'s drummer, Sonny Freeman, and female vocalist Lady Hi-Fi was immortalized.

When presented with a copy of the photograph in the fall of 1982, B. B. King manifested his pleasure, and his close scrutiny of the document stirred up long-forgotten memories: "This is a rare picture. I don't have a copy of this!" King exclaimed. "That would be the only picture I have with Earl Hooker. You know, I'll tell you something else. The first time that I ever had a picture taken with Elvis Presley, I had on this very same jacket! The same jacket I'm wearing on my first album, the very first album titled *Singin' the Blues*. No kidding. That's the best one I had!"

B. B. King's admiration for Hooker's ability went back to their first encounter, and although Earl was not one of King's sources of inspiration, he included Hooker in his list of favorite instrumentalists, along with Charlie Christian, Django Reinhardt, and T-Bone Walker. To this day, he will readily concede that Hooker, if he was no strong vocalist, ranked far above any other guitarist. "He was a good friend, and he was always an inspiration," Kings admits. "I'm sure that had I come along after Earl Hooker, I would have been influenced by him, because I liked his playing, and I still do. To me he is the best of modern guitarists. Period. With the slide he was the best. It was nobody else like him, he was just one of a kind. For me it was two, well, maybe three people: one would be Robert Nighthawk, two was Earl Hooker, three was Bukka White; so those was my three people that I loved the slides. And then Earl Hooker was the more modern of all three. He was younger, but he was more modern, so that knocked me out. I liked him because he had great ideas. Great ideas. In fact, I heard him singin' through his playin'. Quick fingers, very fast fingers, and I used to tell him that he had fingers like Django [Reinhardt] did. Fast move, real fast move; very good execution, real fast, so we used to talk about Django."

Earl's mastery of his instrument has rarely been disputed. In addition to B. B. King, many guitar players and connoisseurs such as Otis Rush, Louis Myers, Bobby "Blue" Bland, and Buddy Guy have testified to his supremacy, but Billy "The Kid" Emerson, a fine pianist-singer whose relationship with Earl went back to common experiences in Florida, once stated that Hooker's styling could hardly stand the comparison with the highly emotional, lyrical content of B. B. King's musical phrases, referring to an informal contest that opposed the two guitarists in 1957. "For years and years, B. B. King was a little jealous of Earl Hooker. Now I'm going to say this, and B. B., don't get mad with me, 'cause you know this is the truth! To say jealous might not be the right word but I'm gonna use that for lack of a better term. Because everywhere B. B. went, somebody always knew somebody could outplay him: 'You heard Earl Hooker?' . . . And so this gonna get to B. B. So I think B. B. came in town looking for Earl Hooker. This was in 1957, at 39th and Indiana. I think it was called the Hollywood. . . . And so, B. B. came inside there. He saw me, and Earl Hooker was in there. B. B. looked up and saw Earl Hooker, and when he saw Earl Hooker, I tell you, you never seen a man's eyes light up! You hear what I tell ya? I think B. B. wanted to hold the people there. B. B. started buying drinks for the whole house. . . . So now *allll* of his life, he'd been wanting to get to Earl Hooker and show Earl Hooker who was the boss. And, man! Earl Hooker got down there and Earl played that guitar that night. Because Earl had his chest stuck out, too. And let me tell you something—B. B. King beat him so bad! Everything he played forward, B. B. played it forward and backward! And B. B. King made him feel so bad until all he could do was just stand up and laugh. Man, I never heard a man outplay a man that far. You know, a horse win a race by a head, he won. But this guy won by forty lengths! That was a walk! And so that ended and so the word got out: 'Man, Earl Hooker can't do anything with B. B.' . . . But Earl Hooker was a very good guitar player."[4]

Emerson may have magnified a friendly guitar battle into a World Guitar Championship, and King's ability and popularity as a singer may well have helped him win the audience, but his impassioned narrative definitely proves that Earl's ebullient nature would leave no one cold. As for B. B. King, he has also kept vivid memories of that night at the Hollywood: "Yeah, we played. I remember the time [Billy Emerson] was talking about, but I didn't cut him bad, no, God, no! Earl Hooker was EARL HOOKER!" B. B. laughs before he adds with gravity, "Nobody, nobody, NOBODY could cut Earl Hooker bad, nobody!"

Hooker's almost undisputed position as a guitar prodigy would tend to account for his propensity to show off and clown in front of large appreciative audiences, while his virtuosity easily explains why he never displayed any jealousy for other guitarists. A competitive musician who played at his best when people were watching him, he liked nothing better than the chance for a guitar battle, despite his peers' tendency toward fleeing from the stage whenever his figure showed in the door. "He always liked to go to sit in and jam," St. Louis stylist B. B. Odom reports. He would love to do that. And when he'd come to a jam session, he would like to go around and say, 'Hey, Grandpa! Let's go around, we g-gonna c-cut some heads.' That was his thing. He loved to play guitar, and everybody that think that they was really tough, he had to go by and check him out."

"He was always ready to challenge anybody, just like he was the top tennis player or something," Billy Boy Arnold confirms. "Yeah, because I remember one time Memphis Slim was playing on 51st at the Barrelhouse, and he had Jody Williams with him, and Hooker said—we was going up there, and Hooker said, 'Man, Jody can't play no guitar!' I don't think he ever ran into anybody who really cut him down 'cause he had so much that he could do on the guitar, he could have the guitar say things and do things that nobody else could do."

"He wasn't jealous," pianist Big Moose Walker stresses. "He wasn't scared of no musicians. He knew he was the best, because otherwise Earl would walk in them places and if a guy couldn't play, he'd say, 'G-g-g-gimme that guitar,' and he'd run the other guy out. B. B. King will honor Earl Hooker as the greatest guitar player because he has did it with five hundred people in the house. B. B. King has said, 'Ladies and Gentlemen, my name is B. B. King, and this is Earl Hooker. I'm gonna sing and let Earl Hooker play the guitar,' because Earl Hooker was just that good. That's right!"

There was one occasion at least when Hooker thought he had finally met his master in the person of guitarist Otis Rush. But as it turned out, it took more than one man to vie in skill with him, as guitarist "Mighty" Joe Young later related humorously: "At the Castle Rock one time, some kinda cabaret license people was comin' around cuttin' the bands down to three pieces. And so that was gettin' next to me; I didn't want to be offa work. I told Otis [Rush], 'Well, hey, man, look. All they gotta do is let me go in that side room there and leave my amp out here and run my cord back there,' you know. And he said, 'Yeah, man, that's a great idea.' I said, 'Let's try it, man, and see. You don't have to worry about the tune, because I know what key you're in, I know what you're doin'!' And that's what we did. Hey, man, that was great. People would come in the Castle Rock, sittin' up there listen at all that music and they didn't know where in the heck it was comin' from! Like Otis would be soloin', and I had a part in there, and I come in and I'd take my thing, people was lookin' and they just couldn't figure it out. One night Earl Hooker came in the joint. Earl was sittin' up there at the bar lookin' at Otis, he couldn't figure out what was happenin'. So finally after we taken intermission and I came out of the back and I walked on over, and Earl looked at me, he say, 'Hey, man, looka here, where you been? What's goin' on up there on that bandstand? Are you workin'?' I said, 'You don't see me, do you?' He said, 'Look, man, I know good and well Otis play good but he don't play that much o' guitar!' I finally told him what was happenin'. Yeah, man, it was really somethin'."[5]

Nineteen fifty-six was an important year for Earl Hooker in many respects. Darker episodes like his bout with tuberculosis were compensated to some extent by the ascending trend his musical career was taking. At last, Hooker was moving beyond the restricted southern boundaries within which he had remained for ten years as he reached wider audiences in midwestern states such as Illinois, Iowa, or Indiana. The reasons for this were many, and they included to some extent the transfer of much of the southern blues scene to the almost near-northern complex of St. Louis/East St. Louis, as well as the fact that Hooker stayed around Chicago more because of his disease.

As Hooker's popularity waxed in the Windy City, the development of a local following gave him access to the recording studios. The first Chicago-based label to show any interest in his music was the Chess/Checker Company run by Leonard and Phil Chess. After the failure of a first proposition at the time of Hooker's stay in Cairo in 1951, Earl was invited again into the Chess studio around August of 1956. Backed up by a piano player, a drummer and producer Willie Dixon on stand-up bass, Earl recorded two instrumental sides that showcased his flamboyant playing. "Frog Hop" and "Guitar Rumba" have remained unissued to this day, and one would have to listen to the tapes stored in box number 4678 in the Chess vaults to find out whether technical problems prevented a normal release. The quality of the material recorded can hardly be questioned, for Hooker and band were back in the studio shortly after this first session to record the same titles again in September.

In its second version, "Frog Hop" is a pure rocking instrumental on which

Hooker displays his virtuosity. After kicking off with an introductory chorus, Earl eases into a basic boogie-woogie pattern before going into inventive single-string guitar pyrotechnics over a strong backbeat provided by the drummer. When the pianist takes over, Hooker showcases intricate rhythmic chordwork before taking back the lead. The most noteworthy aspect of this particular number is to be found in the intro and ending themes used by Hooker, which cropped up several years later in Freddy King's "Man Hole," recorded in 1963. It is impossible to use recording chronology to determine authorship in such a restricted world as the Chicago blues scene where a musician who originates a musical idea is not always the first one to put it on tape, but the fact that Freddy King's song was cut some seven years after "Frog Hop" as well as the fact that King acknowledged the influence of Hooker on several occasions would tend to corroborate once again the radiance of Earl's musical personality.

"Guitar Rumba"—a number in the vein of the Mexican-styled novelty piece taped for Sun three years earlier—is just what its title says, a typical rumba melody deftly underlined by syncopated drumstick work. If this track—recorded at a time when mainstream America danced to the music of Perez Prado, the "King of the Mambo"—can hardly be considered a milestone in Hooker's recording career, it stands as a testimony of his versatility in any musical idiom. Hooker's eclecticism was clearly acknowledged when these sides saw the light. Instead of releasing them on their Chess or Checker series, the Chess brothers used their subsidiary Argo label, devoted to rock 'n' roll and pop-jazz, a category Leonard obviously thought Hooker belonged to.

When Argo 45-5265 was put out in February of 1957 in between offerings by Louisiana-based artists Clifton Chenier, Paul Gayten, and Clarence "Frogman" Henry, it was credited to Earl "Zeb" Hooker, author, composer, and interpreter. "That's what most people called him anyway, Zeb," stresses his friend Arbee Stidham, who met the guitarist in the late forties. "It was a long time later that I knew his name was Earl, and the way that that came about, somewhere we were together, myself, he and John Lee Hooker, we were all the way in Lubbock, Texas. We were all staying at the same big boardinghouse, and Zeb was there and John Lee Hooker called him Earl. But when I was introduced to him, I was introduced to him as Zebedee Hooker." This trend seems to have been started by Mrs. Hooker, who commonly used her son's second Christian name. With time, Zebedee was shortened to Zeb, except when his friends wanted to tease him. "We called him Zebedee," Big Moose Walker laughs. "He didn't like that! Zeb, Zebedee, that's what his mother called him. I used to call him Earl Booker, for fun!"

Hooker's initial contact with the Chicago recording industry led to more projects. After the Chess company, Vee-Jay Records, its most important competitor, provided Earl with his next studio opportunity, when he was used as a session guitarist on a June 13, 1957, recording date by the Dells. Few vocal groups have been as active in show business as the Dells, who first started out as an informal street corner sextet performing doo-wop ballads on the sidewalks of Harvey, one of Chicago's southern suburbs. After an unsuccessful Checker single cut for the Chess brothers in 1954 that led to the departure of a disheartened group member, the five remaining Dells, more than ever determined to make a name, succeeded in hustling an audition with the black-owned Vee-Jay firm.

Next to the Chess/Checker enterprise, Vee-Jay dominated the Chicago R&B industry in 1957 from its 2129 South Michigan Avenue offices with a roster a national black acts that included Vee-Jay discovery Jimmy Reed, Paul "Hucklebuck" Williams, Earl's own cousin John Lee Hooker, and a string of vocal groups like the El Dorados, the Delegates, the Magnificents, and the Spaniels, who provided the rising company with its first hit record in 1954. As for the Dells, since their third Vee-Jay release, "Oh What a Nite," had become a Top Ten R&B hit in the winter 1956–57, they had grown into one of Vee-Jay's top-selling products. They were at the peak of their early career when they walked into Chicago's finest recording premises, Universal studios, found at 111 East Ontario on the near North Side, on that Thursday of June 1957 to record their sixth session for the label.

Vee-Jay studio dates were usually produced by Calvin Carter, whose sister Vivian co-owned the label, but bassist Al Smith was also involved in the procedures, his name being credited on the labels of many issues as bandleader with the company's main vocal groups. The Al Smith Orchestra actually consisted of studio units of variable sizes and qualities who offered their services to local recording companies. Among other mainstays, Smith's ubiquitous outfits included capable musicians like drummers Earl Phillips and Al Duncan, bassist Quinn Wilson, and guitarist William H. "Lefty" Bates, who later explained the origin of his association with Smith: "It was a idea we had. They started formin' a lot of record companies around here, so we went to 'em with a proposition that we could furnish 'em the best musicians available, and it worked out pretty good. Al Smith had the band at the time. Chance was the first company we went to. Then we went to Vee-Jay. And after we went to Vee-Jay we come up with what they call the Chicago sound."[6]

Albert B. Smith and Earl Hooker were on friendly terms, and Smith was responsible for hiring Earl as lead guitarist for the Dells' June 1957 session, thus giving him his sole opportunity to play on a Vee-Jay release. Under the competent direction of Smith, Hooker, with the addition of Lefty Bates, Al Duncan, pianist Earl Washington, and saxmen Lucius "Little Wash" Washington and McKinley Easton, provided a fine backing to the Dells as they crooned their way through "Time Makes You Change" and "O-Bop She-Bop (Cubop Chebop)," both of which saw the light on the flip sides of Vee-Jay 45s respectively released in August and November 1957. "Time Makes You Change," for all its appeal, did not bring Hooker's playing to the fore, both guitarists strumming an unobtrusive chord accompaniment. By way of contrast, "O-Bop She-Bop," credited to Calvin Carter and Vee-Jay co-owner Jimmy Bracken, showcased Earl's versatility in this unusual context as he contributed a rocking intro and spirited guitar punctuations, while Bates propelled the doowopping quintet with a simple though effective driving riff. Already a superlative blues guitarist, Earl proved that he was no slouch either in the emerging rock 'n' roll field.

The cohesion between Hooker, Bates, and Smith was such that the three men went back to the recording studio four weeks later for a session set up by another black-owned firm, the United/States Company. When Leonard Allen and Lewis Simpkins commenced operations in 1951, the R&B market was still dominated by 78 rpm releases. During the company's six years of activity, United and States blues and gospel issues by the likes of Robert Nighthawk, Memphis Slim, Junior Wells, Roosevelt Sykes, the Four Blazes, J. T. Brown, Gene Ammons, the Caravans, and the Staple Singers were released at close intervals. By 1957 changing musical trends and the hegemony of the 45, as well as the development of major competitors like Chess/Checker or Vee-Jay, were taking their toll. Just as United was about to fold, Leonard Allen and his partner Samuel Smith contacted singer Arbee Stidham. "They were losing ground, and they figured that that would help," Stidham recalls. "It was a friendship thing. At that particular time, Allen and Smith also had a cleaner's and they got all of my cleaning. So I take some things of my wife's and I to clean, and when I got out there, they started to talkin'. They started just from that, I say, 'Okay, I'll make you a record,' and that's when I made that record for 'em."

Like Jimmy Bracken and Vivian Carter at Vee-Jay, Leonard Allen and Samuel Smith often entrusted the production side of their business with Al Smith, who would usually rehearse the company's artists in his basement with a set of studio regulars before bringing everybody down to Universal. The United/States session that took place on Friday, July 12, 1957, was a double event. In addition to Arbee Stidham, an obscure vocal group known as the Earls also recorded a coupling that day with the same studio band, including saxophonists Tommy "Madman" Jones and Eddy "Sugar Man" Pennigar, Al Smith on bass, Fred Below on drums, Lefty Bates, and Hooker. Stidham has kept fond memories of Hooker's sense of improvisation: "I can remember that session because we rehearsed it about a week, and Hooker made one rehearsal, he say, 'I don't need to rehearse.' And he didn't! You can hear from the record- ing, he didn't have to rehearse. He played lead, and Bates was playing rhythm on that. I had a lot of respect for him as a guitarist, that's why I asked him to play on this session. I said, 'Well, will you play on that,' I said, 'blues.' Because Lefty Bates, I knew that he was a good guitarist, but for blues, I wanted to hear a blue sound, and I knew I'd get that from Earl Hooker. And that's why I went to the Trocadero Lounge before we started to rehearse the numbers, and he said he'd play."

This July session was a rather long one, for about a dozen takes were taped for each track as the sound engineer erased false starts and re-recorded over un- wanted takes in order to save tape. Of the four tunes recorded that day, only Stidham's were released, when Leonard Allen issued them both in November 1957 on what turned out to be the company's last 78, States 164. Lefty Bates, officially credited as bandleader on the label, stands aside on both tracks—with the exception of one intro—as he weaves a tight network of piano-like chord- ing in the background, letting Hooker drive the band from the front with con- fidence. As usual, Earl adjusts to the situation with perfect ease on "Look Me Straight in the Eye," deftly adorning Stidham's lines with brilliant phrases; his solo feature is a pure gem as he juggles the minor and major modes throughout a superbly flowing guitar improvisation that still baffled Stidham almost thirty years later: "Hooker was amazing, 'cause if you listen to the tune, everything I sang, Hooker said it with the guitar."

Stidham's second effort of the day, "I Stayed Away Too Long," was an attempt at presenting him in a down-home blues setting, and as such it fell short of the previous number. Hooker nevertheless stepped into the limelight for a fine solo midway into the tune, also playing on his Gretsch guitar the low-down introductory passage, as is confirmed by producer Leonard Allen whose voice, coming ghostlike from the control booth, was kept on the tape before the ninth take: "After the intro, go back to your regular way of playing, Hooker."

The second half of this United/States recording date presented less interest, as the Earls did not prove very convincing. Nothing is known concerning this vocal group, but considering the large number of young crooners who patterned themselves on illustrious groups like the Charms or the Dells, it may be surmised that they were but another starting vocal unit, possibly recruited by Hooker himself—hence their name. Various specialists, including Bob Koester, current owner of the United masters, have put forward the hypothesis that soul music star Gene Chandler was involved in the session. Yet, if Chandler later became known in the R&B field for his widely influential "Duke of Earl," these 1957 recordings took place before he got started in the music business, a fact supported by Chandler himself, who once confirmed to Chicago R&B specialist Robert Pruter that he had never been part of the Earls. At any rate, the Earls' sides were cut in the evening with the same studio gang who appeared on Stidham's coupling. Production notes indicate that the group's first song, "Meet Me After School," was recorded a dozen times altogether and that take nine was considered the best of the lot, whereas the fifth take of "I Love You So" retained the attention of the production staff. From a musical standpoint, "Meet Me After School" fares a little better than its follower, due to Sugar Man Pennigar's nice tenor sax solo, but Leonard Allen did not think fit to release either tune, and his company folded shortly after this final session.

This 1957 United/States date put a temporary halt to Hooker's studio work, and it was not until the first few months of 1959 that he was given another opportunity to record. Meanwhile, Earl drifted back into the ghetto, alternating out-of-town performances with local club work. "Nothing was steady with Hooker but the music," confirm those who knew him well. But with all the necessary reserve that must be attached to the adjective "regular," Hooker would work with a selection of regular sidemen at the turn of the decade. During the years 1959 and 1960, his main drummer was Harold Tidwell. Hooker was very fond of Tidwell, billing him with his Roadmasters—the current name of his band—whenever he could. In addition to his full sounding drumming, Tidwell's singing came in handy when no other vocalist was available. Kansas City Red, Earl's friend from the early days, would sometimes replace Tidwell, unless Earl asked his all-time fan from Chicago Heights, Ronald Bluster—later known as Bobby Little—to fill in as MC and drummer with the Roadmasters, giving the young man a chance to get a proper start in the business.

Another talented beginner whose career Hooker boosted from 1959 was Jack Myers, a twenty-two-year-old bass player originally from Memphis, Tennessee, who made the move to Chicago with his family when he was only four. Myers decided to become a musician at an early age, and he took a liking to the four-string electric bass at a time when it was slowly forcing its way into Chicago blues combos. Myers later went on to pursue a prolific career with the likes of Buddy Guy and Junior Wells, but his one-year stint with Hooker in 1959–60 provided him with his initial professional experience. Also in Hooker's outfit then was a pianist known as Cookie, who had appeared on and off with the band since the mid-fifties, especially in the Lawton, Oklahoma, area, where Cookie settled temporarily after Hooker brought him there. Earl rarely used a rhythm guitarist, so he gave a lot of attention to his piano players, as they helped build up his solos by weaving a rhythmic safety net under his virtuoso single-note guitar flourishes.

Early in 1959, Cookie drifted on and left the piano stool empty; Hooker, in need of a reliable pianist, asked his friend Johnny "Big Moose" Walker to take over. Hooker initially met Big Moose in the Delta years before, when Moose was playing bass guitar with Ike Turner, Cleanhead Love, and Boyd Gilmore. Moose and Earl had remained on friendly terms since visiting California together in 1955 and spending the first few months of 1956 at Lawton's Jive Club. At Hooker's instance, Moose moved to Chicago where he eventually ended up as full-time pianist and occasional singer with his longtime associate. "I don't know when I came to Chicago," Walker says, "but I been here a long time. I musta come here with Earl Hooker 'cause I would never have went that far from home with too many other folks I know. You would be a fool to go on the road with some of these musicians I know! I know I had to fight Hooker, but we was never going to hurt each other 'cause we was like brothers."[7]

With this new formula of his Roadmasters, Hooker hustled work seven nights a week, but his stays in the Windy City were constantly interspersed with the usual chaotic trips that would take his group through the familiar cafés, joints, and dance halls of the South. In 1959 Earl and his crew spent several weeks in one of their favorite hangouts, Lawton, Oklahoma, where one of Earl's childhood friends, Chicago guitarist Jody Williams, would often sit in with them when on leave from the Lawton-based Fort Sill Military Reserve, where he was stationed at the time. But soon, more recording work and regular engagements in Chicago's larger venues proved that Hooker had roused the lasting interest of ghetto audiences.

If former recordings for companies like Chess or Vee-Jay did not bring contracts, they cleared the path for the smaller labels that were rapidly developing in the wake of the bigger firms. The first indie to show an interest in Hooker's band was run by Carl Morris Jones, a Texas singer who moved to Chicago a couple of years before World War II at the age of twenty-four after flipping a coin to decide where to seek his fortune: "That's right, that's what I strictly did. See now, when I left Dallas, I was tryin' to make up my mind did I wanna live in Chicago or New York, so this ticket agent fellow he asked me, say, 'Where you wanna go?' I say, 'I don't know.' He says, 'This is the damnedest fella I ever seen in my life, don't know where he wanna go!' I say, 'I really don't,' I say, 'but I'm leavin' here today,' and I just pulled out a quarter, heads I think it was, I go to New York, tail I come to Chicago. Then after I flipped that coin, it said, 'Chicago,' and I came on to Chicago, and I've never been to New York since I've been here! That's true."

By 1955 Jones had started his own record label, which he kicked off with a single by Phyllis Smiley, a female vocalist who later moved on to bigger things with the Duke Ellington Orchestra. Several issues followed, and new releases appeared on the market every time Jones saved enough cash to cover studio expenses and pay his artists regular union rates. Even though no hit record ever came his way, Carl Jones stubbornly helped launch the careers of unknown artists, some of whom, such as Betty Everett, eventually struck gold with more established firms. His position as record label owner was a side occupation for Carl Jones, who usually tended the bar at Theresa's on the South Side, a job that kept him well attuned to the musical scene. It was on the occasion of one of Hooker's engagements in the city that Jones and Earl met for the first time. It did not take the guitarist long to convince Jones to produce his band, although Jones insisted on recording vocal material exclusively despite Earl's usual reluctance at singing in the studio.

"I met Earl Hooker at a dance out on 63rd Street," Carl Jones recalled shortly before his death. "It was a club gig, and two or three more boys was playin', so he was tellin' me that he heard I had a label and he wanted to do somethin' on it, and he asked me where he'd find me, and I told him he could find me at Theresa's Tavern, down at 4801 Indiana. When I started, then everybody wanted to record for me because they was gettin' so many bad deals, and I just started to record them up. Then Earl Hooker and I, we started to gettin' ourselves together. After then he started to comin' up to my house every day, and we started to practice the numbers."

Early in 1959 Earl walked into the International Recording studios on the West Side with the current version of his Roadmasters, including Big Moose Walker, Jack Myers, and Harold Tidwell. When the two songs recorded that day were released on Jones's C.J. label, they were duly credited to "Earl Hooker and His Road Masters." Regardless of Jack Myers's strong bass work, Hooker's first offering was a mediocre version of Memphian Rosco Gordon's influential 1956 Sun recording "The Chicken," retitled "Do the Chickin" (sic).

"Yea Yea," Hooker's second song, showed Earl's more pleasant side as a singer. It was not one of his compositions either, although it was also rooted in the Memphis-St. Louis tradition, being inspired by "Do You Mean It," a Kings of Rhythm tune originally recorded by Ike Turner's vocalist Clayton Love in the spring of 1957. As such it exemplified the strong ties Hooker kept with the Turner gang.

Carl Jones postponed the release of these sides until early 1960, close to one year later, but Earl's instrumental proficiency and musicianship had made a strong impression on him. "Earl Hooker was a musician, and he could play, he really could. And it didn't take him long to pick up anythin', he had a God's gift," Jones stressed. "Listen, if you had a session today, and say you had another fella over there with you, and you just have to tell him one time what to do, and how to do it, then he go ahead and do it, wouldn't you enjoy being with him? Well, that's the way Earl was. I'd say, 'Earl, play it this way, du-du-du-du-

du,' and shhh! Man, he pick it right up! He had a God's gift. And you will find very few peoples can do that. That's true."

During the weeks that followed Hooker's session, Jones brought Earl and his Roadmasters back to the studio, where he used them as a back-up unit behind saxophonist Lorenzo Smith. The resulting sides, respectively titled "Moose on the Loose" and "Blue Change," were immediately put out on C.J. 603, credited to "Lorenzo Smith & His Swinging Changes." It seems that the Hooker outfit was rapidly turning into C.J.'s house band, for Jones offered to take Harold Tidwell back to International Recording shortly afterward, where he and Hooker's musicians cut two additional sides on Saturday, May 23, 1959. By the time this third C.J. session took place, the composition of the Roadmasters had already changed. If Tidwell, Myers, and Hooker were still present, Big Moose Walker had been replaced by pianist "Tall" Paul Hankins, a man originally from Mobile, Alabama, whose unit, the Hot Peppers, were the house band at Theresa's Tavern at the time.

The outcome of this third C.J. session was not very satisfying from an artistic standpoint, for Tidwell turned out to be a rather limited vocalist. His two efforts of the day, "Senorita Juanita" ("Señorita Juanita, please teach me the español") and "Sweet Soozie," a passable dance number, were bland novelty tunes aimed at the pop market, but Jones still released them at once, on C.J. 605. Regardless of the quality of the music, Jones's amateurism, lack of proper distribution, and superficial knowledge of promotion kept C.J. from growing into an established firm, even though Jones made it a point of honor, until his death in 1985 to treat his men in a scrupulous way. "I paid everybody, I don't owe nobody nothin'," Jones insisted. "I think at that time, it was fifty-five dollars for everybody in the band, including the leader. Later on, the leaders started to gettin' more than the other fellows. But at that time, everybody was gettin' the same thing. Then I would press from three to five hundred, and then just like I'd get a reorder, some of the fellows would want some of 'em, then I reordered, and maybe they wanted three hundred for stock or two hundred to send to some disc jockey or somethin' like that." The inadequacy of this recording policy may seem amusing today, but it must be remembered that the music of obscure ghetto artists like Hooker, Tidwell, and Smith would never have been preserved but for the dedication of small-time producers like Carl Jones.

The relative failure of his C.J. recording sessions did not enhance Hooker's position in his hometown, but it certainly didn't discourage him. During the summer he managed to hustle jobs in the city wherever he could. Unusual appearances included sitting in with pianist Eddie Boyd's band for a casual street performance under the bewildered eyes of Marcel Chauvard and Jacques Demêtre. The two French blues enthusiasts were visiting Chicago as part of an extended field trip through the ghettos of black America, and they reported the event in an account of their journey published in 1960 by France's *Jazz Hot* magazine. "A crowd of black people swarmed around a truck parked on 47th Street. Eddie Boyd, who had taken us in his car, pulled up and warned us, 'You're about to see something unusual!' He got out of his car, talked to several black people and . . . climbed with them on top of the truck. We were to learn later on that this was Eddie's regular outfit, including Randall Wilson on tenor sax, Robert Lockwood on guitar, and Cassell Burrow on drums. Guitarist Earl Hooker had joined them for the occasion. He played an electric guitar with two parallel necks; one was that of a regular guitar while the other corresponded to that of a bass. A piano was hoisted onto the truck and the band started playing right in the middle of the street. We learned later that this concert was sponsored by a local car dealer. The crowd started warming up and groups of children began to dance. Everyone clapped their hands in time to the music, while smiling black policemen controlled the crowd so the cars would get past."[8]

Still, such performances remained the exception, and club work was the rule. Among the many music resorts that Chicago's South Side boasted at the end of the fifties, Cadillac Baby's Show Lounge, located at 4708 South Dearborn just south of 47th Street, held a special place. Narvel Eatmon, better known to the world as Cadillac Baby, probably was the city's most colorful tavern owner; with his wife Bea, they tried to promote blues music to the best of their ability, genially providing room and board to the penniless artists who dropped in at their lounge. Cadillac Baby's motivations were not exclusively charitable ones, for the shows featured at his club, complete with comedians and shake dancers, also helped establish his reputation. Cadillac Baby's activities were not entirely restricted to the bar business, and he also played a great part in the yearly Bud Billiken Parade. On this important black holiday, Bud Billiken—imaginary Patron Saint of Chicago's black children—was widely commemorated in the South Side, and Cadillac Bay never failed to hire a blues band to advertise his club on the exuberantly decorated float that he presented every year for the parade. Cadillac Baby's remained a popular haunt among musicians until it was torn down in 1960 to give way to public housing, but the fact that Cadillac Baby started around 1955 his own independent label, christened Bea & Baby, also attracted many young artists who figured that a local hit recorded for a small independent firm was a good way of drawing the attention of bigger record companies.

As he became more in demand on the Chicago club scene, Hooker soon found his way to the stage at Cadillac Baby's. Several musicians recalled later that they became aware of Hooker's potential after he started playing there on a regular basis. "I met Hooker in '59 in Chicago," guitarist Lacy Gibson says. "He was playing a place called Cadillac Bar, it was a little old joint that moved around and got on 47th and Dearborn, around the corner, but he had a label called Cadillac Baby, but he is the same dude."

Someone as versatile as Earl could easily play several gigs the same day; when a job with his regular band required his presence at a specific club for an early evening show, he could still be found later on in the night fronting the house band at another venue. This was true at Cadillac Baby's Show Lounge, where drummer "Cadillac" Sam Burton sometimes acted as house bandleader when Earl Hooker started performing there regularly in 1959. The way he actually got his first engagement shows how competitive the Chicago club scene could be. Most of the time, Hooker's instrumental proficiency and unusual talent accounted for the offers he received from club owners, but he could also give destiny a gentle push at the price of his ethical integrity, as the following story related by guitarist Eddy Clearwater clearly demonstrates: "I first saw Earl Hooker at Cadillac Baby's—I thought he had such a unique sound I said, 'This guy's really outa sight.' . . . Can I tell you a funny story? Jimmy Johnson told me this in Europe—we got on the subject of Cadillac Baby and he said that he used to have a group called the Lucky Hearts and they went and auditioned and got a job at Cadillac Baby's. . . . Cadillac Baby had heard Earl Hooker and knew how good he could play. So Jimmy had set up his equipment in the club and somehow or another Earl Hooker came in and Cadillac Baby said, 'Earl have you got your equipment with you?' Now Earl he stuttered when he talked he said, 'I g-g-got my g-g-guitar in the c-c-car.' Cadillac say, 'Go out and get it. Bring it on in.'

"Now Jimmy's already set up and gone out on intermission. When he came back the doorman say, 'Well, you gotta pay a dollar to get back in.' Jimmy says, 'But I'm playing here.' The doorman says, 'I don't care—you gonna pay to get in here.' So it went on and on—Jimmy says, 'That's my stuff sitting up over there. I'm the band that's playing here.' The doorman says, 'I told you. You gonna pay a dollar.' Jimmy says, 'OK if that's the way it is just let me go in and get my stuff.' The doorman say, 'Well, you can go and get your stuff but you have to pay a dollar to get it.' So finally the drummer got really pissed with the doorman, he's gonna start a ruckus so the doorman pull out his pistol and hit the drummer upside the head. The pistol went off but didn't shoot him. So they had to pay a dollar to go and get their equipment."[9]

"That's true," guitarist Jimmy Johnson confirms, "yeah, that's true. They wanted to battle at the door, I paid a dollar and went on back and got my amp. Yeah, I remember that. Well, I guess [Hooker] was the best player, you know what I mean? I had been playing maybe a year or something like that, and he was a very good guitar player then. What can I say?"

Cadillac Baby's position as tavern owner was as good as any to scout out talent for his label; Earl's flamboyance immediately roused his interest and he decided to record him at the next session set up for Bea & Baby. On Hooker's thirty-first birthday, Friday January 15, 1960, Cadillac Baby took two different bands into the Hall Studios, located in downtown Chicago at 307 South Wabash, and while harmonicist Little Mack Simmons made his own Bea & Baby debuts, Hooker cut one song and one instrumental. Cadillac Baby had an exalted idea of Earl's capacity as a guitarist, but knowing that he was no singer, he picked up a young R&B vocalist named Bobby Saxton to front the Roadmasters. Saxton, a native of Peoria, Illinois, was a newcomer on the Chicago scene at the time of his Bea & Baby date. In spite of the unexpected success of his ephemeral association with Hooker on record, he later settled in Washington, D.C., where he became one of the local club fixtures.

Other than Saxton, Earl brought with him pianist Tall Paul Hankins as well as his new drummer Bobby Little, who enlightened the day's recordings with his fat drum sound and hearty rhythmic support. Cadillac Baby completed Earl's combo with a female bass player called Margo Gibson, besides two veteran saxophone players and session men, "Big" Ernest Cotton and Oett "Sax" Mallard. "I had such a nice sound," Cadillac Baby explains, "everybody asked me, say, 'How do you come up with such a good sound?' And in this that I knew nothin' about how to editor and engineer records and be an A&R man, but by havin' good musicianers, I lucked upon pretty fair hits."[10] More than luck, Cadillac Baby's skill, fine ear, and original lyrics accounted for the appeal of "Trying to Make a Living"—credited to both Cadillac Baby and so-called "business manager" Ted Daniels—two versions of which were put on wax that day by Bobby Saxton with Hooker's support.

The lyrics to this tale of sadness and poverty are very competently handled by Bobby Saxton, who sings this song in a soulful vein, with his elaborate diction and sophisticated, tense voice. The sweet and swinging piano-guitar interweaving as well as the bouncing Earl Hooker solo, adequately spiced up with discreet horn interventions over Margo Gibson's rock-solid bass lines, are also largely responsible for the song's success. "What gave 'Tryin' to Make a Livin" such a sound is, at the time it had kind of an off-key beat," Cadillac Baby reminisces. "This woman was way ahead that played bass, bass Fender guitar. Margo Gibson. She played this thing kind of like she felt, which was way out. And we never heard nothin' sound like. So I must say it was a great record. And he [Bobby Saxton] was an unexperienced artist. I only gave him one side, and Earl Hooker had the other side, was 'Dynamite.' It was instrumental. Didn't do too much. We never played the other side too much."[11]

Hooker's instrumental showcase, recorded in a mood similar to that of Saxton's vocal side, is a tight and well-built up-tempo piece that stands well outside the scope of rhythm & blues; surprisingly the so-called "Dynamite," credited to Earl Hooker, is a fine guitar rendition of bebop trumpeter Clifford Brown's "The Blues Walk," that gives an idea of the scope of Hooker's musical culture. As separate as the blues and jazz worlds are, "The Blues Walk" has remained a classic with blues guitarists ever since, still played today by a musician like Joe Louis Walker, or Magic Slim who knows nothing of its real origin. At any rate, at the time of its initial release, "Dynamite" was largely overshadowed by "Trying to Make a Living," which transformed Bea & Baby 106 into an instant hit record in Chicago, drawing the attention of the Chess brothers. As part of the Checker catalog, the 45 then gave Hooker his biggest record so far. Says Cadillac Baby, "My biggest hit was the record I didn't think would do so much, was the record by Bobby Saxton. 'Tryin' to Make a Livin'.' 'Cause after I sold somewhere around 255,000 records, I released the record to Leonard

Chess, and he sent the record around the nation, wherein the record musta did somewhere around 25 hundred thousand for Leonard Chess."[12]

The accuracy of Cadillac Baby's figures is more than questionable, for sales nearing one hundred thousand copies would have been considered very satisfactory by anyone at the time; yet it cannot be denied that this only Hooker/Saxton Bea & Baby release provided the company with its best seller ever. As such, it brought unexpected publicity to Earl, who cashed in on the record's success by featuring Bobby Saxton in his band during the first months of 1960. Another consequence of this success was that Carl Jones finally released Hooker's C.J. recordings, "Do the Chickin" and "Yea Yea." The comparison between Earl's simultaneous efforts for C.J. and Bea & Baby certainly did not turn to the former's advantage; with the exception of a mention in the February 20, 1960, issue of the nation's second largest trade magazine, *Cash Box*, C.J. 613 went unnoticed, failing to sell more than drummer Harold Tidwell's own C.J. coupling several months earlier. Strangely enough, the undisputable success of "Trying to Make a Living" did not incite Cadillac Baby to record Saxton and Hooker again, probably for lack of financial backing. But if Cadillac Baby failed to bring his winning guitar-vocal duet back to the studio, another label operator with a keen interest in the record industry, Mel London, was about to turn Earl Hooker's potential to the best account.

The London Years

(1960–1963)

O n the fringe of his own productions for Bea & Baby and C.J. in 1959 and 1960, Hooker also took part, as an accompanist to others, in various sessions set up by another local independent label-owner and music publisher named Mel London. London initially launched his Chief record company in 1957, and among other Chicago blues artists, he included in his roster Hooker's friend Junior Wells. At the age of twenty-five, Wells was one of London's favorite bluesmen, with a handful of artistically mature recordings to his credit, including two early Chief singles recorded shortly after Junior's current record company, Leonard Allen's United/States firm, folded during the second half of 1957. In the last half of 1959, Wells found himself looking for a guitarist capable of holding his part in the studio as a replacement for the recently departed Syl Johnson, and he turned to Earl. Besides Hooker, Junior's outfit included for the occasion drummer Eugene Lounge, pianist Lafayette Leake, and Louis Myers's brother Dave on second guitar as well as Willie Dixon, a former heavyweight boxer who had established a solid reputation as songwriter, arranger, and A&R man for the Chess brothers since the early fifties. From 1956 Dixon had a hand in sessions set up by other companies; over the years, his expert advice and strong bass work enlivened countless Chess dates—including Hooker's own Argo sides—as well as numerous recordings made for smaller ventures like Cobra and Artistic.

As usual with Mel London, the Junior Wells session involving Hooker took place at the Universal studios. The two songs recorded for the occasion, "Little by Little" and "Come On in This House," were released in early 1960 on Profile—a subsidiary of London's Chief enterprise, with its elegant sketch in black and white of a Roman emperor crowned with a laurel wreath. If "Come On in This House" was the bluesiest of the two, "Little by Little," complete with London's finely crafted lyrics, had a more up-to-date flavor and was aimed at the R&B market. The song, taken at a medium fast tempo, was irresistibly attractive due to Wells's soulful delivery; yet the tune's highlight was Hooker's masterly guitar solo, which remains one of his best recorded ever; with stunning fluidity, Earl carries the original melodic theme with high-soaring lyricism, before giving way to a flawless major mode improvisation.

After making promising debuts in the Chicago area, Profile 4011 became a national hit and "Little by Little" ended up on *Billboard's* "Hot R&B Sides" charts on June 6, 1960, where it remained for three consecutive weeks, peaking at position 23 on June 13. This gem of the Chicago postwar era was to prove widely influential; reissued a great number of times over the years, its initial release in Great Britain urged Mick Jagger and the Rolling Stones to record an uncredited version of it early in their career.

Wells's Profile 45 turned out to be a two-sided hit, for "Come On In This House" also benefitted from extensive airplay on black-oriented radio stations in Chicagoland. Cashing in on his bestseller, Wells started using Earl's band intensively during the second half of 1960; for Earl, "Little by Little"—his sole appearance on a *Billboard* R&B chart entry—was a worthy follow-up to Saxton's "Trying to Make a Living," strengthening his position on the Chicago scene while comforting Mel London in his opinion that Hooker's playing could contribute to the success of his productions. As such, it marked the onset of a determining stage in Earl's career.

"The blues world owes Mel London more than he ever realized,"[1] *Living Blues* magazine founding editor Jim O'Neal wrote shortly after London died of cancer on May 16, 1975, at West Side's Veteran's Hospital in Chicago. Sitting in a privileged position in the blues world evoked by Jim O'Neal was Earl Hooker, whose association with London's many record ventures was particularly fruitful at a time when blues was neglected by bigger record companies. Earl didn't have a one-way relationship with London; his superlative guitar contributions played their role in the development of London's business, but at the same time it was through London that Hooker was able to bequeath future generations a testimony to his highly creative genius, in the form of blues classics like "Blue Guitar," "Blues in D Natural," "Little by Little," "Messin' with the Kid," and "Will My Man Be Home Tonight." The period between 1959 and 1963 was a productive one, both in terms of quality and quantity. Through Mel London, Hooker was involved in over a dozen recording sessions, and his playing was featured on some forty titles and twenty-five singles, a dozen of which were released under his own name, the rest being ascribed to Junior Wells, A. C. Reed, Lillian Offitt, and Ricky Allen.

Melvin R. London was born in Mississippi on April 9, 1932. His initial interest in music led him to write R&B material, and he rapidly set up his own Melva Music publishing firm. By the time he turned twenty-five, Mel felt confident enough to launch a record company; the very first release on his Chief label was a Calypso offering titled "Man from the Island" that featured London himself. The Chief label, which folded after four years of active business in 1961 due to tax problems, boasted a catalog of forty-one singles, the last ones being mere reissues of items released at an earlier stage. Chief was an eclectic label that included efforts by pop and rockabilly artists, yet its best-selling issues—with the exception of a minor rock 'n' roll hit by Tobin Matthews—were blues numbers featuring Hooker's inventive playing, like Lillian Offitt's "Will My Man Be Home Tonight."

Contrary to what has been inferred by writers who studied London's activities, his Profile label was not started following Chief's collapse. Dates of release show that London was jointly running Chief and Profile at one point; but whereas Chief was mainly aimed at the R&B market, Profile was devoted almost exclusively to pop items; only three of its fifteen issues were blues oriented, which makes it all the more ironic that London's first national chart entry, the bluesy "Little by Little," appeared on a Profile single in 1960, one year before the company collapsed.

When he realized in the spring of 1961 that he would soon have to fold his first two companies, Mel London started the Age label, operated from 1827 South Michigan Avenue, which presented music with progressive overtones. As Junior Wells, who totaled one-fourth of the entire Chief output, disappeared from London's roster, several newcomers were revealed by Age. Hooker's regular sax player A. C. Reed numbered seven sides, and Big Moose Walker recorded a 45 under his name, but singer Ricky Allen got the lion's share with nine out of the twenty-five singles on the Age catalog, Hooker's band being involved in most of the related sessions. Despite a second nationwide hit record with Ricky Allen in 1963, Age died out early the following year when Mel London, plagued by financial problems, realized that his labels had rewarded others more than himself. Although he continued to write songs for Ricky Allen after 1964, London supported his family by working for United Records Distributors, while modernized re-hashes of his old material regularly popped up until the mid-seventies on ephemeral ventures such as Mel, All-Points, or Mel-Lon.

London's career as a producer only lasted a limited period of time, showing that if small blues labels were still emerging in Chicago after the mid-fifties, their owners could hardly expect to achieve real commercial success. Distribution problems and unfair competition on the part of larger companies—which often bribed radio disc jockeys in an attempt at smothering potential hits produced by newcomers—were the usual lot for small label operators in a declining blues market. This would confirm the real talent of Mel London, who succeeded in establishing his reputation and that of hitherto obscure artists as he produced some of the most original blues records of the time. Unlike most other minor label owners, who only spent their spare time making records, Mel was a dedicated businessman with a fine ear and a fair notion of the commercial value of his artists. Lastly, the impressive list of blues standards written by him—including "Will My Man Be Home Tonight," "Little by Little," "Cut You A-Loose," and "Messin' with the Kid"—also evidences his capacity as a lyricist.

In addition to his professional qualities, Mel London was a friendly, warm person who cared sincerely for his artists. The good relations he maintained with his musician friends and associates allowed him to draw the best out of people who liked and respected him, a fact confirmed by an early blues journalist, Neil Paterson. "He is obviously held in high regard by the men he recorded," Paterson reported at the end of a 1964 trip to Chicago. "Both Ricky Allen and Magic Sam showed considerable respect for London's ability. The listing of his labels shows his talent for holding some of Chicago's finest bluesmen. His success then is not merely a matter of luck, but rather a reflection of real talent and hard work."[2] Jim O'Neal, who knew London personally, is of the opinion that "Mel apparently got along well with his artists. He was about the same age and from the same background as most of them; he never struck me as an exploitative or aloof record executive. He was a down-to-earth, West Side blues man."[3]

The fact that London was himself a musician—although his personal production was limited to Chief's initial release—certainly accounted for part of his popularity with Chicago bluesmen, whose respect for a producer was often directly related to the amount of musicianship he exhibited in the studio. This clearly appears in the statement of A. C. Reed, who readily paid homage to London's ability, wit, and musical inventiveness when asked about him: "He was kind of a tall skinny guy, nice guy, though, man. He knew a lot about music, and then he didn't play nothin'. He did a little back-up singin'. We were the types of musicians that knew what they was gonna play, but he had good ideas about tunes, the way he wanted tunes to go. He wrote this tune Junior Wells did, 'Come On in This House,' he wrote that one, he wrote quite a few tunes. He's about the best man I ever worked with in the recordin' studio because he knew what was goin' on, you know, musicwise and everythin'. That bass line that Earnest Johnson played, I don't know that [Mel] started it or not. Anyway all of a sudden, they all started playin' that bass line. It might have been London's bass line."

The relationship that linked Earl Hooker and Mel London was based on mutual esteem and understanding. The liking that London took to Earl's playing soon prompted him to use him as his "house" guitarist, using his band every time he set up an R&B session. Earl's style as an accompanist was exemplary, as he used dry-toned, single-note rhythm patterns with much impact. On the other hand, London never trusted Earl's singing enough to record his vocals even once, issuing a strict diet of all-instrumental 45s to promote his pet guitarist.

From 1960 on, the "house band" heard behind London's various R&B vocalists remained the same until Age died out in late 1963, maybe with the exception of drummers. If Harold Tidwell appeared on several sides in 1960—including a song featuring his vocals titled "Swear to Tell the Truth"—Bobby Little provided most of London's sessions with his crisp backbeat until 1963, leaving way for Ricky Allen's regular drummer Frank Swan on several of the singer's sides. Bobby Little's first encounter with Earl went back to the fifties, when the guitarist played around Chicago Heights, home to Little's grandmother. As a young man, Little often sat in with Hooker's outfit at the Black & Tan and other Chicago Heights locations, and he always received the encouragement of Hooker, who eventually asked him to join his Roadmasters, first as vocalist and MC.

Born in Birmingham, Alabama, on May 2, 1938, but raised in the San Francisco Bay Area, Ronald Bluster (Little's real name) often visited his grandmother in Chicago Heights during the fifties. By 1958, when he moved to Chicago permanently, Bluster had turned into an accomplished drummer. One year later, he wound up at Cadillac Baby's Show Lounge, where he officiated behind the drum kit as "Bobby Little"—a nickname given to him by Magic Sam. During the months that followed, Bobby's position as drummer with the Lucky Hearts of guitarist Jimmy Johnson[4] enabled him to acquire enough proficiency to join Hooker's outfit some time in 1960.

All along this period, electric bass chores remained the almost exclusive work of Lee Thomas "Earnest" Johnson, also known as "Big Train," one of Chicago's most sought-after sidemen, whose playing was featured on numerous later recordings by Buddy Guy, Junior Wells, Magic Sam, and Muddy Waters. During his four-year spell with Mel London's various record ventures, Johnson recorded so extensively that he was known to tell singer Ricky Allen, "Play somethin' on the jukebox, I'm on all of 'em!"[5] Almost as prolific was tenor saxophonist A. C. Reed, freshly back from Lawton, Oklahoma. Hooker and Reed complemented each other perfectly, both from a musical and personal standpoint, as Reed's saturnine nature contrasted with Hooker's ebullient personality, the former's lyrical and restrained horn figures blending beautifully with the latter's intricate solos.

"Hooker met London when I was on the road with Dennis Binder and 'em, because when I come back, he was already associated with Mel London and he got me into recordin' with Mel London," Reed recalls. "It was a studio band, 'cause we's about the best musicians he had to record behind peoples. Everybody played on everybody's record. Anybody that would record, we'd play on it." Within a few months, Reed stopped playing the role of a mere sideman when his singing and tongue-in-cheek songwriting were deemed worthy of regular 45 releases by London. As such, A. C. shared with Hooker the privilege of inaugurating the Age label in the spring of 1961.

When a horn section was needed, London called various musicians, including Julian Beasley, an alto sax player formerly with the Bobby "Blue" Bland Show; Donald "Hank" Hankins, who made occasional baritone saxophone appearances every now and then; and Jackie Brenston, another baritone specialist and the original singer on "Rocket 88." Following the towering success of this 1951 chart topper with the Ike Turner band, Brenston went through dull periods as a solo act, and he eventually resumed his position with Turner's Kings of Rhythm during the second half of the decade. Until 1961, Brenston was the band's baritone saxophone player as well as one of Ike's regular vocalists, featured on several Kings of Rhythm recordings. The arrival of Anna Mae Bullock was at the source of deep changes in the band; by the time Anna Mae became Mrs. Tina Turner, Brenston's singing no longer was needed on stage; he found himself down on his luck, and he was glad to take part in recording sessions whenever his friend Earl needed him.

Other than horns, keyboards held a central position in London's recordings, and Hooker's longstanding friend, Johnny "Big Moose" Walker, joined the rest of the band in the studio at an early stage. Big Moose concentrated on the piano in the beginning, but he rapidly switched over to organ. Hooker was always on the watch for anything new, and he was one of the very first in Chicago to feature an organist in his outfit, following in the steps of the instrument's biggest popularizer, Jimmy Smith, who brought organ playing into the limelight in the late fifties. In Chicago, the organ seemed to have been the domain of gospel stylists up to that time; if church-tinged organ phrases were currently heard in southern soul combos like Booker T. & the MGs in Memphis, the leading Chicago blues players did not start using organists until later on in the sixties, drawing their inspiration from Hooker's example. The progressive side of Big Moose Walker's organ playing was evident on Hooker's Mel London material, Moose's full-sounding style providing various Chief and Age releases with a unique sound easy to identify. London himself acknowledged Hooker's and Walker's anticipatory penchants when he decided in 1962 to dedicate an all-instrumental Age single to Moose's organ playing.

The piano was not banished for all that from Hooker's sessions, as Moose sometimes managed to play two keyboards at the same time: "If you put a organ, or another piano or something else on the side of this piano here, I could play on this piano here and play the same thing with the other hand on the organ," Big Moose explains. At other times, it proved more convenient to hire other veteran session players like pianist Lafayette Leake, whose sweet licks and gentle runs were featured on Junior Wells's "Little by Little." On a later occasion, Earl used his friend Pinetop Perkins, but a disagreement over his salary kept Pinetop away from the studio after that.

To record, Mel London consistently used Chicago's finest studio, Universal Recording, found just north of the Loop at 111 East Ontario Street; he took his musicians there so often that Universal soon became a second home for Big Moose, Earl, and A. C. Reed, who later found it difficult to keep track of the many sessions he did there: "Somethin' like twenty years ago, that was the best studio in the city. Mel London would just be around, but he wouldn't be the engineer. I'm pretty sure that then, the engineer went with the studio. It might be cheaper at night, see, 'cause they'd be recording big bands and stuff and then, we come in late at night. I'd say like nine or ten o'clock at night, and we'd be through by twelve, it depend on how many we'd be cuttin'. Like sometimes, London, he might get another idea and then he wanna change it then it takes us a little longer, you know. Sometimes he cut two peoples at a time. We was doin' 45s in them days. Sometimes like we'd go in there, I would do somethin' like one, and then maybe Ricky Allen would do one, and maybe he might have Junior Wells doin' one. We'd do like four tunes at a time, then maybe we'd go back again."

A. C. Reed's description lays emphasis on London's limited financial resources; studio fees were costly indeed—especially in the light of the fact that the main customers in large recording premises like Universal were not record companies for the most part, but wealthy advertising agencies recording radio commercials. In an attempt to reduce recording expenses, London rented a rehearsal room at low cost. When this proved helpful with most of his artists, Hooker's singularity made him stand out once again. "We had a place over on the West Side, a place that [London] had rented special for rehearsals," A. C. Reed explains. "But Hooker would be a problem when he recorded his own thing, 'cause he would never play one thing the same way. If he tell you to play it like this, you play it and then maybe, if he had to take another take, he might play it a little different, you know, and if it wouldn't fit right, then they'd have to go over it again."

Big Moose Walker on the other hand argued that Hooker's success could be attributed to his conviviality, recording sessions always taking place on a professional though highly informal level: "Earl would just tell us, 'Hey, Grandpa! We g-g-gonna cut some tapes, now,' and he'd give us twenty-five dollars, or I don't care what it was, we'd just do it. I didn't care. As long as Earl was in it I didn't care, you know. I went in the studio for nothin', it didn't make no difference. I had a lot of fun, though, you know." If money was an issue with Hooker, it wasn't the case with London. Most producers then were known for their unethical dealings, but Mel had the reputation among musicians of being a straightforward businessman who respected his artists. "We got somethin' like $54 I think for a session," A. C. Reed remembers. "The leader would get a little bit more, like one of the sessions I did, I got somethin' like $160. But what I liked about [London], he would send all the money through the union man, and you'd get union scales, you know. It wouldn't be no rip-off and things like that. He sure knew the business, man. You know like when we'd go out on the road, like we went up to St. Louis once. Albert King was our house band. Me and Ricky [Allen] went up there, and he went with us, you know, to make sure everything went right."

Hooker's first Mel London session after "Little by Little" took place at Universal on February 1, 1960, less than three weeks following Earl's memorable performance with Bobby Saxton for the Bea & Baby label, and London decided to concentrate on Hooker's band this time. On the bandstand, a large share of Earl's act was devoted to instrumental showcases, but he knew that blues crowds loved singers. So far, he had mostly relied on the vocal talent of his sidemen, but his encounter in late 1959 with a young female vocalist from Tennessee brought an abrupt change to that routine. Lillian Offitt had all of the characteristics that Hooker wanted in a singer. She was not only young and attractive, she was also a seasoned professional with several recordings to her credit, made for the Excello company in her hometown of Nashville, Tennessee.

Offitt's main claim to fame when she reached Chicago in 1958 at the age of twenty-five was a tune called "Miss You So" that almost made it to the Top Ten on *Billboard*'s black charts in July 1957. In spite of that, she wasn't too keen on leading her own outfit, and she had been looking for a solid working band ever since her arrival in the Windy City. It was not until several months later that Earl and Lillian decided to team up. From the start, Hooker's partnership with Lillian Offitt struck Mel London as an interesting one from a commercial standpoint, and he decided to give them a chance to record. In addition to Hooker's usual back-up unit, London hired Tall Paul Hankins, then leader of the house band at Theresa's, while Earl brought in A. C. Reed, fresh back from his long spell in Oklahoma with the Dennis Binder band.

Mel London's main object when he recorded Lillian Offitt on February 1 was to re-create the atmosphere of her Excello bestseller, and the song that the band first put on tape that day was a disguised remake of Lillian's hit, titled "The Man Won't Work." In spite of A. C. Reed's spicy tenor sax work, the song has limited interest, lacking the freshness of the original. On the contrary, the second Hooker-Offitt contribution was a magnificent slow blues titled "Will My Man Be Home Tonight," which fully evidenced London's capacity as a tunesmith. Lillian Offitt delivered this sad tale of a doomed marriage very convincingly, but even more than her sharp-edged voice, Hooker's truly superb guitar work made the song stand out, largely accounting for its success. As Lillian delivers each line, Hooker's instrument prolongs her vocals with poignant, voice-like slide runs that still stand today as definitive blues licks. The tune's climax comes with the stunningly fluent guitar solo that follows the third verse, although its emotional content is somewhat marred by Offitt's crying laments, complete with comforting comments made by a youthful voice: "Don't cry, Mummy, don't cry!"

Both songs were issued within a few weeks on Chief, with the usual Indian chief-head logo printed in black ink on the red label. Against London's expectations, it was "Will My Man Be Home Tonight," with its more traditional blues melody, that transformed the single into one of Chief's bestsellers. Before London realized what was happening, the sales of Lillian Offitt's 45 skyrocketed in the whole Chicago area, giving his company a solid local hit. On the West Side especially, young guitar players instantly added Hooker's guitar licks to their repertoire. To this day, the song can still be heard in the bag of tunes of many Chicago bluesmen—including Jimmy Dawkins and Otis Rush—but its long title has been shortened into the song's first line, "I Wonder Why."

Considerably enhancing the reputation of Hooker and his vocalist, "Will My Man Be Home Tonight" opened the doors for them to a large South Side venue located on South Park, Roberts' Show Lounge, where the tandem was billed at regular intervals in 1960. With three major recordings to his credit released within a few months—"Little by Little," "Trying to Make a Living" and "Will My Man Be Home Tonight"—Earl Hooker was at last winning in his own town the recognition he had long deserved.

Eager to capitalize on the popularity of his duet, Mel London brought Hooker and Offitt back to the Universal studios three months later on Thursday, May 5. The resemblance of this next Offitt single to her first Chief release was striking; coupled with a fine bluesier offering titled "Oh Mama" in which Hooker's vocalist went on with her tales of domestic grievance—"Oh Mama, but you don't seem to understand / I've got somethin' else that chases women, when I thought I had a man"—"My Man Is a Lover" was another adaptation of a current bestseller. This time, London drew his inspiration from "Fannie Mae," the work of New York harmonica stylist Buster Brown and a number-one hit in the rock 'n' roll mold that remained charted for twenty-five weeks in 1960. On Offitt's barely hidden cover, the original horn riff found on Brown's record was duplicated by a female quartet known as the Four Duchesses, giving it an unusual flavor. At all events this coupling, if not as novel as Lillian's previous record, sounded similar to her previous output with Hooker's flawless slide guitar work, and Chief 7015 sold satisfactorily.

True to his usual sparing policy, Mel London invited Junior Wells to Offitt's May session, and the harmonica player used the little studio time left that day to record a brilliant instrumental track taken at a slow, ominous pace on which Junior's saxophone-like chromatic harmonica and Earl's slide guitar duetted at will. Regardless of its musical qualities, "Calling All Blues" did nothing to advertise the two men's proficiency and connivance, as it was mistakenly released a few months later on a Chief issue credited to legendary slide guitar master Elmore James, who had already enjoyed two previous Chief releases with his Broomdusters, and whose "Knocking at Your Door" backed the improperly attributed Hooker-Wells instrumental effort.

Another artist present that day was Magic Sam, whose recording career Mel

London was trying to revive at the time. It is likely that Sam was coming to record at Universal with his band when he ran into Hooker and his men. Someone may have suggested they record something together, and they soon jammed an extended dance number London titled "Square Dance Rock" when he released it shortly afterward in two parts on Chief 7017. Far removed from Sam's usual soul-drenched repertoire, "Square Dance Rock" was one of Earl's usual forays into the country & western arena, partly based on "Steel Guitar Rag," in which Earl and Sam traded licks. Their lead work was supported by two saxophone players, one of whom clearly sounds like A. C. Reed, while the other may have been Sam's current horn man, a former member of Louis Armstrong's Stompers named Boyd Atkins. Throughout the performance, all those present in the studio that day, including the Four Duchesses, laughed and shouted in an attempt at giving the whole proceedings the atmosphere of a Hollywood western hoedown. The result, clearly aimed at the pop market, may not have been exceptional, but as Hooker's and Sam's only common recording, it remains a rather interesting one.

During the summer Earl Hooker with Big Moose Walker, Earnest Johnson, and Harold Tidwell was back at Universal, where London cut a vocal side featuring Tidwell's singing, a novelty number involving Junior Wells, and for the first time a Hooker instrumental. Recorded first, "Swear to Tell the Truth," with its almost surrealistic lyrics, gives a better idea of Tidwell's ability both as a lyricist and vocalist than his earlier C.J. sides. Even more interesting was the unusual keyboard sound of Moose Walker, who experimented with an electric piano, showing a penchant for progressiveness that would soon materialize in his pioneering use of the organ. This probably wasn't enough for London, who waited for almost two years before he put out this song on the flip side of an early issue of his next venture, Age records.

On the contrary, the two tracks taped after Tidwell's side were issued almost immediately on Chief 7016, giving the label one of its best-selling items; the record sold so well, in fact, that London even re-released it on one of Chief's last issues shortly before the label folded in 1961. The record's B side was a nonsensical number titled "Galloping Horses a Lazy Mule" in which Hooker made a convincing imitation of a horse gallop with the bass strings of his instrument before rushing into lightning-quick flurries of notes, while a seemingly furious Junior Wells admonished an imaginary mule: "I know you can't talk, but you can hear! You oughta be able to hear, your ears is longer than mine!" hollered Junior before he tried to tackle the problem from a different angle: "You know I was gonna buy you some gold teeth, but you don't never smile!" "This tune was Mel London's idea," Junior Wells comments. "Mel was a nice person, he had a very creative mind about his thing, and he used to come up with some ideas that were really [funny]. Sometimes I'd have to stop in the studio, and get to redo it right, 'cause I'd get to laughin' about it, you know what I'm sayin'."

But it was not this minor effort which accounted for record buyers' interest. "Blues in D Natural," the third number recorded that day, was a revamped instrumental version of Lillian Offitt's "Will My Man Be Home Tonight" taken at a faster pace. Hooker's virtuoso slide playing replaced Lillian's famous lyrics, each one of her lines being sculpted into vocal slide guitar phrases that Hooker embellished with straight-picked punctuations. The resemblance between the wails Earl wrung out of his instrument and the human voice was so striking indeed that it was almost impossible for anyone familiar with Lillian Offitt's hit not to hear in Hooker's playing the words originally delivered by his female vocalist.

"Another Hooker, another seller" should have been London's motto, as his bestsellers invariably involved Earl and band. After "Blues in D Natural," London's will to diversify his production (and doubtless Earl's club activities) temporarily kept Hooker away from the studio as London concentrated on the likes of Magic Sam, the Four Duchesses, or Melvin Simpson. But on Monday, October 17, Junior Wells was back at Universal with Earl Hooker and Big Moose Walker; Earl's usual tenor sax man, A. C. Reed, was touring Texas at the time, and he was replaced by Junior's current horn men, Jarret "Jerry" Gibson and Donald "Hank" Hankins, while Junior's rhythm unit, bassist Jack Myers and drummer Fred Below, rounded off the studio band. London considered the Hooker-Wells twosome his best asset by far, and he had three songs ready for Junior, whereas an additional track was left open for a Hooker-Wells instrumental duet.

The second and third tracks taped that day were fine, if not outstanding efforts. "You Sure Look Good to Me" was an R&B song in the "Little by Little" vein with unison vocals by Junior Wells and Mel London, while "So Tired" was a version of a familiar Wells blues theme, boasting Hawaiian-like slide licks from Hooker that set up the song's somber mood. Both songs may well have been undervalued due to the exceptional quality of the additional material recorded then, for they were put on the shelf by London, who did not think fit to put them out until 1961.

The London composition first put on wax that day was a brilliant R&B tune titled "Messin' with the Kid," which confirmed Mel London's faculty of selecting and composing material for his artists, as the following story recounted by Junior Wells to *Magic Blues* editor Lois Ulrey shows: "'Messin' with the Kid' was a thing because of my daughter Gina. When she was just a baby, London told me we was goin' in the studio. So he said, 'I'll pick you up at nine o'clock.' . . . Mel London came over there early. He came in talkin', 'Where's your Daddy at? Get him up.' 'No, you said you were goin' to be here at nine o'clock. It's not nine o'clock. . . . You're not goin' to be messin' with the kid.' Just like that. So we was in the studio and he said, 'We need another tune.' . . . And from that, one thing lead to another and . . . it took us maybe five minutes, maybe ten minutes and we had it."[6] Written especially at Junior's intention, the tune was a tight, rocking number that perfectly fitted the image the singer usually projected; it symbolized Wells's personality so well that he rapidly adopted it as his theme song.

As for Earl Hooker, he had his own moment of glory before the end of the session when he cut "Universal Rock"—a tribute to London's usual recording premises—in which he displayed his formidable command of the guitar. "It was my tune," Junior Wells claims, describing the musical understanding which tied him to Hooker. "I writ it, and on our way to the studio, I did one thing, I just hummed a little bit of it to him, and he come up with the beat of the thing. When I first heard the first twelve bars, the music turned out to fit with what I was doin', that was all." Strongly inspired by Muddy Waters's popular anthem "Got My Mojo Working," this driving up-tempo masterpiece, registered with BMI as a Hooker-Wells composition, fires off with a machine-gun guitar intro before Hooker's stinging licks break into a merciless fight with honking harmonica-horn riffs provided by Wells, Donald Hankins, and Jerry Gibson. The latter gets the upper hand during a tenor sax solo, closely followed by Big Moose Walker, whose organ intervention foreshadows the church-tinged sound so characteristic of Mel London's subsequent output. Yet Hooker manages to steal the show in a flash with a breathtaking staccato lead which sweeps the number to its close. Released on Chief 7021, this exceptional coupling achieved rapid success, even spurring Muddy Waters to record a reply to Wells's original, "Messin' with the Man." Four decades later, "Messin' with the Kid" still remains Junior Wells's best-known song, while it takes virtuoso guitarists to carry on the "Universal Rock" tradition.

During the first few months of 1961, Earl Hooker was approached once again by his friend Carl Jones, who wanted to use him on the C.J. session of his new discovery, female vocalist Betty Everett. Everett was still quite removed from the status she eventually acquired in the soul field with more established labels, but she was no newcomer on the scene, with several promising recordings for various minor firms to her credit, including Eli Toscano's Cobra label and Cadillac Baby's Bea & Baby concern. Betty was in search of another promoter when she met Carl Jones in 1960. An audition was rapidly set up, which convinced Jones of the extent of her talent. Her association with Carl Jones yielded only two C.J. singles at the time, but later compilations of unissued material give ample evidence of Jones's fondness for Everett's talent.

Betty Everett's second C.J. 45, cut during the first half of 1961, involved Earl Hooker. With the unfailing help of his friend Ike Perkins, a former guitar player with the Rhythm Kings of boogie great Albert Ammons, who generally officiated as C.J.'s A&R man, Jones brought Betty and Earl to the International Recording studios—known to regular visitors as IRC—located on the West Side at 5619 West Division Street. "Hooker didn't know Betty, I knew Betty," Carl Jones specified in 1984. "Betty met me one afternoon, and she wanted me to come over to the church to hear her, and then after then, I got Betty and Earl Hooker together one day over to my house. Earl Hooker was a good guitar player, and I wanted somebody to bring somethin' out. We was goin' over some of the tunes, and that's when she met Earl Hooker. And then the next time we met, we met out to Mr. Vernon, out to International studio."

The two songs taped then, "Happy I Long to Be" backed with "Your Loving Arms," appeared on C.J. 619 toward the end of the spring; the A side was credited to "Betty Everett—Earl Hooker Allstars," but the flip acknowledged the presence of the "Ike Perkins Allstars," although the same band was used on both tunes. At any rate, Everett gave one of her less convincing studio performances, and Carl Jones was confronted with a failure when this boring coupling—which with time became a collector's item, nonetheless—passed unnoticed, and Betty Everett moved on to bigger things in 1962 with the Vee-Jay company.

Early in 1961 Mel London used Lillian Offitt on a third and last session. Contrary to what was inferred by discographers for a long time, Hooker was not involved this time; this makes the comparison with Lillian's earlier recordings all the more interesting, the dullness of those final sides bearing witness to the crucial role played by Earl in making fine recordings. Chief 7029 was to mark Offitt's retirement from the music scene, as she gave up her stage life to start a family.

For Hooker, the spring of 1961 saw his return to Universal for more work when London decided to concentrate on Earl's instrumental ability. This next recording date turned out to be an unusually prolific one. In addition to Hooker's sides, three efforts by Junior Wells were cut then, as well as A. C. Reed's and Ricky Allen's first vocal appearances. The sidemen used for the session included Big Moose Walker and Lafayette Leake on keyboards, Earnest Johnson on bass, and Bobby Little on drums, while A. C. Reed's raucous tenor sax pepped up the band's efforts. Also present were horn men Julian Beasley and Jackie Brenston, whose contributions could be heard on several of the tracks taped then.

Recorded early in the session, "Apache War Dance" was a forgettable though humorous number inspired by the Five Royales' 1955 "Mohawk Squaw" that illustrated the informality of London's sessions. The featured vocalist was a Hooker associate named Austin, who made uncanny comparisons between the old and the new "Rock 'n' Rollin' Shows" in Chief Yellowhand's and Chief Thundercloud's tribes. "This old boy named Austin, he wrote that tune," A. C. Reed remembers. "We brought him from Lawton, Oklahoma. He was somethin' like our roadie, you know, and he'd clown and dance. He wanted to be around musicians and he thought of the tune." Definitely a number meant for the Chief label, "Apache War Dance" ended up in the late spring of 1961 on the flip side of Mel London's very first Age release.

The next two Hooker tracks were infectious rockers aptly titled "Rockin' with the Kid"—an obvious instrumental response to Junior Wells's bestseller for Chief, "Messin' with the Kid"— and "Rockin' Wild," a superb shuffle that showcased Earl's guitar pyrotechnics as well as A. C. Reed's superlative tenor saxophone improvisations and Moose Walker's rock-solid organ phrases. But the day's noteworthy items were the sides recorded under Junior Wells's name, that turned out to be Earl's final contributions to the Chief label. Junior's first number, "I Could Cry," was a reworking of a slow blues already recorded three years earlier for release both on Profile and Chief. This new version was a slightly modernized one, and it easily stands comparison with the original as Earl, displaying a perfect sense of time through elaborate rhythm figures, contributes a fine solo at the tune's ending. Like "I Could Cry," "I'm a Stranger" was another slow number drawn from the repertoire of the Cavaliers, a West Coast group recorded by Oakland producer Bob Geddins in the late forties. Wells's version was the occasion for Earl to re-create in a Chicago studio the bygone atmosphere of smoky Delta country joints, his slide intro confirming his attachment to his boyhood hero Robert Nighthawk. The session reached a climax with Junior's third vocal, a steaming R&B number titled "The Things I'd Do for You" that Hooker feverishly led with driving staccato riffs. "The Things I'd Do for You," with its gritty tenor sax chorus provided by A. C. Reed, was a model of its genre, its imaginative lyrics bearing the instantly recognizable stamp of Mel London with its tongue-in-cheek humor and long verses: when the vast majority of blues songs usually numbered three verses, London's compositions boasted four or five, as was the case here.

With this 1961 recording session, one of the most creative partnerships in the history of postwar Chicago blues was coming to a close. Although Wells and Hooker were frequent stage partners during the years that preceded Earl's death, it seems unfortunate that such a fruitful combination of talents did not result in a deeper association. Over the years, Junior Wells often raved about Earl's playing and he would not have considered unfavorably teaming up with his friend, but Hooker's instability prevented it, and Junior and Earl never appeared on record together again.

As this protracted session drew to a close, Hooker insisted on having A. C. Reed make his singing debut on record. His knack for digging up new talent proved efficient once again, for "This Little Voice" turned into a fair seller around Chicago when London released it a few weeks later as the initial issue of his newly founded Age company. "I thought of the tune sittin' at my table eatin', man, 'fore my wife died," Reed later recalled. "Me and Hooker we had just come from down South playin', and I just thought of the tune and wrote it. We's playin' in Peoria, Illinois, and he started out on some Jimmy Reed and I sang the tune 'cause I knew it would fit, you know, 'cause I had been doin' it around the house. And Hooker, 'M-m-m-man, why don't you come and record that tune, that sounds good,' and he kept on askin' me and I just recorded it, you know. 'Apache War Dance' and my tune was recorded the same day, 'cause I only had one tune, I didn't have nothin' to go on the other side. In them days, records didn't never get out of the city, just strictly city, and I think London told me it sold somethin' like 9,000 right around there in the city. And after then I started to writin' tunes."

Bringing an end to the day's crop, the next coupling also was a first run for another London-Hooker discovery, singer Ricky Allen. Like Lillian Offitt, Allen was originally from Nashville, Tennessee, where he was born on January 6, 1935. After a first recording attempt on a local label named Look, Allen settled in Chicago in 1960. "I didn't do nothin' [in Nashville] because I was immature," Allen modestly confesses. "I just didn't know, you know. I was singin' spirituals at the time, see. 'Cause we used to follow the Skylarks, the Golden Harps, Fairfield Four, Harmonizing Four. See, we'd go around to each funeral, and we'd do a number. But we never did have a amplifier or guitar, we had to do strictly harmony. In other words, I was just a kid singin' in a group, just ragged and unexperienced, see. I had a record out, but it didn't do anythin'. I came here [in Chicago] back in '57. I left and then I came back again in '60, and I've been here ever since. You'd be surprised how I came. Two pair of pants, a half a pack of Camels, and thirty-five cents."

The influence of the church was essential for Allen, who soon crossed the line and moved into the secular music world. By the time he started working on a regular basis at the White Rose—a rough joint located in Phoenix, a working-class suburb of Chicago—R&B material had replaced Allen's gospel repertoire. "By me runnin' around, gettin' around with the crowd, that's when I met Bobby Little," Allen continues. "See, [Bobby Little] was playin' with Syl Johnson's brother, Jimmy Thompson. They was workin' in Phoenix at a place called Hawk's White Rose. It was a gamblin' joint, it was a hotel, a restaurant, and whatever. It was just a party place, see; it never closed at that time. And him and my brother, I don't know what happened. I think he returned one favor for Bobby, so he told Bobby, 'Let him sing.' So after that song, me and Bobby got to be tight. We'd run around, we got along good together. So I stayed out there at Hawk's I think about three years. The whole time Jimmy [Thompson/Johnson] was there. But Bobby had been knowin' Hooker a long time, 'cause he used to tell me about Hooker all the time, and I used to be very inquisitive about Hooker's music, and I met Hooker at his house. Bobby Little, he got me to meet Mel and Mel, he was big stuff then."

Ricky Allen's meeting with Mel London in 1961 was the start of a fruitful collaboration—the vocalist turned into London's favorite and most prolific artist on Age, with a total of nine of the label's twenty-five releases. An appealing singer as long as he confined himself to strong R&B material, Allen was a limited vocalist when he tried to interpret the bland ballads that London too often provided him with. Yet, it was with Ricky Allen that Mel London got the long-awaited recognition his production work deserved. As the public's interest for straight blues declined, Allen adjusted himself to the demands of the era by singing soul-blues offerings.

It was almost by accident that Allen put on wax his initial contribution to the Age catalog. He explains: "When we went down to the studio to cut 'This Little Voice' and those things by Hooker, I did 'You'd Better Be Sure' and 'You Were My Teacher.' Junior Wells was there. It was about eight tunes did, not countin' mine, 'cause mine wasn't even supposed to be cut. But what happened, they finished up ahead of time, see. And so they said, 'How much time we got, Ernie?'—Ernie, he was the vice-president at Universal—and Ernie say, 'We got fifteen more minutes.' So Mel remembered mine, and Hooker had played it already. Mel couldn't even remember my name, man. He really couldn't. I was impressed, 'cause the first session I had, man, I was a youngster. So I told 'em what I wanted, I explained to the band, and we did it in two cuts. Two cuts, that's all."

The two sides recorded with Hooker's band then show Allen's better and worse sides. "You'd Better Be Sure," a take-off on Clyde McPhatter's "What'cha Gonna Do" with the Drifters in 1954, was a nice and swinging R&B effort, whereas "You Were My Teacher" was a slow ballad unworthy of a high school prom through which Allen painfully crooned his way. On account of "You'd Better Be Sure," Allen's initial Age record was a fair hit on the Chicago market. To begin with, it boasted fine lyrics by Allen—who, for obscure reasons, used his grandmother's surname, McAdoo, as a pen name when the song was registered with BMI; but most of all, Hooker enhanced the song's appeal by emphasizing in his playing the song's melodic resemblance to "Hide Away," Freddy King's instrumental hit that could be heard on every black radio station in the spring of 1961.

The success of his record took Ricky Allen by surprise: "And so we did it, and I left town. I went to Nashville and stayed a while, and then all of a sudden I got a telegram tellin' me to come here, that 'You'd Better Be Sure' was number one. [W]VON was playin' it, and every time we changed the station, boom! It was on there." The commercial impact of this initial Ricky Allen Age release was such that London soon produced, without Hooker's help this time, enough material for two additional Allen 45s.

Age's sixth issue, an awkward coupling, was the label's bluesiest number as well as one of the company's best-selling items. Yet, Mel London did not expect much of it when he put it out in the early spring of 1962. For want of more recent material, this hastily packaged issue included on its B side "Swear to Tell the Truth," the unreleased vocal track recorded by Harold Tidwell two years earlier. As for the A side, a slide guitar instrumental titled "Blue Guitar," it had been improvised the previous spring at the beginning of the long session that produced Allen's initial sides. If Allen's initial Age recordings were accidental, it also was by a stroke of luck that London captured Hooker's masterpiece.

"In them days," explains A. C. Reed, who shared with Big Moose Walker, Lafayette Leake, Bobby Little, and Earnest Johnson the privilege of cutting this gem, "they wouldn't hold you as long as you would be now in the studio, man, you know, like a couple of takes and you'd have your thing together. Now when Hooker cut that 'Blue Guitar,' only one take. One take! We was just warmin' up, you know, we wasn't even gonna cut the tune, and Hooker just started out on it. Mel London just happened to hold the tape, why I don't know. We was just gettin' ready to record for somebody else, gettin' the horns and stuff in shape so we could record, and he just cut the warm-up tape, it just sound so good, I guess he went ahead and do it, and all of a sudden he put it out, and then it was a good tune. Hooker was just somebody like you have to catch him at his best, you know, unpredictable, like when we did the 'Blue Guitar,' it was no rehearsal, no nothin', we just let him play."

"Blue Guitar," Earl's own favorite, is the epitome of modern blues guitar as it combines the ultimate in taste, virtuosity, sheer simplicity, and pure creativity. From the first bars, a slide intro in a Robert Nighthawk vein sets the mood of this slow-paced blues. With majestic dignity, Hooker then carries the simple melody line at a quiet tempo as the rest of the band rely on the strong backbone provided by Earnest Johnson's powerful bass. With the exception of a Moose

Walker organ solo, Earl has ample room to display the fascinating accuracy of his slide work. With astounding ease, he alternates singing guitar runs and straight-picked passages, the colorful use of his guitar tone complemented by his impeccable phrasing giving the song a truly ethereal dimension.

Advertised in *Cash Box* from April 14, 1962, "Blue Guitar" went on to pursue a unique career following its release on Age 29106. At a time when soul music was the thing on black charts, Earl's record sold unusually well for an instrumental blues side. Before the spring was over, every band in the Chicago blues belt included "Blue Guitar" in their bag of instrumental showcases, along with warhorses like Bill Doggett's "Honky Tonk" and Freddy King's "Hide Away," and it joined a string of immortal classics in the pantheon of modern Windy City blues. The implications of this unexpected success were many; the tune had barely started making noise around the city when London was approached by Leonard Chess, co-owner of Chicago's major black-oriented record business. In an attempt to rejuvenate his aging house star Muddy Waters, Chess offered to use "Blue Guitar" on Muddy's next record. By late June, an agreement was reached between Chess and London, and Muddy Waters walked into the Chess studios with a Willie Dixon composition titled "You Shook Me," which he recorded over Earl's original track. Far from burying Hooker's playing in the background, Muddy's vocal enhanced the beauty of Earl's work. Released on Chess 1927 with a new matrix number corresponding to the overdub, "You Shook Me" emphasized the similarity of "Blue Guitar" to the traditional "Rock Me Mama" theme, and Muddy's performance met with favorable reactions from his fans despite the presence on the flip side of "Muddy Waters Twist," an inferior recording cut with an unknown band at an earlier session.

Leonard Chess and brother Phil, cashing in on the relative success of "You Shook Me," turned toward Earl Hooker once again in order to generate renewed interest in Muddy Waters, who had steadily been losing favor with record buyers since the release of "Close to You," his last chart entry in 1958. In July the Chesses brought Earl into the company's recording premises at 4750–52 South Cottage Grove in the heart of the South Side, and they insisted on cutting him with the same band that had played on "Blue Guitar," with the addition of Jackie Brenston on baritone sax. This time, the session was intended for Muddy Waters from the very beginning, but Earl and band sat down to record in the absence of the singer, who was touring Ohio with his regular unit. Under the supervision of the Chess brothers, Hooker taped three instrumental tracks that were used in early October when Muddy Waters overdubbed his vocals on them. While a version of "Black Angel" remained unissued, "You Need Love" backed with "Little Brown Bird" were released before the year was over.

The trick seemed rewarding enough, for Chess 1839 sold better than Muddy's early sixties recordings—with good reason, since these sides represent a rare sparkle in a decade's worth of dull Muddy Waters material. "Little Brown Bird" presents Muddy in a moody slow blues setting featuring Hooker's fine slide licks and Moose Walker's heavy organ sound, whereas "You Need Love"— complete with overdubbed percussion—ranges even better. From an anecdotal standpoint, this modernized version of Muddy's 1952 "She's All Right" had an impact well outside the Chicago city limits, rock group Led Zeppelin's 1970 smash hit "Whole Lotta Love" being directly borrowed from it.

Shortly after his July session for Chess, Earl was invited to record four more instrumental cuts with A. C. Reed, Jackie Brenston, and Moose Walker, this time under his own name. As a sign that Leonard and Phil Chess were attentive to the rapidly changing musical trends, the brothers tried to present Hooker in a completely different setting. "Tanya," recorded first, was a West Coast favorite borrowed from the repertoire of Joe Liggins, whose Honeydrippers had cut a version of it as early as 1946 for the Exclusive label. Hooker usually performed "Tanya" on stage as an accompaniment to the go-go dancers he sometimes carried in his show, and his rendition of the song featured nice slide passages. Earl's second effort stood even farther away from the Chicago blues tradition; light years from the delicacy of his "Blue Guitar," "Put Your Shoes On Willie" was an inept pop attempt that made little noise when it was released along with "Tanya" on the Checker label at the end of 1962. However uninteresting, "Put Your Shoes On Willie" must have appealed to Earl's childhood chum Bo Diddley, who included a version of it in his Bo Diddley and Company Checker LP, put out shortly after Earl's single. The sales of Hooker's 45 probably did not live up to the expectations of the Chesses, for the rest of the material put on wax for them—"Everything Will Work Out Fine" and "Sweet Brown Angel"—was shelved, marking the end of Hooker's association with the Chess/Checker concern.

His temporary dealings with Chess didn't keep Hooker from doing more work with Mel London, and his band was back at Universal in mid-1962 to cut enough material for three singles by three different artists. In addition to Hooker and A. C. Reed—who had become one of London's regulars since the release of "This Little Voice"—this prolific event involved another great, if underrated, Chicago guitarist, Reggie Boyd.

Also present that day was Hooker's friend Pinetop Perkins, whose piano licks were to complement Moose Walker's organ work, but Perkins didn't complete the session after getting into an argument with Earl over his financial compensation, as was all too common with Hooker. "I played a couple songs, but I didn't do too much, see. We done got into it, and so just like I tell you, I never did fight him; I'd just leave him. I walked off, after I got angry. I just got into my old car and left," Perkins says philosophically. Apart from this incident, the session went on smoothly, considering the amount of material recorded; within a few hours, Hooker, Reggie Boyd, and A. C. Reed had cut enough songs for a single each. When the two guitarists confined themselves to a strict diet of guitar instrumentals, Reed sang his way through "That Ain't Right" and the hilarious "Mean Cop," both of which enjoyed a late 1962 release on Age 29112.

The Boyd-Hooker coupling was a weird one, for if Boyd managed to feature his intricate chordwork on "Nothing But Poison," "Nothing But Good" should have been credited to Hooker, who stole the show with his stratospheric slide guitar acrobatics. As Hooker and Boyd got into each other's way, A. C. Reed took advantage of the situation and finally made the best of it. "Nothing But Good," the title of which referred to a 1961 hit for Hank Ballard & The Midnighters, was a guitar rework of another bestseller titled "I Want to Know," contributed in 1959 by West Coast female singer Sugar Pie DeSanto. Originally released on the Veltone label, "I Want to Know" had sold well in the San Francisco Bay area, and it eventually reached the Top Ten in the fall of 1960 after the Checker company leased it from Veltone; this time again, Hooker's slide re-created in a baffling way DeSanto's vocals, his guitar literally singing the original lyrics.

Hooker's own titles perpetuated the "Universal Rock"–"Blue Guitar" traditions. Recorded first that day, "How Long Can This Go On" was an instrumental cover of a current Junior Parker chart entry, confirming the tight bonds that linked Hooker to the Memphis scene. Far less influential than "Blue Guitar," this magnificent guitar-saxophone duet still emerged under the title "Easy Go" on an album recorded in 1971 by Otis Rush, one of Hooker's most gifted disciples. In a different vein, Earl's second instrumental was deeply rooted in the Delta tradition, as was suggested by its title, "These Cotton Pickin' Blues." In spite of the updated sax-organ arrangements typical of London's productions, Earl's slide work retained the rough southern flavor learned firsthand from Robert Nighthawk, and it was the logical sequel to the sides waxed a decade earlier in Florida under Henry Stone's guidance.

Although none of the Age issues resulting from this long session sold above the average, London brought Hooker back to the studio before the end of the year. In an attempt to diversify his production, London decided to present Earl's music in a different setting and used on two sides the questionable vocal talent of the Earlettes, a female twosome who regularly appeared on the Earl Hooker Show. The advent of back-up units such as Louis Jordan's Jordanettes, Ray Charles's Raeletts, and Ike Turner's Ikettes had started a female-group epidemic on the R&B scene. Hooker, always attentive to the latest fad, was one of the first Chicago blues artists to include a vocal team in his act. The Earlettes were better known offstage as the two Taylor sisters, and they can hardly be viewed in proper perspective as Hooker's most memorable invention; they wouldn't even be remembered today but for Age 29114, credited to "Earl Hooker & The Earlettes," issued during the first of 1963. This coupling actually displayed very little originality; "Win the Dance" was a below-par number based on the "Yea Yea" melody, and "That Man" was a Hooker-penned rewrite of Lillian Offitt's classic "Will My Man Be Home Tonight," its lyrics just giving Earl an excuse to reiterate his influential slide guitar phrases in between the Earlettes' irritating twitters.

The rest of the session yielded more rewarding results, proving once again that London's ideas ranged from the not-so-good to the best. In the spotlight was Earl's main keyboard specialist, Johnny "Big Moose" Walker, who contributed two strong guitar-organ instrumentals. "Off the Hook," a powerful shuffle with a vigorous organ intro, allowed Walker, Hooker, and Reed to solo at will; as was the case with a growing number of instrumental sides at the time, it bore the mark of Booker T. & the MGs, the upcoming Memphis-based quartet featuring organist Booker T. Jones, one of the first purveyors of the Memphis soul sound of the sixties. The influence of Booker T. was even more marked on Moose's second effort, titled "Bright Sounds" by London, who drew his inspiration from one of the countless names used by Hooker for his bands. Copyrighted by Mel London, "Bright Sounds" was a remake of "Green Onions," the MGs chart-topper that was getting heavy airplay on black stations then. However derivative, "Bright Sounds" was an inspired number in which both Earl and Moose managed not to fall short of the original. This must have been the opinion of record buyers, who made it one of Age's four best-selling items when it became the label's last 1962 release, credited to "Big Moose & The Jams."

The session's final song featured A. C. Reed, who crooned his way through his own "Crying Blues," with outside help from the Taylor sisters. London never released this track, and it would have disappeared when his original tapes were lost if it hadn't been mistakenly placed on the flip of a demo 45 that eventually popped up in 1986 on a compilation LP.

After a one-year interruption and a handful of Age releases devoted to musicians as varied as Hooker, female vocalist Robbie Yates, and saxophone player Saxy Russell, Mel London showed some renewed interest in Ricky Allen with a session that produced Allen's second big seller, "Ouch!," released at the beginning of 1963. The next session set up toward the spring of the same year proved even more essential, as Mel London recorded "Cut You A-Loose," Allen's best-known side and the most successful seller of London's career. Earl himself did not take part in the session, probably because he had a more lucrative engagement elsewhere. At the last minute, he asked rhythm guitar player Ivory Parkes, a relative newcomer on the Chicago scene who had been taught most of his technique by Earl, to take his place. Also present that day were bassist Earnest Johnson, drummer Frank Swan, and Sonny Lantz, Ricky Allen's organist, who recorded his own Age 45 at London's request.

As was the case with all of the bestsellers on Chief and Profile so far, the lyrics to "Cut You A-Loose" were the work of London, who modernized for the occasion a song he had written a few years earlier for Elmore James, "Cry for Me Baby." With sales amounting to 100,000 at a time when selling of 10,000 to 20,000 was considered an achievement, Age 29118 stayed on *Billboard*'s R&B charts for a total of four weeks from August 31, 1963, eventually reaching position 20.

His absence from such an achievement was very frustrating for Earl Hooker, who was sanctioned for once for his unreliability. "On the record, it was Ivory," Ricky Allen recalls. "Hooker came in and rehearsed with us some, but what was happenin', he was tradin' spots. Hooker would show up, Hooker'd come around, and he'd show Ivory the tune. But Ivory was consistent, and Hooker was maybe." Earl, as if refusing to be stripped of his share of success, claimed from then on that he was the original guitarist on "Cut You A-Loose," a legend few ever questioned.

Spurred on by Allen's sudden hit—although financial problems already foreshadowed the end of his label—Mel London decided to re-invest the profits he was beginning to draw from the sales of "Cut You A-Loose" in a series of new Ricky Allen releases featuring Ivory Parkes. Hooker was back for the following London session nevertheless, the vocalist involved being none other than his Clarksdale friend Jackie Brenston, whom he had played with many times up and down the road over the years. On this occasion, Earl brought along A. C. Reed as well as a new keyboard player known as Little Ray Charles. "Little Charles, he played with us all the time, you know, like on sessions and sometimes he played on the road with us, 'cause he was a good singer," says A. C. Reed, who had recourse to Charles's services on several of his own recordings. "I don't even know his real name. Like musicians when they start to callin' themselves, they just keep it up, you know. He just disappeared. I don't know where he went to. Hooker would get him all the time to play with him 'cause he could play the organ and sing, see, and he would be Hooker's cover. I don't even think they ever recorded him. That's too bad, 'cause he was a good singer."

Brenston cut two songs, "Want You to Rock Me" and "Down in My Heart." Although both tunes were registered with BMI under Mel London's name, "Want You to Rock Me" of course was the umpteenth version of a traditional blues theme that would soon be brought up to date by B. B. King. "I cut that thing, 'Rock Me All Night Long.' And B. B. covered it and killed it. I couldn't get anything out of it,"[7] Brenston reported shortly before his death. His version sounded quite different from King's, however, its resemblance with "Blue Guitar" being accentuated by Earl's exciting slide licks.

"Down in My Heart" was very different, with a pronounced gospel feel, Brenston bawling out an unexpectedly heathen message in which the singer's worship had clearly been transferred from the Lord to a very worldly girlfriend.

Helped out by Little Charles's church-inspired organ playing, Jackie Brenston did a mock parody of an overjoyed preacher while another Age labelmate, Robbie Yates and her background vocal group the Elites, played the part of an imaginary church crowd.

After a string of generally dull Allen efforts, Brenston's recording session provided London with an enlivening change. Yet Mel London's loyalty to Age's star-vocalist prompted him to put these sides on the shelf, and they were not released until several months later, when they appeared on the initial issue of London's erratic Mel-Lon label, following the end of his Age venture. This Mel-Lon 45, credited to "Jackie Brenston With Earl Hooker Band," sadly turned out to be the final recorded legacy of Brenston, former nationally acclaimed star and truck driver by trade when he died in 1979 in almost complete oblivion.

The end of Hooker's long association with Mel London was drawing near and the Age label was slowly dying out when Earl walked into the Universal studios during the second half of 1963 to put on tape his final instrumental showcase under London's direction. Over time, the quality of London's material was getting poorer, and this last Hooker display is the only one worth mentioning. In addition to a nice piano break contributed by Big Moose Walker, "The Leading Brand" features Earl's exemplary guitar styling at its best, but London was not able to release it on Age; he had to wait for better times before he could put it out on the short-lived Mel-Lon venture.

At the beginning of the following year, Earl Hooker also was present on the very last Age single, featuring the label's most prolific artist, Ricky Allen. Quite symbolically, most of London's house musicians were involved on "Help Me Mama" and "The Big Fight," so that it was in the company of Hooker, A. C. Reed, Jackie Brenston, Lafayette Leake, Sonny Lantz, and Earnest Johnson, with the addition of the excellent drummer Casey Jones, that Ricky Allen put an end to the Age era. "'The Big Fight,' that's when [Muhammad] Ali and [Sonny] Liston was gonna fight. You remember they had such a controversy about it? But we couldn't get it out in time. We coulda made a million off it if we could have got it out in time," Ricky Allen regrets. By the time Allen's topical record was out, Cassius Clay had already surprised everyone by winning the world title against his opponent on February 25, 1964, and the real loser seems to have been London's Age label.

With the collapse of this third enterprise—quite ironically in its most glorious days—ended one of the most creative and productive chapters in the history of postwar Chicago R&B. Plagued by financial headaches due in part to his commercial success, disheartened by unfair competition from bigger firms that looked unfavorably at Age's sudden growth, and despite undeniable artistic achievements, Mel London was finally compelled to close down his business and abandon record production altogether in a tough world that left no room for the small. If sporadic issues on subsequent labels such as Mel-Lon, All Points, or Mel rarely uncovered new material, the fact that most of them included the best efforts cut by the Wells-Hooker team early in London's career testified to his respect and attachment for Hooker's music, one that he no doubt regarded as his finest legacy. By the time London died in 1975, most of his masters had been lost; what was left of his tapes was purchased by Jewel label owner Stan Lewis in Louisiana, who ended up leasing rights to reissue specialists in Great Britain or Japan, at last making available some of Chicago's finest examples of sixties blues music.

Today, London's sessions stand out for many reasons, most notably the genuine talent of their initiator and the genius of the main artists concerned, but also because they were the last ones to keep the improvised, spontaneous feel that made Chicago blues records so original and appealing. Only a few years later, companies of a different kind like Delmark and Alligator would contribute to the survival of the local scene, but their very professionalism eventually robbed the music of much of its impact.

Guitars, Cars, and Women

CHAPTER 7

As extroverted as he was on the bandstand, Earl Hooker was more of an introvert at home, where he focused his attention almost exclusively on his art. It is no secret that life on the road can be tiresome, but professional entertainers generally find time to rest and enjoy life in their off hours; this was not the case with Earl, who spent most of his spare time practicing on his instrument, cutting down sleeping hours to a strict minimum as if he drew his tremendous amount of energy directly from his music rather than from scarce periods of rest.

"When we was in Oklahoma, I guess he got some sleep," Billy Boy Arnold reports. "He'd lay down later on or something, but he got up early in the morning and I'd hear him play the guitar. My room was right next door to his. Early next morning, nine o'clock, eight o'clock, Hooker would be playing that guitar; it would wake me up. It was damning! He'd be by hisself, playing 'Sassie Mae' by Memphis Slim, and he was playing the guitar part that M. T. Murphy did. He had to play. That was everything to him; he was a fa-

147

natic. Everything he was doing was music, you know. Like in the daytime, we'd get up and me and Moose and Smokey—Moose used to follow me around a lot 'cause I had a lot of women who followed me, so Moose liked to be with me, and so we'd go and eat and we'd associate together, but we didn't see Hooker. We'd hear him in the room practicing, and we'd see his car going. Hooker was up at some music store, looking at guitars, finding out the latest gadgets on amps.

"He stayed to hisself sorta like, you know. He talked, but not too much. To me he wasn't the guy that took you as a confidential friend. He was always doing something with music, and there was always musicians with him, I don't know whether to say friends. He had a lot of associates, everybody he knew was musicians. He was a guy who played so well, he didn't have too much time for guys who couldn't play good. He was a very different type of guy. He was unique in his own personality too, he wasn't like anybody else I ever met."

Earl's monomania was so pronounced that he could do just about anything as long as it was related to music; even though he did not particularly enjoy puttering about at home, he would perform miracles when his passion was involved. "Hooker was good at anythin' a little bit that he wanted to do," singer Andrew Odom stresses. "Like a guy's organ broke down one night when we was playin' at the 1015 Club, east on 43rd Street in Chicago, and Hooker fixed it on intermission. He may not have had the proper tools or the education, but he would fix it."

Unlike most of his traveling companions, Hooker never showed any interest in card games, sports, movies, or television shows. "I'll tell you what," says Big Moose Walker. "If he was just layin' up or somethin' like this, he'd watch TV until he'd go to sleep or somethin', and that's it. But so far as wantin' to watch a certain program or somethin', or somebody on TV, no way. He never gambled, never. He did nothing with his money but bought amplifiers, guitars, microphones, tape recorders, radios, cars, and clothes. He couldn't do nothin' but play guitar, wasn't interested in nothin' but womens."

Earl's love of music was almost matched by his penchant for women, his professional unreliability finding its pendant on a personal level. Mrs. Hooker's over-possessiveness kept her son from running his own home in Chicago, but Earl always found some compensation for his solitude in the course of his travels. Much as Cairo or Chicago in Illinois, Clarksdale and Helena in the Delta,

Lawton in Oklahoma, Bradenton and Pahokee in Florida were regular stopovers for Earl, in the course of his hectic road trips, various women over the years intermittently played the role of spouse—often combined with that of full-time mother. Sadie in Cairo, Ann (a girl who worked at a hamburger place on 47th Street) or Dorothy Maholmes (half-sister of saxophone player Bobby Neely) in Chicago, Bertha in Missouri, or Rosemary in Iowa, to cite but a few, provided Hooker with a variety of homes he called his own in scattered locations.

This pattern is common among traveling musicians who, adopting the promiscuity which is usually ascribed to sailors in love matters, keep a wife in every port. This is especially true in the mother-dominated family structure of the African American ghetto, in which many male individuals prove incapable of severing the strong ties that link them to their husbandless mothers, consequently refusing to assume in their turn the responsibility inherent in the status of a head of family. Sociologist E. Franklin Frazier saw in this a reminiscence of slavery when he wrote: "Only the bond between the mother and her child continually resisted the disruptive effect of economic interests that were often inimical to family life among the slaves. Consequently . . . the Negro mother remained the most dependable and important figure in the family."[1]

Earl Hooker developed this fickleness, and he enjoyed among his peers the reputation of a lady-killer with a girl in each town, although his power had a tendency to lose its edge with years as his tuberculosis grew more serious. "When I knew Hooker, he wasn't really that much for hitting on women," Dick Shurman, a friend of Hooker's in the late sixties, says. "But one time when I was with Moose [Walker], somebody made some sort of comment to the effect of how Hooker didn't seem to care much, and Moose said, 'Well, you should have seen Hooker when he was younger and stronger. He could just walk in and walk off with a woman just before you knew it was happenin'.' At one point I guess he was pretty hot stuff."

"Yeah, he was always after some chick," Billy Boy Arnold confirms. "He wasn't the type of guy in clubs that ran after one but in his spare time, when he wasn't playing music, he was always going over to some chick's house. He had some women around, but you never saw him openly with them, you know. He sorta liked to be to himself. He was a road man; where he'd go was home. I remember once, Bobby Fields—he was a saxophone player—and see, Bobby

Fields was a playboy. He went down to Oklahoma with Hooker once, and he brought a woman back. Bobby was married, but he didn't tell the woman that he had a wife. He brought this woman back to Chicago and had her staying with some people. She was in love with the guy, and she couldn't resist comin' up here. So Hooker went by this woman's house to try to get the chick behind Bobby's back! See, he was that type of guy, you know, he was a good-time type of guy."

In addition to the ephemeral households he started in various places over the years, Hooker kept an eye open for potential conquests. Although his attractiveness generally enabled him to find women who gratified his sexual desires on the road, Hooker also had recourse to professional lovers, according to Son Seals, a guitar player and singer who joined the Hooker band in the early sixties: "Earl had women everywhere he went, man. When we go somewhere and he say, 'Well, I'm g-g-goin' to my old lady's house,' I just didn't pay it no attention, 'cause hell, he had that everywhere. He was doin' somethin'! It seems like they'd have somethin', because I know damn well he didn't know all of those places and shit, man, so these womens would be into some money, which I guess made sense, you know. If you gonna fool around, you know, hell! Fool around good."

"I think Hooker had only three things he really loved: that was his guitar, cars, and women," Billy Boy Arnold confirms, before he adds with an arch smile. "I remember in Oklahoma, we were all young guys, and there was a retired soldier and his wife living down at the hotel. And the bottom of the door was about a couple inches off the ground, so Hooker was peepin' under the door at this woman in the hotel, so Moose [Walker] came and got me. I went there and saw Hooker down on the ground lookin' under the door. Well, you know, we had a lot of fun." A similar episode is recounted in the posthumous tribute to Hooker published by his friend Dick Shurman shortly after the guitarist's death: "On one occasion, Earl and Moose [Walker] were forced by a man at gunpoint to sample the wares of a lady whose efforts they had been watching through a motel keyhole, a story that has plagued Earl ever since!"[2]

Earl greatly enjoyed such pastimes in his younger days, but his behavior had more to do with his need to keep his fellow band members laughing than with any lack of sexual balance, as Junior Wells's testimony would tend to show: "Oh, man, he used to do so many crazy things. He had a hole in everybody's door in the hotel. He'd get a drill and put a hole in your door so he could peep in there at you. And we hooked up Moose John [Walker]'s room one night, took the microphone, put the hole way down by the bed, down by the wall, and hid the microphone up there behind the bed and had the amplifier in the other room."[3]

The decline of Mel London's various recording ventures from 1963 on brought about radical changes in Hooker's career that found a parallel in his personal existence. After so many years on the road, Earl finally decided to get married. After a succession of love affairs that seldom lasted long enough for him to acknowledge his children, Hooker finally took the responsibility of a home at the age of thirty-four.

The girl of his choice was Bertha Nickerson, his senior by two years. At the time of their initial meeting in 1962, Bertha was a pretty divorcee who lived with her two children, Regina and John Charles, in Catron, a small southern Missouri community. Catron and neighboring towns Lilbourn and New Madrid are located just off of Highway 61, halfway between Cairo and the Missouri-Arkansas state line. As such, they stand at a strategic point on the route that took itinerant bands from the busy St. Louis scene to Memphis and the lower Delta. Earl's frequent incursions into that part of Missouri at the time of his stay in Cairo accounted for his popularity in the area. During the fifties he further developed his network of professional connections on the western bank of the Mississippi River. His main hangouts in southern Missouri became the country joint operated by Papa Foster and Walter Taylor's, a large club found in Lilbourn five miles away from Bertha Nickerson's home.

Bertha was familiar with the Hooker band through their regular appearances around Catron, but only after she divorced her first husband in 1959 did she start going around the local clubs on the weekend. In 1962 an evening out provided her with an opportunity to get acquainted with the guitarist, and Earl and Bertha saw each other regularly during the following months. In an attempt at being with her more often, Hooker even started giving thrilling performances in Catron. "When he didn't have a big engagement elsewhere, he would just stay here and play at that place called Bill Rotman's Café," Bertha, who still resides in Catron today, explains. "When he would play here, he'd have a crowd, too. That's when people had jobs. Now they don't harvest crops any more by hand. They do it by machinery which they can take about ten or fifteen people and do the whole thing. People just moved off and it's not too many peoples here any more, maybe two hundred. It was three or four times that many people here. When he would play here, just a big sign said, 'Earl Hooker's band is playing in Catron.' It would be so many cars uptown you couldn't find a parkin' place, believe it or not."

From the very beginning, Bertha was impressed by Hooker's musical ability; at the same time, she was an intelligent woman in her mid-thirties with principles and a high sense of responsibility who was not ready to jeopardize the education of her two children for the sake of a short-lived, sentimental affair, regardless of Earl's talent. "I liked his music," Bertha admits very readily. "He could play anythin' on that guitar. He could even play that guitar with his teeth, I don't know how he did that. And he could play that double-neck guitar. That was a miracle to see him do that! But it wasn't really his music that made me marry him. I guess it was just Earl Hooker himself. I just liked him as a person. I've never cared too much for music. I never could understand blues, it never could do too much to me. I guess as a whole, I'm never a blue person."

As for Hooker, he possibly admired the heedfulness with which she ruled the existence of her family. For someone as dependent on his mother as Hooker was, Bertha epitomized a maternal image that made him feel secure. The similarity between Bertha's situation and that of Mrs. Hooker is striking: like Mary Hooker twenty years earlier, Bertha was a dedicated mother with a boy and a girl who had to scuffle to make ends meet. Such elements may not have influenced Hooker's choice consciously, but they probably played a significant role.

On Monday, October 7, 1963, Earl Zebedee Hooker and Bertha Lee Nickerson were married at the courthouse in New Madrid, Missouri, by Reverend B. B. Gillespie, in front of Doris Hampton and Geo. D. Boone, official recorder of deeds. The marriage was to last for close to seven years, until Hooker's death in 1970. Paradoxically, whereas Earl had children with various concubines over the years, his union with Bertha did not bring any because Bertha decided that she was too old to start a new family when she was already responsible for the education and welfare of two children. Judging by the fact that Hooker didn't raise his own progeny, Bertha's decision apparently didn't strain their relationship, although Earl apparently liked being around children. "He got along real good with the kids," Bertha reports. "They liked him. My son, I imagine he got along with him better than my daughter. She was headstrong. All she believed in was those books. Then, you know, once you bring kids things every time you go out of town and come back, they just love you to death. I remember one time he bought my son a motorcycle. We was comin' home from Indianapolis, Indiana, and he saw this motorcycle. I don't know just how much money it was back then, but he bought that motorcycle. And my son is named John Charles, but we called him Bubble. He was about eleven or twelve then, he was still small. And he said, 'I'm buyin' that motorcycle for Bubble.' And he put that motorcycle in the back of one of those old long limousine cars, and we brought that motor-cycle home. They rode it 'til they tore it up."

Hooker's position was more comfortable than his wife's. For the children, Earl represented the appealing figure of the missing father who came home on special occasions and surprised them with gifts. Bertha, on the other hand, was the head of the family who provided for her children's daily needs; as such, she embodied reliability and security but also strictness and discipline in the eyes of Regina and Bubble. As a result, Earl tried to be attentive to his wife when he was at home, although he invariably ended up devoting more of his spare time to his trade than to his family. "He'd always bring me presents. He could buy my clothes better than I could. Clothes, coats, bags, things like that. He was a nice person. He was quiet, pretty well close to himself, and he concentrated on that box more than anythin' else. So if he wasn't plunkin' on that box, he was asleep. Once you stay up all night, I guess if there were times you can get a chance to sleep in the daytime, you would. He really wasn't a talker. He might get in a conversation and talk, you know, and then the next thing, he's disap-peared. He had to play somewhere. Instead of gossipin', he was always concen-tratin' on usin' the telephone to see where he was gonna play."

Although he constantly kept up a joking front with most of his associates, Hooker was a serious-minded and laconic man at home. The only person he ever really communicated with was his mother, with whom he kept in close touch even after he got married. "Earl Hooker was a mama's boy," Bertha says. "I think that she was really closer to him than she were her daughter. She was crazy about Zebedee. And then maybe Earl Hooker was just one of those per-sons who could really talk to his mother. I think he would talk to his mother. I don't know of no great conversations they had, but I know he was crazy about his mother. 'Cause when he'd get home, the next call he would make would be dial Mum, you know. I had no grudge against that, I don't think a child can call their mothers too much."

Bertha was introduced quite early to her mother-in-law. No serious problem ever arose between the two women, but a concealed tenseness generally plagued Bertha's visits to Chicago. The fact that her son spent most of his days off in southern Missouri from 1963 was not to the liking of Mrs. Hooker, who considered Bertha more a rival than a daughter-in-law. Like other girlfriends of Earl's earlier on, Bertha soon decided to limit dealings with Mary Hooker to a strict minimum, especially since Earl refused to tackle the problem. "I told him one time I didn't think his mother liked me very well, and he said, 'Oh, forget it,' that's about all I got out of him," Bertha recounts. "Then, well, I didn't think too much about it because whether she liked me or not, I knew I wasn't gonna be there but a day or two. And if things got too uncomfortable, I wouldn't have to be there at all, so it didn't bother me one way or the other.

"He brought his mother down here to visit us after we had married. And when we would be in Chicago, I'd stay there sometime a week at a time. She did housework, and she was always very neat about herself. Dressed nice, clean. I think that was one thing that she really liked about me. She liked to dress, and I liked to dress. And she was nice to me, but you can always tell when somethin' was there, you know. We wasn't enemies, but we wasn't just that mother-in-law and daughter-in-law stuff. She always treated me nice, it seemed like she made me welcome, but it was just somethin' there. Jealousy, I'd say. And I don't think it would have been just me, it probably woulda been any woman that Earl Hooker married."

Soon after she was married, Bertha realized that much more than his mother, the guitar was fully responsible for estranging her husband from her. Until his death, Earl never stopped traveling for his wife's sake, and Bertha kept track of her husband's itinerary thanks to the laconic postcards she received on the mail: "He'd always report to let me know where he was and how he was doin'. He used to write me some letters, or send me a card, you know, from different places. It wasn't very much on 'em, 'Hello! We're goin' to such a place tomorrow, you know. See you soon.' He would always write 'em," Bertha adds, showing her appreciation of the efforts he made for her, despite the limited education he had received. "But somebody else would address the envelope, 'cause you know two different handwrites. He could write pretty good, but I don't know just how good he could read, 'cause he's been interested in that guitar even in school."

Because he showed no sign of slowing his frantic pace, the only possible way for Bertha to spend more time with Earl was to travel with him. She did so on various occasions, but the presence at home of her two children, as well as the fact that she had a full-time job in Catron, generally prevented her from following her husband when he took to the road: "If I had some time off that I could go with him and I could get back to my job, I did. He used to play over in Cairo a lot, and I used to go over there quite a bit with him because I could drive to Cairo and come back home the same night to go to work the next mornin'. Then I would go different places. Memphis and Mississippi. And we would always go to Chicago three or four times a year. Chicago, Indianapolis, you know, Waterloo, Iowa. He used to play over there a lot. And another little town in Illinois he used to play all the time, Rockford! I went there several times. We went to Indianapolis one time and he played with Muddy Waters. And he played with Brook Benton down in Memphis. Other than that, I didn't go. You know, stayin' here one night, and losin' half of your clothes, it just wasn't my thing."

Although her marriage was not an unhappy one as a whole, Bertha felt disappointed in the long run, and his refusal to settle down antagonized her. By the late sixties, and more especially during the one-year period preceding his death, Hooker did not see much of his wife at all. As his career took a turn for the better, essential engagements on the West Coast and in Europe prevented him from visiting Bertha and the children. Furthermore, the presence in Waterloo, Iowa, of another woman named Rosemary that he had been seeing for years put a strain on Hooker's and Bertha's relationship. As much as love and affection, Bertha needed someone she could rely on. Knowing Hooker's uncommunicative nature, she accepted putting up with a situation that didn't suit her. "I thought that he was gonna get a regular place to play around here close, you know, where we could do the drives, and that he was gonna settle down," Bertha regrets. "He realized he was sick, but he didn't do that. He was tryin' to make a big dollar. He probably could have played here and made about as much money maybe as he would have spendin' it travelin' on the road. It takes a lot of money to travel on the road. But that was his job, that's what he was doin' when I found him, so I didn't interfere with him. But I still think he loved that guitar best."

Other than his consuming passion for guitars and women, Hooker developed early a marked fondness for cars, which went back to his teenage days on Chicago's South Side when a white benefactor, owner of a hotel on Michigan Avenue, had presented him with a secondhand bus. Ever since, Earl had consistently been divided between his desire to parade about in a brand-new Cadillac and his unconditional love of vintage models. Depending on his financial situation, he usually kept a large set of vehicles, which he sold, traded, or tore up with astounding ease.

Cars represented more than a mere status symbol for Earl Hooker. Although his first few years on the road had been spent with others, transportation problems arose after Earl started leading his own ensemble; leaving Chicago for southern Illinois or the Delta could be done by bus or train, but a private vehicle was called for when nightclub engagements took Hooker and band away from their home-base. Earl soon realized that it was better to depend on his own car, especially when disagreements set in among band members. From the early fifties onwards, he never took to the road without his own car, bringing sidemen, stage clothes, and instruments along. "He's crazy about cars," Big Moose Walker shakes his head. "He'd buy 'em and run 'em and junk 'em. Tear 'em up and get another one. Sometime in the fifties, we drove a hundred-dollar Buick all over Florida, New Mexico, Texas, California, 'til it caught on fire, and it ran out of transmission fluid; we stopped and we put some water in the transmission! Then went on to Los Angeles." In a similar way, Hooker's trip to Florida with drummer Kansas City Red in late 1953 had started inauspiciously when the band's car broke down in some remote part of Tennessee.

By the time Hooker took Billy Boy Arnold's band to Oklahoma in 1956, his situation had improved: he traveled in a superb 1949 Roadmaster Buick. "It was maroon with a black top, a very sharp car," says Arnold. "Very beautiful car, in excellent condition; he bought it down South somewhere." The Roadmaster was Hooker's own favorite and remained so for a long time, to the point that he even used its name to identify his group.

Earl was by no means an exception in his milieu; many of his peers shared his love of automobiles, but few of them proved as inveterate as he was in this particular field. An exception was his friend Arbee Stidham, who often bought the same car as Earl's, or vice versa. "We both started with a Chrysler," Stidham reports. "Then I went from a Chrysler to a Roadmaster Buick. I went down and bought a Buick, and it was a color, I never saw that color again until recently. I bought one and Hooker bought one, just alike. He loved the Buick Roadmaster. After he got that Roadmaster, I don't think he ever changed, 'cause I left that for a Cadillac, but he never did. We'd get cars the same color, but you could bet, his would be a Roadmaster and mine would be a Cadillac."

Earl's extended road trips eventually used up the resources of his Buicks, and when time came for him to find a replacement for the Roadmaster model, the many musicians and the bulk of equipment he carried with him urged him to look for a larger vehicle. When most bandleaders in the business commonly drove vans and station wagons, Earl bought one of the eight-door monsters ordinarily used as airport limousines. His mile-long Chevrolet and Chrysler limousines largely contributed to the spreading of his reputation, especially in the small country towns where he took his show. Hooker was not the only one in the business to use such an awkward automobile; Elvis Presley for one impressed his California fans during the summer of 1956 when he hit Hollywood in one of these, and this illustrious example was followed by Junior Parker and Bo Diddley. "In his lifetime, [Earl] had two of those old long limousine things," says Bertha Nickerson. "He had another car, but most of the time, he took the van 'cause it was cheaper, I mean the coach, or whatever you wanna call it, limousine. He bought one. One got bad and he bought another one. 'Cause they would seat the whole band and still have room in the back, you know. That way they just take one car."

For added comfort, Earl installed a carry-all on top of the limousine, and he had his name painted in huge letters on the side. Even when he didn't have the time to post placards to advertise his show, he still drew crowds by driving his conspicuous car around. By the sixties, his limousine had become so famous that it became part of his routine alongside other featured attractions, as Dick Shurman recalls. "In fact, on one of his posters he had a picture of his limousine on it along with the people in the band. He had on his poster like 'Carey Bell—The Wizard of the Chromatic,' 'Little B. B.—The East St. Louis Blues Singer,' 'A Limousine,' and there was a picture of his car on it."

Hooker remained faithful to his limousines for close to fifteen years, ordering them from a specialized dealer in Arkansas, according to Big Moose

Walker: "That old long car, they put two cars and stuff together and make those cars, and these guys make these in Hot Springs, you know. See, they take the cars and they cut them half in two and they stick the transmission and stuff like that, and they put two more doors between that so that makes four doors on each side."

His ceaseless road trips made an incredibly enduring driver out of Hooker, and his energy seemed inexhaustible when he had to cover long distances. But if his associates all concur in saying that Earl was a good driver who rarely entrusted with anyone the responsibility of his road ship, traveling with Hooker was seldom uneventful. When asked about his friend's caution on the road, Big Moose Walker provided a typical answer: "You's kiddin'?! He drove as fast as he could! Yeah, but he was a good driver. Earl did a lot of drivin' too, you know. He could drive, like leave [Chicago] and go to Lawton, Oklahoma, and then go to St. Louis or Cairo, Illinois. You gonna sleep and wake up, you'd be a mile and a half, or two miles, or ten miles from where you was goin'. I've seen him drive a thousand miles. But when he got sick, oh goodness! He was terrible! He'd get on the other side lane. Yes! He'd tell us, 'I-I-I-I ain't gonna need you all here, I'm gonna carry you all with me!' and he'd get on the other side. I'd say, 'Goddam!!!' he say, 'Th-th-th-there ain't nothin' comin', man,' and zoom! He'd get on the other side. Drivin' along like that, and goin' up the hills, a hundred miles an hour!"

Fortunately, Hooker was never involved in any serious accident, but his driving sometimes upset passengers unused to it, as the following story recounted by Billy Boy Arnold confirms: "When we were going to Oklahoma, we were going somewhere in downstate Illinois, and [drummer] Billy Davenport was a very nervous type of guy. Hooker was scaring him the way he was driving; he threatened to jump out of the car and bla-bla. He was mad and trying to stop him from driving too fast, and Hooker couldn't understand what was wrong with the guy. Of course Hooker was driving at top speed, and I remember this guy was back there moanin', saying his stomach was hurtin', he was goin' on vomiting, you know, because he was scared to death. So Billy Davenport took over the driving, and Hooker got asleep, and that's really the reason why he let him drive. We were almost at St. Louis; it was daybreak, and Hooker got real tired. So Hooker let him drive a few miles. Then Hooker saw he couldn't drive, and he took the car away from him."

In his quest for recognition with the members of his community, Hooker was very meticulous about his appearance, spending large amounts of money for his clothing. Until the last few years of his life, Earl remained a strict dresser. "He and I had both those two bad habits, clothes and cars," Arbee Stidham says. "We never dressed alike, but we loved clothes alike, and he'd say, 'Well, I got to go shopping,' and I'd say, 'Well, I've been already, I don't have to go there today,' or somethin'. He was a conservative dresser, but he wore a lot of sport clothes. He liked sport coats, he liked different coats and slacks."

Hooker's love of garments was inherited from Mary Hooker, herself a sharp dresser, especially when she was going out with her son on a weekend evening. On such occasions, Hooker tried to dazzle people with garish outfits, his fascination for loud colors or unusual combinations urging him to brighten up the strict cut of his suits. Singer Lee Shot Williams makes a detailed description of Hooker's wardrobe: "His suits he wore was two-tone. If he had a brown suit, it would be dark brown on this side up this way, this leg would be dark brown, this arm and this chest'd be dark brown, and this other side'd be beige brown like that, that's the kinda suits he wore."

If Hooker dressed with care in every day life—an undeniable asset when trying to impress women—it was on the stage that the care with which he polished his image fully manifested itself. A logical complement to his instrumental brilliance, Earl's flamboyant costumes had much to do with the admiration he aroused in audiences, particularly around the rural areas he visited. "See, at that time, you didn't wear jeans much, jeans were not popular at that time. You only wore jeans if you were goin' to work in the fields," blues star B. B. King explains. "But Earl Hooker would always wear a shirt and tie, and if not shirt and tie, a beautiful shirt, nice, you know, and other clothes to go with. He looked real Chicago. He was a light-skinned black guy, very fair complected, very thin, kinda long-jaw like; slim fingers, very thin fingers. And he'd always wear a hat, and usually very well dressed, most times. Most of the guys in Chicago always dress, they're very dressy."

With time, Hooker's tastes changed. During the second half of the sixties, his wardrobe evolved as he developed a penchant for western attire. In addition to tight-fitting jackets, he would usually wear a large Stetson hat, while leather vests, flashy shirts with frills, and gaudy shoes completed his western look. "The outfit that I remember him best for," friend Dick Shurman reports,

159   *Guitars, Cars, and Women*

"he had a black cowboy hat, and he wore a black suit and a lilac ruffled shirt and lilac shoes, any wild kinda shirts. Now he wasn't a real fancy dresser, but you know he dressed up to a certain extent."

Companionship, cars, clothes . . . being choosy about his standing and appearance was just another way for Hooker to enhance the attractiveness of his shows. As in other fields, Earl would put this meticulousness at the service of his only true passion: his music.

A Man of Many Styles

The circle of Hooker's admirers was not limited to his fellow musicians. The fascination he exerted on his entourage was shared by the club and neighborhood bar audiences he entertained with a zest not equaled by many. In addition to his instrumental virtuosity, Earl always found a way to hold the attention of his public, probably as a way to make the world revolve around his own person. From the late forties, his performances were marked by his use of spectacular tricks, such as playing behind his back or between his legs, picking his guitar strings with his feet or with his teeth, and doing flips in front of bewildered audiences without missing a note. If the use of such gimmicks later became commonplace in the blues community, they seemed revolutionary at a time when most players, emulating big band jazz guitarists, still played sitting down. One of the earliest examples of flashy showmanship in R&B circles was given by Eddie "Guitar Slim" Jones—author of the 1954 hit "The Things That I Used to Do"—whose hair was dyed blue to match an all-blue outfit and who was wont to roam club halls perched on the shoulders of his valet, his guitar connected to his amplifier with a three-hundred-foot cord, but Hooker's own acrobatics, antedating Slim's antics, were inspired by the elaborate stage shows of his childhood idol, T-Bone Walker, who was based briefly in Chicago during the war years.

In addition to his showmanship, the technical improvements that took place in the field of electrified musical instruments from the fifties provided Hooker with a renewed set of effects. When most of his peers used the same guitar for years, Hooker constantly purchased new instruments, always introducing unusual gear. "He got all the new gimmicks, electrical equipment that came out for music," harmonicist Billy Boy Arnold says. "He'd come up with amps that you had never saw before. He had amps five-feet, six-feet tall back then, you know, all kinda weird amps. I don't know where he'd get 'em. I mean, he always had his name on his guitars. He had it written with fancy letters, EARL HOOKER. Anything that came out that was unique. He knew all the latest gadgets, and he was experimenting [with] everything. He had so many things, I don't know what he would do with it. Well, a lot of times, he'd keep it at his house 'cause his mother used to have a lot of different types of amps, guitars, she kept his things."

Besides the loud-colored, weird-shaped instruments he boasted on the bandstand, Hooker became famous quite early for the double-neck guitars that were to become his trademark. Over the years, Earl used at least two different twin-neck models. In the sixties his favorite twelve-string/six-string model—manufactured under the name "Double 12" by the Michigan-based Gibson company from 1958, and priced at $475!—came as a replacement for the initial Danelectro bass-guitar/six-string instrument he sold to guitarist Sunnyland Charles in the early sixties.

Hooker was one of the first musicians in the Chicago community to start playing a double-neck instrument, along with his childhood friend Bo Diddley. Whereas the twelve-string part of his second twin-neck guitar provided him with new harmonies and a different sound, his first bass/guitar model had been chosen less for its musical possibilities than for its most uncommon look, as keyboard man Johnny Big Moose Walker remarks: "He wanted something different. He figured that he'd look even bigger than the rest of the guitar players with the two-neck guitar. He used a six-string, and then he had a bass on the same guitar. He played the bass a while, along behind the other bass player.

He'd just do somethin' on the bass, understand, then he'd go back to the guitar."

With the advent of transistorization, guitar players progressively found new ways to diversify their sound. Most blues players stayed away from such novelties, but Hooker, walking in the steps of innovators like Eddie Durham, T-Bone Walker, and Charlie Christian who had paved the way for amplification before the war, experimented with all the gadgets that came out, often with success. The use of echo chambers and delay units at first, and during the second half of the sixties of the wah-wah pedal, gave his music an extra edge that never failed to rouse the admiration of his audiences.

"Hooker was really into gimmicks," Dick Shurman says. "When I saw Hooker, he'd be playing like maybe a double-neck guitar, but he'd have a wah-wah and he'd have an echo delay unit on his amplifier so that sometimes he'd be playing two things at once. And he'd be playing behind his back or playing with his teeth and playing slide. If Hooker had had the money to have good equipment, there's just no telling what he would have sounded like, because what he did within the limits of poverty was just incredible, and I really think he could have been just an absolutely amazing rock guitar player if he would have just been into that sort of scene. Most blues bands don't even have PAs and Hooker was like that too, and he was stuck with the tools he had to work with, but he got the most out of it, of any blues artist."

Hooker's merit and creativity, more than the fact that he used technical artifacts, was to discover before anyone else ways of turning them to account in order to expand the boundaries of blues guitar. Earl's Chicago peers were not the only ones to benefit from his innovative mind, and a whole generation of guitarists were soon to follow in his wake; one of rock's foremost representatives, Jimi Hendrix, himself a former rhythm & blues musician fully aware of the blues scene, belonged to that category when he emulated Hooker's superlative use of the wah-wah pedal.

Earl's inventiveness was not restricted to sophisticated effects, and he also developed surprising new techniques with basic equipment. The popularization of portable tape recorders in particular allowed him to practice at home in a more efficient way, whereas his urge to baffle the public made him devise new tricks. "Of course, he listened to records a lot, at home he did," Big Moose Walker recounts. "He had a studio in his house, every kind of speaker, every

163   *A Man of Many Styles*

kind of mike, he had all of it in his house. Then, he bought some kind of am-plifier, and he'd sit down at home, and then he'd cut his guitar down and press the button, and play a complete song on the guitar. And a lot of time, he'd leave the bandstand and press this, and leave us up there. He'd go on and walk and sit down in the house, and we'd play behind a recording! He had a tape in his amplifier, you know what I'm talkin' about? He would tape it at home. He could also tape with the band playin', and then he would leave the bandstand and put the tape and we'd go right back over, and he had a guitar playin' just like he was up there. He would take his guitar in his hand and go way up there and leave it, or lay his guitar down, you know, and the guitar started, '1, 2, 3, du-du-du-dum,' and he'd be sittin' over there laughin', with his cowboy hat on, and the guitar'd be playin'. That tickled him, you know. People would be lookin'."

Hooker's delayed playback system found other applications; double-tracking his playing during a song, he could pick simultaneously two solos in harmony, or create variations on a theme. Portable tape machines also proved helpful whenever Earl's tuberculosis kept him in bed for extended periods of time, and his stays in the hospital provided him with opportunities to come up with new musical ideas. But as much as he practiced by himself, Earl never rehearsed with his sidemen, and only excellent musicians were able to follow his unbri-dled guitar improvisations without losing their foothold. "Hooker never re-hearsed. He rehearsed at home, but he didn't rehearse with no band not as long as I knowed him, never. Go on stage and play," Big Moose Walker confirms. "He'd never tell the musicians what key, like 'We're gonna play this in C, like G, or A, or B flat.' He just started to playin', we just pick it up. See, the guys done played with him, they knowed where he playin' at anyway. I did. We didn't care. Then I'll tell you what; if he plays about a bar, and if you ain't found that key, you was fired. He got another bass player or another piano player or another anythin'. 'G-g-grandpa, you m-m-made the wrong chord!' He don't care what you do, you know.

"And Hooker played in every key on the guitar. He liked D, and if he's gonna play like T-Bone Walker, he'd play in B flat, but the regular keys that he really played the blues in was A and D, like that. And Hooker was too good to play with a clamp [capo]. I don't think that he played with nothin' but a straight pick on the bandstand. His fingers was too fast. That's what I can't understand, he used to get all those notes, you know, just with a straight pick, while a lot of guys use their fingers. See, Earl Hooker played so good and so fast, you could hardly tell when he'd jump time. He would put somethin' else in, and get back where he was, and if he jumped any time, you could hardly tell it, see. A lot of guys jump time, then they get scared, and then they'll quit and wait on the other guys; but Earl Hooker just keep a playin', keep a playin'. Earl Hooker could play good enough to back his own time, that's how I see it."

Hooker's improvisations could be hard to follow for his musicians, but they were an asset to his listeners, who were certain never to hear the same song played the same way twice. "The thing about it, like I watch bands, and most times they have a show that they're playin' on stage," says booking agent Herb Turner. "But he wasn't playin' planned shows, you know, and he'd say, 'Okay, fellows, let's hit it!' It was a mood, or the crowd or somethin'. He might use a slide this time, and not use it the next time. To see Earl Hooker was just terrific, each time. It was always somethin' new. If he started on a tune like this, he'd play it like this. Then somebody might say, 'Hey, let me hear that slide, Earl!' and then he would do it, you know."

To a greater extent than his use of spectacular gimmicks and tricks on the bandstand, Earl Hooker's versatility accounted for the faithful following he developed everywhere he played. Besides the fact that he showed relative proficiency on an impressive number of instruments—including bass, mandolin, banjo, harp, and more especially piano and organ—no other guitarist in the blues community was able to play in as many styles as Hooker could.

His repertoire, depending on his mood or that of his audience, could include slow blues tunes, driving boogie-woogie instrumentals, deep soul numbers, be-bop standards, and pop attempts, whereas his show inevitably included at least one country & western favorite. "When the band was goin' for a break, he'd play 'She'll Be Comin' 'Round the Mountain.' It was a gimmick thing. She'd come every time he was off," Herb Turner comments with a smile before he adds: "But he played the hell out of it. It was up-tempo, and it was outa sight, you know, it was a different pace from what people used to hear. It was a catchy thing, and everybody would give a hand. Quite a few blues bands still do that as a joke. But about Hooker, I really don't believe that there was anything that he couldn't play."

"He could play everything," Earl's friend Dick Shurman approves. "He was a great bebop player, he was a great shuffle player, he was a great country player, he was an incredible slide player, he played great wah-wah, he played beautiful slow blues, he could bend strings really well. He especially liked to play shuffles with single-note runs over bebop chords. He played a lot of bebop instrumentals, and swing, you know, like he played 'Flying Home' and stuff like that. God, I don't know what he couldn't play, really."

Even though he was proficient in many styles, Earl always remained a bluesman at heart, by his own admission. "I like to do different things on the guitar," Hooker told record producer Chris Strachwitz in the fall of 1968. "I have never had a job in my life—played music all my life. I like to play rock and roll, jazz and blues—I like to play a little of everything. I once had a jazz group but we couldn't make no money. Well, so I said I'm going back to play the blues—so I got me a blues group and started to make money again!"[1]

Far from copying patterns and licks, Earl constantly transcended the elements he picked up in an attempt at making them his. In the process, he managed to stay ahead of his time, according to Billy Boy Arnold: "The first time I saw him in 1953, he was playin' all the rock 'n' roll stuff that came out in the sixties. I'm talking about all the original beats and stuff, he was playing that. Way ahead of his time. I used to listen to him, I'd say, 'I never heard this kinda stuff he's playing.' No guitar player had ever heard it. He was very creative, very inventive. It was only three musicians I've met that were really impressive like that, very dynamic, very soulful, who would have so much when they played, and that was Sonny Boy Williamson #1, Little Walter, and Earl Hooker. I've met just about all the guys in Chicago, but those are the only three guys that stood out, that were unique when they played." "Playing with Hooker, it gave you ideas," saxophonist Little Bobby Neely stresses. "Certain people, the things that they do on their instrument, it triggers a thought in your mind. The people that was around Hooker at that time, they all thought like me. It was like some kinda magical inspiration. And it wasn't just with guitar players, it was the same thing with me on the horn."

Earl's lack of formal musical education certainly prevented him from knowing as many chord structures and progressions as some of his fellow guitar players who could read notes, but his spontaneity and verve were the positive signs of a natural talent, and his playing radiated with the unselfconscious, boundless creativity typical of an illiterate genius. Hooker himself, far from suffering from being inhibited by his lack of training, had a tendency to look down on educated musicians; he thought that written music was a caricature of human emotions, as the following anecdote, told by Junior Wells, demonstrates: "We was on our way to Lawton, Oklahoma, and we stopped in Detroit. I can't recall the name of the big place that this big white band was playin', but we're drivin' down and goin' through the city and Earl saw the sign, he say, 'Oh,' he say, 'let's go in here and see what they doin'.' So we went in and so when they got off the stage and came back to the dressin' room, Earl was talkin' to 'em, and he axed 'em, say, 'Could me and my band come up and sit in with you? We just tryin' to get a few dollars to get to Lawton, Oklahoma, and we just wanna help out a little bit if we can,' so the guy told him, say, 'Well, I don't know,' he say, 'we don't have any sittin' in,' so Earl went all the way to the promoter of the place, and the promoter of the place say, if it was all right with the group that was there, then it was all right with him, so they said yes, it was all right with them. And we got on the bandstand. The first thing the man axed is, 'Do you read music?' Earl said, 'Read what?!!!' 'Do you read music?' He say, 'No, I don't play no Mickey Mouse music.' He say, 'You call readin' music Mickey Mouse music?' He say, 'That's all it is,' he say. 'If you gotta read it, you can't play it,' he say, 'because when you readin' it, everybody got a little dab here and a little dab there,' he say, 'but if you really wanna play it, you gotta play it from your heart like I do.' And we set the world on fire right there in the end with 'em! Now I won't say their name, it's a great big, important white band, very big one."

From a strictly technical standpoint, Earl's playing was flawless but for the fact that he was not especially good at sustaining notes—a technique he was not fundamentally interested in due to his outstanding instrumental rapidity. This drawback finally turned out to his benefit, as he never became another imitator of B. B. King, uncontested master and originator of this style, as was confirmed by Jim O'Neal in 1970 when he reviewed for *Living Blues* magazine five of Earl's six albums: "Out of all five albums (forty-nine cuts), there are only three overtly King-styled leads, and one is by [rhythm guitarist Paul] Asbell."[2] Unlike most guitarists of his generation, Earl never felt the urge to "squeeze" notes, his mastery of the slide making up for sustain; if the trademark of B. B. King stylists was sustain—actually an artificial rendition with bare fingers of the specific trill obtained with a bottleneck—Earl Hooker's own style was the slide. "He had perfect discipline of his hands," Dick Shurman asserts. "Dave

Myers was the one that showed me that he had just the exact notion of when he was or wasn't touching the strings; now he didn't move an extra—even like a millimeter, like resting without touching, so that it looked like he was hardly moving. He had a light touch. And he played a real short slide too, so he could get the most use out of his fingers when he was playing."

Earl's approach to slide guitar was much more sophisticated than that of other specialists like Elmore James or Muddy Waters. Unlike them, he seldom retuned his instrument, allowing him to switch from slide playing to normal finger style with baffling ease. Instead of using full-chord glissando effects, he preferred the more subtle single-note runs inherited from others who played slide in standard tuning, Tampa Red, Houston Stackhouse, and his mentor Robert Nighthawk, wording them into delicate voice-like phrases that gave one the impression that he made his guitar sing and talk. "That guy was incredible. That man had that thing talking like a person singing a lyric. I said to myself, 'I ain't got no business trying to learn how to play slide. I ain't got no business looking at a slide, the way that man plays,'"[3] Buddy Guy declared to his biographer. "Yeah, it was called talkin' guitar," Big Moose Walker stresses. "I've never seen anybody play a standard thing on a slide like him. And he never did retune. He had old funny tunings that he could tune and practice in, like Spanish or D Natural [open D], but he never did play on the stage like that. He used a steel slide. He made 'em, some kind of old steel pipe, he said he'd get 'em out of used cars, somewhere up in the wheel or somethin', and sawed 'em to make 'em stick to his finger."

Earl Hooker's vocal approach to slide guitar was a direct consequence of his lack of confidence in his own singing; he tried to reproduce with his instrument the sounds he failed to create with his voice. This became even more flagrant after he started using a wah-wah pedal during the last few years of his life, wah-wah and slide styles merging into a human-like presence in an incredibly realistic way. Hooker's vocal complex can be traced to the early days, and it stands out in his recorded output, largely devoted to instrumental showcases. "I always doubted myself on singing," he himself admitted readily to Chris Strachwitz when the latter recorded him in November 1968. "Some people tell me that I sound nice—but I be ashamed of me the way I sing, but I'm not ashamed of playing music!"[4]

It is hard to determine today the reasons behind Hooker's rejection of his singing, but it may be surmised that the emergence of his lung disease at a very early age, and possibly his pronounced speech impediment, prevented him from developing into a powerful vocalist. At any rate, whatever energy he could not spend on the vocal side of his talent he transferred to his playing with unmatched intensity. "He certainly was a guitar player first," Dick Shurman confirms. "He didn't remember words and he didn't have any range. That was basically it, he knew one or two verses of a lot of songs, but it was hardly any song that I knew vocally that he knew all the way through. But the thing with Hooker, he would just come up with a lick and he'd just play an instrumental based around it, and then he could just call somebody else up to sing."

Shurman's testimony concerning Earl's bad memory is interesting, because it would tend to explain why Hooker repeatedly recorded over the years "Do You Mean It," Rosco Gordon's "Chicken," and "Swear to Tell the Truth": they happened to be just about the only vocals he had bothered to memorize. This trait of his personality is consistent with his creativity, inventive individuals usually feeling an urge to move forward. For Earl, playing was gratifying because it provided him with an opportunity to try out new musical ideas, whereas singing was just a matter of repeating well-tried verses; when singing on the bandstand or in the studio became inevitable, he satisfied himself with a limited number of songs he had more or less memorized. "Yeah, he'd do two or three tunes every night, he'd never do it on the whole show. He'd always let [Harold] Tidwell sing, or let me sing, or let B. B. Odom sing. See, he always had somebody to sing," Big Moose Walker explains. "When Hooker sang, he had to stand by and whistle, you know, like Otis Spann. You could tell him the words. By the time he'd get ready to sing, he had done forgotten, so he'd sing the same verse over and over. He didn't care, nothin' but the guitar, that's the only thing he'd remember. Didn't remember anybody's name, called everybody Grandpa. He called all the ladies Grandma."

Various opinions have been expressed about Earl's vocal qualities; some of his friends and associates, like Herb Turner for example, considered him a mediocre singer, but others concur in saying that, although his singing was not outstanding and could hardly match his instrumental potential, Hooker was a pleasant vocalist, especially in a slow blues context. Delmark Records owner Bob Koester of Chicago gives the most plausible explanation for Hooker's failure to draw the attention of producers and A&R men when he ascribes Earl's lack of success to a current trend in blues circles at the time: "I liked Earl Hooker's voice, but that was an age of strong voices. Like Luther Allison was a strong singer, and the guys who didn't have strong voices were a bit put down, like men with a short penis. It's stupid; it doesn't mean anything, but it can mean something if people think it means something. Earl did have a voice for recording, but he wouldn't sing in clubs, and I generally found him to be a bit on the boring side, to me. So it was just like when he had his band at Pepper's. I would just go in, see it was him, and say, 'Well, forget it!' you know. Of course any band in any club would play two or three instrumentals before anybody would sing, but with Earl Hooker, those instrumentals just kept on, I mean there was a whole set, a couple of whole sets of instrumentals. I think that's a terrible mistake, because for me, I'm always glad to hear guys singing."

Koester's reaction epitomizes the recurrent attitude of record label operators, who believe that blues players cannot reach commercial success unless their instrumental proficiency is matched by their singing ability. This partly accounts for the fact that Earl never made it really big in national blues circles despite the respectable status he attained, at first in the southern states and then in the Midwest. The blues being first and foremost a vocal genre, Earl's inability to develop a singing style that neared the distinctiveness of his guitar playing denied him true recording success, at least until the last year of his life. One cannot help feel that Hooker, had he devoted but a small portion of the energy he lavished on guitar on a more personal vocal approach, would have gained recognition on a large scale.

Hooker's distrust in his capacity as a singer, if it played a determining role in the development of his recording career, was not the only factor involved. His versatility, for one, rebuffed narrow-minded blues purists; but most of all, his purposely unresponsive attitude in the studio deprived him of the recording success and nationwide popularity he could have earned but for his short-sightedness and almost superstitious mistrust of others. It is true that the atmosphere of the recording studio is not as challenging as that prevailing in the clubs and dance halls that Earl was wont to play, a fact the guitarist himself willingly acknowledged: "I like any club with lots of people in it," he once told producer Strachwitz. "That gives me real soul to play—when I see them people—I get happy and everything comes out of me."[5] But the absence of a public that he wished to dazzle was not the main reason for Earl's restraint in the studio, as he voluntarily bridled his creative instincts and instrumental skills when he recorded in the hope of deterring potential imitators. "Even when I knew him, he was better on stage," says Dick Shurman, who became friends with Hooker when his sickness had already impaired his abilities. "But Louis [Myers] told me that Hooker gave him some advice. He said, 'When you go into the studio, if you play your best licks, other people will steal them and get rich; so when you go into the studio, you play dummy guitar,' that's the phrase that he used. Which to me is just backwards, because the time you play your own licks is in the studio when you can put them on record, and everybody will know they're yours, or you can play them in a club where somebody will copy them and record them first in the studio. Like Magic Slim is the perfect example, he picks up everything everybody else plays, and that's to his credit. But anyhow, even when I saw Hooker, he was better on stage, and I don't know how much of it was because he was really holding back in the studio, and how much of it was that he was just better live." Shurman's explanation is backed by facts: the most flagrant evidence of Hooker's inhibited attitude in the studio is found in the fact that "Blue Guitar," the title the guitarist is best remembered for and his finest effort on vinyl, was recorded by accident, unknown to Earl, when producer Mel London let the tape run as the band was warming up.

If the slide somehow made up for Earl's lack of vocal assurance, it did not free him from the need to hire vocalists. Realizing the essential role played by singers in the eyes of club audiences, he made it a point of honor to feature in his band talented vocalists. In this respect, one the most positive aspects of Hooker's collaboration with Mel London was his durable association with singers worthy of his talent. Until then, Hooker had merely asked his sidemen to handle vocal chores, unless he was able to lure in his outfit professional singers like Billy Boy Arnold on a short-term basis. Earl knew from the start that crowds reacted to his music with more enthusiasm when a capable vocalist enhanced his show, yet he had a hard time sharing the stage with others. "I always liked to have my own group," Hooker admitted in 1968. "I feel better— I can play what I want—but when you play with somebody else you have to play like they want you to play."[6]

On the other hand, vocalists were reluctant to sing with someone as flashy as Hooker for fear of cutting a sorry figure, and only superior singers could carve their way to front stage when he was around. "Earl really didn't rely on the vocalist," Billy Boy Arnold explains. "He'd just use that to break the monotony, the whole show was his guitar. The vocalist was just a added attraction, just to give some kind of variety. I wouldn't wanna be a singer with a guy like that, 'cause when he got through playin', there wasn't nothing else for you to do 'cause he had the people in the palm of his hand."

Hooker's recording activities in the early sixties made him see things from a different angle, his position as lead guitarist on hot singles paving the way for well-paid shows with his studio vocalists. This was true with Lillian Offitt, Junior Wells, A. C. Reed, Ricky Allen, and Bobby Saxton. No matter how accidental the reunion on vinyl of Hooker and Saxton was, the popularity of "Trying to Make a Living" provided them with numerous club engagements in 1960. After a long spell in Gary, Indiana, they toured the Midwest with Harold Tidwell, young Bob Nelson, and a set of go-go dancers, playing one-nighters at various Indiana, Ohio, and Michigan locations before heading back for Chicago.

By the time "Trying to Make a Living" was beginning to die out on the record market, Junior Wells's "Little by Little" was at its peak after a three-week stay on *Billboard*'s R&B charts in June 1960, and Hooker left Saxton to start working with Junior Wells. The second half of 1960 and most of 1961 were busy years for the Hooker-Wells team, after "Blues in D-Natural" and "Messin' with the Kid" complemented Wells's Profile hit. Mel London's Hooker/Wells releases were hitting the market at close intervals, and because their records sold with regularity, Earl and Junior, with keyboard man Big Moose Walker and saxophonist A. C. Reed in tow, appeared in the city's most prominent lounges in between extensive road trips. Earl's longstanding friendship with Junior certainly helped him get over his reluctance to share the bill with another artist. Junior had already been the featured singer with Hooker's band on previous occasions, but the collaboration between the two men was never as fruitful as during the London years. The feeling of mutual understanding that prevailed between them largely contributed to their reputation as devastating artists, in all the meanings of the word!

"Junior Wells went on the road with us a lot," Big Moose Walker reminisces. "He went on down with us to Sikeston, Missouri. We were just young guys, you know, we did everything! We made the hogs drunk! This man had a nightclub, and then he had a farm where a lot of people would come from Memphis. The band stayed free, and we all got food free, so we'd take whatever money he'd give us, you know. We didn't really care. The guy wanted us to chop cotton, because we was just playin' Friday, Saturday, and Sunday. They chopped cotton during the day, but we wouldn't go out to chop cotton. The guy said, 'You all gonna stay here, so okay, you all gonna kinda cut the weeds around in the yard.' So we went to the store, we go in Hooker's car, we got five gallons of wine, and we feed the man's hogs, you know. He said, 'You all feed the hogs.' He had about fifty hogs out there. So we mixed the wine up in the trough, Hooker, Junior Wells, and I, and then we pulled the hogs out. It was hotter than it is now, about 100, 105, 110. The hogs, they just ate and ate and ate, and after a while, they started staggerin' all over the place. Junior Wells was sittin' down cryin'. He'd taken a firecracker, one of these big things, and it was a old rooster used to run outside around the house. And we caught the old rooster, you know, we roped the old rooster like they do it, and we tied the firecracker in his mouth with a cordstring and lit it. It blew his beak off! So when the guy came back, Junior Wells looked at me. The rooster was tryin' to eat but he didn't have any beak. And Junior Wells started to laughin', so that made the guy suspicious. He looked at me, he said, 'What's wrong with my rooster, Moose John?' I just burst out, started laughin', you know, so the man went and got his pistol, said, 'I'm gonna blow your brains out!' I said, 'It wasn't none of me. It was Junior Wells!' and Junior Wells just fell out, and he put it all on me. The man kicked us out."

As eventful as road life was with Hooker, the prolific session that produced "The Things I'd Do for You" signaled the end of the partnership with Wells after financial disagreements set in. "He's reversible. He did his thing, and when I come up or whatever, he pushed the issue just as hard behind me as he did for his own little self. Now this is when I really feel that an artist is an artist," Junior Wells emphasizes. "So I'd still go places with Earl, but not too often because the money that he told me he was gonna pay me he didn't pay." With time, Hooker's unstable nature finally got the best of him, and Wells drifted on to play with other bands, although Earl and Junior remained great friends and occasional bandstand partners until the former's death.

Hooker's experience with Lillian Offitt, Bobby Saxton, and Junior Wells incited him to use full-time singers in his band even when he did not work with one of London's appointed vocalists. If Junior was an experienced artist capable of forming his own outfit, Offitt was precisely the type of singer Earl needed, someone with a vocal talent and no specific desire to become a band-leader. Her withdrawal from the blues scene and the end of the dynamic team he formed with Wells compelled Hooker to look for other vocalists, including drummer Bobby Little, Jesse Anderson, and Lee "Shot" Williams.

Lee Williams, originally from Lexington, Mississippi, made the move to Illinois with his family in the early sixties, and he was beginning to gain recognition on the Chicago scene as Lee "Shot" Williams when he first met Earl. "My people used to call me 'Shot,'" the singer recalls about the genesis of his nickname, "but now it's like, 'You're a big shot,' you know." Hooker was all the more prone to hire beginners that he could easily underpay, and Lee Shot gained his first stage experiences between Earl's Roadmasters and the band of harmonicist Mack Simmons. "I met Hooker in 1961," Williams remembers. "I met him in Chicago, he was playin' down at Theresa's. Earl couldn't sing, but he was, whooo! one of the guitar-est players, oh man! He could make a guitar sing, talk, you know. He used to do this tune that Ike and Tina Turner had, 'Baby It's Gonna Work Out Fine.'[7] He'd play it just like Tina sing it. So one day in '62, when I had my record out, 'Hello Baby I Ain't Got Long to Stay,'[8] he asked me to go on the road with him. We went from coast to coast, and my record wasn't nationwide, but we played everywhere." Regardless of his unde-niable talent, Lee Shot's easygoing nature and eagerness to learn a trade that was new to him appealed to Hooker, whose band featured Williams's elaborate B. B. King/Bobby Bland–style singing at regular intervals until the mid-sixties.

In addition to the usual Chicago engagements at Theresa's or at Pepper's, in between recording dates Hooker found the time to take his combo through Missouri, Arkansas, and Mississippi, where Lee Shot never failed to visit his relatives. "We had one of those long airport limousine cars. We had it painted green, 'Earl Hooker and the Soul Twisters,' the name of the band. We used to go down to my home, about three miles from Tchula, and then six miles from Lexington. Me and Moose [Walker] used to rabbit hunt, but Hooker was into like recorders, organs, and stuff like that, his guitars," Lee Shot recalls.

Considering the way he generally misused his musicians, Earl Hooker could hardly rely on one vocalist only; around the same period of time, he also started hiring in his band a powerful singer named Andrew Odom. Hooker met Odom in St. Louis, where they had often worked the same stages in the late fifties. Earl enjoyed Odom's singing a lot, and he expressed his appreciation of it at the time of their initial encounter by calling him "B. B. King Jr." Earl tried to entice the vocalist away from his home in East St. Louis on various occasions, to no purpose, until one cold day of January 1960, when Odom abruptly left southern Illinois for Chicago on the spur of the moment: "One day I just packed my suitcase without thinking much about what I was doing and had did till it was time to get off the bus in Chicago. Man, you talkin' about somebody feelin' sad—it was me! Here I am in great big ole Chicago with no money in my pockets, or, as a matter of fact, no money nowhere else either! No money, nowhere to stay; didn't know nobody here. I remember thinkin' to myself, what is this I done done? And, oh Lord, what am I gonna do?

"The first thing I did was go down on the South Side—on 43rd Street. I went in some little club and started talkin' to this fellow sittin' next to me and telling him what I had did. He told me, that down the street was a club that had bands and I went down there. . . . That club turned out to be Pepper's. . . . After that night, I would always be at Pepper's. After a few days, Hooker came in, and then I started working short trips out of town with him and his band. That was my start here in Chicago. I stuck with the man all the way, much as I could, because we both loved music the same way. . . . Hooker used to tell me, 'Junior, with your voice, man, and the way I play guitar, man, we got to make it some day, ain't we?'"[9]

Andrew Odom's vocal style complemented Hooker's playing well, especially when he didn't try to plagiarize B. B. King. Unfortunately, Odom stuck to the B. B. King mold all too often, especially when Hooker introduced him on stage as "B. B. Junior" or "Little B. B." As club gigs followed road trips, Hooker and B. B. Odom got closer, and Andrew gradually became Earl's bodyguard and friend. As such, the singer's duties included paying out other band members when Hooker had promised more than he was ready to give, or collecting performance fees from reluctant club owners. "I was his backbone," Odom proudly states. "I took care of his business, I took care of his drivin', I took care of him when he's sick, I took care of him when somebody tried to misuse him, and stuff like that. I was his right arm. If he'd be late to come, then I would take the guys where he's supposed to go and get 'em there on time, and stuff like that. I could tell him about his contracts, I used to lift all his amplifiers and stuff like that. Hooker was just like a brother to me, I really cared a lot for him. I had quite a few guys try to jump him one time. And I fought his battles because I knew what type of condition he was in. His health was bad. And I couldn't stand watch around and see somebody else do somethin' to him to hurt him."

B. B. Odom's stay-at-home nature prevented him from traveling as much as Hooker would have wanted him to, and he kept a day job in addition to his musical activities. As a result, Earl would pick up people like Lee Shot Williams or Jesse Anderson when he left the city over extended periods, but in Chicago, B. B. Odom never missed one of Hooker's gigs. He would also travel with the band as an added attraction for weekend appearances in neighboring Illinois, Iowa, Wisconsin, or Indiana localities, as was the case on New Year's Eve, 1962, when the Hooker band featuring guitarist Ivory Parkes and sax man A. C. Reed shared the bill with Billy Boy Arnold at an East Chicago, Indiana, dance.

Quite symbolically, the day of May 1961 when Hooker ended his collaboration in the studio with Junior Wells witnessed Ricky Allen's recording debuts for Mel London. Allen's initial success, "You'd Better Be Sure," opened the door for more studio work, and as the young singer grew into Mel London's most reliable asset, Hooker started featuring him more and more on his show. "Ricky was somethin' like a freelance singer," A. C. Reed explains. "He just come around and sing with us, he never had a band. When he started doin' his records then, even when he'd go on the road, we would be his band." Allen may not have been an exceptional singer, but his large following in the black Chicago community was a sure sign of the public's taste for commercial soul/R&B material. By keeping Allen with him, Hooker got more exposure than most traditional blues musicians in the Windy City. The release of "Cut You A-Loose" in 1963 confirmed the trend, especially when the record climbed up the national charts in the late summer, and club gigs offering good exposure around town alternated with promotional tours. Over the summer, Allen and Hooker could be heard on a weekly basis at a West Side location called the Copa Cabana, found off Kedzie Avenue in the 3200 block of West Roosevelt Road. Managed and owned by DJ and booking agent Big Bill Hill, the Copa Cabana had opened its doors earlier in the year. Playing there was more rewarding than most appearances at larger venues, for Bill Hill broadcast on his radio shows the live performances of acts he hired at his place. When Allen and Hooker played the Copa to capacity crowds, they were heard over the air by a large share of Chicago's African American population, and their popularity was only rivaled by the success of Muddy Waters's nightly stand at Pepper's.

Hooker enjoyed the situation to a certain extent, but his pride was hurt to be hardly more than Allen's guitar player, at least in the public's eye. Once again, his eagerness to recover a freedom he had rarely given up over the years impelled him to act, and he started cheating on his vocalist. Their collaboration stopped all the more rapidly as the collapse of Age in 1964 marked the end of their studio work. "I's supposed to been on salary," Allen says. "But see, the man's dead. I know this, but see, the man never paid me a quarter. [Drummer] Bobby Little paid me about three times, and the whole band got together and paid me one other time, 'cause he slipped out. He had his ways, man, when you look back on it. I was sittin' in a room one night, man, Hooker come by, and you know how he stuttered. He said, 'M-m-m-man, c-c-come on, g-g-go with me down here to S-S-St. Louis, I'll g-g-give you $135.' I said, 'Man, you crazy,' I say, 'You didn't give me my $25, now how am I gonna get $135?' 'M-m-man, c-c-come on!' So I's sittin' there, and I called Bobby up, and Bobby come up, 'What happened?' I say, 'Man, Hooker talkin' about givin' me $135 to go to St. Louis.' I say, 'But I'm gonna check this out first.' And I called, and the people gave me $395 for one show! On Page Avenue, that was the American Legion. And that's when I really got hip to him then."

Much in the same way Hooker and Junior Wells had decided to go separate ways two years earlier, Earl and Ricky merely stopped working together, with the only difference that the band chose not to stay with the guitarist this time. The future undoubtedly looked more promising with Ricky Allen, for Earnest Johnson, A. C. Reed, and Bobby Little stuck with the vocalist under the leadership of Earl's former student and rhythm guitarist, Ivory Parkes, while Earl was left to an uncertain fate. "Well, see, I paid," Allen confirms. "And after 'You'd Better Be Sure' came out, see, I had more motivation than he did, and I was gettin' more airplay, and we's workin' like nine nights a week. And then every month or so, he had to go in the hospital, so that kinda left 'em stranded too. Hell, they had families, you know what I'm sayin'."

Concurrently with the standing of his vocalists, Earl Hooker's bands improved as a general rule in the sixties, another consequence of his four-year association with Mel London. London's sense of business and his professional approach urged him to make sure that the live performances given by his bands were up to the standards set by his Chief or Age releases. To a certain extent, Hooker also understood that the popularity of his recordings was in part due to the handful of sidemen who had helped create the "London" sound. Because audiences expected to hear on stage the same organ or tenor solos they had liked on his 45s, Hooker could no longer hire and fire his accompanists with the regularity and carelessness that had been his trademark so far. Johnny Big Moose Walker and A. C. Reed more especially, both of whom knew firsthand about Earl's unpredictable moods, remained the keystones of Hooker's unit during most of the decade. Earl's truthfulness was not as pronounced with his rhythm section, and if bassist Earnest Johnson often traveled with him, he was sometimes replaced by Bob Anderson, James Green, or Nick Charles, whereas drummers Harold Tidwell, Bobby Little, Frank Swan, and Larry "Big Twist" Nolan—later to lead the internationally acclaimed Mellow Fellows—shared rhythmic chores, among others.

With the development of his career, Hooker also featured more elaborate acts. He could still perform as a trio if the situation called for it, but his constant need to move ahead made him want to emulate the example of better-known artists. A symbolic example of Earl's longing for better things was the addition to his band of the two Taylor sisters, billed on his shows as the Earlettes, whose questionable talent was exposed on a 1963 Age single. In addition to the usual string of vocalists of both sexes who took turns at the microphone, Hooker's show in its most glorious days also included dancers. The tradition of shake dancers in Chicago goes back to the hootchy-kootchy contortions of dancer Little Egypt, one of the highlights at the 1893 Columbian Exposition. By the twenties, female dancers like Louise Cook, Princess Aurelia, and Tondelayo had synchronized their undulations to jazz rhythms in select venues, starting a trend that gradually affected smaller outfits after the war. "He had a whole show," Hooker's wife Bertha explains. "Go-go girls, he called 'em. They would strip. Not all of the clothes down, though. And he had one man called Lightfoot. He was a dancer, and he really could dance. He would always do a thing called the floor show. He was really good. He was exactly what they named him, Lightfoot." "He had girls like Marie, used to shake dance and stuff like that for him," B. B. Odom approves. "And he had quite a few others, but I can't call their names right now, but when I was with him, he didn't have that many. Only time he had go-go dancers was when the club owners wanted dancers or somethin' like that. He would just come up with 'em just like out of the clear blue sky."

Few of Hooker's advertisement placards printed during that period have survived, but a 1960 poster announcing Earl's weekly gig at Gary's Tri-State Inn shows a smiling Hooker proudly boasting a double-neck instrument in his lap. In addition to Roadmaster Bobby Saxton of "Trying to Make a Living" fame and drummer Harold Tidwell, Hooker introduces Miss Linda Lou—a shake dancing artist cashing in on the success of the "Linda Lu" dance craze launched during the summer 1959 by Ray Sharpe—complete with pictures of Saxton and Linda Lou, along with an alleged list of their latest recordings.

Even though Hooker was not the only one on the Chicago scene to feature female contortionists, he was a leader in this field too, the instrumental side of his playing being well adapted to the dancing acts in his shows. Shake dance numbers may not have been the ultimate in taste, but they were always crowd-pleasers, according to A. C. Reed: "In them days, man, if you played a job, if you had a dancin' show, it went over better. There was one girl there called Laura, she'd do a lot of dancin', and we'd use her a lot on some shows. Sometimes we'd play 'Tanya.' That's why he recorded it, 'cause we played it a lot of times for the dancer. We would like start with ordinary playin', and then we would call her up for the act, and then we would go over bigger like that. Man, we could keep a job like that."

Club Gigs and Road Trips

arl Hooker's reputation grew from 1960, and his professional
lifestyle changed as he became more in demand in the studio.
His presence on regional R&B hit records and the growing number of singles issued under his name brought him more and better
club gigs in Chicago and other urban centers in Illinois, Indiana,
and Iowa. During most of the fifties, Hooker's main support in his
hometown had come from West Side tavern owners; quite natu-
rally, he still made regular appearances there in the sixties, even
though his mother's apartment was located in the heart of the
South Side at 3921 South Prairie Avenue—a trifle off the
north–south South Park axis and a stone's throw from the busy
east–west Pershing thoroughfare. On the West Side, Hooker's
main hangouts were Walton's Corner at 2736 West Roosevelt
Road, owned by drummer T. J. McNulty; Dee Dee's Shangrala
Lounge on North Sacramento; and a string of neighborhood bars
scattered along Madison Avenue: the Seeley Club, the Avenue
Lounge, the Happy Home Lounge, the Kitty Kat, and Chuck's—

both found at the intersection of Damen Avenue—and more especially Curley's Twist City—a busy venue featuring two bands, one upstairs and one downstairs—at Madison and Homan.

Through his success, Earl was also getting recognition in the South Side, where he had long been underrated by club owners. A fine example of this new situation is that of Roberts' Show Lounge, a posh club specializing in top-class acts located at 6622 South Park, which hired Hooker's band featuring Lillian Offitt shortly after "Will My Man Be Home Tonight" became a bestseller. At last, Earl found himself in a class with better-known figures like Muddy Waters and Howlin' Wolf, and finding a gig on the South Side no longer proved difficult. Besides the Blue Flame and Theresa's Tavern—a tiny basement club situated on Indiana Avenue at the corner of 48th Street—Earl also played the Tuxedo Lounge and Turner's, also found on Indiana; the Duck Inn Lounge at 5550 State Street, and various 63rd Street locations. Another favorite hangout from the late fifties was the Trocadero Lounge. Singer Ricky Allen, who worked there with Hooker on several occasions, remembers: "It was on 47th and Indiana, in the basement. It was [owned by] Banks, who ran the Tropicana Hotel. You go down there, man, you could see everybody. Dinah Washington, she used to come in there sometime, and Lefty Bates, he would come in. See, we start like on Mondays about seven o'clock and we'd work a couple hours; another band come in and work a couple hours. It was a thing all day long, no intermission. Then you had bands comin' to sit in, and I remember Jackie Brenston, Billy Gayles, Billy "The Kid" Emerson, they'd always come in to sit in. You either worked there, or Pepper's Lounge, or you would go on Oakwood at the Blue Flame."

With time, Hooker moved his home-base to Pepper's Lounge, at 43rd and Vincennes. Johnny Pepper, when he opened his club at 503 East 43rd Street in 1956, had no intention to feature live blues entertainment: "At that particular time there wasn't too much demand for blues. Just a good band, you know, everyone loves to dance. I say Pepper's got started good about 1959 and '60 after I started to havin' top entertainment. I started usin' Muddy Waters, Junior Wells, Magic Sam, and Howlin' Wolf, that was about 1960."[1]

During the first half of the sixties, Hooker managed to hustle engagements there at regular intervals on week nights; with time, Pepper's Lounge, advertised on an outdoor sign as "The Home of the Blues," became his favorite spot in Chicago. "I saw him around Pepper's more than any place else," Dick Shurman, who became familiar with Hooker from 1968, reports. "Like he'd play there on Wednesdays most of the time. And Otis [Rush] would play there in the middle of the week too. It wasn't the sort of thing that people would wanna do for a weekend, but they'd do it for a fill-in like Tuesday or Wednesday or something. And they'd have somebody like L. V. Banks or Buddy Scott on the weekend a lot. Probably because they got along better with the gangs on the street, which was really a bummer at Pepper's. The gangs were just really terrible. They did rob people in the club, and there was just a lot of wild things going on. People'd get into fights and would start shooting. People would rob you at gunpoint or knifepoint, people would get jumped in. I was robbed once at Pepper's. It was funny, but they gave me almost all of my money back. They surround me on my way out to the street, and there is like five guys, and me and a friend. That friend had a quarter and they took it, but I had four one-dollar bills in my wallet. They took the money out real fast and they split it up and then shoved the wallet back in my hand so fast that I was just surprised to see it there, so they said, 'What's the matter, man, don't you want your wallet?' like they were gonna grab it too, and I said, 'I didn't expect you to give it back.' Then I said, 'You know, this is a really cheap watch but it has sentimental value, and you might wanna consider just not taking it as I'm sure it's not worth anything.' And so they left it and said, 'Okay, that's cool.' Then I said, 'Listen, I know this is carrying things kinda far, but could you give me a dollar so I can get home?' and three of them started to hand me back the money, but then this other guy that probably got bummed up by how flexible they were with me, he said, 'Hey, man, we gotta get outa here, the cops're gonna come,' so they split."

Playing every night in the ghetto neighborhood bars of the Windy City could sometimes be an unenviable experience. If it took a certain amount of self-control to keep one's head under normal circumstances, things changed for the worse later on in the sixties, especially during the months that followed the assassination of Dr. Martin Luther King Jr. in April 1968. The situation was not any different in the area around Chicago. Besides Chicago Heights, where Hooker and his band still performed at the Black & Tan or at the Domino Club owned by Johnny Pepper, Hooker often found shelter in Phoenix—a working-class suburb situated south of the Chicago city limits—either at the White Rose, a rough gambling joint operated at 905 East 153rd Street by a man named Hawk, or at the Rose Inn or the Royal Sportsman, both standing right down the street from the White Rose.

Another blues center of importance was Joliet, found in the heart of Will County thirty-odd miles southwest of the Loop, where itinerant acts found regular engagements in a number of nightspots like Joe Howard's Club 99, or a beer tavern known as the Shed. "Just about everybody used to play the 99 in Joliet; Ike & Tina [Turner], Ray Charles, everybody played there," says Hooker's friend and occasional promoter Herb Turner. "The bar was down in the basement, the restaurant was on the first floor, and it was like a motel there, too. The whole business, you know." When they did not play Chicago's suburbia, Hooker and band drove across the Illinois State line straight east to Gary, Indiana. With a population of nearly 200,000, Gary was an entertainer's paradise, with a large number of black steel-mill employees who worked and lived there, patronizing a string of taverns and lounges that hired live shows every single night of the week. Earl appeared for a long time on a weekly basis at the Tri-State Inn at 2576 Jennings in Gary, where he hosted the traditional Blue Monday night jams. When he was not appearing there, Hooker entertained rowdy crowds at a gambling den known as the Roadhouse, where most top R&B acts played. "An old place out there in the sticks called the Roadhouse," Vee-Jay recording star Jimmy Reed remembered later. "And this cat, we call the cat Sticks, because this place was way back out in the bushes. They had a nice little club out there."[2] Herb Turner draws a rather forbidding picture of Reed's "nice little club": "That Roadhouse, that was somethin' else! When you come in the door, they had like a check-room and you'd check your weapons and everythin'. And they stayed open all night. I think that place even operated on Sundays. The Dells used to play over there constantly; just about everybody played that Roadhouse in Gary. And now Joe Green's Club was right down the street from it. That was another one, but Joe Green's was a different type of class." "The Roadhouse? We called it Steve's place," A. C. Reed confirms. "That's where Otis Rush and a lot of 'em played, they had gamblin' and everythin' in there."

Other than the Roadhouse, Earl's favorite spot in Gary was the F&J Lounge, a popular black rendezvous described by British writer Paul Oliver, who visited it in 1960, as Gary's "principal blues center," the audience of which consisted of "steel mill workers and their women with a sprinkling of army personnel."[3]

The F&J, a large venue operated by brothers Fred and Jay—hence its name—at 1501 Adams Street at the corner of Washington, was open nightly from nine o'clock until two in the morning; for a fifty-cent admission fee it featured a different blues band every night. Among other Chicago musicians, Eddy Clearwater gave weekly performances there: "Everybody used to play the F&J like Muddy Waters, Howlin' Wolf, Otis Rush, Magic Sam, myself. We all had what you call a night like Tuesday Muddy Waters, Wednesday Otis Rush. Harold Burrage was around then too, Earl Hooker, everybody—a real famous blues club."[4] "They called it the border . . . and the border means hustlers, pimps, whores, it was the night thing and everybody went to the F&J,"[5] saxophonist Little Bobby Neely confirms.

Some way or another, Hooker became friends with the owners of the F&J Lounge, who hired his band every Thursday for what was known as "talent night." A. C. Reed's fond memories of these days prove that this was no mere figure of speech: "Me and Hooker was the house band on Thursday nights, and then sometimes we played there on weekends, that'd be around '61. It'd be big crowds on Thursdays 'cause it'd be Talent Night. The Jackson 5, they'd win it all the time, 'cause they was kids and the little kid, Michael Jackson, he was about like that horn, he'd be dancin' bad and I couldn't hardly play for laughin' at him, as little as he was, he'd be dancin'. And he'd steal the show, he was that good!"

All the contestants on Hooker's amateur shows were not as young and gifted as the 1958-born Jackson, but the presence in places like Gary of musicians of Earl's caliber contributed to the discovery of local talent. Just as Hooker was a hero for Herb Turner, Bobby Little, or Andrew Brown in Chicago Heights a decade earlier, several Gary teenagers got their first musical thrills out of watching Earl's flashy performances. One such youth was Bob Nelson, from Bogalusa, Louisiana, who spent his summers with an aunt in Gary. In 1960 Bob was only sixteen, but Hooker would sometimes let him sit in with his band on harmonica. These initial attempts were conclusive enough, and Nelson soon found himself hired as an added attraction with the Roadmasters, winding up in Chicago, where he started his own career under the moniker of "Chicago" Bob Nelson, later moving to Atlanta, where he worked with different bands—including the Heartfixers—before leading his own ensemble. Earl Hooker may have been infamous for shorting his musicians, but he also gave unstinting encouragement to fledgling musicians. "He gave me a lot of tips," Dick Shurman reports. "I'm not really much of a guitar player, but he would take me aside and show me little things all the time. Like he was encouraging to other people, but on the other hand, the fact that he was helpful to them still wouldn't stop him from not paying them their money. He gave a lot of young guys a chance to get some experience on the bandstand, and showed them how to play slide and things like that."

The end of the eventful London period brought abrupt changes to Hooker's way of handling his business. With the defection of Lillian Offitt, Junior Wells, and Ricky Allen, Earl needed engagements that would compensate for the well-paid club appearances his star singers had brought him. This challenge became all the more acute as Hooker spent more time in southern Missouri with his wife Bertha from 1963, and he finally got in touch with Ricky Allen's occasional booking agent, Herb Turner. "When I first saw Hooker in Chicago Heights," Turner says, "I was about thirteen, fourteen. That was about 1950, '51, and I was just completely interested in music. Later on I got a TV shop, and then I had a record shop. At one time, I had one in Peoria, Chicago Heights, and Chicago. By being in that field, I knew a lot of entertainers. I was workin' with Ricky Allen at the time and then I had a group called the Mighty Marvelows. It was a pop group, they had two hits that made the charts.[6] So this was '64, I think. Earl came to me then, and he wanted me to do some bookin' and do some work with him. Earl was just lookin' for places to play, see. So we did shows like Rockford [Illinois], Kankakee [Illinois], and I guess I worked with Hooker until about '67."

Working in collaboration with a booking agent in the Chicago area was a great help to Hooker, who no longer needed to hustle work every time he came back from his wife's Missouri home. In addition to Pepper's, Curley's, and Walton's Corner in the city, the club gigs Turner set up in smaller Illinois urban centers made it possible for him to concentrate on his road trips. Whenever he was struck with the fever of the road, Earl hurriedly packed his instruments into his car and put a band together. Earl's travels invariably took him south, where he followed the circuit mapped out by countless black entertainers before him. From the late forties, Hooker's trips started off in the Cairo, Illinois–Sikeston, Missouri, area, where he was to meet his wife, unless he made a first stopover on the lively St. Louis–East St. Louis scene. In the sixties Earl started using his wife's house in Catron as a home base, raiding familiar southern Illinois locations like Mounds and Cairo and making forays into Kentucky, where the clubs of Ohio River town Paducah welcomed rambling bluesmen.

In southern Missouri, in addition to Catron, Hooker and band played their way through Sikeston, New Madrid, Lilbourn, Caruthersville, and Hayti, sometimes making incursions into nearby Arkansas country towns. From there Earl would head west to Kansas City, Missouri, where he had relatives on his father's side and where he usually performed at the Black Orchid on 12th and Vine, proceeding to drive to Wichita, Kansas, or Oklahoma City and Lawton in Oklahoma, before ending up in Fort Worth, Texas. Eastbound, his wanderlust led him through Evansville, Indiana—the hometown of his cousin Joe Hinton—to Owensboro, Louisville, and Danville, Kentucky, into Cincinnati, Ohio, and back to Clarksville, Tennessee, before winding up in the Delta area that he knew like the palm of his hand, sometimes going as far down as Louisiana. "Ike Turner and 'em used to work the same circuit, what you called the chitlin circuit," Herb Turner explains. "The chitlin circuit was a little circuit that everybody played, you just follow the way, that's all. He had a route that took him through there, and he would be gone for two or three months."

"I guess if there was such thing as a black gypsy, then you would have to call Earl Hooker that," bluesman Little Milton Campbell adds. "He traveled all the time. He seemed like a very restless type of person, a very good guy, and a tremendous, tremendously good musician. I would frequently run into him in different places; if I played, say for instance Memphis, Tennessee, or some parts of Arkansas, or some parts of Louisiana, he'd be on his way to some other place and he'd always stop in, and in most cases sit in. Earl Hooker worked everywhere, all the time, man. If he didn't, he'd be there anyway."

The chitlin circuit, a self-deprecatory term for black entertainment referring to a typical soul dish, runs from Florida through Georgia and Alabama, then along the main north–south axes that link New Orleans to Chicago, the Mississippi River, Highways 51 and 61, and the Illinois Central tracks. Playing the chitlin circuit had its good aspects; the state of Florida was a harbor of warmth to traveling musicians who provided live entertainment at night during the fruit season for music-hungry orange pickers. By way of contrast, the tiny country clubs and crossroad juke joints where Hooker and his peers performed were not Chicago's slick lounges, and the atmosphere that prevailed there could be hotter than hot. "We played in Lambert, Mississippi, we played Cleveland, we played Leland, we played in Brooksville, all in Mississippi. We played juke houses, all out in different places, barns and stuff cut in two, just anywhere. And I seen guys get killed for fifteen cents. They would kill you for a dime, you know, for a dime!" Big Moose Walker insists.

Herb Turner remembers how easily Hooker would work his way out of difficult situations: "It was rough in there. That was the chitlin circuit. Every time, you'd make about $100, $125 a night, and some nights you worked for the door. That's sayin' that it's supposed to be whatever you make off the door. I remember once Hooker told me about it. He said they were playin' a club in [Lake] Charles, Louisiana, and he was playin' for the door. They had had quite a crowd there that night, and so the owner come to Hooker after the end of the gig, he says, 'Well, you ain't much comin'.' So Hooker says, 'Hey, man, I saw them people stand in the house. I got more than this comin'.' And the club owner says, 'You said you was playin' for the door, that's all we got at the door.' So Hooker figure out he had to do somethin', so he told the owner, he said, 'M-m-man, you damn right I played for the door!' Hooker said he went with some of the fellows in the band, and they removed the door. So the owner goes like this, says, 'Hey, what you all doin'?!' And Hooker says, 'We just played for the door, so now its mine.' And so the guy got real mad then, but there was nothin' he could do, and he had to give him—I don't know exactly what he paid him to get his door back. That was Hooker!"

In spite of the problems this system could breed, Hooker liked playing for the door better than any other type of payment, the sensational side of his performances making it all the more rewarding. Guitarist Son Seals, who worked the Delta club scene extensively during the sixties, gives an interesting account of the economy of the business: "We would like to play for the door because guarantees then wasn't about shit, you know. When we go and try to book a job or somethin', you go in and ask the guy, say, back then, man, for forty and fifty dollars, and that's for the whole band, he used to say, 'Oh, no! No, no!' You know, he say, 'You have what you make on the door,' that's the first thing he would say. And then we said, well okay, because a lot of times, we would make a heck of a lot better by takin' the door. Then you could get away with chargin' like a buck or seventy-five cents a head or somewhere like that, and that was a lot of money back then. Like it really depend a lot on the weather. Back then, see, like people that worked in the fields and things liked for it to rain over the weekend on Saturdays and Sundays, so they could work on Mondays, 'cause every time it rained, the price of choppin' cotton would go up, because the grass would grow faster. So like if people had a good week in the fields and things, well then they wouldn't mind comin' out durin' the weekend and spend a few dollars. But if they didn't get a chance to work because of the rain or somethin' else, then it was no need to say, 'We'll pack the place this weekend,' and you're not gonna do it because you'd be better off just let 'em come on in free, and the man just give you a salary."

Hooker's stage shows were improvised to a large extent, and his chaotic road trips were hardly ever planned, since he could afford setting up a gig wherever he decided to drop anchor. "He is the only freelance artist so well-known all over the USA," guitarist Jimmy Dawkins wrote in a tribute to Hooker published by British magazine *Blues Unlimited* in January 1969. "He never uses a booking agent, he books his own jobs. He will order his placards, put them in his car, and go out over the country booking jobs and leaving his placards to be put on display. Then he comes back, gets his band and goes play his dates. If not that, he can call anywhere and book himself, just like that, because he is so well-known by club owners all over."[7]

"He'd go everywhere," Billy Boy Arnold stresses. "You see, he had places where he had established hisself, and when he came back it was like a celebration. 'Earl Hooker is in town!' the word was all over town." Never one to rest on his oars, Hooker regularly scouted out new playing grounds in the course of his travels. His recordings came as a help, since his reputation sometimes preceded his coming, but his matchless performances were by far his safest asset. "See, we was goin' through towns where didn't nobody know him or me," vocalist Lee Shot Williams explains. "We'd get the club owner to let us play, the club owner didn't know if we could play. The people be at the door fussin' about payin' their money, 'They probably can't even play!' That's what we'd be hearin' 'fore we start. But the minute he hit that guitar, the house would just go up. They never heard nothin' like that; he had 'em spellbound." "Yeah," stresses Big Moose Walker, "he was so good, the guys would come in and hear him play, and book him right in the end for different jobs. Like they'd say, 'Hey, will you play for me in St. Louis, for such and such a time?' 'Yeah, I'll be there.' Then while we were playin' in St. Louis, somebody else would come and do the same thing, and then we'd play anywhere like that. Anywhere! Like he might leave St. Louis and somebody call him in Texas. He'd leave for Texas, you know."

The fact that Hooker never had a steady booking agency didn't keep him from working regularly over the years with local promoters who lined up tours for him. "In 1963 we did thirty-three one-nighters through the state of Florida, and Alabama," vocalist Andrew Odom recalls. "It was a guy called Buddy May. He's one of the top black promoters down that way. We played all the way down, as far as Cocoa, Florida. And we played at the Barn in Sarasota. We played on the same show with Ted Taylor in Fort Myers, we played at the University down in Florida, Miami."

Yet Hooker's reluctance at parting with his money prevented him from hiring booking agents most of the time, using people like Herb Turner in Chicago or similar acquaintances down South only when he couldn't do otherwise. "He would mostly do his own bookin'," Herb Turner explains, accounting for his limited prerogatives. "But see, sometimes I'd make phone calls or connections, 'cause I guess maybe he'd had rough dealings with 'em, and he wants somebody that they don't know. So that's how he set me up. He had a couple of bookin' agents in the South too. I think he's tellin' me about Rockin' Ed, a disc jockey out in Greenville [Mississippi]. He had a record store and he was a disc jockey also, and he'd book his gigs. But mostly he said he didn't even advertise in the South. On his way into town, he said they be out there pickin' cotton, and they'd see that long car, that's all. And he wasn't a guy like a lot of musicians, you know, at the last minute, they don't show up or anythin'. I'd say, 'Hey, man, you've got a gig in such and such a place.' He was livin' down there in Missouri, and he'd be comin' here, then go back and forth."

Hooker's reliability has been the object of contradictory accounts. When Herb Turner expresses his trust in Earl's professionalism, drummer Kansas City Red reports that he left the Hooker band in the fifties because of the guitarist's unscrupulous ways: "That was one guy that didn't have no bookin' manager; he would go get his gigs hisself. He would pick up a deposit so he kept him some money to travel with, and a lot of 'em places, he didn't even do his show. That's what started me to thinkin', I said, 'Well, I'd better let that guy alone,' 'cause peoples would think that I be part of it." It seems that Hooker became more reasonable with time. It is not known whether his attitude evolved after getting in serious trouble somewhere down the line or merely because he finally realized that he could no longer afford to alienate club owners. At any rate, later associates concur in saying that Earl became more dependable in the sixties.

Hooker's main asset on the road, especially in the small towns he went through, was the sensational side of his personality. For blues-hungry Southerners, he was this incredible showman who traveled in an eight-door limousine and walked on stage with a double-neck instrument that he played with his teeth and toes. As if his colorful show was not enough, Earl often provided club owners with bright cardboard posters that never failed to arouse the curiosity of local populations. "Most times, the club would do the advertising," Herb Turner states, "unless Earl was goin' down through there, then he would put up his placards. He would call clubs and tell 'em, 'Okay, set up a gig.' Then he would call Tribune Press in Earl Park and have 'em send the placards to the owner, and the owner would put up the placards. Tribune Show Press Company. All the blues artists you could find, just about anybody had his placards or posters made there, with pictures of 'em."

Whereas most blues entertainers ordered promotional placards only when they played important engagements, Earl Hooker had more advertising posters to his credit than any other artist of his caliber. In order to keep the legend alive, his appointed photographer, found on Chicago's South Side at the corner of 59th and Morgan Streets, would take promo pictures of Earl, his singers and dancers, not to mention the guitarist's favorite cars and vans. With a set of shots in his pockets, Hooker would then head to Earl Park, a small Indiana town situated sixty-five miles south of Chicago on Route 41, where the Tribune Press Company was operating under the competent management of owner Arvel A. Furr, a soft-spoken and enterprising Midwesterner with a solid sense of humor: "We specialize in showcards and bumper stickers, and people connect the name more with showprint, and that's the reason we changed," Furr reports, accounting for the company's name-change from Tribune Press to Tribune Show Print in the early seventies. "We started out as a weekly paper in 1896 or somethin' like that. Then we started to get into the showcard business, right after World War Two, and the first cards we printed were for a hillbilly act. This outfit had a big Cadillac. They had the horns in front of the Cadillac and all of the entertainers in this one car, and they got us started in this showcard business. But the business's kept growin' and growin', and most of our business advertisin' has been word of mouth. Now a lot of our business is the card trade out of Chicago, and South Chicago. We've been workin' for blues musicians for twenty-five or thirty years. They play all the clubs up there, and most of 'em drive down and pick up their cards."

Many blues entertainers, especially in Chicago, ordered sets of posters from Tribune Press through their current agent, but Hooker transacted directly with Arvel Furr, making the ninety-minute drive down to Earl Park. When interviewed for this research in 1984, the printer clearly remembered their frequent encounters, as well as the guitarist's impressive eight-door vehicle: "The street out here is great, big and wide as you notice, but he had trouble trying to turn this great big limousine around out here. I got quite a kick out of him. I can remember him for the simple reason he would always—we had the print-shop next door, and we'd bring him over here, this would be the barroom, it was called the G&T Tap at that time. And I don't remember what Earl Hooker drank, but he was quite a kidder, you know that? See, when he'd come over, he tried to arrive here at that time, late in the afternoon, so he could come over with us, 'cause nobody in the shop has a drink or anythin' during the daytime, until the presses are all shut off. And I remember him quite well for the way the boys treated him; they always kidded him and stuff.

"We used to sit in the booth right up here in the front of this room, and the biggest thing I remember about him is his sense of humor. He was quite a boy! He had many stories. Most of the stuff he was tellin' us would be about, like they'd be buildin' an apartment-buildin' or somethin', and the colored families wouldn't appreciate it, see. The minute they would have a fireplace in, the first thing they know, they haven't got anythin' to burn, so they start burnin' the woodwork and stuff, and he says, 'It just makes me sick,' he said they tried to help 'em and they just wouldn't take advantage of it, and things like that. And he said, 'You fellows don't have that feelin' against colored people like they do up there, see.' And, boy, we grew up with 'em down here, and we only had two families, but I was raised with the colored people, so that's one thing that never made any difference to me, and most of these fellows down here are farmers, and they enjoy bein' around colored entertainers and stuff."

This is one of the rare instances when one of Hooker's acquaintances mentioned his interest in the social and political environment of his day. For someone born on a dirt-poor Mississippi plantation and raised in the black Chicago ghetto during the worst of the Depression, whose career developed at a time when *Brown vs. Board of Education* was making front-page news, when young Chicagoan Emmett Till was murdered in Mississippi by Southern bigots, when Rosa Parks refused to give up her seat on a Montgomery bus, when the Little Rock Nine were mobbed by segregationists for helping bring widespread integration to public schools, Earl seems to have had little concern for the social movements that were unleashed at this critical period in the history of race relations in America. His conservative positions, as recounted by Arvell Furr, would tend to show that his political consciousness didn't quite match his revolutionary artistic temperament, although it is possible that Earl made such antisocial comments in an attempt to please his nonchalant, patronizing white interlocutor. Later on in the sixties, this was confirmed when Earl worked briefly in California for Denny Bruce, a young Caucasian agent who was struck by the fact that he "never looked me in the eye when we spoke," a sign that would tend to show that Earl, like many prewar Southerners, felt uneasy in the presence of white people. Contrary to committed artists like Sam Cooke, Hooker certainly was no strong civil-rights advocate, his love for the guitar taking precedence over everything else.

At any rate, the unusually large number of placards advertising Hooker's countless bands and ephemeral shows that have been traced to this day bear witness to the guitarist's marked taste for the cardboard posters he ordered from Tribune Press. They stood out in the current production of blues performers for their varied layouts and eccentric illustrations; in addition to his cars, Hooker's guitars were often glorified as he usually presented himself holding one or two twin-neck instruments at the same time, or playing one behind his head, unless a clumsy photographic montage showcased one of his go-go dancers sitting in his lap. "We'd see him probably once a month," Arvel Furr asserts. "And every time he'd show up he'd have somethin' different, he'd be playin' some place else. He'd bring pictures, and we'd have the cuts made. The Trio Engraving makes the cuts at Lafayette [Indiana]. Most [blues artists] have one picture, and they stay with that for quite a while, but [Hooker] had several, and another thing, sometimes, there's two or three cuts on the card, you know, different ones."

Hooker's placards were so unique that Arvel Furr felt the need at one point to send off copies of Earl's most sensational posters to his son, enhancing Earl's reputation far beyond the boundaries of his usual playing ground. "My son, Johnny Furr, when he was in Vietnam," Arvel Furr chuckles, "when we'd get a good card or a funny card, we'd always send it over. And he was a sergeant in the Marine Corps, and there's a lot of colored in his outfit, and we'd have colored shake dancers and things like that on Hooker's cards. Back then it was go-go dancin'; they'd get mail, and it'd be one of our showcards, out in the middle of nowhere with a big nigger shake dancer on it, and those boys would just go wild out in the field."

Earl's placards inevitably boasted his name in large print, but his band name changed often, appearing in turns as "The Roadmasters," "The Soul Twisters," "The Soul Thrillers," "Bright Sounds" or "The Electric Dust Band." "'Earl Hooker and the Soul Twisters,' 'Earl Hooker and the Hookers,' he'd just come up with anything. It was Earl Hooker, you know," Herb Turner confirms. Hooker's Tribune Press posters were typical of a pictorial genre that prevailed in the music business from the late fifties. Although some were in black bold type on white or yellow, many were printed in black over a blended, three-color background according to a printing technique perfected by Arvel Furr: "This rainbow card was invented by myself, and almost by accident. I was washin' up the press one night, and we had in a couple colors, just two colors, and I's takin' it out and we were washin' up, and then I saw that they blended together when you'd add some kerosene. And so we tried it, and we had quite a time to get 'em to blend right, and then we finally developed it, and we keep it pretty well secret how we do it, and then we had it copyrighted. Pink, yellow, and green is the most popular for gospel and evangelists and things like that; and a lot of blues entertainers enjoy the blue at the bottom. I believe there is some kind of relation with the music."

Although Earl ordered new posters with clock-like regularity, his promotion hardly kept abreast of his continuous travels. The fact that he rarely stayed in one same place more than a couple of nights in a row prevented him from ordering showcards advertising specific engagements, so he started ordering cards with a blank space left at the bottom to grant them a universal function. "Now the reason he would do that," Arvel Furr says, "like if he played some date until maybe twelve o'clock on a Saturday night, maybe he'd get a date from twelve-thirty to four-thirty or six o'clock in the mornin', where he'd play two dates on the same night in two different places, and that's why he needed to have those cards, and then fill it in at the bottom."

With time, Hooker's hectic musical travels underwent deep changes. If the late forties and fifties had seen Earl concerned primarily with the South, the sixties were marked by a progressive evolution of his usual circuit as he slowly became familiar with midwestern territories. Tuberculosis may not have been the major reason for such changes, but it played a role. As his sickness compelled him to stay in Chicago more and more, Earl would no longer find the energy to drive his band around the Deep South as casually as he used to. Another consequence of his contagious disease, combined with his amazingly careless and easygoing attitude with regard to it, was that he made himself undesirable in several states—including Texas and Florida—after running away from the anti-infectious wards of several hospitals.

The main cause of Hooker's sudden liking for the Midwest was that more money could be made there for a Chicago-based blues artist of his stamp. With the surge of his recording career, Hooker built a strong following not only in the vicinity of Chicago but also in neighboring states where black working-class populations were exposed to his regional hits. Bestsellers like "Little by Little," "Will My Man Be Home Tonight," and "Trying to Make a Living" provided Earl with a passport to hitherto unprospected land, and he soon adopted a new trail that went through Indiana, Ohio, and Michigan. Further hits like "Blues in D-Natural" or "Blue Guitar" confirmed the trend, until Hooker grew into a widely acclaimed act in Iowa, Wisconsin, and Minnesota urban centers, to the point that the Midwest eventually superseded the South in his traveling priorities. By the mid-sixties Earl and band had explored most of this new territory, thoroughly working out a new route that took them from Chicago north to Milwaukee and other Wisconsin locations on their way to Minnesota. After performing in Minneapolis-St. Paul—sometimes in the company of local bluesman Mojo Buford, former harmonicist with the Muddy Waters band—they headed south for Iowa cities like Davenport, across the Illinois state line on the Mississippi River, and more particularly Waterloo, a music center that eventually turned into the midwestern equivalent of Earl's favorite base in the west, Lawton, Oklahoma.

In the early sixties Waterloo was a heavily industrialized urban center numbering a population of 75,000, of which 15,000, or 20 percent, were African

Americans. At that time, the black community dwelt in a ghetto area known as the North End, situated north and east of the downtown part that spread over the Cedar River. The Illinois Central railroad line that went straight through town provided the original impetus for black settlement by importing migrants from central Mississippi before the Second World War, at a time when workers were needed to break local strikes. Into the sixties, Waterloo's active black labor worked mainly for the city's two largest employers, the Rath Packing Company and John Deere Tractor Works. This gave a plausible explanation for the great number of clubs and bars scattered around the city's main thoroughfare, East 4th Street, located immediately north of the Illinois Central tracks in an area where street singers and traditional Mississippi fife and drum bands still performed on worthy occasions. Although most of Waterloo's nightlife featured out-of-town artists like Earl, Jimmy Reed, Howlin' Wolf, Smokey Wilson, and Joe Hinton, Hooker's first cousin, a local blues scene developed there under the leadership of organists Wayne Carter and Lincoln Reid, guitarists Jimmy and Sonny Bunch and Lonnie Flowers as well as vocalist Bud Harper, whose sophisticated Bobby Bland–influenced singing was featured on releases by the Houston-based Peacock label in 1964 and 1965; another R&B artist from Waterloo was Jimmy Holiday, whose "How Can I Forget" reached the R&B Top Ten in 1963. Also leading his own ensemble around town was Steve Miller, a white keyboard player whose Prophets earned a reputation for playing fine rock-blues music (not to be confused, as was the case often over the years, with rock superstar Steve Miller).

The comparison with Lawton, Oklahoma, was all the more obvious; Hooker also returned to Waterloo on a regular basis for personal reasons. Concurrently with his Catron, Missouri, home, he set up another household there after getting involved emotionally with a woman named Rosemary Walker on the occasion of an early visit to Iowa. From a professional standpoint, Hooker's main performance grounds in Waterloo were the Super Chef Lounge, a small storefront bar located at 1007 East 4th Street, and Jimmie's Cocktail Lounge, unless he decided to sit in with Steve Miller and the Prophets, whose current hangout was a white downtown club named the Tic Toc Tap. Jimmie's Lounge, Earl's steadiest spot, was a larger venue found at 115 Summer Street, just north of an area known by locals as "Blood Alley;" Hooker never failed to perform there when he was around town until 1968, when owner Jimmie Hunt got into heavy trouble after a drug and prostitution bust.

Other regular features at Jimmie's then were Wayne Carter, Delta-born guitarist Smokey Wilson, and Ironing Board Sam, a native of Rock Hill, South Carolina. Sam's connection with the Waterloo scene was Hooker because both men knew each other from Chicago. Ironing Board Sam is an outstanding figure whose main claim for originality lies in the fact that he plays an ironing (key)board of his invention. After getting to Chicago in 1964, his first step was to approach the Chess brothers in the hope of signing a recording contract. His art may well have been too progressive for the time, and Leonard Chess turned him down. Sam's one-year stay in the Windy City did not prove useless, for he was able to perfect his technique with some of Chicago's most versatile players, including Hooker. Together, they played devastating gigs at Pepper's, where they competed in eccentricity. As a token of his respect, Earl tipped Sam off to the wide open Waterloo scene, where he became a notorious personality from the mid-sixties, especially at Jimmie Hunt's Lounge where the ironing board wonder enjoyed an almost continuous residency for nearly two years.

Hooker's own stays in Waterloo usually lasted several weeks. Chicago sidemen who visited Iowa in the Hooker outfit included Sammy Lawhorn—a superb guitarist whose vibrato owed much to Earl's slide-playing—as well as the Muck Muck Man, a cranky Memphian who settled in Chicago, where he became famous for his outrageous stage act. Muck Muck was also known for going barefoot all year long, a habit he apparently kicked after his feet got badly frostbitten during a particularly harsh winter in Waterloo.

The fact that Hooker kept another "home fire" burning in Iowa explains why he was being considered one of the local celebrities by full-time Waterloo residents. His reputation must have gone far beyond the black ghetto tavern business, since his guitar playing aroused the interest of the white community. While R&B was in high favor with Waterloo's black population, country & western remained a favorite genre with white Iowans; Hooker's perfect ease in this field allowed him to give surprising performances at the I See Inn, found in the downtown area at 913 East 4th Street across the Illinois Central yards, to the bewilderment of the club's exclusively white patronage. "I went to Waterloo," Hooker later recalled in a rare interview, "went to a hillbilly joint where some hillbilly boys were playing—I asked the guy to let me sit in and he said,

'Man, you don't play no rock and roll, do you?' I said, 'Well, I can play some rock and roll and I can play some of that stuff you playin' too.' So he said, 'If you can play this good old hillbilly music, you're welcome to play,' and he called me up on the bandstand. Everybody was lookin' at me—they said this is something they got to dig—a colored guy playing hillbilly music in a hillbilly joint! I went to playing my guitar doing 'Walking the Floor over You' and some of Hank Williams's numbers like 'Your Cheating Heart.' Now those kind of numbers I can sing—I used to watch Gene Autry and Roy Rogers as a kid! The man liked the way I played and told me I was about the best guitar player to come through there, so I was playing hillbilly music for six months!"[8]

One of Hooker's stopovers on his way back to Chicago was the northern Illinois city of Rockford, where Earl and band regularly entertained capacity crowds at Joe Turner's Place or at the Rock Tavern. Thanks to Herb Turner's resourcefulness, better-paying gigs were regularly set up there on the weekend, such as the show organized at the Ross Pearson Post of the Veterans of Foreign Wars organization, located at 922 7th Street, which left Turner with unforgettable memories of Hooker's reckless attitudes. "The Marvelows was on the bill too," Turner giggled as he evoked the event. "'Cause I remember there was a fight after that night between him and the band. They got into it about the money. For a gig like that, he might make four hundred dollars, which was pretty good money. And Hooker wouldn't pay! I had my money, and Hooker had decided he wasn't gonna pay [the band], because of somethin', I don't know what it was. And so what they did, they took his guitar and they carried it to the police station. And so Hooker goes into the police station, and I go with him—I remember 'cause we was ridin' with Hooker in the long car, it didn't have no heat in it, and it gets colder than hell in Rockford; I could have frozen. And they said they was gonna stay in Rockford, and they wanted that money. They wanted the police to make Hooker pay 'em that money, to give him his equipment back. And it was a big hassle, a big argument, but we finally got out of Rockford I guess 'round about three-thirty in the morning."

Hooker's niggardly ways had plagued his relationship with his musicians since the fifties; far from abating with time, it had grown out of proportion by the following decade, accounting for the terrible reputation he had with sidemen. Earl's uncontrolled attraction to money, no matter how easy to explain in the case of an individual born into poverty, urged him to devise farfetched schemes in order to keep in his pocket the band's salary. "He paid me more than he paid the rest," singer Lee Shot Williams reminisces, "'cause me and him was like this. I would help him drive, and me and him would hang out together, you know. A lot of times, I worked the door, so he couldn't lie to me about the money because I know how much it was. But he lied to the others. He'd say, 'It wasn't b-b-but a hundred dollars come in,' and it'd be five or six hundred. He had a drummer out of Cairo, Illinois, named Bobby Joe Johnson. Him and Bobby Joe used to fight every night, just about that money. And then, after he got real sick, Bobby quit jumpin' on him 'cause he wasn't able to fight. Yeah, he wanted to kill him bad, he told him, says, 'If you wasn't sick, I'd kill you.'"

Besides telling fellow band members at the end of a performance that playing for the door had not been lucrative that night, another technique consisted in leaving very early the following morning without the ones he had decided to short. As was the case with guitarist Jimmy Johnson, it generally took a couple days of cotton picking to earn enough pocket change for a train fare home. "He did it, yeah. He was just a funny guy," Jimmy Johnson laconically comments. "He got in trouble time after time, though, oh yeah! He got in fights and stuff like that, but he escaped really getting hurt. Like me, I used to always have a cool head, see, like trouble is easy to get into, but it's hard to get out of, and you really wouldn't wanna go through life knowin' within yourself that you really hurt somebody, but on the other hand you have to protect yourself. So after a while you'd get to understand he don't really mean harm. He didn't know no other way, people just said, 'Well, okay, I just won't mess with him no more. It's okay. He took my money, that's all. He can have it,' you know, somethin' like that."

With time, it became harder for Hooker to find Chicago sidemen naive enough to go on the road with him as the word spread around the city that he couldn't be trusted. While he was not the first bandleader in the blues world to act like this, Earl perfected the art of cheating his musicians to a point never reached before. In this respect, the influence of his guitar mentor Robert Nighthawk was tremendous, the latter being notorious among musicians of the older generation for walking off with the band's earnings. Earl's friend Kansas City Red, who started out in the music business under Nighthawk's guidance, can bear witness to the strong similarity between Nighthawk and his disciple on payday: "Nighthawk, he's another guy that pulled that stuff to me. He'd get

2000th broadcast of *King Biscuit Time*, 1949: announcer Peck Curtis, Dudlow Taylor, and Earl Hooker. Ivey Gladin/Collection of Sebastian Danchin.

EARL ZEBEDEE HOOKER, self taught guitarist and son of Mrs. Mary Hooker of 3361 Giles ave., has been going great guns on the station KFFA's "King Biscuit Time," beaming in the Helena, Arkansas area "King Biscuit Time." recently completed its 2000th broadcast over station KFFA. Young Earl has been with the group about 6 months.

A 1949 press release in the *Chicago Defender*. Collection of Sebastian Danchin.

Roberts' Show Lounge, Chicago: Eddie Boyd, B. B. King, Lady Hi-Fi, Earl Hooker, Louis Myers, and Sonny Freeman. Collection of Sebastian Danchin.

Earl Hooker and saxophonist Little Bobby Neely, late 1950s. Collection of Sebastian Danchin.

Earl Hooker with a double-neck Danelectro instrument, mid-1960s. Collection of Sebastian Danchin.

Earl Hooker, guitar and organ. Collection of Sebastian Danchin.

Tribune Press poster for Earl Hooker. Collection of Sebastian Danchin.

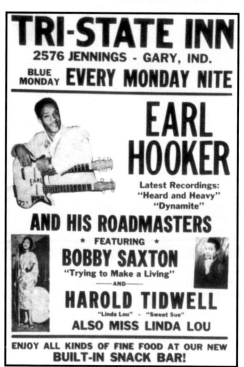

Tri-State Inn poster, 1960. Collection of Sebastian Danchin.

Earl Hooker and wife Bertha with her two children. Collection of Sebastian Danchin.

Alex Club, 1968: Pinetop Perkins, Odell Campbell, Arthur "Dogman" Jackson, and Earl Hooker. Willie Leiser/Collection of Sebastian Danchin.

Earl Hooker and Big Moose Walker, May 29, 1969. Phil Melnick, BluesWay Records/Collection of Sebastian Danchin.

Earl Hooker, trying out a strange instrument in a Geneva music store, October 1969. Willie Leiser/Collection of Sebastian Danchin.

"Blues in D Natural," Chief label.
Collection of Sebastian Danchin.

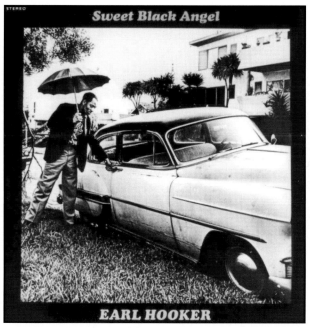

Sweet Black Angel, Blue Thumb album cover. Collection of Sebastian
Danchin.

The American Folk
Blues Festival '69
roster: Earl Hooker,
Clifton Chenier,
Cleveland Chenier,
Juke Boy Bonner,
Magic Sam, Carey Bell,
Whistlin' Alex Moore,
John Jackson, Robert
St. Julien, and Mack
Thompson. Willie
Leiser/Collection of
Sebastian Danchin.

Hooker makes front page
news, *Blues Unlimited*
magazine, 1970. Collection
of Sebastian Danchin.

that money. Me and him had it out there in Future City. I had to run him out through the corn fields. And he messed Ernest Lane. Ernest Lane went to his house to collect the money. I went with him. Ernest Lane jumped on him in the bed, and next thing I know, Robert had done left me and Ernest Lane both."

For all his natural charm and charisma, Earl could hardly expect to come off well every time; it took both his luck and the presence by his side of unweary-ing friends like Big Moose Walker or Andrew B. B. Odom to prevent tragedies. Although occasional fits of violence should have warned him against the out-bursts his attitude didn't fail to generate, the lure of money was just too strong, and Hooker could not help running the risk of alienating his associates. "If he get a good day, he say, 'Man, the people came through the window,'" Big Moose Walker laughs. "I had to keep a guy from shootin' him down in Indianola, Mis-sissippi, once. This guy blow a horn, I forget his name now. This cat had a pis-tol. I said, 'Man, don't shoot that man, you crazy!' There was about seven or eight hundred peoples in the house, and they charged about $3.50 at the door. Easily can make $1,500, you know. Hooker came along, gave me 'bout a hun-dred dollars. The other guys were waitin'. He said, 'Uh-uh, m-m-man, you don't make bu-u-ut $20 in Chicago. I-I-I'm gonna pay you $5.' 'Man, I want more money than that. Look at all these peoples.' Hooker said, 'Man, s-s-some of that p-p-peoples came through that hole up there, man, 'cause don't nobody come in the door!' So a fight was goin' on, and we stopped it. [Harold] Tidwell and I, we stopped it."

As unpredictable as Hooker was, it was difficult for his musicians to deter-mine beforehand whether they would get paid or not on a particular night. Most of those who had been tricked once refused to work with him anymore, but others devised their own way around the difficulty. The lack of mutual trust such relationships were built on speaks volume for the suspicious atmosphere which reigned at times in the Hooker band. "Matter of fact, Hooker did not keep too many dudes too long," guitarist-singer Lacy Gibson comments sourly. "I'm gonna tell the truth. I hate to be the one to say that but you may print that, a lot of times, he ran off with your money, so I ain't planting no roses on him. With Hooker, you'd ask for your money and he'd say, 'Well, I'm short so much,' and then you get mad. I played with Hooker so many times, on and off, but I never dared go out of town with him. He would call me periodically, but he wouldn't call me unless he just didn't have a guitar player, because he knew that I was gonna get the money. I would say, 'How much are you paying?' 'Twenty-some dollars!' and I'd say, 'I played two shows. Give me fifteen dollars,' and then I knew I had five dollars left, and I could have a half pint of whiskey, for my pleasure. Then I would have nothing coming for that night, and then if he don't pay the rest of the guys, well . . . you know, you shouldn't be naive enough as not to know different people."

Regardless of the reputation he had in the Windy City, Hooker had no trouble convincing new accompanists to go on the road with him, even though most of them were aware beforehand that they would not come back any richer than they left. Dick Shurman accounted for this paradox in the short written tribute he published shortly after Hooker's death: "There was always that slight hope that he really would pay the fantastic amounts he promised, and besides it was such a pleasure to play with him that musicians did it just for the fun and education. Seeing veterans of thirty years' work having a ball on the bandstand is a very beautiful experience, and Earl's accompanists were always laughing and shaking their heads."[9] Similar arguments expressed by some of Hooker's closest associates back up Shurman's views, while all of those who knew Earl agree in ranking him as the most exciting bandleader they ever played with. "He was a lot of fun to be around," A. C. Reed says, supported in his statement by Junior Wells, Herb Turner, Billy Boy Arnold, and Little Smokey Smothers, who remembers Hooker lifting watermelons off a truck stopped on Highway 61 with a flat tire, trying to steal corn whiskey from a moonshiner without knowing the jug was wired up to a shotgun, and rescuing Earl and Moose Walker from a perilous situation: "We was at the state line of Arkansas and Missouri one time. [Hooker and Moose] had been arguin' all day. And while we was hookin' up and gettin' tuned up, they grabbed one another, fell off the stage into a sixty-gallon drum head first. Just four feet stickin' out of the barrel! We had to turn the barrel over to let them out. . . . But Earl Hooker was an outstanding guitar player."[10] "He was the onliest musician that could come to Chicago and get some of the star leaders, piano players, and bass players and drummers, and they knew they wasn't gonna make any money before they left, but they would go with Hooker," Big Moose Walker insists. "Earl and I was the best of friends, but we knew that we was gonna fight after every show, but I didn't quit. I still played the next time. You know, everybody in Chicago played with him because they knowed he was a good musician, but they didn't play with him for the money, 'cause they was not gonna get any. But we liked him anyway. I went out of town, California and everywhere, without a dime in my pocket with Earl Hooker because I knew that with Earl I was gonna have a lot of fun.

"There was always somethin' goin' on when you were with Hooker. Like once, we was out and we had a flat on the car. It was about six or seven of us. This was down on the way to Missouri or Mississippi or whatever. So we find this guy's door, and this cat was a farmer, you know. So we was all out there, three-thirty or four o'clock in the mornin', cussin' and arguin', and this cat comes out there with a shotgun. 'You guys get the car from out front of my door! I gotta rest, I gotta work!' 'It's okay, as soon as we put the wheel.' He say, 'No, move it now!' And this cat, he was gonna shoot all of us I believe, so we got up and picked the car up, about eight of us, to get the car out from front of the guy's house. You should have seen us! Everybody wanted to fixin' the tire then, to get away from there. It tickled the hell out of the cat, he laughed and went on back in the house."

Herb Turner concurs with Moose and Billy Boy Arnold in saying that Earl managed to remain on good terms with most of the people he cheated, but his opinion is more moderate as a whole: "Most times, after the guys cut Hooker loose, they still stayed friends with him but they wouldn't work for him no more. They didn't want no part of him 'cause he taught 'em a lesson, and he taught 'em well. A lot of 'em said he taught 'em how that you could make a man out of anybody, how to survive. When they would look over and see him, everybody would start impersonatin' him, start stutterin' like that, 'Uh-uh-uh-uh-uh.' Hooker'd walk by or somethin' and they'd say, 'C-c-c-come and g-g-g-go with me, I-I-I-I'll t-t-take you down to A-A-Arkansas, and g-g-give you three dollars,' and everybody would just go laughin', and that was it. This was Hooker, and he wouldn't even turn around, he'd just keep goin' and just forget it!"

While money exerted a real fascination, Hooker was not devoid of a basic sense of human psychology that would keep him from going beyond the breaking-point. Besides the inexperienced sidemen he picked up in the southern states, only the most easygoing individuals were shamelessly misused, as if Earl consciously knew the ones he could afford to short with impunity. Big Moose

Walker, although he was not Hooker's only close friend to suffer from the guitarist's ways, endured more than his share of undeserved mishaps during the fifteen-odd years he spent with Hooker. It must have taken Moose's deep admiration for Hooker as well as his natural kindness to put up with Earl's inconsiderate attitude. Next to Moose on Hooker's list of drudges was drummer Bobby Little, whose dedication to Earl made him overlook the worst sides of an artist he had admired since his teenage days in Chicago Heights. As was the case with Big Moose, the various vexatious measures Earl imposed on Bobby inevitably led to verbal disputes that were the occasion for consenting victims to let off steam.

Earl's attitude was all the more odd in that he wouldn't treat everybody unfairly; he acted like a dependable employer toward a handful of privileged associates, including Herb Turner, Kansas City Red, and A. C. Reed. "He always treated me fair," the latter admits readily. "Sometimes, we'd go on the road, man, and everybody in the band get a different salary of money, and I'd get more than any of 'em. He give me this much and he give this one this much and all the way down the line. But lots of time, like the guys that knew him well, they would always argue and fight over money. He got in a fight with Bobby Little once when he was sick, over money, and Bobby Little hit him in the chest. To me, he's more of a friend than a good musician. He was a good musician, but he's more of a friend, I just liked him some kinda way, I don't know why."

Another privileged associate was vocalist B. B. Odom, of whom Hooker was genuinely fond; a flagrant illustration of Earl's attachment for him is to be found in the following episode, recounted by B. B. Odom with moving simplicity: "In 1963 we played at the state line of Missouri and Arkansas, the Club 61, and that's the time that I got stabbed tryin' to stop a fight between the saxophone player and the drummer. His name was Bobby Joe [Johnson], he's out of Cairo, and the saxophone player was out of Chicago, his name was Sammy, I can't think of his last name. But anyway, I got stabbed that night, and I was taken to the Lutheran General Hospital in Blytheville, [Arkansas]. And the only thing I remember when I passed out, I heard that Earl Hooker told this doctor, 'Save my star.' That was the type of guy he was. He got me to the hospital right away, and got the best doctors."

At the same time, Hooker was too self-centered to let friendship be his only guide. In many instances, a dose of guileless self-interest complemented his altruistic inclinations, Herb Turner argues quite soundly: "Pinetop and Earl were good friends, and I think Earl always paid Pinetop, the same way with me. When I would carry my group out with him, I'd always get my money. One thing about it, a lot of times Earl would be comin' from Missouri or somethin' like that, and he was short of money. He'd run by the place, say, 'Hey, Herb! I need fifteen, twenty dollars, twenty-five dollars,' and he's always had 'em. You gotta pay some debts, I guess, keep somethin' where you can come back to, so he's always paid me."

According to his associates, irrespective of his failings and weaknesses, Hooker was a very likable person who seemed unconscious of the harm he could do others. "He was just a guy hustlin' to make money, without meanin' to hurt anyone," B. B. Odom says. "Now regardless of what type of guy he was in music, he always talked about religion. You know, because his cousin was a pastor and if he was in town, he would go to his cousin's church, Reverend Blair. And sometime he would even play, you know." "He never really meant to permanently alienate people—he would always do whatever was necessary to patch up friendships, and would go out of his way to be nice and associate with people," Dick Shurman wrote after Hooker's death. "He was a mixture of an extrovert and a man who felt a little defensive. It can't be denied that Earl was most friendly to those who could do the most for him. He was always my partner when he had an amplifier to be brought in, or wanted a coke. . . . But he was glad to reciprocate, and was a genuinely friendly person who inspired a lot of affection. He just had a Machiavellian view of life and thought that whatever happened would be because of his efforts."[11]

"I liked him very much," Kansas City Red concedes, describing Hooker's ebullient nature. "He made me awful mad some time, but he was the type of guy, you couldn't stay mad with him. He'd come up with somethin' funny and make you laugh, so there was no need to be tryin' to stay mad with the guy. Hooker would talk big but he was no fighter, you know," Red goes on, stressing Earl's physical harmlessness. "He tried to bluff you if he could—me and him ran into it out in the hills once, had a flat tire. Cold! Me and him and Lee Kizart, right out of Greenwood [Mississippi], in them hills out there. We didn't have no spare tire, so Lee gonna walk about three miles in town and see if he can get a tire. So while he was gone, I had a idea. We had some old clothes and things in the back of the car, so I said, 'Earl, will you help me jack this car up?' I said, 'I'll pack up the tire full of rags and stuff, to make it on to the station where it's warm at.' And he wouldn't get out of there and help me, and I lost a tom-tom out of my drums, I throwed it at Earl Hooker and missed him. The drum went down them hills somewhere."

Maybe the most distressing aspect of Hooker's constant need for money was the futility with which he spent it, buying yet another guitar he would inevitably lose or trade, another secondhand car he would be forced to junk on a lean day for lack of the money needed to have it fixed, or another glittery stage costume that would rapidly fade out in the closet of one of his ephemeral homes. Guitars, cars, and clothes were a high price for the lost friendship of those who didn't know him well enough to disregard his urge to cheat others. But the fact that Hooker felt the need to keep fat wads of dollars in his pocket all the time showed that money helped him feel secure. While establishing his status with other members of the blues community, it made up for the lean years of cold and hunger he had spent in the ghetto.

Similar behavior is currently noted in others whose climb up the rungs of the social ladder has been long and painful. Hooker's craving for large amounts of cash, a sign of his newly gained financial security, takes on different forms with others. In the case of Little Milton Campbell, an artist of great talent and renown, shoes give him a sense of fulfilment, as he explains: "Man, when I was a kid, my mother couldn't afford to buy us no shoes, and winter or summer, we would go barefoot all the time. And even now, if you come to my home, I can show you two closets full of shoes; I might have two hundred different pairs of shoes, because every time I pass a shoe store, I just can't help it. It's very rare that I don't stop and get me a pair of shoes; it makes me feel comfortable to know that whenever I want to, I can buy shoes."

B. B. King is another personification of such a complex. King, whose international career and success have been equaled by few black artists in his generation, still feels the need to purchase everyday goods in large quantity. "Evidently, he is acquisitive," Charles Sawyer wrote in 1978 in his authorized biography of King. "He never buys one of something if it might possibly break or wear out. He returns from his road trips with luggage bulging at the seams from all the goods he has acquired. It is probably a compensation for his harsh childhood, so fraught with deprivation, but whatever the reason, B. B. is a pack rat who hoards belongings as if he were expecting a famine. Some of his hoarding makes sense, like his record collecting, but other times he packs things home that defy explanation—like stationery and office supplies that surely must be available at the local office supply store. Perhaps Boy Riley, ever worried where the next pound of lard and sack of flour will come from, still lives in the heart of this man."[12]

The logical consequence of Hooker's way of treating his musicians was the fluidity of his entourage, and most sidemen stayed in his band barely long enough to learn firsthand about his questionable behavior. Confronted with a constant need to renew his outfit, Earl couldn't hire new talent as much as he wanted to due to his bad reputation. The typical reaction of someone like Lacy Gibson was far from being an exception in Chicago; if Hooker didn't have much trouble setting up a band when he performed locally, convincing musicians to take to the road was not always easy. The tales of misfortune recounted by Earl's victims were there to bring back to reality dashing newcomers elated by the guitarist's matchless instrumental skills, and even Hooker's faithful accompanists usually acted with caution. "I never went to California with him," Lee Shot Williams laughs. "He wanted me to go. I never did go, 'cause I know how Earl Hooker was, and that was too far away from home to be messin' with Earl. One day he was goin' to California. He said—he called me Grandpa— 'Grandpa, I'll be by to pick you up,' I say, 'Okay.' The sun would come up, so he's out there blowin', and I's peepin' out the window, so I told my sister to tell him I wasn't home. Three thousand miles with Earl Hooker, gee! That's too far."

Hooker's only alternative was to set up bands as he proceeded along the chitlin circuit. With the development from the mid-fifties of new openings there for ambitious talents, the St. Louis-East St. Louis blues scene was swarming with starving instrumentalists who were eagerly waiting for an opportunity to show their ability, and they would accept taking chances to do so. Earl's safest bet when he drove through town in search of accompanists was Ike Turner's East St. Louis home, where he could find musicians temporarily out of a job. Despite his reluctance at paying his men, Earl didn't want second-rate musicians, unhesitatingly firing those who didn't meet his standards.

The South stood next to St. Louis as a source of talent; to that extent, the dense network of personal connections Hooker had built up in Mississippi,

Arkansas, Missouri, and southern Illinois since the forties provided him with a rich well of potential sidemen. In the list of musicians who followed Earl to Chicago, several names stand out: Big Moose Walker, Pinetop Perkins, Andrew B. B. Odom, as well as more obscure ones like Mississippian J. J. "Harmonica Man" James, bassist Nick Charles, and John Gastin, a talented vocalist and a native of Cairo, Illinois, who toured Florida with Hooker and Kansas City Red in the mid-fifties.

Over the years, Hooker perfected a technique that enabled him to lure naive musicians away from the South. In rural areas, young and eager musicians were easy prey for Earl, who shamelessly took advantage of their ingenuousness, depicting Chicago as the capital of the land of plenty. As he traveled through remote country towns, driving around in a shiny green eight-door limousine, proudly boasting on stage customized guitars bearing his name in large type, wearing fancy cowboy hats and loud-colored outfits, Hooker radiated wealth and achievement. The verbal assurance of a generous salary was enough then for Earl to lay hold of any number of blues-playing field hands, trading upon their ignorance of the music scene. "He put bands together like he had 'em made," Herb Turner laughs. "I guess he brought more musicians to Chicago than any other musician. That's why Chicago is loaded with musicians, you know. Right now I'd say one tenth of the musicians that's in Chicago was here because of Hooker. I remember, Hooker told me how he would do it. The guys, they didn't make much money in the fields pickin' cotton, maybe two bucks or somethin' like that, and Hooker said he gonna give you five to take you to Chicago, so hey! They'd go! And the long car and all the women hollerin' and everythin' when Hooker was down there. And they didn't stay around, 'cause when they'd get here, they'd get down at Pepper's and they'd see that they can make fifteen or twenty dollars a night, so they'd split."

From a financial standpoint, this system was profitable for Hooker, who ran one of the cheapest combos in Chicago, much to the dislike of established Windy City sidemen who looked very unfavorably on those newcomers who innocently drove down musician's pay. But this wasn't enough for Earl, who managed to draw back a large share of the meager wages he paid his sidemen while making sure of their trustworthiness as long as possible, according to Herb Turner: "See, that long car, everythin' he carried in it, all the equipment belonged to him. Guitars and everythin'. He just asked the guy if he could play, so he could come and work with him and that was it." "And if they didn't have an instrument, he'd bring 'em and let 'em play with him, and charge 'em rent for the instruments and stuff, so he didn't have to pay 'em. That's how he'd get his money back," A. C. Reed confirms.

Regardless of such methods, Hooker should be given credit for the musical education he gave upcoming musicians; in the absence of financial compensations for their efforts, Earl's sidemen largely benefitted from the advice he lavished on them. Lee Shot Williams, recalling his personal experience, stands up for his leader: "Me and Hooker would leave Chicago a lot of times in that long car, and we'd pick up musicians down the road. Earl would teach 'em how to play. Well, see that's what I told 'em too, I say, 'You can't grumble too much 'cause really you don't have your own instrument. You playin' the man's instruments.' Listen, we always had somethin' to eat every day when we's on the road, we always had a place to stay. No money, but then it was experience that I probably wouldn't have got, see, 'cause I would have just been right there in Chicago on the corner. A lot of fun, and a lot of experience; that was schoolin' for us. For this day now, what Earl Hooker taught me, this is the Lee Shot that you see now. He taught me how to survive, and how to entertain."

The example of guitarist Frank "Son" Seals, whom Hooker kept in his band over a period of several months in the winter of 1963, illustrates Hooker's ways with young musicians eager to learn. Seals was born in 1942 in the Mississippi River town of Osceola, Arkansas, where his father owned a small café, the Dipsy Doodle. When Hooker and Seals met in the late fifties, the latter was a mature teenager who played drums and guitar. Although Earl never performed at the Dipsy Doodle, Osceola was a regular stop on his way to the Delta, and Son Seals would catch his show at any one of the main local clubs.

On their first encounter, Hooker let Son sit in with his band on guitar. Over the years, this initial experience was repeated several times until Hooker had a fair notion of Son's potential. By the early sixties Seals was proficient enough on his instrument to travel around Arkansas, Missouri, and Kentucky with his brother-in-law, Little Walter Jefferson. He eventually wound up in Little Rock, where he played the local club scene over a period of several months. In 1962 Son was just about ready to move on to bigger things when he visited his sister in Chicago. "From the first time that I sit in with Earl, he'd always try to get me to go back and work with him, said, 'If you ever come to Chicago, look me up,'"

Son recalls. "I think it was in '62, the first time that I went up there to spend some time. After gettin' settled in, I decided I wanted to play, and I knew I had to get a hold to Earl, so I asked my brother-in-law, I said, 'Where do Earl and all of 'em guys play at?' and he say, 'Well, Earl, the few times that I ran up on him, he was playin' at a place on Homan and Madison called Curley's.' And sho' nuff, he was in town, and I think that was on Monday that he was gonna play at that place. He played there like on a weeknight. And Freddy King came by and played some with him, just sittin' in."

Son Seals was hired that very night at Curley's, staying with Earl until the spring and spending most of the time on the road. In the summer Hooker drove down South, staying at his wife's home in Missouri, but the coldest months usually saw him in Wisconsin, Minnesota, and more particularly Iowa and the Waterloo area, where another "wife," Rosemary Walker, resided. By Son's recollection, "Popeye was on piano, that's what they called him. And Bobby Joe [Johnson] played drums, he was from Cairo, and the bass player, and myself. And then we ended up in Waterloo. That's the first thing we did, and the snow was so tall. He had his limousine bus–type thing that had all these seats in it parked up behind his old lady's house up there, but we couldn't see the bus."

The fact that Earl deliberately chose to work the midwestern states during the worst of the cold season may seem strange. If the Delta's scorching summer weather was not adapted to his failing health, Iowa's bleak winters did little to help him cure his tuberculosis. "He got sick in fact once up there in Iowa," Son Seals remembers. "I think he spent about a week in a hospital, and hell, we left and went on back to Chicago. That musta been the second time that we went up there." In Waterloo, Rosemary Walker could look after Hooker, and her house was home for Earl and his band members. "She had a big house there, and we stayed down in the basement of the house. They had a room fixed up down there, damn nice. They had about four or five beds down there, so we stayed there, I'd say about ten days," Son explains.

On the weekend Earl appeared with his band at Jimmie Hunt's Cocktail Lounge, and the rest of the week was spent in neighboring localities: "Earl had booked a few more places around close. Because he played not only Waterloo, it was a lot of other little towns around close, little suburbs or whatever. Earl knew a lot of places that he'd book, so out of that ten days, I guess we played at least seven of 'em. Earl always had some beautiful posters and things made up all the time, with him on it with the big double guitars and things. He had pictures of himself, and also Big Voice [Odom], and I think he had Bobby Joe [Johnson]'s picture on some of 'em."

As they proceeded with their travels, Hooker and band visited new clubs almost nightly. Wherever they went, Son was surprised to note how popular Hooker was, even in remote country towns: "He was usin' his head. See, Earl I guess kinda spaced himself, like each year he would go into certain areas and play for so long. Just like when he come down South, he would stay three or four months, and then if he go back North, he spent the rest of the time up there playin'. So everywhere he went he had a followin', and people would come to see him because they didn't get a chance to see him so much to where he'd burn 'em out. I guess he knew the places that he would be sure to draw somebody, because he would always have somebody on the door. That was one thing he'd do, now. He'd have his old lady or somebody there with him and he would do pretty good, because like I guess for the simple reason that he had been goin' there playin' for so long."

With the presence of a trustworthy person at the door, Hooker had full control over the money situation. That way, it was difficult for club owners to underestimate the night's gains, and Earl could manipulate the band's account, although he never took advantage of the situation with Son: "I never did have no problem with Earl. Now I don't doubt that guys had problems about it, but I guess that it was certain people that he just didn't wanna fool around with, 'cause I would have been immediately pissed off, and wouldn't have played no more." At the time of his collaboration with Earl, Seals not only was a dynamic player, he was also a capable singer. As such, he opened the show for Hooker: "Earl didn't sing, I sang most of the time. Now, Voice [Odom] a few times went out with us. But if it wasn't Voice, I would sing, and then he had this boy Popeye playin' the keyboard, he did a little singin' himself. Even Bobby Joe [Johnson] sang a little bit. By the time the band start playin', people start to comin' in. Now Earl was spendin' the early part of the evenin' on that door with his old lady tryin' to see that money bein' right. But after everythin' kinda settled down, then he come on up there and get with us."

The harshness and competitiveness of the blues scene and Chicago's freezing climate eventually got the better of Son Seals's enthusiasm. Like many of the young players Earl lured into the city over the years, Son went back down to Arkansas. "At that time, I was a little bit undecided myself, whether I was really gonna try to stay there at that time or not," Seals, who moved to Chicago permanently in 1971, says. "So it was a good thing for me to get a little bit more experienced, like on that road. So I worked with Earl myself like about three or four months before I finally decided to go back down South. But it was good, because I had been knowin' Earl for a long time, and so to get a chance to work some with him like that was good. 'Cause Earl, he was good to sit and watch, but it was even better to play with him, because you could feel all the licks and shit, you know, when you'd get up and play with him."

Hooker and Cuca

(1964–1967)

The disbanding of the tight and widely acclaimed Mel London recording unit led by Earl Hooker in the late winter 1964 sent Earl looking for a new back-up group. Quite typically, the successive bands he set up then consisted of newcomers chosen at random in the course of out-of-town trips, with a sprinkling of reliable players. While A. C. Reed and Earnest Johnson stopped traveling with Hooker on a regular basis, keyboard man Big Moose Walker refused to abandon his leader in the storm. Another regular organist during the sixties was one of Earl's cousins on his mother's side. Edmond Blair, a dedicated Baptist preacher during the day, sometimes traded the pulpit of his father's South Side church on week nights for the more secular boards Hooker treaded in Chicago clubs.

Occasionally Earl also entrusted piano chores to his longtime friend Joe Willie "Pinetop" Perkins. Earl and Pinetop had played together on and off since the forties, around the Delta and in the Cairo area at first, then in St. Louis after Pinetop moved there in the mid-fifties. Hooker and Perkins seldom performed together in St. Louis, unless Earl happened to sit in with Johnny O'Neal's Hound Dogs. After O'Neal's death in the early sixties, Hooker put Pinetop back on the blues trail, and the pianist eventually moved to Chicago at Earl's behest, sharing his time between casual appearances with various local bands—including Earl's Soul Twisters—and the development of a more gainful family business. "He was more often with Moose [Walker] than he was with me," Perkins says. "He had different bands all the time, 'cause he'd mess up with the money, and he'd get into fights. Me and him never did fight. When I'd get ready to about fightin', I'd go and leave him. And I loved him like a kid, you know, 'cause he started with us when he was a kid, but he just wouldn't do right with that money. He'd say, 'M-m-m-man, the m-m-m-man didn't pay me off, m-m-man, y-y-you'll get somethin' next week!'"

Although sidemen would come and go, Hooker's outfit during the years 1964 and 1965 included regulars like guitarist-singer Cecil Norman, saxophonist J. J. "Jump" Jackson, bassist James Hamilton, and a drummer known as Stevie. Herb Turner, who kept in close touch with Hooker at that time, recalls: "The majority of the time, he didn't have a sax, so you might catch him with three pieces, and when he was goin' to Mississippi or Arkansas, he'd get maybe five pieces but his bands mostly was just three or four. Now Stevie, he was from Greenwood, Mississippi. Stevie came here with Ike Turner. He was a hell of a drummer, then he left here and went to Utica, New York. I think Cecil Norman came here with Earl out of Missouri, but he was originally from Arkansas. He's dead now. He got killed in Charleston, Missouri, in a car accident on his way back from Mississippi or from Arkansas. Cecil Norman, all of 'em was with Jump at the time, they was based out of Waterloo, Iowa."

Aside from Hooker himself, the nucleus of this outfit was a versatile two-some who displayed on stage their instrumental and vocal showmanship. The first member of this team was drummer Bobby Little, a rare survivor of the London era, who resumed his seat with Hooker after a spell in the band of Ricky Allen; the second one was an obscure bassist and singer known as Little Tommy Isom. Not much is known concerning Isom, other than the fact that he was connected in some kind of way to the Waterloo scene. "I recall a man calling himself Little Tommy," remembers blues critic Jim DeKoster, who grew up in the Waterloo of the sixties, "no doubt Tommy Isom, but passing himself off successfully as Little Tommy Tucker, who had a big hit at the time with 'Hi-Heel Sneakers.' Little Tommy was a small man who looked rather like the pictures of Tucker, and he was playing—or faking—piano. He worked with local bluesmen, guitarist Lonnie Flowers plus bass and drums."

It was around that time that Earl, whose personal appearances at Waterloo's North End clubs recurred at regular intervals, spotted Little Tommy. With the complicity of both Bobby Little and Little Tommy, Hooker was able from late 1964 to use a technique perfected years before, one that could prove both perilous and profitable. His collaboration with popular singers like Ricky Allen or Junior Wells resulted in bigger touring benefits, as engagements in better-paying clubs became more frequent. At the same time, the presence in his band of star singers meant that Hooker had to give up a larger share of his performance fees. The only possible way out would have been to pay well-known acts the salary of ordinary sidemen; the equation seemed as simple as squaring the circle, but Earl still managed to solve it. "You see," Hooker's guitarist friend Jimmy Dawkins reported in a 1969 magazine article, "anytime a hot record is out, Hooker will go out seeking till he finds someone that can imitate it, or sing like the artist that made the hit record. Then he will print placards and go around claiming his vocalist is the one that made the record."[1]

This questionable way of seeking the favors of the public was a trick Hooker had kept up his sleeve for some time, since the early fifties at least, when he roamed the southern states in the company of Little Walker—a harmonica player audiences would generally mistake for the famous Little Walter—or Albert "King," whom Hooker introduced as B. B. King's brother. Another imaginary relation to a renowned artist was saxophonist Aaron Corthen, billed at first as "Little Jimmy Reed." Under this identity, Earl's tenor saxophonist went on to pursue his own recording career, claiming to whoever cared to listen that he was his namesake's half-brother. "I just picked up the Reed when I got heavy into the music. Hooker was the one that had me to do it," A. C. Reed confesses. With time, only the "Reed" stuck, and Corthen started using his actual initials as a first name, still claiming that he was related to Jimmy Reed, probably more out of nostalgia than for the sake of a publicity he no longer needed.

On the strength of such experiments, Hooker's strategy progressively reached a high degree of sophistication, and his act grew into an "All-Star R&B Show." At one point, Earl carried in his band singer Bobby Rush; in order to offer club owners a more glamorous show, Rush first stepped out in a glittering suit and stick-on mustaches to avoid being recognized by audiences, playing the role of MC and comedian under the identity of "The Tramp." While Hooker kept the crowd waiting with one of his dazzling instrumentals, Rush would then change costumes, coming back a few minutes later to sing his regular repertoire in his normal guise.

With Bobby Little and Little Tommy in his band, Hooker soon moved a step further. His impersonators, no longer claiming a close relation to nationally acclaimed recording stars, would assume on stage the actual identity of Tommy Tucker, Ricky Allen, or Junior Wells, much to the dislike of these artists, who were sometimes preceded by more than their reputation, Herb Turner explains: "I remember one night, Ricky [Allen] came to me and said, 'Hey, man, thanks to the snow I'm plannin' about goin' South, all the way into Greenville [Mississippi] and then Lake Charles, Louisiana.' So I said, 'Okay!' and he said, 'Listen, when I get ready to leave out there, try to book somethin' here.' So I set up a night in Joliet, and Ricky and I goes to Kankakee and we set a night up in Kankakee. Ricky had blank placards, so we goes out to put off these posters, and there's posters already, you know. RICKY ALLEN. He's gonna be in another club down the street that Friday night, and we was tryin' to do that for the Saturday night. And Ricky says, 'What's this?!!' And when we saw that and the Soul Twisters, I said, 'Man, that's Hooker!' Hooker had Ricky's picture put up and everythin'!

"Earl had him a Junior Wells one time, and any hit blues record that hit the market, that was in the Earl Hooker's Band, he would take a show on the road with that artist. And I used to ask him, I said, 'Earl, you know, why you do that?' And he stuttered, "'H-H-Herb, I-I-I-I can't help it! If I c-c-can't get no gig, I c-c-can't work. One thing about it, all I want somebody t-t-to do is get a hit record, then I-I-I put anybody in a red suit, I c-c-can't help it.' And this was Hooker! He would constantly do it! Right here in Chicago Heights, he would have a Ricky Allen right here! It was next door, you know. And now he'd get caught! I remember one time Hooker said, he was playin' this gig in southern Illinois, and Junior Wells happened to be comin' through town, and he saw the posters that he was appearin' there that night, with Hooker. So then Junior Wells waited until the show's over, and then Junior Wells, the real Junior Wells went to the promoter and got his money. So Hooker went mad then. Hooker tried to make a deal with him, for settin' up the show and everythin'. Said, 'I-I-I'll tell you what Junior, j-j-j-just gimme my part of it, and forget the rest of 'em.' You know, he'd try! I know Junior was mad about it.

"So in Kankakee, we told everybody where Ricky was gonna be when we put our posters over, because a lot of people that would get there on Friday night, they wouldn't wanna come unless they could see Ricky Allen. And he better look like the picture on the poster. But I'll tell you who Ricky Allen was at the time, who was singin' 'Cut You A-Loose.' It was Tommy Isom! Tommy Isom was the impersonator. And to me Tommy don't sound nothin' like Ricky Allen, but Hooker'd get away, though. And Bobby Little used to be Tommy Tucker, or Junior Wells, or whoever got a hit record. That was their job, copy that record."

Keeping in his band vocalists who assumed the identity of others apparently did not satisfy Hooker. In order to hustle better engagements, he would go as far as to "borrow" club gigs, abusing the good nature of local promoters, Ricky Allen explains: "Hooker used to put us in some trick bags. See, as far as hustling gigs, he got 'em, regardless how he got 'em, see. If he found out I'm goin' on a road tour for Rockin' Eddie and JoJo Gun, DJs out of Greenville [Mississippi], he would ease his way in their office and get a hold to the addresses of the places I was goin', like Peppermint Lounge in Yazoo City and Peyton's Place in Greenville, and he'd beat me to it! I remember one time, we was at B. B. King's ex-mother-in-law, that's in Indianola, Mississippi. So anyway, we pulled up, I had my truck and my name all over it, all my records and everythin'. We un-load the organ, and bass, Earnest [Johnson]'s amplifier was like that high. And we go all the way through—pass these kids. And they gamblin', havin' a good time; it's wide open, see. So when we start to get ready to set up, we tuned up, a little guy come over. He had a roll of money, man, and it looks like the oldest one in this thing was seventeen. If that old. He say 'Hey! You supposed to be Ricky Allen, aren't you?' I say, 'Yeah, I'm Ricky Allen.' He says, 'Earl Hooker come down here with a guy called Ricky Allen, and he didn't know but two verses to "Cut You A-Loose."' See, now, if you don't sing "Faith" [the flip side of "Cut You A-Loose"] we kickin' your ass.' So I got mad, I told Earnest, I told him 'Gimme my pistol out of that case.' My pistol was in the back of that amplifier, that's where I kept my stuff, right? Hey, I didn't go no place, to no small town with nothin' on me, hey, man! Average musician be crazy. And what made me feel more secure and protected, it was like forty or some people there from Chicago, they go over there on vacation. And they all behind us, and about three of 'em was policemen. Friends of mine. So I wasn't gonna sing 'Faith.' You know you just be pushed so far, you get as stupid as they do. So one of 'em kept sayin', 'Sing "Faith," sing "Faith,"' so I did 'Faith' and the kid come down and he put his arm around me, say, 'Looka here, now you Ricky Allen. But anybody else come by here tellin' us about they're Ricky Allen again, we kickin' their ass.' We couldn't do anythin' but laugh, though. But just to think how close you can get to havin' problems.

"Hooker had a guy that looked like me at Pepper's one night, and I'm gonna show you how Hooker was at that time, I mean he'd put you in a trick bag in a minute to get hisself off the hook. We just came off the road, and this is right after this incident I was tellin' you. And I walk in, and Hooker jammin'. Aw, man, we sittin' there, and the place—he'd pack a house. He didn't have to use no phonies, but he want more money, he'll get any name to go with him. See, that's a double crowd, that's twice the money. So anyway, I walked in, and he had a guy up here, I see him every once in a while now, I don't know his name. Anyway, he says, 'Here's Ricky Allen.' I'm lookin' around. 'No, I ain't talkin' about you, I'm talkin' about you, come here, man.' The cat walked over there that made all that money imitatin' me. He won first prize doin' 'You'd Better Be Sure!' So he say, 'H-h-h-hey, Ricky, I want you to m-m-meet Ricky Allen.' Man, I like fell out, he was just that bold."

Hooker was not the first and only one to use such dubious methods, but his unparalleled nerve placed him well ahead of other bandleaders, whereas his natural talent at uncovering acceptable impersonators came as a great help. Over the years, in addition to A. C. Reed, Bobby Little, and Little Tommy, he featured a succession of singers and groups in his band under various billings. If things usually went smoothly, Earl occasionally stirred up the thunder of audiences who did not enjoy being played for fools, A. C. Reed recalls: "We was playin' in Clarksville, Tennessee, and he had this group out of Gary, Indiana, they was supposed to be Hank Ballard and the Midnighters. It was a lot of soldiers in the club, man, we had a packed house, and some of 'em knew Hank Ballard, and they knew this wasn't the Midnighters, and they started askin' for their money back, and they started to fightin'. They called the police, and I just stopped goin' on his phony deals. It could be dangerous, impersonatin' other peoples. I remember he had a package deal once, and I refused to go. He had great big placards, lot of peoples on there didn't even exist," Reed laughs at the recollection.

The collapse of Age Records in 1964 was more disastrous for Earl's recording career than the disbanding of the tight studio unit that followed; finding another record company, and more especially a producer of London's caliber, sounded nothing as easy as hiring new sidemen. Since the fifties recording activities had played a leading role in the development of Hooker's following, and he found himself quite helpless when London went out of business, bringing an abrupt end to a promising experience that didn't last long enough to bear all of its fruits. During the years that followed, Earl tried his best to arouse the interest of record producers. If he ever dreamed of drawing the attention of a major record company, his illusions must have vanished with the failure of his own Checker release in 1962. Even though the early sixties were a time of great popularity for instrumental groups in rock 'n' roll and R&B, Earl's position as a leading instrumentalist on the Chicago blues scene—an essentially vocal field—put him in an awkward position, especially at a time when Afro-American music was undergoing drastic changes, compelling major firms to reconsider their artistic policy. Such considerations easily accounted for Chess's desperate attempt at rejuvenating the sound of house star Muddy Waters, but the efforts Phil and Leonard Chess were willing to make did not include investing money on the launching of new blues artists.

Undaunted by the lack of interest Chicago label operators showed in his talent, Hooker tried to work out deals with other firms outside of the Windy City during the mid-sixties. The success some his friends like Junior Parker, Rufus Thomas, and his own cousin, singer Joe Hinton, enjoyed with major recording ventures like Duke or Stax in the South, clearly showed that Chess and Vee-Jay in Chicago no longer had the monopoly on rhythm & blues releases. In an attempt at drawing the attention of a large company, Hooker stopped in Memphis, Tennessee, around that time, on the occasion of a trip South. Like most black entertainers, Hooker usually stayed at the Lorraine Motel, at 406 Mulberry Street—the site of Dr. Martin Luther King Jr.'s assassination in April 1968—when he was in town, and his friend Arbee Stidham remembers seeing him there: "I went there on business to see [producer] Willie Mitchell. And somebody had seen me and told Hooker that I was in Memphis, Tennessee. We were stoppin' at the Lorraine Motel, and he came through there because he wanted to see the guy that had Stax Records, Stewart." Hooker's music probably did not fit into any of the categories represented in the Stax catalog, for nothing came out of his encounter with Jim Stewart, president of the company.

This left Hooker with no other possibility but to turn toward small independent firms. In Chicago he made various attempts during the five-year period that followed the collapse of London's record business, but his only releases on the Chicago market were an average C.J. single recorded in 1965 under the auspices of Carl Jones, as well as a fine two-sided Bobby Little/Little Tommy vocal 45 issued on the ephemeral Jim-Ko label. Actually, the largest share of his recorded output was taped outside the city limits, as a function of the recording facilities he stumbled upon on the occasion of his wanderings through the midwestern states. Many short-lived experiences stopped at the making of demonstration tapes; to that extent, obscure material may well pop up unexpectedly in the future, whereas only released efforts can be documented with some adequacy.

"See, Earl had a bad habit," Herb Turner reports. "If he was goin' around anybody who had a recordin' studio, he was like Lightnin' Hopkins. You know Lightnin' Hopkins recorded for just about anybody who is related to the business. If there was a studio and anybody said, 'Hey, let's tape this and let's do it,' Earl would do it. Just like I recorded him, I didn't contract him because you couldn't contract a person like Hooker. It wouldn't do you no good if you did. I have master dubs that he gave me. Some pretty good stuff. Then I've never seen it issued. He'd say, 'Hey, check this out. This is a session I did,' you know."

It was not in Chicago but in a tiny Wisconsin town that Hooker came across the record company that was to fill, to a certain extent, the gap left by Mel London. The various sessions that this new firm originated from 1964 were not as numerous as the ones set up by London; nonetheless, they resulted in over two dozen different songs and instrumental tracks, some of which were put out on a handful of 45s whereas the largest share later saw the light on Earl Hooker's very first long-playing record.

Earl's favorite circuit when he took to the road during the sixties often brought him to northern Illinois and Wisconsin on his way to Minnesota, hustling jobs in the bars and taverns of Rockford and Milwaukee. Rockford more especially boasted a large black population, and Hooker performed there frequently, sitting in with local R&B musicians. Rockford's most popular black outfit at the time was led by Sidney Banks, better known to the music world as "Birdlegs." In addition to Birdlegs's wife, Pauline Chivers-Banks, his band included two fine horn players Earl Hooker knew well: Julian Beasley, once alto saxophonist with the Mel London studio band, and Adolph "Billy" Duncan, a seasoned Memphis player whose back-up work included Hooker's first recordings for Sam Phillips in July of 1953.

Birdlegs & Pauline and their Versatility Birds, including Beasley and Billy Duncan, started making noise in the early summer of 1963 when their initial 45, "Spring," entered the national charts. Even though the single was distributed by Vee-Jay, the songs were recorded by an independent firm operator named James E. Kirchstein, who released them at first on his own Cuca label. Kirchstein's Cuca Record Company was based out of Sauk City, a small town of two thousand located in Sauk Indian territory on the Wisconsin River, some twenty miles northwest of Wisconsin's state capital, Madison. Kirchstein, whose studio and offices were found in the basement of a compact building at 123 Water Street, specialized in the folk repertoire of the various ethnic communities scattered around the Sauk and Dane counties. Cuca presented the polka music and yodels of locals of Polish, German, and Austrian origin, but its catalog also included jazz, gospel, and R&B releases.

Kirchstein relates the history of his enterprise: "In '54 when I got out of service, I decided to go into the University. At that time, in order to get a little extra income—'cause at that time we were getting $160 a month from the government, which was fine except it didn't quite support a family—I started the Hi-Fi Record Shop in Sauk City in the basement of a toy shop that my brother was running, and sold records for a couple years and did fairly well. I had got the idea at one time to get into the recording business and release a record and see what it was like. Luckily the second record hit. It was called "The Mule Skinner Blues," by the Fendermen. The old Jimmie Rodgers song. That sold within the United States over a million. So in the early sixties, we got involved in ethnic music, and from about 1961 to 1970 we recorded and released over three hundred albums of what we call old-time polka music of all nationalities, and put about another two hundred in the can that were not released. At the same time, of course, we were doin' a lot of country music, a lot of rock music, and a lot of R&B music.

"In the early to mid-sixties, we got a call from Sidney Banks from Rockford, and he says, 'My name is Birdlegs and I'd like to come up to record,' and I just said, 'Sure, when do you wanna come?' And I'd never heard of him, but I thought, 'Why not?' So they came up within a week or so, and it was one of the neatest bands I ever heard. Pauline was just a super singer, his wife. And they came in to record a session for us, I think about four songs. Two of 'em were 'In So Many Ways,' which was kind of a ballad Pauline'd sing, and 'Spring' was the name of the other one. I released that on a 45, completely sponsoring it myself, this was on Cuca. And I sent it to O. C. White, a DJ in Milwaukee, who I happened to just get to know at that time, and it did very well. He had the entire black population in Milwaukee listening to him, and he broke that thing wide open, and [Ewart] Abner, who was the president of Vee-Jay at the time, called and said, 'I think you got a record,' which was his way of saying, 'I think you've got a hit,' and we leased it to Vee-Jay, and they sold several hundred thousand copies, and we got paid for some of 'em."

The success of this initial Birdlegs & Pauline record brought Cuca Records to the attention of several black performers. Among these was Earl Hooker, who got in touch with Jim Kirchstein around 1964 after getting his address from Birdlegs. A first session was scheduled for several weeks later, which gave Kirchstein a rough idea of the extent of Hooker's talent. On the strength of this initial session, several others followed over a period of close to four years, during which Hooker never failed to visit Jim Kirchstein's recording studio whenever he felt ready to put on tape his latest material. Kirchstein's way of working with his artists was quite different from what Hooker was used to. When Chicago producers had a tendency to rush up things because of high studio rates, Kirchstein worked in his own self-made premises, taking whatever time was needed to rehearse his bands. In Hooker's case, recording a handful of tunes usually lasted until dawn, more particularly as Earl and band were wont to arrive in Wisconsin at all hours of the night.

"I do remember they would have a seven o'clock session," Kirchstein, a very articulate man with a genuine interest for black music, recalls with fondness. "Almost at all times at eleven-thirty that night, I felt somethin' went wrong and they weren't coming, and I'd be ready to lock the door when a couple cars would pull up. So at midnight, they'd be bringing in their instruments, and luckily my dad had his supermarket next door and I had a key, so we got some bread and some baloney, and everybody ate a little bit. Then if things didn't really click, we'd run downtown and get a couple bottles of wine from a local liquor store—Sauk City is only about two thousand people, but the taverns number about twelve. So about two o'clock in the morning, some of the finest music I ever heard was starting to happen, and by four or five when I'd be going home, my mother would be just getting up, and we'd have some pretty good stuff in the can. It was just that much fun. Everything was improvised. It wasn't ever a session of labor. It was just more or less a session of enjoyment from Earl's end and from ours. Sometimes they came in, rehearsed and ran maybe four or five songs. Other times, they came in and just worked on a song. They might say, you know, 'Run this, will you?' So we'd run it off, they would stop after maybe thirty-two bars. And very often after you played back thirty-two bars, they would sit there in complete silence, for maybe four or five, ten minutes, without saying a thing. And all of a sudden, they would try something different. When they were ready, it only took one or two takes. Generally after the session, the next day, I loved to go back to the studio in the morning. Everything was nice and quiet, smoke had cleared the air, and the walls had stopped vibrating and you pulled off the tape and really heard what they sounded like. And almost always, they really sounded greater than what you remembered."

From the very beginning—unlike most producers in the field of popular black music who remained faithful to the 45 market—it was Kirchstein's intention to put out a whole album of Earl Hooker, but he knew it would take time before he had enough valuable material for an LP. Consequently, Earl's Cuca LP did not see the light until 1968, at a time when Hooker's health was severely deteriorating. Pending the release of the album, he put out two 45s, in late 1964 and early 1967 respectively, that Hooker sold to club audiences when he traveled on the road, while a third was put out concurrently with the album. "I guess I put out the 45s more or less to keep Earl's spirits up while we worked towards the album," Jim Kirchstein confirms, "'cause I really didn't think the 45s were gonna return much, basically, 'cause my only sales in R&B at that time were jukebox sales. So a jukebox dealer in Wisconsin that has a couple hundred jukeboxes might buy a box of twenty-five, and that's the end of the sale. The 45s was to get Earl some side money. But I had a lot of confidence in the album."

If Hooker's Cuca output was a strict diet of guitar showcases, several vocalists—including A. C. Reed, lyricist Frank Clark, and Chicago-based James "Muddy Waters Jr." Williams, in addition to Earl himself—managed to slip in occasional songs, as was illustrated by Hooker's very first Wisconsin session. Of the various Cuca dates, none was as productive as this initial event. Taking place in the second half of 1964, it yielded a total of eight sides, three of which boasted fine vocal efforts. One of Hooker's main assets that day was the presence by his side of a tight unit, including Bobby Little on drums as well as Hooker's longtime friend, tenor saxophonist A. C. Reed. Reed would still take to the road with the Soul Twisters episodically at the time, until he eventually joined the Buddy Guy band from 1967. Since the breaking up of the London studio band, Earl and A. C. had performed together at longer intervals, and the Cuca tracks they cut then marked the end of their collaboration on record.

Reed's recollections of his trip to Wisconsin with Earl are somewhat hazy. Other than bassist James Hamilton and drummer Bobby Little, he recalls a young organ player whom Hooker picked up in Champaign, Illinois. "We didn't even get paid for the session, man, we just go up there with Hooker and do it," Reed reports. "I even sang a tune, 'My Baby's Fine.' I remember we went up there, and [Hooker] had this little boy named Richard playin' the organ. Hooker's tellin' me about the organ player was as good as Jimmy Smith. He could play piano, too."

This first session set up a pattern consistently used on later sessions: after a set of inspired guitar instrumentals in which both the saxophone and organ players held a place of honor, several vocal efforts were waxed before Hooker brought things to an end with one of his fine country & western renditions. On Hooker's C&W menu for this initial trip to the Cuca studios was a cover version of Ernest Tubb's 1942 hit "Walking the Floor over You," bearing witness to Hooker's proficiency in this idiom. It came as a fitting follow-up to the rendition of "Guitar Rag" Earl had taped in Memphis for Sam Phillips in the summer of 1953. A revisited version of Earl's 1962 hit, "Blue Guitar"—retitled "Mean Guitar" at the time of the session, although it eventually saw the light on the Cuca label as "End of the Blues"—proves that Hooker had not abjured his faith in the blues. Hooker did not want to neglect the pop market, however, and he also put on wax his version of the 1959 Santo & Johnny guitar instrumental "Sleepwalk." The song was a crowd-pleaser he often played on stage that he chose to call "Bertha" as an affectionate tribute to his wife. "I don't know why he decided to make that record," Bertha Nickerson said twenty years later. "One day I heard it playin', I said, 'What's the name of that record?' He said, 'Just listen, I made that special for you.'"

The most interesting instrumental items recorded by the Hooker-Reed team that day did not belong in any of the above mentioned idioms, "Dynamite" and "The Foxtrot" being part of Earl's R&B repertoire. In a little under two minutes, Hooker reaches close to perfection with "The Foxtrot," a track that makes up in a formidable manner for the weaker numbers cut in Sauk City over the years. The tune's brilliance is the work of the whole band, including Reed on tenor and Richard on organ, whose spirited playing perfectly fits the song's infectious atmosphere. Hooker takes advantage of the band's inspired playing, exhorting his gang to pursue their efforts for an additional chorus with a vigorous "Hey, baby, I said one more time!" But even more than his sidemen, Hooker sweeps the song to a superior level. A mere listen to the breathtaking guitar break that follows the organ solo and to the subdued accompaniment that propels Richard's licks with astounding accuracy will give the measure of Hooker's creative genius.

Whoever was familiar with Earl's Chief output would have recognized in this driving instrumental a track already waxed for Mel London in May 1961 under the title "Rockin' Wild." The fact that the tune's title had no relation with its Chief counterpart was a proof of the lack of importance Earl attached to the icing on his musical cake. As a general rule, he let fellow players or producers name his instrumental pieces, unless he came up with a catchy name on the spot. And if one same tune could be recorded under different titles, the opposite frequently occurred as well. Such was the case with "On the Hook," a title identifying a 1953 Rockin' cut that reappeared under the slightly altered form "Off the Hook" on three occasions over the years. Hooker's other R&B offering waxed during this initial Cuca session provides another example of this phenomenon, "Dynamite" bearing no resemblance to its Bea & Baby predecessor. Pretty similar in mood and verve to "The Foxtrot," this new "Dynamite" is another fine instrumental shuffle featuring Richard's rocking organ styling.

The vocal part of the session was no less rewarding, especially as Earl Hooker contributed two of the three songs cut that day, a rare treat, considering Earl's usual reluctance at putting his singing on wax. Hooker's choice first went to one of his own favorites, "Swear to Tell the Truth," a song that previously featured the voice of drummer Harold Tidwell on the flip side of Earl's bestseller, "Blue Guitar." Next came a rendition of "Reconsider Baby," originally a 1954 Checker hit for Lowell Fulson. The impression emanating from these tunes is one of perfect cohesion as the band supports Earl's swinging vocals like one man. If Hooker proves sparing of solos on both songs, the impeccable guitar phrases with which he punctuates his lines testify to his ultimate taste and sense of backing. But the biggest surprise comes from Hooker's singing: he sounds in good vocal form here, his voice radiating a warmth one would not have suspected in him, considering the limited confidence it had inspired in record producers so far. For the last vocal offering of the day, Hooker went back to playing his guitar as A. C. Reed sang one of his own compositions, "She's Fine," boasting excellent lyrics as usual. Unfortunately, Reed's effort remained in the can, and A. C. recut it two years later with Earl's former pupil Ivory Parkes. Although it fell short of the Cuca original, Reed's "My Baby Is Fine" was a commercial success for the Chicago-based Cool label.

The quality of the vocal material recorded on this first Cuca session made Earl's and Kirchstein's joint decision to release all-instrumental singles quite surprising. Following their agreement, Kirchstein and Hooker put out "Bertha" and "Walking the Floor (Over You)" at once on Cuca J-1194, credited to "Earl Hooker & the Soul Twisters." According to the Cuca files, a total of three hundred copies were pressed in mid-November 1964—making it a much sought-after item today. By Earl's instructions, Kirchstein kept in stock two hundred copies for promotion and sent twenty-five records to Mrs. Hooker's Prairie Avenue address, while the remaining seventy-five were forwarded to Earl in care of the Chicago TB Hospital at 1919 West Taylor, where the guitarist was currently undergoing treatment. "I never recorded anything without the idea of releasing it," Kirchstein says to account for his policy. "We had a fairly decent offer. First of all we guaranteed the session. If someone came in and recorded and did not like the sound, they didn't have to pay us a thing. And in the seventeen years that we had the studio, we never had that happen. Secondly, if they decided to release a record, they would pay only for the records they bought. And if we saw what we felt potential on a record, then we entered into a contract and paid a royalty to the bands. Generally, Hooker got a hundred records, and then we put it on the books until his royalties would come along and pay for what he owed. And then after that caught up, then we would pay Earl. I realize that in those days, the black groups didn't have very much money at all. And of course I guess back in their mind was always the idea of the thrill of having a hit record, and everybody makes a lot of money."

The label used for Cuca 45s was a particularly elaborate one for a small company, especially in the light of the limited number of records pressed, requiring the use of no less than seven different colors. While the name of the artist and song titles appeared in silver print on glossy black paper, the Cuca logo—a pot-bellied Mexican man caught in the middle of a meditative siesta—deftly mixed touches of orange, red, white, and blue, the words "Cuca Record Sauk City Wisc." standing out in bright yellow letters at the bottom of the label. Kirch-stein traces the label's name to its origin: "When I got out of service, I wanted to put a label on the first record that would create some attention. And it did. I used the swastika. It was a dumb thing to do, but around this area, the swastika is a good luck sign, okay? And I was too naive to realize the implica-tions of the Nazi era were still that strong. So RCA pressed three hundred records on the Swastika label, and it had a swastika on it. They started to press the second record when Bill Leonard—he was the head of the Chicago office of RCA—calls me. He says, 'We've an awful lot of eyebrows rise around here.' He says, 'We can't use that label any more.' At any rate, once we found out we couldn't use that label, I had to come up with something real fast, and a cousin of ours who is a Mexican girl, her name is Ruth, and the nickname for Ruth is Cuca. She was quite a pretty green-eyed Mexican girl. So I said, 'Heck! I'm gonna use Cuca!' And then I created the little Mexican figure. I thought it would be colorful with the little scarf and sombrero as long as Cuca was a Mex-ican name, and it worked out pretty well."

The same label layout was used in March 1967, when Kirchstein thought fit to release another coupling taken from Earl's first Cuca session. Earl's rocking "Dynamite" backed with "End of the Blues," credited this time to "Earl Hooker & the Soul Thrillers," saw the light on Cuca J-6733—namely, in Kirchstein's numerical jargon at the time, 1967's third month's third release. The fact that Kirchstein drew material from this initial recording date when he decided to is-sue another Hooker single two and a half years later, although he had at his dis-posal additional numbers put on wax in 1966, speaks volume for his satisfaction at the end of Earl's first session. Consequently, the high standards set on the occasion of this first trial would make most of Hooker's following Cuca efforts all the more disappointing.

It was not in Wisconsin but in Chicago that Earl made his next recordings, when Herb Turner, his usual promoter in northern Illinois, entered into partnership with a white independent label operator named James Kolb in the course of 1965. Kolb started out in the music business recording white garage bands like the Revelles and the Cave Dwellers. By the mid-sixties Kolb decided to try his luck at R&B with his Jim-Ko label, when he noticed that young Whites were developing an interest for the popular black sounds of the day. After a first failure involving a female soul group, Kolb made a deal with Turner in order to benefit from the latter's experience in the black music business. "What happened," Herb Turner recalls, "James Kolb didn't know how to deal with black disc jockeys, because they was carryin' him to the cleaner's. So he came to me, and he told me he couldn't pay me but what he would do, he would give me half of the record company. And so we became partners. And one day I was tellin' him, I said, 'Hooker called me today,' and he say, 'Who?! Not THE Earl Hooker?!!' I said, 'Yeah, he calls me quite often.' He said, 'That's what I wanna cut, I wanna cut some blues.' And he say, 'I think that the Whites is startin' to dig the blues, so why don't we give it a try?'"

In between erratic trips out of town and frequent hospital stays, Hooker still found the energy to grind out fluent instrumental showcases, and he was glad to accept the offer. At Turner's suggestion, he left some of the recording time granted for his Jim-Ko session to vocalists Bobby Little and Little Tommy, but the first part of his recording date was devoted to his usual guitar pyrotechnics. Turner was aware of the vocal appeal of the blues, and having little faith in Earl's capacity as a singer, he was convinced that Bobby and Tommy deserved better than their restricted stage role. The recording session took place in the basement home-studio of CBS sound engineer Frank McNaultry in Highland Park—a Chicago suburb situated ten miles north of the city limits—where Patti Drew and the Drew-Vells had recorded "Tell Him," a modest hit for Capitol Records, early in 1964.

Two under-par Hooker vocals were first put on wax that night, followed by a set of guitar numbers, before Isom and Little cut two fine R&B efforts co-penned with Turner for the occasion. The latter's account of the event faithfully documents a typical evening in the studio with Hooker and band, pointing to Hooker's shortsightedness when he recorded, an attitude that can easily be compared to the guitarist's everyday behavior. His decision to put on wax Rosco Gordon's "Chicken," regardless of the fact that he had already recorded it for the C.J. label six years earlier, proved that Earl gave little attention to his vocal material, accounting for Turner's reluctance to record his singing. Earl's lack of preparation prior to the session, as well as the fact that part of his back-up unit was under-rehearsed—if rehearsed at all—give fair indications of the essential role someone like Mel London had played in the studio in order to come up with successful results.

"Hooker came in with Bobby and Tommy, and Hooker wanted to do instrumentals. He liked to do things like 'Doin' the Chicken' or somethin' like that, 'cause he always sang that song, 'I wanna chicken, I wanna chicken with you.' The other thing was a slow thing. But Hooker really, he was a good guitar player and he played the blues good, better than other artists and everythin', but when it comes to doin' a vocal thing, the material that Hooker had, it just really didn't hit me, you know. So I said, 'Hey, this thing Bobby and Tommy got,' I said, 'Let's do it.' They had an idea, but they didn't have a tune; so they really had like a cliché, 'You can run but you can't hide,' but I had to finish the tune, so that's how I ended up writin' on it.

"I think Hooker had a new band. James Hamilton, he was on bass. He had this boy on the horn from Milwaukee. This boy's name was Charles, but I never did know his last name. I guess this boy was about seventeen or eighteen, clean-cut, kinda heavy set, a nice-lookin' guy. He's a good horn man, but he's very young. On the Bobby and Tommy, Bobby might have played drums, 'cause Bobby was a drummer. It was cut all the same night. We went in there, it was about eight at night, we started about ten and we stayed until twelve-thirty or one o'clock. We was in there about three hours, I think. We did six sides on [Hooker] and two sides on Bobby and Tommy, but we just issued the Bobby and Tommy. The other sides, at the time I didn't think it was up to par. I done forgot the names of 'em. The band just started, it was really just like a jam session, a cookin' thing, that's all it was. There wasn't nothin' there that was unique about it."

In spite of Turner's initial intention to put out the Hooker material, only the Isom/Little coupling saw the light, and the rest of the tapes cut that night eventually disappeared along with James Kolb. Issued on the Jim-Ko label without any serial number, this only release was credited to "Little Tommy & Bobby Little with Earl Hooker and his Soul Twisters." Both sides, titled "Won't Be Down Long" and "You Can't Hide," were jointly signed by Herb Turner, Tommy Isom, and "R. Welch"—actually Ronald "Bobby Little" Bluster, who used his stepfather's name for the occasion.

"Won't Be Down Long" was largely inspired by Tommy Tucker's 1964 hit "Hi-Heel Sneakers," the intro and melody of which were borrowed by Little and Isom, who merely added their own words to it. The sophisticated mood that radiates from the tune, with its elegant organ-sax flourishes and counterpoint vocal duet, connects the song more with the southern R&B scene, and more particularly with Junior Parker, who recorded a similar tune entitled "Cracked Up over You" for the Mercury label shortly afterward. The highlight of Hooker's own contribution to "Won't Be Down Long" is a fine slide passage slipped in after the second verse, the unusual sonority of which owes to the fact that it is played on the twelve-string neck of Earl's double guitar. "You Can't Hide"—based on a popular Afro-American saying popularized by Joe Louis when he used it in the forties as a boxing slogan—is another nice R&B vocal duet that Hooker's alto player provides with a weeping solo.

Although this Jim-Ko 45 was a tasty effort, it suffered from poor distribution and failed to become a bestseller. The single, meant originally to lead to bigger things for Hooker, Bobby, and Tommy, ended up leading to the breaking up of the Soul Twisters' nucleus because of the unsatisfied hopes it had roused. "They got into it all of a sudden with this record," Herb Turner recalls. "I guess Earl hadn't had a thing to do for a pretty good while, and that record caused a conflict. The record hadn't really did somethin', that's what it was. It sold I guess about fifteen thousand or somethin' like that. I would see 'em arguin', but I just decided to stay out of it. Bobby decided to go with J. J. Jackson and the Hitch-Hikers, and the whole band broke up. Tommy would call me then and say, 'I'm goin' by myself,' and Bobby said 'I'm goin' by myself.' Earl would do what he wanted to do anyway, and Earl had him another band, a whole new band for everybody except Pinetop [Perkins]."

If this failure did not affect Earl Hooker deeper than previous ones, the same could not be said of Tommy Isom, whose career came to an abrupt end. Drifting back into the North End of Waterloo, he assumed the function of farm worker at first before he became a forklift operator at the Engineering Equipment Company, according to city directories, which listed him under the name Tommie E. Ison. By 1973 Tommy had left Waterloo for an unspecified destination.

After spending some time as drummer with J. J. Jackson's band, and in spite of occasional stints with the Hooker band, Bobby Little progressively gave up his activities as a musician and became, in the course of time, personal driver for blues star Little Milton, disc jockey for various radio stations in Mississippi, and promotion man for small-time record companies, eventually moving to Clarksdale, where he led his own blues band on the weekend.

Hooker's next recording was a 1965 C.J. release that did little to enhance his career. Rather than the music itself, the choice of material was responsible for the weakness of C.J. 643, Carl Jones making sure as usual that the Hooker band was thoroughly rehearsed prior to the session. After two nights' work, Jones decided that the musicians were ready, and he brought them to the International Recording studios on Thursday, April 29, 1965. Taped first, "Wild Moments" is a simple and effective up-tempo number that showcases Earl's proficiency, his lightning-quick fingers running from one end of the guitar neck to the other as he picks the song's lilting melody to the swinging sound of Big Moose Walker's organ and Charles Lange's sax.

The second title shows Hooker under a less favorable light, as Earl manages to squeeze in yet another rendition of his overworked "Chicken," six years after the one he recorded on his first C.J. session. Three takes were recorded, the first two being instrumental, while the third one, chosen for release on the flip side of C.J. 643, featured weak vocals by Hooker. The main point of interest for listeners is to be found in the brassy intro passage, borrowed note for note from Junior Parker's first nationwide hit on the Houston-based Duke label in 1957, "Next Time You See Me." Although C.J. 643 was the label's final Hooker release, Carl Jones did bring Earl back to the studio shortly afterward, where an unknown vocalist fronting Hooker's band cut a mediocre track titled "I Can't Understand." The event was badly documented, due to the fact that it took place at the end of a session Carl Jones had set up for another group, but the poor quality of this forgettable item certainly accounts for its obscurity. It was put on the shelf until the late seventies, when Carl Jones decided to put it out on an uneven compilation album, but it doesn't add much to Hooker's musical heritage.

229   *Hooker and Cuca (1964–1967)*

The end of Hooker's partnership with Bobby Little and Little Tommy may seem regrettable from an artistic standpoint, but it didn't hinder Earl's course in the slightest. In no time, the guitarist put up the umpteenth version of his Soul Twisters around faithful partners like Johnny Big Moose Walker and Pinetop Perkins. This time Hooker's outfit was enlivened by the presence of one of his finest recruits, a young man named Freddie Roulette, who started to work probation periods with the band from late 1965. Unlike most bandleaders in Chicago, who chose their sidemen within a limited circle of musicians, Hooker had the knack of uncovering obscure talents whose musical capacities lay beyond the restricted scope of twelve-bar blues, and Roulette was no exception to the rule. Roulette was born in the Chicago suburb of Evanston on May 3, 1939, and his prime musical interest was in the country & western sounds that Hooker himself was so fond of. The influence of C&W was so compelling that when Roulette decided to take up the guitar as a youth, he favored the "lap steel," an eight-stringed instrument, placed flat on the guitarist's lap and played with a slide, whose slurring glissandos typify most C&W recordings.

Roulette lived his first blues experience in the Hooker outfit in the early sixties, after sitting in with Earl one night on the West Side at a club run by Hooker's former drummer and friend, Kansas City Red. "This was at the Boola-Boola," Red recalls. "I used to try to get the guys to join in with me, 'cause by me runnin' the club, I couldn't be on the bandstand too much. I would have a drummer there to play, and I would go up every once in a while. But I liked the way this guy [Roulette] played this thing, he was good. Earl Hooker always had some good musicians with him." Roulette's performance sounded promising enough, and Earl started hiring the young man with regularity because he was particularly keen on Roulette's ethereal slide style. When asked about his main source of influence, Roulette definitely states country & western: "I stem from C&W to R&B and then to pop, and then to blues. See instead of starting up from blues like most black musicians, man, I was in a bag. . . . I don't want to sound like anyone else. That's why I like steel—just make your own sound. . . . I only have played blues, real good blues, since I've been with Hooker. . . . I met him in some village joint called Kansas City Red's on the West Side, Lake Street. . . . He was sick then and didn't have any group. So I said I wanted to play with him. . . . The newest thing is that he is playing on a Gibson guitar, double neck, and with a slide...

accompanied with a steel guitar. That's the combination difference. That's why I started to play with Hooker because he plays slide and I play slide guitar. We blended so well. . . . We started playing a lot of local dates. With blues bands, this, that and the other, but we stayed together."[2] On the strength of the success that they met when they performed together, Hooker decided to feature Roulette's fluent playing on his next recordings. Instead of turning to Carl Jones this time, Hooker made arrangements over the phone with Jim Kirchstein in Wisconsin; after hastily putting together a pick-up unit in mid-1966, the two slide masters headed for Kirchstein's Sauk City studio, where Roulette's initial sides were cut.

Three instrumental tracks were put on wax on that occasion. The first two brought Roulette's playing to the fore, Hooker taking over on "Off the Hook" as Roulette swiftly tripped through clever steel guitar chordings. The resulting sides are slightly frustrating, for they are far from reaching the high standards that both guitarists would set on later recordings. "Two Bugs in a Rug" especially—its title alluding to Hooker's tuberculosis, which he humorously referred to as the "TB bug"—is a monotonous exhibition of Roulette's technique that drags on unnecessarily. "Hold On . . . I'm Coming" is a much more lively performance. This impressive instrumental rendition of Sam & Dave's number-one hit, aired on all black-oriented radios in the spring of 1966, does full justice to Roulette's proficiency, giving a fair idea of the way his playing blended with Hooker's intelligent chordwork. As for "Off the Hook," an average shuffle marred by a clumsy organ solo, it proves that the Hooker/Roulette combination is just as successful with Earl's playing to the fore.

For the second part of the session, Freddie Roulette put his lap steel down. Hooker, testifying to his versatility, stepped back out of the limelight to back up an unknown gospel singer who shared session time with him. Various gospel classics were recorded then with a fitting guitar/organ/bass/drums accompaniment, including a fine version of "Didn't It Rain" that Hooker deftly adorned with crisp runs. Before the day was over, Earl and Roulette were given another chance to play together when James Williams—a vocalist known as Muddy Waters Jr. on the South Side that Earl picked up at Theresa's Tavern before setting off for Wisconsin—fronted the band on one song. First drawing his inspiration from Little Walter's 1959 "Everything Gonna Be Alright," Muddy Waters Jr. then drifted into a medley of popular blues lyrics. Despite a vocal-like slide solo from Hooker, the song never really gets off the ground, partly because of the singer's bland styling and bad sense of dynamics.

As a whole, this second Cuca session suffered from Hooker's carelessness and inadequate choice of accompanists—with the exception of Roulette—and only the first three instrumental numbers were released when Kirchstein marketed Earl's first LP in 1968. Similar remarks apply to Hooker's next session, although technical problems were an added source of criticism this time. Earl's next recorded efforts, taped around late 1966, were not realized in the Cuca studio in fact, and if Jim Kirchstein presently holds them with the rest of his Hooker material, they were sent to him by Hooker, who originally intended to have them released on Cuca singles, according to a letter dated February 20, 1967 sent from Waterloo, Iowa: "Dear Sir, The tape that you have I want the two fast numbers from it. One is 'Hard and Heavy.' The other fast number I can't remember the name of it. So we will make a different name for it: call it 'The Yo-Yo.' The tape that I am sending you now—the third song is 'Hello Babe'—'Monrovia.' I want you to put 'Hard and Heavy' on one side and 'Hello Babe' on the other. Make one record with those two. Put 'The Yo-Yo' with 'Monrovia' on one record—making a fast side and a slow number. I want this above record pressed up and put out first. But make the other record and send it too," specified the guitarist who signed "Famous Earl Hooker and his Soul Thrillers."

Judging from the poor sound quality, this material was probably cut on a portable recorder, possibly by Hooker himself. Partly because of the questionable audibility of these tracks, it is difficult to assess their artistic value. Standing out are "Hello Baby"—a song that features a fine vocalist strongly influenced by Junior Parker, backed by Hooker's tasty playing—as well as a version of jazz pianist Mal Waldron's and saxophonist Gene Ammons's "Blue Greens and Beans," a driving bebop number propelled by Bobby Little's fiery drumming that provides Hooker with a fine opportunity to display his flawless technique. At any rate, poor sound and lack of preparation on Earl's part accounted for Kirchstein's decision not to release these recordings. As compensation, Kirchstein issued Earl's second Cuca single, but he gave preference to tighter efforts drawn from his initial Cuca session with A. C. Reed in 1964, and "End of the Blues" backed with "Dynamite" were put out in March of 1967 on Cuca J-6733.

In the perspective of the album he wished to devote to Hooker's playing, the limited number of worthy sides he had in the can incited Kirchstein to bring Hooker back to the studio; his confidence in Earl's potential was fully rewarded on the occasion of the next session that took place on a Sunday evening of April 1967. The seven tracks taped then presented Hooker in a favorable setting because he came to the Cuca studio with drummer Bobby Little and a well-rehearsed band. As was customary with Kirchstein, who seemed to be fond of organ players, a syncopated keyboard instrumental showcase with a flowing sax solo was taped first, quickly followed by one of Earl's favorite R&B dance themes, "Hooker Special." The band then moved into a bluesier bag with a fast guitar rendition of Otis Rush's "All Your Love (Coming Home)" boasting a fine saxophone solo. Other instrumental offerings that day included an inspired guitar-saxophone version of Albert Collins's widely influential "Frosty," as well as "Something You Ate," a lyrical number in which a Hooker in fine form poured forth fluid slide guitar lines.

The session's highlight came when Frank "Crying Shame" Clark—a singer Earl picked up in Waterloo, Iowa, on his way to Wisconsin—was asked to sing the session's two vocal numbers. Clark, in addition to his singing talent, was a gifted lyricist, as his coupling shows. Recorded first, "You Took All My Love" opens up with a terrific slide guitar intro from Hooker, who returns to the limelight after Clark's second verse long enough to deliver a breathtaking chorus. The other Frank Clark tune, a humorous tale of bad luck and misery titled "Got to Keep Movin' (The Misfit)," also features a fine Hooker solo, but it is the inventiveness of Clark's lyrics that makes it shine: "Run out of Rhode Island / Shot out in San Antone / Kicked out of Kansas City / I'm just like a rollin' stone." With such a list of woes to his credit, it doesn't take much to figure why Clark simply has to keep moving. Although the song wasn't released until 1985, its catchy lyrics emerged on "Bad Luck," a recording made for the Memphis-based Stax label in the early seventies by guitarist-singer and former Hooker disciple Albert King. The fact that Clark knew personally many southern bluesmen, including King's friend Larry Davis, would tend to indicate that King drew his inspiration directly from Clark.

Kirchstein's personal inclination for instrumental material made him discard "Got to Keep Movin'," but the musical density of Hooker's work on "You Took All My Love" encouraged him to use it when he released Earl's third

Cuca single in 1968 concurrently with Hooker's album. The flip side of Cuca J-1445 also belonged to the blues tradition. "Dust My Broom," recorded shortly after the April session that yielded Clark's palatable efforts, was taped on Earl's final Cuca date around the early summer of 1967, along with other instrumentals. This over-recorded standard, originally waxed in 1936 by Delta master Robert Johnson, was popularized in 1952 by another slide specialist, Elmore James. In his 1967 instrumental version, Earl succeeded in giving Robert Johnson's theme some freshness, his intricate straight-picked lines and elaborate slide variations placing "Dust My Broom" in a modern setting. Hooker's most effective licks come shortly before the band brings the number to a close as Earl makes a stunning display of his talking-guitar styling.

The rest of the session is a mixing of various musical idioms, bearing witness one more time to Earl's stylistic eclecticism. Rhythm & blues at first with "Hot & Heavy"—actually a reworking of the "Hooker Special" track recorded on his previous date—and the heavily syncopated "Screwdriver;" soul with an instrumental cover of James Brown's 1965 hit "I Got You (I Feel Good);" and country & westen with Bill Monroe's "Blue Moon of Kentucky." Other than Hooker, the work of a cousin of Ike Turner's and occasional member of Hooker's band, veteran saxophone player Bobby Fields, is worth mentioning, especially as he contributes a wild solo on "Hot & Heavy."

This mid-1967 recording date turned out to be Hooker's last one for Cuca, as Hooker was hospitalized in the late summer of 1967 for close to a year in Chicago, interrupting abruptly his musical activities; but for all of its dire consequences, this forced period of rest did not put an end to Earl's relationship with Kirchstein. With more than two dozen Hooker recordings in his vaults— only four of which had already been released on singles—Kirchstein was ready for a Cuca album release. The seriousness of Earl's condition came as a shock to Kirchstein, who realized that Hooker might not overcome his sickness. Not wanting future Hooker releases to be posthumous ones, he decided in 1968 to put out Earl's long-awaited Cuca LP before it was too late, opting for an all-instrumental release, although he had a handful of fine vocal sides at hand.

Around the same period of time, another producer came up a similar idea. With the development from the mid-sixties of the album market, label operators who had restricted their activities so far to the production of singles were beginning to follow the trend. One of these was Mel Collins, owner and manager of the Giant/Palos enterprise that also comprised subsidiary labels like Globe and Glory. As such, Collins was a well-known figure in the Chicago R&B community; Hooker knew him all the better because he was then his friend Ike Turner's brother-in-law. Some time in 1967, Collins and Hooker discussed the possibility of working together; an agreement was reached, and Earl walked into the Sound studios in downtown Chicago, where he and his band, including keyboard man Big Moose Walker, cut enough instrumental material for an album.

Very little is known about this session, for Collins never found the time to release Hooker's LP. "I had so many other things to do!" Collins said laconically during the summer of 1978 when asked about it as part of the research for this book. Even though he was later invited to lease his Hooker tapes, he was never able to locate them.

With time, Hooker's condition kept getting worse as he persistently refused to slow down. As hospital stays grew more frequent, it became harder for him to go on the road over extended periods of time. By 1967 his health had deteriorated to such an extent that he could no longer keep his sidemen busy enough to hire them on a lasting basis, and he started using hastily put up backing units every time he felt well enough to play an engagement, accounting for the unpredictability of his performances, whether live or recorded. Another source of work was the presence in Chicago of visiting acts like Junior Parker, Ike Turner, and Joe Hinton. Parker's friendship with Earl went back to the early postwar period in and around Memphis. Parker, who regularly hired top Chicago musicians when he played engagements around the city, often invited Hooker as a guest attraction on such occasions. Until 1968, when Parker finally decided to settle permanently in the Windy City, the "Little Junior Parker Show" was often billed at Chicago's famed Regal Theater, in the heart of the South Side. Parker's popularity also resulted in frequent club engagements throughout the sixties, thus providing Earl with opportunities to perform in front of appreciative audiences. More than just a way to keep him working, his on-and-off association with Parker proved profitable for Hooker, who was able to keep in touch with a source of inspiration that had already strongly marked his formative years. Subsequent signs of this showed in some of his recordings, his instrumental rendition of "How Long Can This Go On" for Age and his 1965 version of "Chicken" giving strong evidence of Parker's influence.

Besides Parker and Ike Turner—who hired Earl when the Ike and Tina Turner Revue visited northern Illinois—another artist who regularly used him when he appeared in Chicago at the time was Joe Hinton. Joseph Lee Hinton, born in 1929 in Evansville, Indiana, was a beautiful singer with a very moving voice and subtle delivery technique, who started out in the gospel business before he was persuaded to cross over to the rhythm & blues field; after gaining his professional start with the Blair Gospel Singers—he was related to the Blair clan—he started traveling with the Spirit of Memphis Quartet, appearing as lead tenor on many of their Peacock recordings. By the late fifties Peacock owner Don Robey realized that there was more money to be made in the secular field than in gospel for talented vocalists, and he urged Hinton to renege on his gospel roots.

Reluctantly at first, Hinton swapped his gospel robe for the tuxedo of a rhythm & blues balladeer, later joining the "Little Junior Parker Show" and achieving relative success on Robey's Back Beat label with "You Know It Ain't Right" in 1963 and more particularly "Funny (How the Time Just Slips Away)" one year later. On the strength of his bestsellers, Hinton left the Parker show and started a career on his own, traveling across the country at the head of his own Pinetoppers or Invaders. Joe Hinton was also the son of Mrs. Hooker's own sister. Earl particularly enjoyed performing with his cousin, and he often fronted Hinton's back-up unit, not only in Chicago, but along the one-nighter trail as well. "Yeah, we played a lot of shows with Joe Hinton up in Indiana, Evansville, Owensboro, Kentucky," Lee Shot Williams, himself a singer with the Hooker band, remembers. "Joe was livin' in Texas, in Houston, so he would come home [to Indiana], and him and Earl would play some dates together. Earl would be the band, and Joe would be the star. I'd be an openin' act. I know we played for him when he had out his record 'Funny How Time Slips Away' for Don Robey. We played with him a lot of times." But in the summer of 1967 a page was about to be turned, and Hooker would soon have to stop performing altogether: his tuberculosis was finally getting out of hand.

Two Bugs and a Roach

(1967–1968)

Bringing an end to the three-year period that followed the climax Hooker reached with Mel London, illness brutally interrupted Earl's career when he was rushed into the Illinois State TB Hospital with a particularly severe attack of tuberculosis in September 1967. This dark episode left Hooker with hardly any room for choice, for the medical staff warned him that he could either keep on with his work and meet a rapid death or accept forced rest in the TB ward until full recovery, and with reluctance, Earl submitted to his doctors' advice. Adding to this setback, his long stay in the hospital prevented the making of a commemorative photograph with rock 'n' roll star Chuck Berry scheduled for late 1967 at Berry's request.

This development hardly came as a surprise for Earl's entourage, who had long given up convincing him to attend properly to his health. Even though consumption was an almost endemic disease among Afro-Americans before World War II—segregated medical facilities being the rule in insalubrious, over-

237

populated ghetto communities—things had improved since vocalist Victoria Spivey put on wax her famous "TB Blues" in April 1927 for the OKeh company. At that time," Miss Spivey explained in 1960 to English blues historian Paul Oliver, "I had been lookin' at people who had the TB in part of the country and at that time if you had the TB nobody would have no part with you; they put you away in hospital and you was just doomed then, you gonna die. So I figgered it was a nice thing to write about."[1] Another major artist who evoked TB in his repertoire was country music pioneer Jimmie Rodgers, whose "TB Blues" and "Whippin' That Old TB" were courageous social commentaries on a disease that would kill him in 1933.

Since the chance discovery of the virtues of penicillin by Sir Alexander Fleming at London's St. Mary Hospital in 1928, additional research made during the war by the Anglo-Australian team of Chain, Florey, and Hartley had led to the development of powerful antibiotics that brought about miracles in the treatment of tuberculosis. Cases of consumption were still frequently detected in America during the fifties and sixties—especially in members of underprivileged social classes—but patients could now be cured if they received adequate medical treatment. By the time penicillin became widely used, it is likely that Earl's tuberculosis had reached a stage too advanced for doctors to restore his health completely, all the more when he started to develop a heart condition. As he stubbornly refused to get proper rest in a sanitarium where the medical staff could make sure he took his medication with regularity, his frequent hospital stays over the years barely enabled him to rekindle enough fire to keep up with his work until the next outbreak. "The main thing is that he didn't take care of hisself," Mrs. Hooker deplored. "I remember he was in Florida once, and he just didn't wear the right kind of clothes. Some peoples say that it's awful hot in Florida, but it's awful cold in Florida, too. By not takin' care of yourself, you can give yourself very bad things. In the hospital he got out, but it's a lot of times when he wouldn't go to the hospital, that's the main thing. Instead of stayin' in the hospital, he traveled on the highways."

Inadequate clothing and lack of proper food made Earl's condition worse. Mrs. Hooker, although she enjoyed a reputation as a fine soul food cook, grieved to see that her son made little account of the meals she prepared: "Earl wouldn't eat much, he was very thin. His daddy was the same. When you don't eat good, it's no good for you. And Earl, he didn't eat properly, he didn't like it.

No, he used to put it down like a pig." "He wasn't a big eater," Hooker's wife Bertha confirms. "I was after him about eatin', 'cause I know he was out on the road all the time. You can't eat on the go. He needed solid food in his stomach."

In spite of Earl's careless behavior, most of his friends voice their amazement at his resistance to a disease that is known for using up people's will as well as their bodies, but Big Moose Walker has an explanation for it: "The guitar kept him alive for fifteen years after he was sick. He loved the guitar as much as he did his life, I think. You take that guitar away from him, he wouldn't have lived that long. He was taken sick in the fifties. The reason he caught TB, I'm pretty sure it was exposure. Like not gettin' enough rest, not gettin' no sleep, maybe drinkin' or smokin' the wrong thing. And he didn't do anythin' for it, so it just grew and grew and grew. See, he was in a bad state because I remember, we was playin' in Sikeston, Missouri, and they gave him four hours to live. They got him out of Missouri, called an ambulance and drove him to Chicago. He got up and he got healthy and boom! you know. Every time he would get good enough to get back on his guitar, he'd leave the hospital. He joked a lot about it and laughed about it."

If Hooker adopted a carefree attitude about his illness toward the end of his life, he had tried to hide his sickness for years, as if refusing to acknowledge the seriousness of his condition. In fact, most of his associates were not even aware of it until they witnessed one of his scary attacks. This was the case with A. C. Reed, who knew nothing about Earl's tuberculosis for a long time even though the two men worked together extensively from the late forties: "I realized he was sick, I would say around the early sixties. We played up in Columbus, Ohio, once, and he got so sick he had to leave, and he coughed up blood in the car all the way to Chicago and went straight to the hospital."

More especially after 1963, Hooker's health deteriorated to such an extent that he was forced to get rid of the unconcerned front he had put on until then. As his illness grew, his incredible energy started running out, and he was compelled to reduce his stage acrobatics, the weight of his instrument becoming burdensome with years. "Hooker wasn't that sickly when he was young," Big Moose Walker reminisces. "Well, he always coughed a lot but he'd play standin' up all the time. He didn't start sittin' down 'til way out close to '64, from '64 on up to '69. He would stand up a while, then he would sit down and play." Another major change in Hooker's lifestyle came as alcohol progressively became intolerable. By the time he got married in 1963, he had already stopped drinking, according to his wife Bertha: "I heard that he used to drink, but after we got married, Earl Hooker did not drink. You'd hardly ever see him take a sip out of a beer. I always liked beer myself, and like they would stop playin', and if I's sittin' there at a table with a beer or somethin', he might have woulda taken a sip out of my glass. But beer, no. He always wanted juices, or 'Order me a cold pop!' He didn't even drink coffee, he would just drink pop, milk, and juices. But like I say, I don't know what he did before I got him. He probably was a drinker."

Bertha's feeling is supported by Big Moose Walker: "He quit drinkin' about six years before he died, but he used to drink. Me and him used to outdrink each other, he'd drink his gallon and I'd drink mine. But what I had on him in drinkin', see, when I went to the army, they taught me how much food and how much water and stuff, don't care how much alcohol you drink, and what to do for it. We drinked everythin'. Antifreeze, gas, shoe polish, canned heat, we drink it all. And I never lost appetite, see. I could drink, and then eat up everythin' I had, and drink plenty of water and next day, boom! I could do the same thing, still keep it goin' on for years. But Hooker didn't know that, so it was hurtin' him, see."

Drinking—like smoking in this respect—was more of a social habit than anything else for Earl, who lived in a milieu where many people smoke "reefers" and drink large quantities of alcohol, and he didn't seem to have much trouble stopping altogether, orange juice and Coca-Cola replacing beer and whiskey. "He didn't really like to drink. He wasn't a drinker," Billy Boy Arnold states. "One night we was going down on 63rd [Street], and somebody in the group said, 'Let's get a drink' and Hooker told him, said, 'Drinking's gonna be your downfall.' A lot of people will be sick and they can't stop drinking. But that wasn't his thing." Whereas his sister Earline was a true alcoholic, Earl considered drinking more a distraction than a need, making it easier for him to get away from it, but his loose attitude with regard to his sickness sometimes urged him to stretch his principles. "Every now and then, he would take a drink of alcohol," says B. B. Odom. "A little whiskey or beer, or a little shot of wine, anythin'. Because I used to get at him about it. He know he shouldn't drink, but he would do it anyway. 'Grandpa, I just got to get a little drink. I'm not gonna drink that much, this ain't gonna hurt me,' I said, 'No! Don't do that,' but he went on. He knew he was sick, but he knowed that if he didn't stay in the hospital, there wasn't no cure for him, and I think that's what really made him feel that he didn't give a damn. Enjoy hisself while he was livin'. Like he said, if music was to kill him, he didn't mind dyin'.'"

The most noticeable change brought by Earl's sickness was his ever-increasing need for sleep, an obvious sign that his condition was worsening. Until the mid-sixties Earl's stamina was legendary among his friends. "Earl would drive from [Chicago] to California by hisself. Earl ran that road so fast, he wouldn't close his eyes," Lee Shot Williams remembers. By the end of his life, Hooker expressed an increasing need for sleep, as if his energy was slowly running out. "He liked to sleep, that's one thing, and he don't wanna be bothered when he restin'," Mrs. Hooker recalls. As for cigarettes, the fact that nobody smoked in Earl's family proved helpful. In the same way that he wasn't a drinker, Earl wasn't a smoker, except for an occasional reefer, according to several early associates. The main problem he was confronted with when he performed was the thick clouds of smoke that couldn't be avoided in the crowded bars and taverns where he played most of the time. Herb Turner explains: "He just coughed constantly. Like if he was in a club playin', you know how it is. In fact, during intermissions, he'd leave out of the club. He'd go outside 'cause he couldn't stand the smoke. He'd go outside, and had milk, plenty."

Turner's account would tend to prove that, with time, Hooker was willing to compromise as long as it didn't keep him from playing and traveling. Still, he worked more than his body could stand. From the early sixties, forced hospital stays became more of a reality, and Hooker was hurried in a coma to the nearest medical facility on several occasions. It is likely that he would have met his fate earlier than he did but for the devotion and courage of his fellow musicians. This was especially true of Andrew B. B. Odom, who progressively got used to Earl's frequent hemorrhages and who always found a way of stanching spectacular blood flows, as was reported by guitarist Jimmy Dawkins in an article published in 1972: "Earl Hooker told me many times before he died, that Voice [Odom] saved his life—you see, Voice was with Hooker on the road most of the time in the last ten years and Hooker's health was very frail. Sometimes Hooker would play too hard or stay on the stage too long, and would start bleeding, due to his TB. Many times they would be way out—in the country where there is no doctor for many miles, and Voice, or Jr. as Earl called him, would somehow get help every time. Hooker felt that without Voice, he would have died long before his time came, in 1970."[2]

About ten years before he himself disappeared, B. B. Odom related with characteristic modesty two dramatic episodes related to Hooker's illness: "I probably did save his life a couple times. In Florida in '63, some big club, I forgot exactly what name, he had called me on the stage and 'bout the time I got to the stage, he said he had to go to the bathroom. So he stayed so long, and when I walked in the washroom, man, the cat was spittin' up lumps of blood that big, you know. Told 'em to bring me some towels and stuff, and I told the band, say, 'Hey, man, the man is sick, man. If you all gonna play, just keep on, but I got to take him to the hospital. And when he took sick in Waterloo, Iowa, we had to rush him back to Chicago. The doctors gave me a slip, just in case the police and state troopers would stop me, and show 'em this and I would have no problem. Which from Waterloo to Chicago takes quite a while, but the way I was drivin', I got him back here to the hospital in Chicago."

For obscure and somewhat superstitious reasons, Hooker was unwilling to undergo any kind of surgery, and his first reaction every time he woke up in a hospital ward consisted of scheming a way of escaping what he regarded as discretionary detention. Such a provocative and challenging behavior was not to the liking of Hooker's attending physicians. According to his wife Bertha, it plagued to a certain extent his relationship with his doctors: "Earl got along with those peoples, except runnin' off when he thought he was well enough, and they wouldn't let him go. See, I guess he felt that he felt all right, and he would just take off without bein' dismissed. Then when he used to get so run down he had to go [to the hospital], that's when he'd go. When he had to. At least about once a year. Sometime twice a year. He had medicine to take, and shots. It would help, but then he would go so long. But that guitar was his life. He really loved that guitar."

Earl's ways also exposed him to the disapproval of his band members. Understandably, they were reluctant at sharing the stage with a contagious consumptive patient. Big Moose Walker remembers: "We used to chase him off the bandstand. He got to the point we didn't want him out, he got contagious like, you know. So we wanted to take him back home, and Hooker would look and see me, and zoom! We didn't know one thing, he was gone! But I got him out of the hospital in Midland, Texas, and I got him out of the hospital in Florida, in Tampa. I signed for him. I told the peoples that I was gonna take him back to Chicago. We had to play the jobs and everybody in the band signed." Hooker did not always depend on the goodwill of his men to get a release from the hospital, and his resourcefulness proved useful on various occasions, as is shown by the following episode related by Herb Turner: "He went to Florida. He went down there on a tour, and he got sick. They carried him to the hospital, and they found out he had TB, and they had Hooker locked up, but he broke out. He tied his sheets together to get out, and he beat the band back to Chicago. He got back before they did!"

The safest way of luring Earl Hooker into a hospital was to invite him to give a free performance for patients, a request he rarely turned down. Earl was aware of the reality that confronted the sick, and he regularly played benefit gigs at various locations in the sixties. Over the years, such informal concerts took place at the Chicago Municipal Tuberculosis Sanitarium on Pulaski Road, in the northwestern part of the city; at the State TB Hospital; or at the Veterans Administration Hospital, two medical institutions standing opposite each other on Taylor Street in the near West Side. On another occasion, a special appearance was set up within the walls of an institution where blues patriarch Howlin' Wolf was undergoing treatment.

Hooker's own sojourns at the Municipal Sanitarium, and more especially at the State TB Hospital, where he was usually sent, had a tendency to last longer with time, to the point that he sometimes told business relations like Cuca Records' Jim Kirchstein that they could reach him "care of the TB Hospital, 1919 West Taylor in Chicago." Every time Earl underwent treatment, giving a concert was a good way of breaking the monotony of his existence and of keeping in touch with his friends. A habitué of these impromptu concerts was drummer Kansas City Red, who clearly remembered a gig Hooker had set up: "I know they had him at the hospital out here, 'cause I visited him at this sanitation, what d'you call it. I went to see him 'cause he give a party out there, we went out there and played, me and him and Morris Pejoe. We played for the peoples in his ward. And after that, he would slip out so much and the next thing I know, he would be back down that road. He was really hard to keep up with."

"He wanted us to come out there and play for other sick peoples," A. C.

Reed confirms. "He was a patient then, but they're gonna let him out so we put on a show for the sick peoples there before they let him out." By B. B. Odom's recollections, such performances were unpaid, but the musicians were usually rewarded for their efforts: "You wouldn't get paid, but they would give you a little donation for comin' by. They would send you a check for twenty dollars, twenty-five dollars. Then you have food and stuff there for you to eat, a few drinks, you know."

In spite of his strong distrust of medicine and surgery, Hooker got along well with doctors, and more particularly with nurses, who in their turn took a liking to their unruly patient. "He just liked to have fun with 'em," Andrew Odom remembers. "He was always talkin' about leavin' and gettin' up; he was just a jokeful guy. You blocked up in a place, man, you got to do somethin'. So you have to joke when you can, because, hey! If you're not used to these things, man, it's kinda rough on you." The friendly relations Hooker entertained with most staff members indicate why he did his best to show his gratitude; as a benign move, he even agreed to appear on a poster advertising an Illinois Medical Board campaign against cancer, which Mrs. Hooker still proudly showed her visitors long after the death of her son.

September 1967 marked the start of Hooker's ten-and-a-half-month stay at 1919 West Taylor Street, the Illinois State TB Hospital, where he was taken after suffering his most critical attack of tuberculosis ever, according to Big Moose Walker: "That time, he stayed longer than the other times. That's when he did cough up some of his lungs, that's why he stayed in the hospital that eleven months. Like I never seen a man—well, he had nine lives anyway. I never seen a man bleed that much, man. Yeah! We were steady carryin' him out of the house."

Earl's was a familiar face both at the State TB Hospital and at the Municipal Sanitarium in Chicago, where he inevitably wound up every time his sickness got out of hand; in fact, they were the only institutions that a black Chicagoan like himself could afford to go to. The fact that many nurses were fond of Hooker probably made it easier for him to endure his misfortune. Another diversion came with the frequent phone calls he made to Jim Kirchstein in Sauk City, trying to find out about the release of his album or plugging new talent for Cuca. One such talent was Minnie Singer, who actually ended up doing recordings for Kirchstein, as the latter recalls: "Yes, he called a lot. Collect.

But I never even gave it a thought about accepting a collect call from him, because you kinda knew in talking with him that things were going to end up better at the end of the conversation, even though you didn't know what the conversation was gonna be about. The Minnie Singer recordings was a result of a phone call from Earl asking if I would record the groups that were at his hospital, and I agreed. Miss Singer was a nurse that helped Earl. Minnie was attractive, probably about thirty-five at the time, and delightful to work with. Earl was too ill at that time to make the trip, but [guitarist] Jimmy Dawkins was with her."

Other than phone calls, Earl Hooker received visitors, including his mother and sister, his wife Bertha, and various lady friends with his children, as well as close friends like Big Moose Walker, Pinetop Perkins, and Louis Myers. Hooker's main confidant during this whole period was guitarist Jimmy Dawkins, who was himself treated for tuberculosis in the same ward. Dawkins, a guitarist whose proficiency earned him the nickname "Fast Fingers," was raised in the Mississippi town of Pascagoula on the Gulf of Mexico, in the southeastern part of the state. After making his professional debut in the New Orleans of the mid-fifties, Dawkins made the move to Chicago in 1957. By the time he met Earl Hooker during the summer of 1965, he had become one of the most promising upcoming talents on the West Side, and their first encounter was the start of a lasting friendship. "I met Hooker back in August 1965," Dawkins wrote a few years later. "He was sitting on top of an old upright piano, playing his guitar. I could see he was the best around, even then. As he sat up there playing he was making his guitar sing and talk. He had a slide on his finger an' he was playin' 'No More Doggin'" and making his guitar sing it. I just walked in because I heard the band, but I stayed 'til closing time just to dig this crazy music man. So that's how we became good friends from then on."[3]

Through the force of circumstances, Earl and Fast Fingers saw a lot of each other when they both happened to be hospitalized at 1919 West Taylor in 1967. The presence of a fellow musician with whom he could practice and trade musical ideas was a tremendous help to Hooker, who usually found it hard to remain cooped up in a hospital room all day long. Even after Fast Fingers was allowed home at the end of his treatment, the two men stayed in close touch. Dawkins visited his friend whenever he could spare an hour, whereas Hooker made frequent phone calls to the Dawkins family apartment at unpredictable hours.

Throughout this extended period, Hooker's favorite occupation was to play his guitar by himself. With the help of a portable tape recorder, he spent most of his time putting his latest licks on tape, in order to test them out and keep a trace of his constant innovations, much to the despair of his mother, who strongly disapproved of his keeping all of his instruments at his bedside. Mrs. Hooker knew that her son would never get the rest he needed to fully recover as long as his guitar was within reach. "Oh yes, God, oh yes don't ask me!" Mrs. Hooker chuckled when asked if Earl was allowed to keep his guitar in his room. "I had to lock it up to keep him from playing, but he'd get up and try to get that guitar! Oh yes, Lord! The doctors helps him, they helps him! They would go and slip that guitar to him, because the doctors was so sweet to him."

Hooker seemed to enjoy a privileged status at the hospital, a fact confirmed by Jimmy Dawkins in the following description he wrote for a portrait of Hooker published in England shortly afterward: "Whenever Hooker goes in the hospital he never stops playing, he has all his instruments there too. He has the band come out there too as often as he can, and then he plays with the band for the other patients. His doctor nearly has a fit! But he must have his guitar, and I am steady carrying him tape as he loves to record his playing while he is in the hospital. When he is well enough the doctor lets him play his guitar in a room by himself—they feel he will worry himself to death if they don't let him have his guitar. Although while there he is sick, he has his guitar and amplifier, organ and tape recorder all around his bed and any other places he can put it. That's the way he is. Then he always calls me anytime night or day to see what I think of his latest idea he has just put on tape, and he plays it over the phone to me. He is Mr. Music himself!"[4]

Hooker's inability to rest properly ended up tying him to his bed longer than anticipated, and it was not before the summer of 1968 that his attending doctor decided he was strong enough to leave Room 309. In late July Hooker was free to go home at last, as was reported by Jimmy Dawkins in a letter dated July 22 to British blues magazine *Blues Unlimited*: "Earl Hooker is in the TB hospital, but doing fine and looking to go home any day now. I went to see him early today—he has been ill eleven months now."[5] This long-awaited release should have been a happy one, but it was saddened shortly afterward by the sudden death of Earl's cousin Joe Hinton. Afflicted with a particularly dire case of skin cancer that hindered the last years of his career, Hinton passed away in a Boston hospital at 4:00 A.M. on August 13.

In late July 1968 Earl Hooker was back on his feet again, released from the grim routine of the TB ward. Having almost recovered, he felt well enough to proceed with his career, but doctors recommended a well-balanced life involving proper rest, appropriate food, and adequate clothing for Chicago's blistering cold winters and sticky hot summers. Through the force of circumstances, Hooker spent his first few days of freedom at his mother's apartment located in the heart of the South Side at 4025 South Park. Getting back to a normal existence again was not as simple as might have been expected. Since his arrival at 1919 West Taylor ten and a half months earlier, things had changed in the Windy City, particularly in the black ghetto, where many South and West Side residents had not yet recovered from the violence that erupted following the assassination of Martin Luther King Jr. on Thursday, April 4, 1968. At the time, urban Blacks in anger rioted in more than a hundred American cities. Chicago was one of the hardest hit, with nine African Americans dying in the process, after Mayor Richard Daley sent his police his infamous order to "shoot to kill any arsonist, and shoot to maim or cripple anyone looting."[6] On April 5, as rioting broke out on the West Side, twenty blocks were burned to ashes. The South Side was not spared, and April 6 saw angry rioters move into the vicinity of the University of Chicago as more fires were set and more white-owned stores looted. In late July the scars of these terrible events could still be seen in many ghetto areas. On the last day of July, Hooker's own street, South Park, was even symbolically renamed Dr. Martin Luther King Drive by a falsely repentant Mayor Daley, who eulogized Dr. King in public while calling him "a rabble rouser, a troublemaker" in private, according to veteran Chicago journalist Mike Royko.[7]

Earl Hooker had a good occasion to renew his ties with the Chicago music scene at an All Star Blues Show given at the Regal Theater, located at 4719 South King Drive—a few blocks down the street from Mrs. Hooker's apartment. The Regal, with its oriental-looking street front and Moorish-style showroom, was a remnant of a breed of black theaters that included the Howard in Washington, D.C., and the famed Apollo, operated by Frank Schiffman in New York's Harlem, the tradition of which went back to the Swing Era and the big band sounds of Cab Calloway, Erskine Hawkins, and Duke Ellington. Over the years these temples of black popular music managed to keep abreast of constantly changing beats and trends; with time, rhythm & blues and soul acts noisily tiptoed their way to these much respected stages. Still, theaters like the Regal were no longer suited to accommodate the large teenage audiences that supported the popular soul bands of the late sixties. With the development of roomier and more modern concert venues, these historically prestigious monuments were becoming anachronistic, and the Regal finally pulled the curtain late in 1968.

Until the end, the Regal remained Chicago's best-known jazz, blues, and soul showcase. Early 1968 shows included the James Brown Revue in February, Jackie Wilson and Wilson Pickett in March, Stevie Wonder, Maurice & Mac and the Detroit Embers in June, as well as the Vibrations and the rapidly rising Jackson Five for a July 12 concert. R&B and jazz players were regularly featured there as well on the occasion of marathon shows that never failed to attract, in addition to Chicago's black middle class, significant members of the local blues milieu. The concert attended by Earl Hooker and his friend Jimmy Dawkins on Wednesday, August 7 clearly belonged to that tradition; for a three-dollar admission ticket, an enthusiastic all-black crowd of a several hundred were treated that evening to the stage shows of no less than six name artists—Albert King, Little Milton, Fenton Robinson, B. B. King, Bobby "Blue" Bland, and Junior Parker—whereas the concert provided Hooker with a chance to get back into the mood when he was invited to sit in with his friend B. B. King.

Hooker's first decision following his release from the TB Hospital was to set up a new outfit. This proved no easy task, since most of his former sidemen had gone their own way when they realized that Hooker's hospital stay would last longer than usual. Johnny Big Moose Walker was temporarily unavailable, and A. C. Reed, Earl's favorite tenor saxophonist, had joined the Buddy Guy band on a permanent basis. After making the rounds of the ghetto taverns and clubs, starting with Pepper's Lounge at the corner of 43rd and Vincennes, where freelance blues musicians were known to hang around in search of a gig, Hooker managed to pick up a drummer and a bass player. Hiring a capable keyboard specialist was slightly more difficult, but the obstacle was rapidly overcome after Earl's old friend Pinetop Perkins agreed to resume his seat in the Hooker band, temporarily entrusting Perkins Jr. with his South Side laundry and cleaning business. "My son here can take over when I have somewhere to play a gig," Pinetop explained then in an interview. "That boy is big enough to do good work while I'm gone."[8]

Next on Earl's list was lap steel wizard Freddie Roulette, whose novel sound blended particularly well with Earl's own playing, evidence of this being found in the handful of recordings made for Cuca in 1966. In the late summer of 1968, Hooker also welcomed in his band a new addition, Carey Bell, whose adroit harmonica blowing developed the overall sound of the band and compensated to a large extent for the absence of a saxophonist. "When the riots happened (April 5, 1968) I was in Morton Grove working in a car wash," Carey wrote the following year in the liner notes to his first album. "I made it home but the building was burned down. I lost everything but my wife and four kids—guitar, amps, clothes, everything were gone. I needed money so I went on the road with Earl Hooker."[9] Bell, a disciple of "Big" Walter Horton and "Little" Walter Jacobs, had remained in relative obscurity so far, although he was at thirty-two one of the most promising harmonicists on the Chicago scene. His mastery of the chromatic harmonica in particular marked him as a worthy heir to Little Walter, who had dominated blues harp playing with his original song-writing and creative playing for nearly two decades before meeting a brutal death earlier in 1968. In addition to his proficiency on the harmonica, Bell was a fine bass player, and his highly personal singing style was featured on the bandstand in between efforts by both Hooker and Pinetop Perkins. Yet the band's appointed vocalist was Earl's protégé Andrew B. B. Odom, who resumed his seat as lead singer in Earl's outfit as soon as the latter returned to the stage.

This ace band first started out locally around Chicago, but Hooker soon managed to set up one of his instant-made tours across the midwestern states, as was to be expected. By mid-August Earl left the Windy City with his double-neck guitar and his new recruits, disregarding the strict instructions of his doctors, who advised him against such exhausting road trips, at least for a period of several months. "Even now I am trying to talk him out of playing his double-neck guitar as it is very heavy," Jimmy Dawkins wrote in the *Blues Unlimited* column at the time. "He is in and out of the hospital every year, but he has not been back since he's been out this time. . . . He is up and about playing, but he is not very strong as of now, but he won't take it easy, so it is sad to see."[10]

This late summer 1968 tour saw the band burn up the usual route that led from Chicago south to Evansville in southern Indiana, on to Guthrie—right at the Kentucky-Tennessee state line—north of the Clarksville, Tennessee, area. Hooker then headed back toward Illinois through Owensboro with a stopover at the Ohio River town of Paducah, Kentucky. After playing a set of dates in southern Missouri, where his wife Bertha still lived with her two children, Earl visited his favorite Cairo haunts before driving back up through Champaign-Urbana on his way to Kankakee; the string of one-nighters eventually came to an end at one of the various taverns found in Rockford, Illinois, where Hooker always performed when he went through town.

It did not take long before this exceptionally brilliant outfit started making noise on the Chicago blues scene. By the time Hooker and his gang moved back to the Windy City after their successful tour, they had gotten into their stride. As a tight and coherent unit, they rapidly made a name for themselves outside the boundaries of the South Side club world. Somehow Hooker had managed to create a perfectly balanced show that appealed to the most critical audience, with the right amount of vocal work ranging from Pinetop Perkins's traditional boogie-woogie tunes to Carey Bell's and Andrew Odom's modern urban idiom. The instrumental side of Hooker's act, more developed than was the case with most blues performers, remained exciting at all times with its constant dialogues between Hooker's guitar and Roulette's lap steel.

Another innovation was Hooker's recently acquired wah-wah box, an electronic device just put on the market at the time that Earl, constantly in the vanguard of his art, was one of the very first to control to full effect. To this day, critics concur in the opinion that Hooker stands as the most proficient master of the wah-wah technique, on a level only with Jimi Hendrix. "Hendrix and Earl Hooker are the only cats I've heard who use the wah-wah pedal effectively,"[11] blues-rock guitarist Elvin Bishop once told *Guitar Player* reporter Tam Fiofori. Legend often has it that Hooker "invented" wah-wah, but the truth is more simple. Long before manufacturers of electronic equipment developed wah-wah pedals in the wake of the psychedelic rock wave of 1966–67, a handful of gifted electric blues guitarists perfected a similar technique, obtaining wah-wah sonorities with the tone control of their instrument. Since the fifties, Earl Hooker in Chicago and Johnny Heartsman in California had used in their playing this vocal-like style that evoked the "talking trumpet" sound created by jazz players as early as the 1920s, and the advent of electronic pedals—unquestionably generated by such pioneer efforts—made it possible for Earl to take this art one step further.

To that extent, his long hospital stay proved beneficial, since it enabled him to master this new device that he experimented with on the bandstand as soon as he returned to the stage, his friend Dick Shurman explains: "They started to make them around like late '67 or early '68, and that's about the time he got his. I know he was using one right after I came here. I was talking to Louis [Myers] and he told me that Hooker had come by to sit in with Louis, and Hooker had brought his wah-wah even when he was sitting in. I would imagine by the fact that he would carry it around, that he probably got into it not too long before that and was really kinda obsessed. Despite the fact that some very conservative blues fans are down on wah-wah, to me it's a thing that's really well suited to blues because it's a very vocal sort of a thing, and that's what blues instrumentation is about. And he used it with taste."

With time, Hooker proved that the wah-wah pedal was not a temporary diversion for him. As his mastery of the device increased, its vocal sound became part of his personal styling and even turned into his trademark, playing in the last two years of his life a role similar to that of slide. Far from giving up on his slide style on account of the wah-wah box, his combined use of both effects accounted for part of his success throughout his last year of musical activity, as he managed to draw from his instrument the most stunning, almost human, sounds.

A spirit of mutual understanding prevailed among the various members of Earl's new outfit, and despite regular changes that took place at the level of the rhythm section, Hooker, Pinetop Perkins, Carey Bell, Freddie Roulette, and B. B. Odom stuck together until the end of the year. The cohesion and drive of this ensemble were widely acclaimed everywhere they played by both black club patrons and white blues aficionados, most of whom considered this group one of the best Earl had ever carried with him. The band even succeeded in drawing the attention of Bob Koester, owner of Chicago-based Delmark Records, who still spoke of it admiringly ten years later: "I'm far from a student of Earl Hooker, and I was always interested in singers, and when I'd go to clubs, Earl would never sing in clubs. But that other band he had with Carey and Roulette, boy, that was a hell of a band! He had enough good singers in that band. Roulette didn't sing, but he'd play so fine. Pinetop was with them, claim-ing that he wrote 'Pinetop's Boogie Woogie.' Of course we found out later that he didn't, although he did record it for Sun. That band was really amazing, and they got even better after that. I remember one of the times I went to see them. Chris Strachwitz was in town, and he said with his Polish accent, 'I'm going to record Earl Hooker,' and he invited me to come along and we went to the White Rose out in Phoenix, and I was just astounded at how good a band it was."

The one-year gap tuberculosis made in Hooker's career led to major changes on the studio front. Between 1964 and 1967 Jim Kirchstein's Cuca company was Earl's main recording opening, but Kirchstein progressively gave up his ac-tivities after he accepted a position with the University of Wisconsin, and Hooker stopped recording for Cuca. In fact, he never returned to Sauk City af-ter his release from the hospital, although he kept in touch with Kirchstein, who finally released twelve Hooker tracks on a Cuca LP in the fall of 1968. But most of all, the rapidly developing blues album business was going to provide Earl with new opportunities to record.

Surprisingly, practically all the offers Earl received during his last year of ac-tivity emanated from California-based labels. The first person who put on tape Hooker's new sound was Chris Strachwitz, a Silesian count by birth whose un-canny taste for ethnic music induced him in November 1960 to start up his own Arhoolie record company on the West Coast. A large share of the early Arhoolie catalog was dedicated to rural blues albums by southern artists, but af-ter 1965 Strachwitz interspersed his production work with the amplified Chicago blues sounds he recorded on the occasion of regular visits to the Windy City. In anticipation of a forthcoming trip to Illinois, Strachwitz asked the advice of guitarist Buddy Guy, who was playing a set of concerts in north-ern California in June 1968. By Strachwitz's recollections, Guy's reaction was very spontaneous: "If you ever ask a Chicago bluesman about who is the best guitar player in town, they will admit it's Earl Hooker. Some time ago I asked Buddy Guy about other guitar players in Chicago who should be recorded more extensively and he immediately said, 'Earl Hooker' and even gave me his ad-dress which in the world of blues is a rare treat!"[12]

A first letter to Hooker brought Strachwitz an audition tape containing part of the material Earl had taped in Wisconsin for Cuca, along with a couple of

Lillian Offitt sides for Chief, interspersed with DJ-like narrations. Strachwitz was slightly put off by what he heard, for it failed to give a clear picture of Hooker's potential. Besides the fact that it presented him in a largely instrumental setting, it hardly showcased the guitarist's bluesier side. Strachwitz actually postponed any decision to record Hooker and band until he arrived in Chicago in early November 1968, when he heard them for the first time on Saturday, November 9, at the White Rose—the gambling joint mentioned by Bob Koester, located in the suburb of Phoenix at 153rd and Vincennes.

"So when I got to Chicago in November I called Earl and he told me to come by that night to hear his band at the White Horse Inn [actually the White Rose] on the South Side and with Delmark Records' Bob Koester I went and was indeed pleasantly surprised," Strachwitz reported. "I am not a musician myself but I know what I like and Earl Hooker really got to me. Not only was I overwhelmed by his incredible guitar playing—with impeccable taste and using his instrument to its fullest—his beautiful 'slide' guitar style and clear picking—the haunting use of the wah-wah effect—but also by Earl's pleasant singing and his fantastic band!"[13]

Strachwitz was so overwhelmed by Hooker's talent that he offered on the spot to record the band, and an agreement was reached with Hooker that very night at the White Rose. Things started moving fast; after making the necessary arrangements, Strachwitz invited the band to join him at Sound studios, found in downtown Chicago at the mouth of the Chicago River at 230 North Michigan Avenue, where they started working with engineer Dave Antler on Tuesday, November 12.

As contradictory as it may seem, this session remains Hooker's most unhurried one. Strachwitz, who had in view an elaborate full-album-length date, organized things to the best of his ability. And although it had hardly been planned, this session turned out to be different from most of Earl's previous fly-by-night dates—with the notable exception of his first Cuca session—when he would merely improvise enough material for a single release. At last, he was granted enough studio time to concentrate on the quality of his guitar tone and the choice of his repertoire. Strachwitz also understood the implications of Earl's sickness, and it didn't take him much time to realize that the standards of his album would be higher if Hooker was given a chance to stop whenever he felt too weak to play. Consequently, this first Arhoolie recording date took place over a full three days—November 12, 14, and 15—so Earl could give his very best.

The band used for these extended sessions was for the most part the one Hooker had been using since the summer, and the results were all the more convincing now that Earl and his men were used to working with each other. In addition to Freddie Roulette, Pinetop Perkins, Carey Bell, and B. B. Odom, drumming was shared between Levi Warren and W. Williams, and Earl used his regular bass player, a white musician named Chester "Gino" Skaggs, who usually worked during the daytime as a cab driver, his wife taking over when her husband performed with the Hooker band.

Another change of note from Earl's previous output was that the session was shared equally between vocal and instrumental sides, Hooker himself handling two of the songs, leaving the remaining three in the care of Carey Bell and B. B. Odom. Earl's own vocal attempts were the most attractive ones, and they proved that his voice deserved more attention than it had been granted so far. This was obvious on "Anna Lee," recorded first on Thursday, November 14 as a tribute to Earl's mentor Robert Nighthawk. The song's history sums up quite well Hooker's slide styling. Initially waxed in Chicago under the title "Anna Lou Blues" by the most proficient of early slide masters, Tampa Red, in the spring of 1940, the song emerged as "Annie Lee Blues" on a Robert Nighthawk 78 released in 1949 on the Chess brothers' first label, Aristocrat. The contrast between Tampa Red's urbanized work and Nighthawk's rougher Delta technique was strongly marked on those early efforts, but Earl Hooker managed to transcend his masters in his rendition of the theme as he combined the sophistication and airiness of Tampa Red's elaborate touch with the brutal sensitivity of Nighthawk's turbid playing. After he successfully re-creates with a pure Nighthawk intro the lazy atmosphere so typical of postwar Delta sounds, Hooker lets loose his musical imagination. Surprisingly, his singing never falls short of his guitar work, and his phrasing even sounds quite elaborate for someone who had always been considered a limited vocalist. Throughout these six minutes and thirty seconds of genuine perfection, Earl's work is perfectly complemented by the band's, including Willie Williams's fat drum sound, strongly reminiscent of the Delta beat, and Pinetop Perkins's piano lines, which take him back twenty-five years to his days in the Robert Nighthawk band. As for the fine Little Walter–influenced harmonica part featured on "Anna Lee," it is the work of Earl's childhood friend Louis Myers, who unexpectedly stopped in at Sound studios that day. Myers insisted on making a surprise appearance on this only track, but he was in such a hurry that he did not even take off his coat during the performance.

Earl's second song, "You Don't Want Me," is a retitled and slower version of the "Yea Yea" track cut nine years earlier for Carl Jones. Although no spectacular rendition of this Clayton Love–Ike Turner composition, it features fair vocals, innovative slide/wah-wah passages as well as a flowing steel guitar solo contributed by Freddie Roulette, complete with spirited variations on the venerable "Dust My Broom" theme. "Two Bugs and a Roach," the track that gives its name to the album, is a rocking instrumental showcase already present on earlier Cuca rehearsal tapes that Hooker intended as a tribute to his long stay in the hospital. "He figured that he had accomplished a thing about bein' recoverin' from TB," singer B. B. Odom explains. As such, the song was introduced by a conversation between Odom and Earl, in which the latter acknowledges the role played by his guitar in his bout against consumption—the "TB bug" in Hooker's own words:

-Hey, Earl Hooker, where you been so long, man?
-Aw, man! I been out there at 1919 West Taylor!
-What you was doin' out there, man?
-Aw, man I was out there messin' 'round with Randy and Doctor Newhower, man! I had to get rid of them two bugs and that roach I had.
-How you do that?
-Aw, man I hit it somethin' like here, Jack!

This question-and-answer rigamarole was one of three Odom contributions at the time of these November sessions, after "Take Me Back to East St. Louis" and "You Don't Love Me." When the album was edited a few weeks later, Strachwitz decided to put the former on the shelf, where it remained until 1998, when it was finally included in an Arhoolie reissue CD. Unlike "Take Me Back," "You Don't Love Me" didn't have to stay in limbo, and it gives a fair idea of the mutual understanding between Odom's singing and Hooker's sparing guitar lines, subtly underlined by Roulette's steel guitar licks. These sessions also were a premiere for Carey Bell, who made his very first appearance on record with "Love Ain't a Plaything"—a personal composition showcasing fair vocals and inspired harp sentences—and a barely reworked version of Little

Walter's widely influential "Juke" titled "Little Carey's Jump." Probably because of its derivativeness, Strachwitz didn't see fit to put it out until thirty years later.

As usual, Hooker insisted on recording a set of powerhouse guitar instrumentals on which he could let loose his formidable imagination. Recorded last on Friday, November 15, "Off the Hook" is a brilliant bebop number Earl cut with Gino Skaggs and drummer Levi Warren. Despite the use of the same title on former Hooker recordings, this so far unrecorded number shows the extreme care and taste with which the guitarist used the tone range of his instrument. As for "Earl Hooker Blues," taped three days earlier, it clearly belongs to the R&B bag, this wah-wah track actually being an instrumental cover of Little Milton Campbell's "Long Distance Operator," released a decade earlier on the St. Louis–based Bobbin label.

As was already the case earlier with "Anna Lee," the reference to Tampa Red and Robert Nighthawk is obvious in Hooker's next instrumental piece, an updated version of the classic "Black Angel Blues" theme created by Lucille Bogan and popularized by Tampa Red. More than a mere display of his matchless command of the slide, this "New Sweet Black Angel" is a masterly lesson on the history of postwar blues music as Earl re-creates step by step the evolution of the down-home Delta style, starting with a faithful imitation of Nighthawk's flowing slide licks, then moving on to some excellent electric picking, before he alludes to the future with his own progressive wah-wah contributions. Earl's new styling is even more to the fore in "Wah-Wah Blues," this flawless demonstration of Hooker's mastery of the wah-wah pedal proving that it is very well suited to blues as long as it is used with taste and feeling. This slow blues in the line of Hooker's 1962 bestseller "Blue Guitar" shows the range of Hooker's musical palette, ranging from straight picking to slide/wah-wah passages.

At the end of three active days of work, Hooker's first Arhoolie session thus came to a close, and when Chris Strachwitz left Chicago that same Friday heading for St. Louis, Missouri, he had on tape more tracks than he could possibly fit onto a long-playing record. Compiling the album and deciding the numbers that needed to be deleted was no easy task for Strachwitz when he released Hooker's *Two Bugs and a Roach* a few months later, but at any rate, this fine crop proved that Earl's music could be presented at his best if both care and time were given to the production of his recordings.

Bob Koester, owner of Delmark Records, deeply impressed by Hooker's band when he heard them in early November at the White Rose, was pleasantly surprised when he discovered that Hooker had put Carey Bell back on the blues trail after almost two years of musical inactivity. He approached the harmonicist shortly afterward, and Bell agreed to start working on his own set for Delmark. In the meantime, Koester offered to use him on the forthcoming session of Tennessee-born guitarist and singer "Sleepy" John Estes. In an attempt at revitalizing the old player's repertoire, Koester's fourth Estes release was intended as a humorous answer to Muddy Waters's latest Chess-Cadet LP, *Electric Mud*. Looking for young blues talent in anticipation of his *Electric Sleep* John Estes session, Koester put together an urban combo that included, among others, Carey Bell on harp and Jimmy Dawkins on guitar. On the first Tuesday of December, as Estes and his electric band were about to start recording at Sound studios, Earl Hooker showed up with his sister and asked to sit in on a couple of numbers.

Koester felt reluctant at letting Hooker take Dawkins's place, but he found a way to use him anyway, as he recalls: "He looked very sick, he was in a state of exhaustion and he asked to sit in, so we decided to use him on bass. He had his two-neck bass I think, and Carey had brought his bass player along as well." Of the four tracks on which Hooker appeared, "Newport Blues" remained unissued until 1991, while "May West," "How to Sing These Blues" and "If the River Was Whiskey" saw the light on Delmark LP 619. At the time of release, Koester made a mistake on the personnel listing printed on the album sleeve, and part of Earl's bass work was credited to Joe Harper and vice versa. This inversion is easy to detect, since the styles of Harper and Hooker have very little in common, Earl's busy bass lines showing that his supremacy as a guitarist didn't have much influence on his mediocre bass playing.

Earl managed to keep busy around the city following that session, although he was plagued with recurring health problems. A major event was the release of *The Genius of Earl Hooker*, the long-awaited Cuca LP Jim Kirchstein finally decided to put on the market in December. Kirchstein requested Earl to make suggestions as to the choice of material, and additional help was sought from Jimmy Dawkins, who undertook to give titles to Hooker's instrumental efforts.

"I've always let the bandleader decide what they wanna put out. Hooker picked the songs. He decided. He even told me what order to put 'em in," Kirchstein says to justify this all-instrumental release. "You see, it was a little hard to see Earl when he sang, because he's sitting down. He had the mike in front of him, where most of the other guys were standing up and kinda performing as they were singing. He'd get his old head down and his body was just moving in the rhythm. He was just like a bird sailing through the air."

The front cover of the Cuca set boasted a portrait of Earl painted by Otto Junkermann, a Rhinelander, Wisconsin, artist responsible for the artwork on several Cuca LPs. Junkermann's painting, realized in a range of blue shades, shows a neat and well-groomed Hooker staring into space with soft and dreamy eyes as he strums his electric guitar. The twelve selections chosen by Kirchstein for the album—with the exception of "Walking the Floor"—were credited to Hooker, who unashamedly claimed to have authored well-known themes like Sam & Dave's "Hold On . . . I'm Coming" or Robert Johnson's "Dust My Broom." "'Hold On . . . I'm Coming' sounded awfully familiar, and so did the title," Kirchstein laughs, "but Earl said he had written that many years ago. Then 'Walking the Floor,' he said that might have been someone else's!"

This compelling need to embellish the facts of his life was confirmed by the fantastic account of his career Kirchstein printed in all good faith on the back cover of the album, including a fanciful training at Chicago's Lyon & Healy School of Music and an appearance with the Beatles on a British television show. Also mentioned in the notes were "Boogaloo" and "Sorry About That," two tracks Hooker was hoping to record for Cuca at the time and that he presented as his latest single release. Regardless of such trifles, some of the music presented in the LP evidenced the genius of Earl Hooker better than fabricated tales. This was particularly true of side two, which took the listener all the way back to 1964 with four fine sides taped on Earl's first Cuca session. As a whole, this set somehow suffered from its uneven quality. Kirchstein could hardly be held responsible for it, considering the lameness of some of Hooker's bands and the precariousness of his health at the time of recording. Yet it is unfortunate that he did not choose to replace some of the album's weaker tracks with stronger sides like "Dynamite," A. C. Reed's "She's Fine," Frank Clark's "Got to Keep Moving," or Hooker's own version of "Reconsider Baby." Kirchstein may well have been aware of this shortcoming, since he concurrently put out

Hooker's third Cuca single in an attempt at balancing Earl's all-instrumental LP. For the first time, Hooker was presented in a vocal setting on a Cuca release: it boasted—in addition to the fine version of "Dust My Broom" included on the album—the magnificent "You Took All My Love," featuring Frank Clark's vibrato-laden singing, recorded in April 1967. In the end however, it didn't do much to enhance the sales of the original album. "Selling an LP is like selling a book," Kirchstein explains. "Selling a 45 was like trying to sell a brochure. Brochures are fine for advertising and keeping the name, and I loved to send 45s out to radio stations, but it was the albums I was gearing up for. I think we had a thousand LPs pressed, and I would think we sold three to four hundred. Of course Earl got three hundred. But we sampled every radio station we could find that handled R&B music."

One of Earl's regular nightspots in the fall of 1968, besides the White Rose in Phoenix and Pepper's Lounge on the South Side, was the Alex Club, found at 1815 West Roosevelt, a stone's throw from 1919 West Taylor, where Hooker had spent the first half of the year. This is where Belgian blues fan Georges Adins, who knew Hooker from previous stays in the city, recorded him on a portable machine. When two of these live recordings finally made it to vinyl in 1985 on a Dutch release, I wrote in the liner notes to the album: "Very few people have succeeded in capturing the raw intensity which emanates from blues musicians when they perform in front of black working-class neighborhood bar audiences, and only someone like Adins, with a genuine feel for the blues and a sincere interest in the people behind it, could succeed."[14] Before his death in 1999, Adins failed to retrace in writing his impressions of that night at the Alex Club, but Willy Leiser from Switzerland, another blues aficionado who also happened to be in town at the time for a ten-day visit, fortunately took abundant notes after seeing Hooker on stage. Leiser wrote a diary of his American trip, and following his return to Europe several weeks later, he had his memories published in an illustrated booklet under the title *I'm a Road Runner Baby*. In a league with the account of their own visit to the black ghettos of America written nine years earlier by Jacques Demêtre and Marcel Chauvard, Leiser's recollections are a fascinating insight into the Chicago blues scene of the late sixties.

Leiser was deeply impressed by the overpowering performances Hooker gave on the weekend before Christmas at his favorite West Side haunt with his band, including Pinetop Perkins and Freddie Roulette. After catching their last set on Friday night, December 20, under the tutelage of Willie Dixon, Leiser took the time two days later to spend the whole evening at the Alex Club in order to attend Earl's entire show, a preferential treatment he gave no other artist on the occasion of his marathon tour of the Chicago blues scene. Leiser's description of Hooker's music and showmanship, written in his own brand of English, remains a unique testimony. The picture he draws of a typical Hooker performance on a weekend night at an ordinary West Side neighborhood bar, complete with descriptions of crowd response and improvised jam sessions, has an almost photographic crispness.

It was around three o'clock in the morning when we got to the Club Alex [sic] back on the West Side on 1815 West Roosevelt. The place was jammed with people drinking, talking, dancing and mainly listening to the fabulous music that was roaring from the bandstand. Dixon and I fought our way to the front (I mean Dixon fought my way) and assembled two chairs close to the five musicians standing or sitting in line on the narrow stage. From left to right Pinetop (Joe Willie Perkins) on organ, Odell Campbell on bass, Arthur "Dog-man" Jackson on drums, a little bit ahead of them Earl Hooker and his double-neck guitar and behind him Freddie on steel guitar, who made that "Puppy Howl Blues" with Big Moose John.[15] The music they produced was fascinating and really turned the people on who showed their appreciation like nowhere else. Some used to walk to the bandstand and offer Earl some drinks; others just tapped him on his shoulders while he kept playing. Behind me, Carey Bell, a man in his thirties got up and joined the band with several harps in his pockets and a big hand microphone. He started singing and playing. Little Walter must have been his idol. He performed well and added an extra dimension to the band.

The combo sounded tough and tight. They breathed and performed like one man. That's what you call togetherness! Willie Dixon showed a big smile on his face. He caught me looking at him and just said: "He's gooood is he?!" Willie was talking about Earl "Zep" [sic] Hooker, the giant of the guitar. His phrasing and all the sound effects he produced with his instrument were strictly his. Of course he could play like Elmore James, B. B. King or others but when he did it still sounded like Earl Hooker because he played their music in his style. A very original artist, he made his guitar talk, laugh, moan and cry like if it was so easy. Although his inventiveness and his technical abilities had no borders, he never overdid anything and his musical speech always was logical, well built and told a story from the opening to the end of his solo work. He also was very active in the background, advising and inspiring his musicians and filling every empty spot. What a great artist! . . . So the joint was rocking and I was floating until the band stopped playing around four in the morning. I had cold chills several times on that night.

* * *

Back to the Club Alex [Sunday, December 22, 1968]

Around 8:00 P.M. I took a cab down to the "Club Alex" to catch a full show with Earl Hooker. Buddy Guy was there and Earl invited him to play. Buddy was terrific, playing a whole lot and really getting into his act, even playing with his mouth. Ain't no big thing but then it's cute! By that time Earl decided that Buddy had fooled around enough with his guitar: he took it back and outplayed him in a flash, also doing quite some action, with his guitar on top of his head, behind his back, between his legs until Buddy said he was going to catch the next bus (his wife had a car accident on that morning) home to get his axe! I believe he finally did catch a bus but he never came back. Actually Buddy admires Earl very much.

It must have been around eleven o'clock when David Blume [sic; in fact David Bloom] and Tim Kaihatsu sat in on guitars and left Earl Hooker available for an interview. . . . "Zep"—that's how everyone calls Earl—has a lot to say and I hope someone will realise it and take time to get more of his terrific music on record. I know how difficult it would be but somebody should try and record him live. How about it Chris [Strachwitz]? I suggest a three LP's anthology entitled "Earl Hooker is alive and well in Chicago Illinois!" . . . Earl took over on organ for quite a while and I felt quite frustrated. . . . Earl finally switched back to his guitar and thrilled me with a completely different version of "Dust My Broom" than the one of his Cuca record. What a remarkable creator! Needless to say that Earl is a very nice person, confident in his talent but modest when he comes to talk about it. His witty smile does not hide the fact that he had it very hard, spending too much time of his life in hospitals. He travels a whole lot but does not seem to take care of himself like he should, a fact his mother and friends later confirmed. He has got a sister who also is a very able singer, harp and guitar player but I only saw her picture. Long life Earl Hooker and get what you deserve, that's what I wish you from the bottom of my heart.[16]

On Monday, December 23, Carey Bell and Willy Leiser called on Hooker to find out through his mother that he was not at home. Faithful to his reputation, Hooker was already busy putting a band together for an improvised road trip to New York state, a fact Earl himself confirmed to Leiser over the phone later on the same day, minutes before he left for Buffalo in upstate New York, close to the Canadian border. Buffalo boasted an active blues life at least since the thirties, when itinerant bluesmen Johnny Shines and Robert Johnson visited the club scene there. Three decades later, Buffalo's main blues venue was the Governor's Inn, owned and managed by guitarist and singer James Peterson. When he wasn't entertaining crowds with his own band, sometimes including son Lucky—a four-year-old prodigy whose "1-2-3-4" would hit the R&B charts in August, 1971—Peterson booked name acts at his clubs. By the late sixties Peterson's had become a regular stopover for blues bands touring the East Coast, and it was one of Earl's favorite stops in the later years of his life. Hooker's December 1968 gig there lasted through Christmas weekend, and by the first of January he was back in the Windy City with a young Buffalo drummer named Roosevelt "Snake" Shaw, whom he picked up while playing at the Governor's Inn.

Nineteen Sixty-Nine

Nineteen sixty-nine, the final year of Hooker's career, was both active and successful: after twenty-five years of dues paying, Hooker saw at last the acknowledgment of his genius outside the restricted boundaries of the blues underworld. For one thing, recognition enabled Earl to take part in no less than ten album recording sessions in less than six months, while he was at last able to perform for European audiences in the fall. The development of a growing consciousness for Afro-American popular music among the younger white generation in the United States and in Europe came as a major help for obscure artists of Hooker's caliber. As early as May 1968, in answer to a survey set up by British staff members of the leading blues publication *Blues Unlimited*, readers were asked to name "the artists active today who you really feel are worth recognition and in need of a first or second trip to Europe, and who you'd like to see more written about." With great unanimity, they listed "Fred Below and Earl Phillips (drums); Elmore Nixon, Lafayette Leake,

Henry Gray, and Katie Webster (piano); Earl Hooker (guitar) and Jack Meyers [sic] (bass)."[1]

Interestingly enough, not only was Hooker the sole blues guitarist cited by readers, but the other Chicago musicians selected—Lafayette Leake, Fred Below, Jack Myers—had all worked and recorded for him, confirming his superior status in the Windy City. As a result, Hooker's story, jointly told by reporter Keith Tillman and guitarist Jimmy Dawkins, appeared seven months later in the January 1969 issue of Blues Unlimited in the form of a three-page feature titled "Mr. Music Himself!" At last, this article provided the growing community of blues fans around the world with a portrait (in words and pictures) of a legendary player whose public image had so far been restricted to a handful of influential guitar solos available on rare singles, and to a hazy reproduction of a 1956 picture taken with B. B. King published on the back cover of the February 1967 issue of the same Blues Unlimited.

Around the same time, Earl's Cuca LP was followed by the release of the Arhoolie set waxed in November 1968. And if The Genius of Earl Hooker received only half-hearted writeups—a logical reaction with regard to the unevenness of Hooker's performances—Strachwitz's first attempt at capturing Hooker's music on vinyl was widely acclaimed, although it was not perceived in quite the same way by Hooker's black following and by white fans. Blues Unlimited editor Mike Leadbitter and reviewer Harry Hussey expressed their unwavering admiration for Hooker's proficiency and creativity—Leadbitter even hailing Earl's cover of Tampa Red's "Anna Lee" as "probably the best Delta blues recorded this year"—but both Leadbitter and Hussey also had reservations with respect to Hooker's progressive use of the wah-wah pedal.[2]

On the contrary, Hooker's home admirers acknowledged his utter sense of creation, urging Chris Strachwitz to put out, alongside the LP, a single featuring Earl's more modern tracks. Backed with "You Don't Want Me," the superb "Wah-Wah Blues" rapidly became a favorite of black neighborhood crowds in Chicago. "They used to have that on the jukebox at Pepper's, people would listen to it a lot," Dick Shurman remembers. Despite the growing interest of white blues enthusiasts, Hooker's followers until 1969 were still to be found for the most part among ghetto tavern patrons. Regular engagements in Chicago during this last year included Pepper's on 43rd Street; Theresa's at 4801 Indiana; and the Blue Flame at 39th and Cottage Grove on the South Side, not far from Mrs. Hooker's King Drive apartment. On the West Side, Hooker could be found at the Alex Club on West Roosevelt Road, Kansas City Red's Jamaican Inn at Madison and Loomis, and saxophonist Eddie Shaw's Place at 4423 West Madison. An impromptu jam session also took place on Friday night, February 7, at the Burning Spear, a classier venue found at 5523 South State on the South Side, where nationally known blues acts like Little Milton, B. B. King, Bobby Bland, Tyrone Davis, and Albert King usually performed. Earl was so proud of the tremendous response he obtained from the Burning Spear's all-black audience that he recounted the event to his European friend Willy Leiser in a letter dated February 10. "Dear Willy—Dropping you a line, hope you are well & enjoying life. . . . You should have been with me Friday night I appeared at the Burning Spear with all the celebrities was called back on stage 3 times. . . . I ran all the guitar players out of the club, I played with my teeth and my toes," wrote Hooker, who signed "Your friend Earl Hooker The Guitar King."

On the health front, Hooker's physical condition did not improve during the first few weeks of 1969, and he even went back to the hospital for a little while in January. His disease keeping him from taking to the road until the spring, he played many weekend gigs in neighboring towns like Kankakee, Rockford, Joliet, and Chicago Heights, where Hooker's friend and occasional booking agent Herb Turner was operating a new club. Besides Ricky Allen and the Jackson Five—a then rapidly rising soul unit—Turner's club often billed the constantly changing Hooker band, with bassist Gino Skaggs, guitarist Freddie Roulette, and various vocalists including Lee Shot Williams, B. B. Odom, and a nephew of Pinetop Perkins's named B. J. King. "In '69, we leased a place down here in the Heights, at 12th and Center Avenue. It was called the Grapevine Lounge, 'cause Marvin Gaye was hot at the time with 'I Heard It Through the Grapevine,'" Turner remembers. "We opened on New Year's Day, 1969. And then I decided to put live entertainment in there, and I called up all the blues guys I knowed, 'Hey, gimme a night, see what you can make on the door,' and they worked for me, makin' a hundred and a quarter a night or somethin' like that, a hundred and fifty. Hooker was here every weekend when he was in town." In many ways, Hooker's routine was unchanged, but this was only an appearance as a whole new audience for blues music was rapidly emerging.

Hooker's initial contact with the young white public came with the increasing number of college performances set up by students with an interest in the blues. Those college gigs were rewarding in many respects, first of all because bandleaders usually made in less than two hours twice the money they would have received for three long sets in a ghetto tavern. Less immediate but more relevant was the tremendous development of record sales, the young college crowd forming a whole new market for blues albums when Afro-Americans still went with the 45 format. Hooker was quick in realizing this, especially after he witnessed the rising success of campus favorites like Otis Rush or Magic Sam. For that reason, he was eager to make his own breakthrough in this milieu when Dick Shurman, then a student at the University of Chicago, offered to hire him there: "The first time I saw him at a gig, I was talking to him because I was booking a series of dances at the University of Chicago. Like I had Otis [Rush] and [Magic] Sam, and the Aces and Chuck Berry, and I asked Hooker whether he'd want to play, and he said a certain amount of money. And I said, 'Gee! That's too bad we really can't go that high!' because it was over our budget. And he immediately said, 'Well, okay, we'll set a price, but I'll play the thing.' So that would have been like about $400 for the gig or something, which was respectable money but not super money. Like you couldn't have got Buddy [Guy] for that price."

Hooker's act was particularly well received by the young public, who were thrilled by his dynamic performances and stage acrobatics. His display of showmanship rapidly enabled him to make a name on this wide-open market, resulting in better-paying gigs. Besides college dates, the Hooker band featuring Junior Wells was offered to play as a support act at a rock concert in early 1969. The event took place at the Kinetic Playground—a large warehouse-like ballroom located on the North Side of town, just off Lawrence Avenue on Clark Street—where promoter Aaron Russo booked rock acts at the peak of the hippie wave. If Hooker's sensational guitar playing was becoming increasingly popular, his shows were enhanced by Junior Wells's hot vocals and soulful blues harp. Several years after their glorious Mel London recordings, the cohesion and spirit of mutual understanding that still dominated when the two men shared the stage even drew the attention of Wells's booking agent, Dick Waterman. Eager to include Earl in the roster of exclusive artists featured by his Avalon Productions booking agency, Waterman invited Hooker to team up with Junior in anticipation of major nationwide college tours. No doubt this would have been the easiest way for Hooker to make a name on the college scene, but this plan failed due to his general distrust of agents and his reluctance at sharing the limelight with another leader on a lasting basis. Giving up the idea of an "Earl Hooker and Junior Wells" team, Waterman finally replaced it with the widely acclaimed "Buddy Guy and Junior Wells" formula, tested on various occasions since the mid-sixties but truly inaugurated on the occasion of a European tour with the Rolling Stones in the fall of 1970.

Waterman's proposal was not the only one, and the idea of making Earl Hooker a party to a talented vocalist sprang up in the mind of another promoter around the same period of time, A. C. Reed recalls: "There was a agent in New York wanted me to get teamed up with Hooker. That was in '68 or '69, that's when I was travelin' with Buddy [Guy] before Hooker died. But it was a agent out there tryin' to get me to quit and team up with Hooker, some guy, he was the Chambers Brothers' manager and agent. His name was Whitey, and he asked me to ask Hooker about it. He said, 'If you all team up together, you can really go, because you all did a lot of recordings together.' So when I asked Hooker about it, Hooker said, 'Yeah,' but it never happened 'cause Hooker is the kind of man you don't get along with him no way unless he's out front. I don't know how they was gonna bill it, 'A. C. Reed and Earl Hooker,' but they was gonna put me out front because I was more known with most of the whites than Hooker was, see. But we never did get a chance to organize it before he died. If he was still livin', I probably would have done it."

Other than local college dates and occasional concerts with Junior Wells around Chicago, Earl's initial contact with the rock scene took place in early April 1969 under the auspices of his friend Ike Turner, on the occasion of Earl's first trip that year to California. Turner was in a better position than anyone else in the R&B trade to introduce Hooker to the Los Angeles scene; after settling there with his wife Tina in the mid-sixties following a decade in the St. Louis area, Ike had built a tight network of connections with the developing Californian musical milieu. In the spring of 1969, he was making a strong comeback in the business with a new band and a new deal with an upcoming record firm, Bob Krasnow's Blue Thumb company, whereas a nationwide tour with the Rolling Stones was already in the works for the end of the year.

Turner's friendship with Hooker went back to the "good old days" in the Delta two decades earlier, and it was strengthened by years of playing together in St. Louis and Chicago. Hooker's trip to California barely lasted a week, but Earl still found the time to meet various influential personalities, including Blue Thumb owner Bob Krasnow. Back in Chicago, Hooker was so thrilled by his West Coast experience that he made up his mind to return there as soon as possible. "i bind over in Calfornia," he eagerly told Willy Leiser in a letter dated April 23, written by Mrs. Hooker under Earl's dictation. "i played for ike tunner one weak—it was just some people thair—i went out in Hollerd Wood Calfornia—I met so minny stars I nowed." Drummer Kansas City Red, whose club Earl visited upon his return from the West Coast, clearly remembered the guitarist's enthusiasm: "I had a place called the Jamaican Inn. I got that right after that riot they had here. Freddy King, B. B. King, a lot of guys was stoppin' that I knowed, and we had a pretty nice time. Earl came there after he went [to California]. He stayed out there with Ike Turner for a while and he was tellin' me about Ike's home."

The future looked promising at last, but Hooker, for lack of obligingly incorporating rock elements into his playing, didn't quite belong to the privileged category of blues musicians who enjoyed great popularity with rock audiences. Among the latter was Muddy Waters, the aging blues figure. Through the efforts of Marshall Chess, son of his record company's owner, Muddy desperately tried to modernize his music in an attempt to make it more accessible to the young public, inviting white rock-blues stars like Michael Bloomfield and Paul Butterfield—who appeared that summer at the famed Woodstock Festival—to play on some of his recordings. Even though this policy was successful from a commercial standpoint, the lack of authenticity and relative sterility of the music it generated was typical of the superficial side of the relations between the dollar-dominated rock world and the scuffling blues scene.

The following anecdote told by Dick Shurman exemplifies the artificial nature of blues/rock connections. Referred to is the "Fathers and Sons" concert, an ephemeral encounter pompously baptized "Super Cosmic Joy—Scout Jamboree" that involved blues fathers Muddy Waters, Otis Spann, and James Cotton and rock sons drummer Buddy Miles, guitarist Mike Bloomfield, and harmonicist Paul Butterfield, taking place on Thursday, April 24, at the Auditorium Theater in the heart of the Chicago Loop. The gulf existing between the commercial success generated by the Fathers and Sons' derivative sounds and the complete indifference Hooker's amazing music was confronted with in a South Side neighborhood bar on the very same night, emphasized by the presence at both places of harmonica master James Cotton, evidences the derisory way young white America failed to pay its true debt to the blues masters. "I remember the night of that 'Fathers and Sons' concert with Muddy and Butterfield and all of them," Shurman says, "I went to that thing, and then on the way home, we stopped at Pepper's and Hooker was there and I remember it was such a strange thing because the Auditorium Theater was just totally packed and just going crazy for the 'Fathers And Sons' thing, and the main thing that they were waiting for was Cotton, because Cotton came late; he had a gig in Wisconsin and was flown to Chicago by helicopter from it. And so they were sort of stalling, saying, 'He'll be here,' and then there was this big cheer when he showed up. Well, when we got to Pepper's, Hooker was playing and Cotton was there just hanging around, and that was where he had gone from that other thing, and there was like maybe a dozen people in the club and it was just a fantastic display of that really mind-blowing guitarist."

Another consequence of the rising interest for blues among college students was the emergence on the Chicago scene of dedicated white musicians. Most of these aspiring bluesmen were merely content to sit in with established artists, but a handful of them tended to forgo their college education to become professional players. Hooker, whose knack of detecting odd sidemen was legendary, got involved with two unconventional white artists currently in the band of drummer Sam Lay.

Harmonicist Jeffrey M. Carp and guitarist Paul Asbell regularly sat in with the Hooker band from late 1968 until the first few months of 1969, when the abrupt departure of several of his sidemen compelled Hooker to recruit Carp and Asbell, at Sam Lay's expense, of course. First to leave and soon to join Muddy Waters was piano man Pinetop Perkins, who decided to quit Earl's Electric Dust Band while they were playing in Iowa following an argument with vocalist B. B. Odom. Next was lap steel wizard Freddie Roulette, who went his own way after several years on and off with Hooker; his seat was taken by Paul Asbell, whereas Jeff Carp's articulate harp blowing filled in the gap left by Carey Bell, then busy recording his own debut album for Delmark Records. A sign of the changing times, the presence in Earl's outfit of bassist Gino Skaggs made it an almost all-white group. As Dick Shurman explains: "Asbell and

Carp were more like students who'd come to Chicago, and who'd got into the blues scene sort of thing, and Gino [Skaggs] was more like sort of a greaser. Like he was into old cars and stuff, and I thought he was apparently more of a guitar player than a bass player even though he played only bass with Hooker. That's what Louis [Myers] told me. Gino was a nice guy, I always liked him. He was a little bit older than Carp and Asbell.

"Now Asbell is another guy who was pretty interesting. If you told him a number, he could automatically tell you what the square and the cube root of the number were. And Carp was really a character. He and Paul Asbell were real tight, and when Hooker worked with Carp, he was using Carp and Asbell together. Carp was one of the smartest people I've ever known. He had almost a perfect grade in the hardest division of the University of Chicago, even though he spent all his time fooling around. He was in what they call New Collegiate Division, studying some kind of music. I knew a guy who was his roommate when he was a freshman, and this guy was very, very straight. Apparently what happened a lot of times, in the room in the dormitory, this one guy would be on one side of the room studying with his head in a book, and on the other side Carp would be in bed with some lady.

"Carp used to come by me 'cause I had a big collection of records, in order to learn songs note for note, so he had me play them for him. He was one of the most interesting people I've ever known, Jeffrey M. Carp. He was Jewish, New York I'm pretty sure. I'd say he would have been born in the late forties. Otis [Rush]'s rhythm guitar player, Billy Prewitt, lived next door to Carp and he hated it, because he said the 'narcs' were always watching Carp, and he couldn't make a move without them watching him. Carp was friends with Little Walter, and Janis Joplin and Carp were very good friends. Carp was a really technically proficient harp player. He still had a lot of derivativeness in his playing when I knew him, but he was good. I mean that guy was so smart, he was astounding."

As usual with Earl, Jeff Carp and Paul Asbell rarely got paid what they were promised before a gig, but the fact that Hooker, Carp, and Asbell played for each other in turn enabled the two white players to pay the guitarist back in his own coin at least on one occasion. Shurman reports: "On May 8, 1969, Hooker worked with their band on an early evening gig on campus. Then he drove me and my tape recorder to Pepper's, where they backed him. Actually Carp had the gig and hired Hooker, so they cheated him on the money like he always did them. Either Carp or Asbell told me laughingly that they all knew what was happening; they shorted him, then he shorted them."

The home base of this tight ensemble, rounded off by drummer Roosevelt "Snake" Shaw from Buffalo, New York, was Hooker's old South Side hangout, Johnny Pepper's Lounge, where most of their Chicago appearances of April and early May took place, often in the presence of Dick Shurman, who made tapes of the proceedings on May 1 and May 8. Although Earl's music was exciting— witness the many bandleaders, including Bobby King, L. V. Banks, or King Edward, who tried to catch one of Earl's late sets with the hope of sitting in—it certainly didn't rate as his best. The harsh winter months and Hooker's refusal to settle down after his hospital stay in January were suddenly taking their toll. By the spring, his disease seemed under control, but Earl was in such a state of exhaustion that he could hardly sing, play standing up, or use his heavy double-neck guitar any more. It may not have been the most appropriate time to bring Hooker back to the studio, but it still didn't keep producer Al Smith from recording him with his band in early May.

Smith and Hooker had known each other for a long time. The former, previously bandleader and occasional A&R man with various record ventures in the fifties—including United/States and Vee-Jay Records—had been instrumental in bringing Earl to the studio in 1957 for sessions with the Dells and Arbee Stidham. After the collapse of Vee-Jay Records, Al Smith kept an eye on the recording business, but his main activity consisted in managing Vee-Jay star Jimmy Reed. In addition to Reed's studio work, Smith helped produce sessions by John Lee Hooker and others for the ABC affiliated Bluesway label during the second half of the sixties. With Bluesway's temporary decline, Smith launched his own company, Blues on Blues/Torrid Productions. Hooker was sitting high on his list of potential recruits, and a session was hurriedly set up.

On Monday, May 5, Hooker took his current band, including Carp, Asbell, Skaggs, and "Snake" Shaw, with the addition of keyboard player Boots Hamilton, into the studio. Within a few hours, the sextet jammed enough titles for a whole album, under the lenient guidance of Al Smith, who failed to devote enough time to the careful production of a coherent musical assembly. This lack of preparation and regrettable shortsightedness on the part of both Smith and Hooker unsurprisingly led to uneven results. For one thing, Hooker did not concentrate enough on the sound of his instrument. For obscure reasons, instead of bringing the double-cutaway SG-standard Gibson guitar that he used in clubs at the time, he walked into the studio with a lesser National instrument that limited his range of sonorities, and his wide use of electronic devices could not fully compensate for this shortcoming. But even more than his sound, Earl's choice of material was to blame. As could be expected when nobody made sure that his repertoire was properly balanced, Hooker stuck to a strict diet of guitar instrumentals, vocals being featured on two over-recorded blues standards. The first one, but for its lack of originality, was a palatable rendition of Robert Johnson's 1936 classic "Sweet Home Chicago" that Hooker managed to make his own with his idiosyncratic guitar lines and mentions of "Marie," possibly a current lady friend. Without questioning the sincerity of his singing, his vocals sounded weak due to his physical condition, but the track still stands out in a myriad of versions of the tune with its very vocal wah-wah/slide choruses. The second vocal effort of the day—a cover of Chuck Willis's 1954 hit "I Feel So Bad" retitled "Ball Game on a Rainy Day" featuring Jeff Carp's mediocre singing and a nice guitar solo by Paul Asbell—paled in comparison.

The instrumental side of the session kicked off with "Wa-Wa Blues," doubtless one of Hooker's favorite themes that already appeared twice on his Cuca album under the titles "Hooker Special" and "Hot & Heavy." Two different takes of the song—pompously labeled "Part 1" and "Part 2" when Al Smith released his tapes—were cut this time, with Hooker interspersing touches of reverb and wah-wah gurglings, even managing to slip in the first few bars of the traditional "O Suzanna" theme among other quotations. More low-down blues settings were also re-created, first with "Soul Cookin'"—an underrehearsed excuse for wah-wah/slide variations on the "Will My Man Be Home Tonight" theme—then with "The Real Blues," its ominous atmosphere owing much to Earl's gloomy guitar breaks.

Hooker's most remarkable contributions of the day didn't belong to the blues repertoire; the band got into a bop groove with "Hooker Cooker" and "Huckle Bug." This sarcastic tribute to Earl's "TB bug" was a modernized version of the venerable Paul Williams classic, "The Huckle-Buck," which topped *Billboard*'s "Race Records Juke Box Charts" for a record fourteen weeks in 1949. Largely inspired by Charlie Parker's "Now's the Time," it had already been covered by Hooker in 1953 for the Sun label. Raising the uneven standard of this May 1969 session, Earl's "Huckle Bug" is an unprecedented journey through musical genres as diversified as blues, bebop, and country & western, as was noted by critic Pete Welding in 1976. "Listen to his gripping treatment of the venerable jump-blues classic, 'Huckle Buck.' Within two choruses Earl has taken a simple blues riff through several of its permutations: first into the 'Huckle Buck' theme, then into its bebop incarnation as 'Now's the Time,' then Charlie Parker's 'Ornithology' (the altoist's paraphrase of 'How High the Moon') for two bars, followed by a fleeting variation on that, and then off into his own spontaneous inventions. Simply astounding."[3]

In a similar vein, "Hooker Cooker" is a breathtaking instrumental borrowed from the repertoire of saxophonist Gene Ammons. Originally called "Blue Greens and Beans," this brilliant composition of jazz pianist Mal Waldron had already popped up in the demo tapes Hooker had sent to Cuca Records' Jim Kirchstein two years earlier. This 1969 version is much more elaborate due to the band's cohesion, and Hooker's creativity can explode; a mere listen to the incredibly fluent unison vocal-guitar chorus found midway through the tune— recorded nearly a decade before George Benson's exploratory forays in this field—shows how much ahead of his time Hooker was.

As a whole, even though the quality of Earl's music could hardly be doubted, this experimental journey lacked the accessibility required of commercially successful productions. This didn't escape the notice of Al Smith, who waited almost two years and until Hooker's death before he finally released this hastily recorded session on his Blues On Blues label in a cheaply packaged memorial album titled *Funk—Last of the Great Earl Hooker*. Due to improper distribution and bad pressing quality, the album was marketed barely long enough for the specialized press to publish lukewarm write-ups. It was not before 1976 and their reissue on the California-based Antilles label that Hooker fans were at last treated to a properly pressed, re-edited version of Smith's tapes, along with excellent liner notes by Pete Welding.

The second in a series of six recording dates involving Earl Hooker, set up within one same month by various producers, brought Hooker back to Los Angeles, where Ike Turner had worked out an album deal for him with outside help from a young manager named Denny Bruce. California then boasted the most active rock scene in the country. Its foremost representatives, in an attempt at expressing their sincere appreciation to the members of the blues community, were quick to pay homage to their initiators. One of the first in the record business to catch on with this phenomenon was Bob Krasnow. This self-called "con man with ethnic credentials" ("I had all the ethnic qualities—I was white, I was Jewish, they could invite me over to their house for dinner, and I could talk to black people,"⁴ Krasnow once said in his usual blunt way) started out plugging country hits for the King company in 1958 before he did A&R work for Warner Brothers, eventually becoming head of Elektra Records in the 1980s. In 1968, Krasnow launched his Blue Thumb label—operated out of Beverly Hills at 427 North Cañon Drive—after hitting upon the idea of re-leasing black blues albums aimed at the white rock-blues market. Among the artists Krasnow contracted for initial Blue Thumb releases were Ike & Tina Turner, who knew Krasnow from their 1964 stint with Warner Brothers, and a first album of pure blues and R&B material was cut during the first of 1969 by the husband-and-wife duet. On the strength of this initial experience, Krasnow set up a second Ike & Tina session involving Texas guitarist Albert Collins in the spring, before turning to Ike for advice, and the name of Earl Hooker cropped up in conversation.

Sixteen years after the legendary Sun demo session likely initiated by Ike Turner in the early summer of 1953, Krasnow invited Earl Hooker out to California to record an instrumental album, and through Denny Bruce a date was set. Turner's musicians were to be used for the session, but Earl wished to visit California clubs in the process, and he drummed up his favorite sidemen, leaving Chicago on Friday, May 9, heading for California. Other than the current members of his rhythm section, Roosevelt Shaw, Gino Skaggs, Jeff Carp, and Paul Asbell, Earl brought with him vocalist B. B. Odom, who kept vivid memories of the event: "I was singin' up with Junior Wells in Buffalo, New York, at the Governor's Inn. And when I called my wife, she told me that Hooker wanted me to go to California. He had got an offer to come and he axed me to go. He say, 'If you don't go out, I don't wanna go without takin' you, because you're my star singer.' So anyway, I left Junior and them on the road and I came back to Chicago, and I stayed there for about two days. Then Hooker and the band, we driven out to California."

Hooker's Blue Thumb session got under way shortly after his arrival on the West Coast. The event was jointly produced by Bob Krasnow and Ike Turner, whose current bassist and drummer provided the backing heard on the dozen tracks taped for the occasion. "He was sick as hell when we contacted him," Krasnow recalled later in *Rolling Stone*. "When he felt well enough, he came out and did the session and a couple of Los Angeles jobs."[5] In spite of Hooker's health problems, the outcome of this session was interesting for various reasons, not the least being the presence of Ike Turner's superlative piano playing on every track, while Chicago harp man "Little" Mack Simmons, currently touring southern California, guested on several tracks. On a less favorable note, Turner was also responsible for marring half of the tracks with fussy brass arrangements, and this was, once again, an uneven session.

Alongside a forgettable instrumental version of "Cross Cut Saw," the Tommy McClennan classic popularized by Albert King in 1966, one could find the slow-paced "Funky Blues"—"by Earl Chicago-No-Thinkin' Hooker," as announced humorously by a voice coming from the control booth—in which Hooker's guitar sounds lost behind a solid wall of horn punctuations. Also featured was yet another version of "Sweet Black Angel" that saw Hooker exhibit his best slide work before moving into unspirited improvisations studded with honking brass. This left "I Feel Good"—an instrumental rendition of James Brown's 1965 hit—as the only song in which Ike Turner's brass arrangements were used to good effect, as Hooker deftly replaced Brown's hoarse vocals with sweet wah-ed slide lines.

The other half of the session fortunately made up for previous inadequacies, the band's simple backing providing Earl with a fitting occasion to display his proficiency and versatility in all freedom, first paying homage to the boogie-woogie tradition with "Boogie, Don't Blot," a lightning quick piano-guitar duet highlighted by Turner's keyboard playing and Little Mack Simmons's powerful harp blowing. This side was so infectious, in fact, that it was released on a 45 in the fall to boost the sales of the album. In a different vein, "Country & Western" shows the extent of Hooker's debt to the hillbilly sounds of his youth, with more quotations from "O Suzanna," while "Shuffle" is an impeccable wah-wah festival with touches of T-Bone Walker interspersed all along. The Delta tradition was not forgotten, with a revamped version of the old "Catfish Blues" standard in which Little Mack's naive harmonica licks balance the progressiveness of Earl's wah-wah phrases, the tune reaching a climax with a stratospheric slide chorus.

For his only vocal effort of the day, Hooker didn't reach very deep into his memory when he chose "Sweet Home Chicago," sung just days earlier at his Al Smith date; this second version—played this time in the key of E, one full step higher than the previous version in D—if it illustrates Earl's lack of originality with regards to his vocal material, fares better than its predecessor due to Ike Turner's strong left-hand work. As for Hooker's singing, it radiates an unexpected strength and range that seems to indicate that the warm southern California climate suited his health better than the Chicago spring, so much so that the unusual geographical notions of the original creator of the song, Robert Johnson, take on their full meaning in Earl's mouth: "Come on, baby don't you wanna go / Back to the land of California, sweet home Chicago."

The session's finest item probably is "Drivin' Wheel," the venerable classic of piano master Roosevelt Sykes popularized by Junior Parker on his definitive 1961 cover. Ike Turner deserves a special mention for the way his subtle piano backing supports Earl's superlative work. And even though *Sweet Black Angel* was chosen for the album title when it was time for Bob Krasnow to release these tapes, "Drivin' Wheel" crystallized the two men's complicity more than any other track. Mention should also be made of "The Mood," which saw Ike take up guitar chores to show Earl that his guitar lessons had been fruitful.

At the conclusion of the recording, Krasnow set up a photo session with a fine photographer named John Hayes, in anticipation of the album artwork. The picture kept for the back sleeve commemorated the reunion of Chicagoans Hooker and Simmons in front of carefully emptied bottles; as for the cover shot, it was a superb black-and-white portrait of Hooker in a typical southern California street setting, opening the passenger door of an old car while protecting himself with a dark umbrella from an imaginary shower of rain.

Already in Los Angeles for the Blue Thumb recording, Hooker wished to familiarize himself with the local scene, and he immediately set about visiting clubs with his band in the hope of finding engagements while they were in town. Until 1973 when it finally closed down following a fire, Ed Pearl's Ash Grove on Melrose Avenue in Hollywood was a rare club in L.A., outside the Watts ghetto, where blues musicians could find work. This folk hangout was used as a home base by local artists Pee Wee Crayton, "Big Mama" Thornton, and Don "Sugarcane" Harris, but rock celebrities like Mike Bloomfield, Janis

Joplin, Bob Hite and Al Wilson of Canned Heat, and Jimi Hendrix regularly dropped in for informal jam sessions.

The band currently playing at the Ash Grove was that of Albert Collins. Collins, whose flamboyant showmanship almost equaled Hooker's dynamism on the stage, was another eccentric guitarist with a strong penchant for instrumental showcases; Hooker had even borrowed his guitar tour-de-force, "Frosty," at one of his Cuca sessions. In the spring of 1969, Collins had barely finished recording the lead guitar parts behind Ike and Tina Turner for their second Blue Thumb set, and his act at the Ash Grove was spiced by the presence on stage of both Hooker and Little Mack, who sat in with his band several times, much to the delight of the club's capacity crowds.

At the Ash Grove, Hooker and band also got a chance to meet various rock stars, including Janis Joplin, who was on friendly terms with harp man Jeff Carp. "She was around at this club, and she was a hell of a artist, man," B. B. Odom reports. "That's where we met a lot of the Blood, Sweat & Tears, and guys like that. We all got together and we did a lot of jam sessions. That's when Jimi Hendrix was there. In fact, it was about six or seven bands a night in this place we played in." Jamming with someone like Hendrix may well have been the dream of most guitar players at the time, but it left Hooker quite unimpressed, according to Dick Shurman: "Jimi Hendrix obviously had a tremendous respect for the blues scene, like there's a long period when Elmore [James] and Albert King and Hubert [Sumlin] was the main influence on him so he was obviously aware of that scene. After Hooker came back from California—that's the kinda guy Hooker was—I was asking what it was like out there and he said, 'Oh, I had a good time,' and I said, 'Who did you play with out there?' and he said, 'You see, there was this one guy, he plays left-handed with a big head of hair, played real loud,' and I said, 'Jimi Hendrix?' and he said, 'Oh yeah, that was his name!' You know, he played with him but he didn't even bother to remember his name!"

Earl's attitude may seem surprising, but the following anecdote recounted by Bob Krasnow at the time of Hooker's death illustrates the gulf that separated a scuffling bluesman like Hooker from an adulated rock icon like Hendrix. "One night we were driving to a club and I started telling him about Jimi Hendrix, how he was where it was at now . . . how he got $50,000 for one night's work. '$50,000 for playin' the guitar?' he said. 'Shit. I'd climb inside the guitar for

$500.'"[6] Denny Bruce, the agent currently booking jobs in California for Earl and band, was also struck by the sharp contrast between Hooker's genius and his limited means: "I lent him money to buy a $75 Japanese guitar that had three pickups and all kinds of knobs. After one night he broke a string and when a set of real strings were put on the sound was cheap and horrible. One of the pickups worked itself loose and was hanging out—it was funny, but sad at the same time."

In order to keep his group working while he did his Blue Thumb session, Hooker had come to an understanding with Denny Bruce, who eventually worked out a deal with Earl's cousin John Lee. "He brought B. B. Jr. Odom and five or six other guys (it was supposed to be a trio!), so they made hardly any money, and I booked him on a show with John Lee Hooker," Bruce recalled. This encounter enabled Earl to stay on the West Coast longer than antici-pated, opening the door to a string of recording sessions. John Lee Hooker, one of the best-known and most lavishly recorded blues artists in the trade, started out hiring Earl's band as a traveling unit for a set of club dates in California be-fore he offered to use them on an upcoming recording session for the ABC-Bluesway label, programmed for late May. Earl had admired John Lee since childhood, and he was glad to accept his cousin's offer, although it alienated Denny Bruce, who didn't particularly like the fact that the ABC deal was made behind his back.

As the new recording session loomed ahead, Earl considered adding a key-board player to his band. Rather than pick up an unknown sideman in Los Angeles, he sent for his old road companion Johnny "Big Moose" Walker, who flew in from Chicago at his request. "What happened," Big Moose explained, laughing at the recollection, "I flew a plane up there. He sent me a plane ticket and I just came by myself. And Hooker got mad because the plane didn't fall, 'cause I got there safe! I walked out of the plane and he said, 'This j-j-j-just ain't my day, man!' And then he showed me, in his pocket he had a life insurance on me! He took insurance on me! He figgered one way around he had to have some money if the plane fall down. I got off the plane and that cat got mad, 'Y-y-y-you m-m-mean that thing didn't fall d-d-down? Looka here, man, w-w-what I had if the p-p-plane had fall down.' I laughed, man, I said, 'You crazy!'"

Managing to recover from this major disappointment, Earl, with his band in tow, finally walked into the studio for John Lee's session in the very early afternoon of Thursday, May 29. This was John Lee's fourth recording date for the ABC subsidiary Bluesway, but quite a few changes had come up since John Lee had recorded his previous LP one year earlier, after ABC's artistic management left New York City to settle in Los Angeles at 8255 Beverly Boulevard. In the wake of this move, former jazz and blues A&R man Bob Thiele was replaced by Edward Michel, a talented producer with a much keener ear for blues than his predecessor. Michel had met and worked with John Lee Hooker before, and he arranged to record him on the occasion of his visit to Los Angeles, but he had no inkling of who John Lee was currently playing with. It was not until the musicians arrived at the Vault recording studios that he got to meet Earl.

Things went both smoothly and quickly. Michel, after taping eleven sides featuring John Lee within a matter of hours, was so taken by Earl's work that he offered on the spot to record an album with him. "I knew that John was carrying a good band, but I didn't know how good," Michel reported later. "I got to know everyone when they showed up in the studio with John Lee for his date: Moose Walker, Gino Skaggs on bass, and Roosevelt Shaw on drums, and adding two white Chicago players, Jeff Carp on harp and Paul Asbell occasionally on guitar. Things went so well that we recorded Earl's album later the same day, with the same personnel, adding 'Voice' Odom—Earl was quite insecure about his vocals, and felt he needed extra singers. At that point, Bluesway productions were very low-budget, quite quick—usually one-day—affairs, with everyone showing up in the studio usually around noon, for sessions which would, again usually, be over by six in the afternoon. I was recording in four-track at that point, using Vault Studios, which was cheap and adequate, and we didn't dawdle, getting enough material for an album and knocking off. There were usually some leftover takes of things, but, quite frankly, they weren't good enough, or they would have been used in the albums. There wasn't time or budget enough to go for the degree of fineness I would have liked."

May 29 was a very busy day indeed, and over twenty titles were recorded altogether in the afternoon. Regardless of the limited amount of time and money involved, most of these tracks are up to the standard—both technically and musically—of the finest blues recordings of the era. If Earl's band members certainly were gifted musicians, Ed Michel must get credit for his fine work, especially taking into account Earl's usual unpredictability. This double session proved thoroughly tiresome for everyone nonetheless, things being made worse by the exhausting heat that rapidly built up in the studio and that accounted for the large quantity of Pepsi-Cola consumed that day. Bluesway's appointed photographer Phil Melnick made countless shots of the musicians all along the proceedings. Judging from his abundant crop, if Hooker's polka-dot cowboy shirt was neatly buttoned up when the band started working, if wasn't long before Earl stripped to the waist. Jeff Carp followed his example, blowing his harp bare-chested, wearing a pair of psychedelic pants, whereas Big Moose Walker's fading hair process had him looking as shaggy as Carp.

John Lee Hooker's own set was quite a contrast due to the different approach to blues music displayed by the two cousins. To tremendous effect, Earl's progressive accompaniment pushed into the limelight John Lee's rougher, more primitive guitar styling, making this old times/new times reunion a true success. Eleven tunes were recorded, with only two alternate takes, Earl Hooker giving up his seat to Paul Asbell on two tracks. If results were excellent as a general rule, the fast boogie items that made John Lee's reputation didn't prevail this time; slow sullen numbers like "I Wanna Be Your Puppy, Baby" or the exceptional "Lonesome Mood," showcasing Earl's discreet wah-wah, Moose Walker's brooding organ, and Carp's moody harp, contributed to a large extent to the day's success. A noteworthy effort was "The Hookers (If You Miss 'Im . . .)," a weird tribute to the Hooker dynasty. Highlighted by Earl's moving slide phrases, this uncanny tale of clannishness benefited from the piano work of Big Moose Walker, who set the pace with his emotion-laden figures before John Lee started rapping:

> Looka here! I'm gonna tell you a story—about the Hookers . . . Me and Earl Hooker went down on 47th Street one night—you know, on 47th—for gas. We went into a club—we was standin' at the bar that night—-and some cat— he started to riotin'—with Earl. I said, "Earl, you got 'im?"—That was on 47th Street. . . .
> [Same pace—Earl Hooker and Jeff Carp join in with the rest of the band]
> He said, "Yeah!" The Hookers! If you miss 'im . . . I got 'im—If you miss 'im . . . I got 'im. I said, "Everythin' cool, baby, I got 'im"—The Hookers! Don't mess with the Hookers.

Unsurprisingly, this statement of family pride gave its title to the *John Lee Hooker featuring Earl Hooker* album that was released one year later, with a nice front cover picture of the Hookers standing in neat cowboy outfits under the hot Californian sun. The set was well received by the musical press. As much as the music itself, reviewers acknowledged the talent of Ed Michel, who managed to revitalize John Lee Hooker's music. "Earl Hooker, Big Moose and Jeff Carp lend a lot of weight to all the performances providing us with an above average set. Excellently recorded and very well played, it should delight fans of John Lee 'Today,'" *Blues Unlimited* founder Mike Leadbitter wrote in the January 1971 issue of the magazine.[7]

A parallel can be drawn between this John Lee Hooker session and the tracks recorded by Hooker for Muddy Waters in 1962. In both cases, Earl's innovating styling helped present an aging bluesman in a new light. Critic Fred Stuckey implicitly accepted this as a fact when he stated in *Guitar Player* that John Lee Hooker's "best cuts were made with Eddie Taylor for VeeJay records [in the fifties and early sixties] and 'spot' records like the one he made for Bluesway featuring his cousin, the late Earl Hooker, as second guitarist."[8] This assertion, published in 1971, proves once more that recognition came too late for Hooker, who met his fate several months before Stuckey's laudatory comments. Fortunately enough, Earl's own Bluesway material was marketed during his lifetime, and he was at least able to read some of the positive comments that started coming out before his death the following spring. Pete Lowry, hailing Earl's Bluesway set as "the best blues album I've heard this year"[9] in the December 1969 issue of *Blues Unlimited*, did not exceed reality, for these sides stand today as Hooker's finest musical legacy, along with his first Arhoolie album and the Mel London material.

Ed Michel's main achievement—helped in this respect by sound engineer Ed Fournier—was to give the whole session both coherence and consistency, qualities Earl normally lacked. When Mel London had provided Earl with an instantly recognizable sound in the early sixties, Michel managed to capture on vinyl the tone quality and wide range of shades Earl squeezed out of his instrument. Michel quickly realized that the presence of competent vocalists by Hooker's side would diversify his output, but like Strachwitz six months earlier, he insisted that Hooker overcome his vocal shyness and tackle a couple of songs. Results went far beyond all expectations, for Earl contributed two strong vocal numbers deeply rooted in the St. Louis R&B tradition—both belonging to the repertoire of Ike Turner's Kings of Rhythm: "You Got to Lose," an uptempo side borrowed from Earl's friend Jackie Brenston, and "Don't Have to

Worry," a retitled version of a 1956 Federal recording by singer Billy Gayles originally called "Do Right Baby." The strength and wind needed for the proper delivery of such tunes, as evidenced by Brenston's bellows on the original version of "You Got to Lose,"[10] apparently were not within the reach of a man whose lungs amounted to very little. Yet for all his weakness, Earl still sounded credible as he obviously took pleasure in singing, even managing to squeeze a reference to his Waterloo, Iowa, girlfriend Rosemary in "Don't Have to Worry." The listener will find further confirmation of Earl's vocal conviction in the fact that his guitar work was limited here, since it was Paul Asbell who played the song's brilliant, flowing solo.

Hooker's fingers hadn't grown numb for all that, and the instrumental support he gave his guest vocalists was as spirited as ever. Big Moose Walker's own two offerings were of unequal interest; in particular, his rendition of the Jazz Gillum classic "Look over Yonder's Wall" turned out to be the most insipid effort cut that day. On the contrary, his version of "Is You Ever Seen a One-Eyed Woman Cry?"—a traditional theme with uncanny lyrics, already recorded by Lightnin' Hopkins in 1959,[11] that poet Langston Hughes once recalled hearing sung by early jazz players in Paris in 1924[12]—featured forceful piano parts and Earl's deeply emotional slide/wah-wah work. On this latter offering, Big Moose proved that he was a capable singer, even though his rough technique was hardly as elaborate as B. B. Odom's.

The latter's own three vocal contributions, in a class with Hooker's "You Got to Lose," presented him in a very favorable light as he wisely stayed away from his idol, B. B. King. In addition to two self-penned numbers, "Moanin' and Groanin'" and "Come to Me Right Away, Baby," Odom's most worthy effort was a masterly version of Elmore James's "The Sky Is Crying," Odom and the rest of the band succeeding in instilling freshness and emotion in their rendition of this widely covered standard. Earl's haunting wah-wah slide, Big Moose's faultless piano touches, Jeff Carp's sensitive harp and Odom's earnest delivery all contributed to the subtle recreation of the dreary, rainy atmosphere conjured up by Elmore James and producer Bobby Robinson when they jointly wrote the original on a cold and torrential November afternoon in Chicago a decade earlier.

The instrumental side of the Bluesway session proved slightly disappointing. When the Arhoolie date presented previously unrecorded ideas and techniques, this one yielded two updated versions of Mel London classics and a lengthy adaptation of Bill Doggett's 1956 hit "Honky Tonk" retitled "Hookin'." "Blue Guitar," although not a bad track in itself, falls short of the original because it lacks the spontaneity that made Earl's Age hit so poignant. The same cannot be said of "Universal Rock," Earl's modernized version unquestionably matching the drive and authenticity of its 1960 forebear, with its staccato guitar lines and deft wah-wah work propelled by Snake Shaw's punchy drumming.

Thus ended this prolific double Bluesway event. On the strength of his rewarding crop, Ed Michel decided to postpone the release of John Lee's LP in order to issue all except two of Earl's own sides. In the meantime, he was determined not to let Hooker and his men vanish from his sight without capturing more of their thrilling music on tape, and additional sessions for both B. B. Odom and Big Moose Walker were set up for the following week. The days after these first Bluesway recordings saw the Hooker band busy playing club gigs in California with John Lee Hooker. This period was not free from minor hassles, especially after arguments over financial issues developed between Earl and some of his sidemen. Underpaid by their bandleader, Jeff Carp, Paul Asbell, and Roosevelt Shaw decided to play safe and go back to Chicago with their share of session money. This was the last time Earl would ever work with Carp, whose promising career came to an abrupt end on New Year's Eve 1972, when the harmonicist was last seen jumping off a boat in Panama after one of the people he was celebrating with pulled out a knife and started using it on other passengers.

By the following Wednesday, June 4, it was time for Earl, B. B. Odom, and Moose Walker to return to the studios located at 2525 West 9th Street in Los Angeles—today a Korean Baptist church—for Odom's own session. Michel's idea when he decided to cut an album with B. B. Odom was to place the vocalist in a different setting from the one used a few days earlier, in order to show that Earl's singer was not just another Chicago-based B. B. King stylist. First of all, Michel insisted on having Odom use his own material, only two of the tracks cut then being King songs. Next, Michel hired two expert jazz veterans, drummer Panama Francis and stand-up bassist Jimmy Bond to create a more relaxed, after-hours atmosphere enhanced by the presence on guitar of Hooker, who was asked to put aside his wah-wah pedal and steel slide temporarily.

With the exception of the session's first item—a slow blues titled "I Got the

Feelin'" reminiscent of the first Bluesway date—this jazz groove was retained throughout the session. The singer's main claim to success was his faultless collusion with Hooker, whose spirited backing complemented Odom's inspired work on both slow and fast numbers, the bouncing "Don't Ever Leave Me All Alone" as well as the pensive and profoundly sad "Long About Sunrise." One of the date's highlights was the old T-Bone Walker warhorse "Stormy Monday" that Hooker turned into a tribute to his most influential source of inspiration after Robert Nighthawk as he appropriated and transcended Walker's famous guitar licks with adroitness. Although allusions to T-Bone Walker were not as obvious on the remaining titles, the influence the old Texas master exerted on Hooker's playing shines through each one of the forceful straight-picked phrases heard behind B. B. Odom. Unfortunately, this project was not very well received by critics, and the material put on wax on that early June afternoon passed almost unnoticed when it finally appeared on the Bluesway label in 1973. Some fans especially failed to grasp the fact that Hooker wasn't a mere pursuer of the Delta tradition; British specialist Mike Leadbitter expressed this utter incomprehension when he wrote at the time: "What a bitter disappointment! Muffled sound, endless boring songs and a total lack of variation. What have Bluesway done to my heroes?"[13]

On the other hand, the same Mike Leadbitter was responsible for the dithyrambic write-up published in the January 1971 issue of *Blues Unlimited*, following the release of Johnny Big Moose Walker's own set, recorded five days after Odom's album: "He plays piano with the sort of boogie-woogie drive you just don't hear any more, and has a nice husky voice—this is an exceptionally good blues album. Earl Hooker really puts his all into the accompaniment and Otis Hale blows good raunchy sax. Rocking goodtime music that is almost an echo from the past."[14]

The odd musical setting of the Odom sampler, which had taken aback conservatory blues fans, was replaced on the Moose Walker album by the type of accompaniment expected from a rough Delta-born pianist like Moose. If both Hooker and saxophonist Otis Hale did acknowledge progressiveness in their playing—as evidenced by their systematic use of wah-wah pedals—their music reassuringly belonged to the pure Chicago tradition. As such, it certainly didn't run the risk of offending conservative ears. Several parameters kept this from being a predictable set, notably the fact that most titles were Moose's own compositions, bearing evidence to the man's talent as a tunesmith. Another reason was related to the awkward circumstances that led to the presence of saxophonist Otis Hale, recruited on the eve of the session to fill in the gap left in the band after Jeff Carp's abrupt departure, Big Moose Walker explains: "Otis Hale? I picked him up in a park! I went out there 'cause they was sellin' hot dogs and stuff out there. I sit out there for a half hour and heard him blow, see. I's on a bench. He asked me for a hot dog, and I told him, 'Yeah!' I said, 'Hey, you wanna make some money?' He said, 'Yeah, how much?' I said, "Bout fifty, a hundred dollars.' He said, 'You gotta be kiddin'!!!' I said, 'Yeah, I mean it. I'm gonna cut a record tomorrow and I want you on the LP.' I first wouldn't wanna use a horn, I's gonna use a harp, but when I heard this cat playin', I said, 'Jesus Christ, I can put this cat on the record.' Because he was blowin' the blues on my style. I wanted to make sure that I'd get this guy on the LP. I took him to my place and kept him all night, I was watchin' the door, I didn't want him to get out and leave me."

On the next day, Monday, June 9, Moose Walker and his slender, long-haired sax player walked into the Vault studios, where they joined Earl Hooker, bassist Gino Skaggs, and Paul Humphrey, a punchy soul and jazz studio drummer whom Ed Michel hired for the session. Busy immortalizing the event was photographer Phil Melnick, while soundman Ed Fournier stood at the board. "It took me three hours and forty minutes to cut the ten sides," Big Moose Walker recalls. "When I got to the studio, I just told everybody, 'Play blues just like you play on the bandstand.'" Ten selections were released on Moose's Bluesway album, but a total of twelve were recorded altogether, "She's Got a Good One" and "All My Love" remaining in the can.

Big Moose Walker opened fire on the organ with a version of "Rambling Woman," a favorite of his that he had already cut two years earlier with lap steel guitarist Freddie Roulette. This time, Hooker was responsible for the hot guitar parts on this new version; his arpeggio runs frenetically drive the rest of the band from the front while Otis Hale contributes a long solo midway through the song, giving the impression that he has played with Hooker and band for years. "Rambling Woman" was followed by "Baby Talk," a superb organ reworking of Moose's "Talkin' About Me," recorded in 1955 already in Los Angeles for Johnny Otis's Ultra label. This traditional boogie theme was brightened by one solo spot each from Earl Hooker and Otis Hale, who both hinted at the superlative performance that they were going to give throughout the session. For the third number, Moose moved to the piano stool and went on with "Footrace," the springy intro passage of which he borrowed from his own electric piano contribution to Earl's 1960 Age side, "Swear to Tell the Truth."

Big Moose's repertoire also included a fine version of "The Sky Is Crying" featuring Hooker's stately slide passages that Moose's hoarse, unpolished vocals made utterly different from the more sophisticated B. B. Odom version taped on May 29. The virtuosity of the musicians was featured on two lengthy instrumental pieces, both of which sounded familiar. The first one, aptly titled "Moose Is on the Loose," was an updated rendition of a number Hooker and Moose had recorded for Carl Jones in 1959 with Lorenzo Smith. As for "Moose Huntin'," it was an improvisation on the "Two Bugs and a Roach" theme that soon turned into a wah-wah conversation between Hooker and Hale, ending with a breathtaking call and response duet. With this unconventional instrumental dialogue, Moose's session came to a close and put a temporary end to Hooker's association with Bluesway and its artistic manager, Ed Michel. As for Otis Hale, after making a brilliant contribution to the blues of the late sixties by a strange combination of circumstances, he quietly walked out after receiving his performance fee.

As was customary with Bluesway, outdoor pictures were left to the care of Phil Melnick. With the skill that characterized him, the label's appointed photographer caught a serious looking Hooker proudly leaning on the side of a newly acquired bus, while a laughing Big Moose Walker was immortalized in a fancy black-and-white Western costume, and both pictures later appeared on the covers of the two men's albums.

Instead of driving back to the Windy City with the secondhand bus he had just purchased in Los Angeles, Hooker and band chose to hang around California for a while and work the nightclub scene in both Los Angeles and San Francisco, hoping to make their stay worth their while. This decision presented Moose Walker with a serious problem, for the pianist didn't have his musical equipment near at hand, and he had to make the return trip to Illinois to pick up his electric piano and amplifier before he could join his friends in the San Francisco Bay area. "We's out there about a month, and Earl played some gigs with John Lee," Walker explains. "We was in California anyway and we was there so we played some jobs. John Lee did that to help us, because otherwise we was short on finance, you know, so he just let us play to make some money."

On the strength of John Lee Hooker's well-established reputation, Earl's Electric Dust Band rapidly turned into a relatively popular one in California. The tremendous response they got in the colleges and clubs where they appeared provided them with continuous engagements through the month of June in various San Francisco locations, such as the Log Cabin or the Matrix—the city's "folk-rock club," operated by Jefferson Airplane founder Marty Balin—as well as on the Berkeley campus or in the various black neighborhood bars of Oakland, across the Bay from San Francisco.

As time passed, it almost seemed that Hooker's band was going to settle on the West Coast for good, and Hooker did greatly enjoy his stay. The five recording dates he had done and the engagements he obtained with relative ease, even though he could hardly be considered a local blues figure, were a positive sign of his growing reputation. In San Francisco especially he developed a local following, even giving guitar lessons to young musicians like Joe Louis Walker: "At the time, I was opening with my band for people like Earl at the Matrix and, man! Hooker was incredible! He taught me a lot about the slide, he had such a light touch, it was amazing to see him play."

In the Bay Area, Hooker also got to meet one of his idols, "sepia Sinatra" pianist Charles Brown, and he ran into several friends. One of them was Charlie Musselwhite, a Mississippi-born harmonicist who had spent several years in Chicago before settling in Oakland. Musselwhite's current band, the Chicago Blues All Stars, included Earl's former lap steel guitarist Freddie Roulette, who had recently made California his home. But most of all, fronting Musselwhite's outfit during the summer of 1969 was Earl's childhood friend Louis Myers. Moose, Hooker, and Myers would often hang around together during the day, appearing with each other's band at night. Sitting in with passing bluesmen was one of Earl's favorite occupations. Always eager to outplay his peers, he found it very gratifying to perform in front of appreciative audiences in the concert halls at the invitation of major artists. Earl was given one such opportunity at a concert B. B. King was giving at the Fillmore West, San Francisco's temple of rock music. According to Ed Michel: "I remember B. B. King telling me about one night at the Fillmore West when he was besieged by every guitarist in San Francisco's sitting in with him—most of the rock 'n' roll players idolized B. B., but he was getting a little bored with all of them. However, he said that Earl came in and played a couple of choruses with his teeth that blew everyone away. I could hardly believe that until I caught Earl with his band at a club in Chicago, and I heard him play better with his teeth than almost anyone else could do with their hands. Absolutely amazing!"

The fact that Hooker was becoming in demand at last had many positive implications. One of them was that his income followed the ascending trend of his success, with fees he collected from his various contributions in the studio and the money he received to play college and club dates. After his bus, his next purchase was a fine semi-acoustic Trini Lopez Standard Gibson guitar— easy to recognize with its diamond-shaped sound holes and single-sided head-stock—that replaced his Gibson SG model. The next step was to get an amplifier. The one that Big Moose had brought back from Chicago along with his electric piano was a particularly worthwhile $1,500 Ampeg model that Earl had coveted for quite some time, and that he wanted to get at all costs. Anticipating Moose's refusal to part with his gear, Earl decided to take the offensive and concocted one of his shady schemes.

Hooker was aware that the situation of his sidemen was uncertain when they depended on his goodwill to survive in a strange territory. When it was time for him to pay Moose for his club work, Hooker pulled the usual rabbit out of his hat, in the presence of Louis Myers, who later told the story to Dick Shurman: "Louis [Myers] was in Moose's room rapping, and Hooker called him up to say that he could only pay him five bucks for the first two weeks' worth of work. They had this big argument, and Moose was so mad that he slammed his phone so hard that it broke. Hooker said he was coming over at the hotel, and so Louis ran down with Moose to meet Hooker. Moose grabbed Hooker by the collar, and Hooker said to Moose with this really angelic voice, he says, 'You can't hit me, 'cause if you hit me I'm fixin' to die,' and Moose started shaking. He knew he was right but he couldn't punch him 'cause he was so sick that it probably would have killed him, and he would have got in a lot of trouble, so eventually he just sort of let it fume for a while." In the end, as he needed to get back to Chicago, Walker had no other option but to let Hooker have his precious amp. However pathetic, this incident did not mark the end of Moose's long-standing friendship for Earl, proving that Hooker undoubtedly displayed some sort of psychological understanding; if his reckless behavior often was on the verge of getting him involved in fatal trouble, he obviously knew how far he could go with the people he misused.

The band's stay on the West Coast was drawing to a close. B. B. Odom left first, because his wife was anxious to see him, heading for Chicago with John Lee Hooker. As for Earl, he eventually drove his new bus back to the Midwest in late June with Big Moose following in his own car. Before he left, Earl secured additional recording engagements, and his return to Illinois was a brief one. While in the Bay Area, Hooker had taken the time to visit Chris Strachwitz in Berkeley, where the latter operated his Arhoolie label. Among other topics, the two men considered the possibility of cutting a second Arhoolie set, and a session was set up for July 18 at Berkeley's Sierra Sound studios.

Hooker's first Arhoolie set, *Two Bugs and a Roach*, was out since the early spring, and initial sales indicated that it would be a firm seller for the company. Strachwitz's expectations were confirmed during the following decade, as the company ended up selling over twelve thousand copies of the LP, quite a feat for a blues album then. The laudatory reviews published when the record came out were certainly helpful. While the album rated four and a half stars in *Down Beat*, Arhoolie and Earl Hooker held a place a honor in the July issue of England's *Blues Unlimited*. Apart from a half-page variant of the fine portrait of Earl found on the Arhoolie cover, *Blues Unlimited*'s review section boasted a vehement eulogy of the record that would embarrass the most immodest artist: "This should have been called the Earl Hooker Show!" wrote Mike Leadbitter. "There's a whole lot of fine talent packed into one LP. . . . The greatest track is 'Anna Lee,' probably the best Delta blues recorded this year. . . . Both vocal and slide work can only be described as stunning. . . . Hooker is a musician's musician. His command of his hefty instrument is incredible. On this album he lives up to his huge reputation. . . . Leave 'Wah-Wah' to the new breed, you'll dig nearly all the rest—and it's that rest which makes this a must for anyone who wants soul Chicago blues. Fine cover, fine notes, excellent recording quality. Chris is a jolly good fellow, or so says one of us."[15]

Apart from the remark concerning Earl's use of the wah-wah pedal, the musician and the producer could hardly expect more, but Hooker's second Arhoolie set re-created only to a certain extent the auspicious circumstances that had led to the first's success. Even though similar moments were reached at points, this second attempt was not as masterly, in spite of the presence behind Hooker of a competent rhythm unit including Gino Skaggs on bass and his longtime Cairo drummer Bobby Joe Johnson. The session's main shortcoming was its vocal side; this time again, singing chores were not left under Earl's sole responsibility, but the additional singers featured on this date didn't compare with B. B. Odom or Carey Bell.

As a whole, the event sounded too much like a musical reunion, as Strachwitz conformed to a fashion initiated by rock producers that consisted in throwing indiscriminately in the studio or on a stage the largest possible number of name artists. Such artificial gatherings yielded worthy results on some occasions, but most of them were disappointing, as was the case with Earl's second Arhoolie session. Sharing the spotlight with him was rock-blues organist Steve Miller, whose Prophets had sometimes shared the bill with Earl when he worked the clubs of Miller's Iowa hometown, Waterloo, earlier on in the sixties. By 1969 Miller had moved to California, when he ran into Earl Hooker, and Strachwitz thought fit to commemorate the event on vinyl, aiming at reaching a larger share of the young white public in the process.

The idea could have produced interesting results—for Miller actually was a talented keyboard player—if the session, initially planned as an "Earl Hooker featuring Steve Miller" event, hadn't become an "Earl Hooker *and* Steve Miller" record. This was epitomized in "Hooker 'n' Steve," the jazz organ-guitar duet that eventually gave its title to the album. This track suited Miller's style well, but it could not appeal to the blues purists who raved about the first Arhoolie set, especially as Earl acted the humble part of guest attraction. The two vocal tracks featuring Miller's affected singing carried this paradox even further, for if Hooker did provide the organist with an adequate slide accompaniment on the rather lifeless "Strung-Out Woman Blues," his playing was hardly audible on "New Riviera." Earl's trouble did not end with Steve Miller's vocal performance, for Strachwitz had a second singer in store. Although "I'm Your Main Man"—a variation on the traditional "Rock Me Baby" theme— boasted uninspired vocals from Gino Skaggs, they were redeemed by Hooker's moving accompaniment, which recalled at times the ominous atmosphere of the original "Blue Guitar."

The instrumental side of the session was no exception to the "guest-star" policy that ruled this recording date, the first non-vocal effort of the day being a harmonica showcase that left little room for Earl's guitar; "The Hook," a brilliant up-tempo number, features the harp acrobatics of Hooker's friend Louis Myers, who volunteered his assistance when he learned that Earl was going into the studio. Fortunately, the rest of the session was devoted to Hooker's playing and singing. "Earl's Blues," despite the cumbersome presence of Miller's organ, was one of Earl's very personal bluesy numbers, in which he alternates conventional picking and talking-slide verses. "Guitar Rag" illustrated Hooker's penchant for country & western music, but most of all it was an occasion for him to display his formidable command of the slide. Yet what the song gained in complexity it lost in drive, and this version came short of the more forceful rendition Hooker had contributed at Sam Phillips's Memphis studio in 1953. As was the case with its Sun predecessor, this new cover is plagued by the fact that Earl's sidemen were unfamiliar with the song's chord structure. What could be overlooked in the case of an informal demo session was unforgivable here, and Strachwitz should have known he couldn't expect much from Hooker if his band wasn't properly rehearsed.

Of Earl's two vocal attempts, the first was nothing new, since "Conversion Blues" was a retitled version of Harold Tidwell's "Swear to Tell the Truth" recorded in 1960 for Mel London and recut for Cuca four years later. That left as the session's highlight "The Moon Is Rising," a Delta gem in the vein of "Anna Lee," also featuring harmonicist Louis Myers. Like "Anna Lee," "The Moon Is Rising" had been learned firsthand from Earl's mentor Robert Nighthawk, and it provided Hooker with an ideal support for his soulful slide contributions. Convincing vocals, haunting slide licks interspersed with subtle touches of reverb, driving bass lines, a strong backbeat, gentle piano figures from Miller—all contributed to the making of a masterpiece that probably outmatches Robert Nighthawk's 1953 creation.

The session's shortcomings and qualities accounted for the contrasting reviews published when Arhoolie 1051 was released in 1970 shortly after Earl's death. When the newly launched *Living Blues* magazine from Chicago stated that "side one"—with Hooker's own two vocals and two guitar instrumentals—"is probably better than any side of any other LP," Mike Leadbitter voiced his bitter disappointment in *Blues Unlimited*: "Well, here's another super-group. Earl and Steve Miller combine forces to come up with yet another set of samey, uninspiring, just-about-blues."[16] In a posthumous tribute, *Guitar Player* acknowledged the album's technical qualities, whereas a rather objective description appeared in *Billboard*'s review section with the mention "A Billboard pick": "Hooker, one of the older more respected talents in the blues bag, comes on strong with a potpourri of blues tunes interspersed with jazz/rock undertones."[17]

Shortly after the conclusion of his Arhoolie date, Earl Hooker went back to Chicago, leaving Gino Skaggs in California, where he eventually became the bassist with John Lee Hooker's Coast to Coast Blues Band. For the rest of the summer, Earl played regular engagements around the Windy City in his favorite spots, including Theresa's Tavern and Pepper's. His following in Chicago, far from diminishing, seemed stronger than ever, and his return after his extended stay in the West was marked by his searing performance at Chicago's first Blues Festival, on a blazing hot afternoon in late August. "The blues capital of the world, Chicago, played host on Saturday, August 30, 1969 to the world's largest Blues Festival—a nine-hour extravaganza in Grant Park, where a youthful, exuberant but orderly crowd of about 10,000 whites and blacks together occupied the parkland in front of the Band Shell," Paul and Victoria Sheatsley reported in the October issue of *Record Research*. "The Festival was sponsored by the federal Reach Out program and the Chicago Park District, but the organizing genius behind the affair—the man responsible for assembling the dozens of artists and organizing the show—was the ubiquitous Willie Dixon, coordinating with co-producer Ed Winfield. . . . Though the Festival was called 'Bringing the Blues Back to Chicago,' the blues of course have never left Chicago. Indeed, almost all of the artists participating in the Festival made their reputations in Chicago and are still based in Chicago."[18]

The event, emceed by prominent R&B DJs Big Bill Hill and E. Rodney Jones, started at 10 A.M. with Willie Dixon's own Chicago Blues All Stars. During the eight solid hours of blues music that preceded Muddy Waters's closing set, the cream of blues stylists—including Victoria Spivey, Koko Taylor, Otis Spann, Big Mama Thornton, Junior Wells, and B. B. Odom—kept the large outdoor crowd asking for more. It was no easy task for Earl Hooker to focus the attention of the public when, next to last on the show, he walked on stage at half past five in the afternoon, but his playing and sensational stage dynamics soon won the audience over to his cause: "Earl Hooker then came on to electrify the crowd (and one was afraid, himself) with his wild guitar playing which wound up with him playing the instrument with his teeth,"[19] the Sheatsleys wrote.

Hooker was clearly at a turning point in his career, but the summer was not free from major hassles. As several months of frantic activity were taking their toll, he was hospitalized for a short period of time in early August. Despite his general state of exhaustion, and although this clearly confirmed that his bout with tuberculosis had not ended with his long stay at 1919 West Taylor in 1967–68, Hooker refused to acknowledge it as a fact and would not even admit to his friend Dick Shurman that he had been under medical care when the latter came back to Chicago in early September after spending some time away from the city.

Hooker and Shurman saw quite a bit of each other during the first half of September; since Shurman liked to spend time in the clubs where Hooker performed. Shurman was not merely an ardent listener, and his admiration for Earl's music urged him to capture it on tape. "When I knew Hooker," Shurman explains, "I didn't have a car and so when I'd go to a gig, he'd drive me to see him play. I still can't believe the nerve I had. People like Hooker and [Howlin'] Wolf, they would pick me up and drive me over to make some tapes of them. When I think back it seems so amazing. He never complained. He liked to listen to it later. He was the one guy of all the people that I recorded that sometimes would make me go some place and play the tape before he would go to bed and let me go; we would often drive to his place and listen to the tape." Such informal live recording sessions took place on various occasions from the spring of 1969, and the several hours' worth of tapes that have remained in Shurman's possession are a priceless testimony to Hooker's genius. Even though they were not recorded when Hooker was at the peak of his form, they are the only possible way today of assessing the guitarist's true potential on stage.

In this respect, the recordings Shurman has kept of the guitarist's performance on the night of September 12 perfectly illustrate the progress of a typical Earl Hooker show in a ghetto club. That Friday night, the crowd at Theresa's Tavern was a mixture of neighborhood patrons and South Side blues aficionados, with a sprinkling of musicians who had come by in the hope of sitting in. Earl's band was limited to a trio, with Arthur "Dogman" Jackson on drums and Dave Myers on bass. The first set that night started with an up-tempo instrumental rooted in the R&B tradition, followed by a more funky guitar improvisation. With the end of the third number—a shuffle later titled "Swingin' at

Theresa's"—Hooker swiftly moved into "Hide Away," the Hound Dog Taylor theme made famous by Freddy King. Halfway through the first set, Earl then called on the bandstand vocalist Muddy Waters Jr., who kicked off with "Everything Gonna Be Alright," a Little Walter offering he had already recorded with Hooker for the Cuca label in 1966. Muddy Waters Jr., a mainstay at Theresa's, then jumped into the traditional "Rock Me Baby" theme before he ended his performance with a strong rendition of Willie Cobbs's "You Don't Love Me." Next on Hooker's list of sitting-in vocalists was Little B. B. Odom, who got into a bluesy groove with his own "I Got the Feelin'." Earl then brought this first set to a close with a guitar rendition of Bill Doggett's "Hold It" before the band took a break.

The second part of Hooker's performance more or less patterned itself on the first set as the guitarist displayed his proficiency and sense of stage dynamics with four extended instrumental showcases, including James Brown's "I Got You (I Feel Good)" and his own "Earl Hooker Blues." By the time Hooker brought an end to his instrumental features, the noisy crowd at Theresa's were ready for the blues, and it was time for Earl's protégé B. B. Odom to show the extent of his talent. Odom's "Don't Ever Leave Me" was aptly followed by a cover of Bobby Bland's 1957 Duke hit "Farther Up the Road" before the vocalist acknowledged his admiration for B. B. King, at first with "Sweet Sixteen," then with "Why I Sing the Blues," a King composition that had worked its way up the charts in the late spring.

In the tavern that night was Jimmy Reed, one of the most popular blues artists to emerge from the Chicago scene of the fifties. Although Reed hadn't had a major record out in years, he was still a favorite with club audiences in 1969, accounting for the enthusiastic response he got everywhere he played. This was no exception, and Reed's renditions of his old hits "You Don't Have to Go" and "Honest I Do" were greeted warmly by a Friday night crowd elated by the subtle interaction between Reed's singing and Hooker's playing. Earl's spirited improvisations on Albert Collins's "Frosty" ended this second set appropriately, and the band was able to go on intermission.

When Hooker's trio came back for the night's final set, three vocalists were ready to join him on stage. The first one was Ernest "Elmore James Jr." Johnson, a disciple of the famed slide master. The influence of James was obvious on Johnson's repertoire that night, which included "The Sky Is Crying" and "I Believe," two of Elmore's anthems that allowed Hooker to come up with superb slide licks. Also included in Johnson's bag of songs were Junior Wells's "Up in Heah," and Bobby McClure's "Peak of Love" as well as "Get Off My Back Woman," a B. B. King tune that could be heard on every black radio station at the time. Elmore Jr. was followed by Muddy Waters Jr., who came back for two standards, "Drivin' Wheel" and "You Don't Have to Go," a strange choice in the light of the presence that night of Jimmy Reed, who was then called back on stage. With Earl's support, Reed put a fitting end to an eventful musical night as he crooned his way through "Baby What You Want Me to Do" and "Big Boss Man."

This description hardly does justice to Hooker, and only his music can truly document his versatility. Indeed, the tunes cited above might give the misleading impression that Hooker's shows were limited to lifeless renditions of stereotyped standards, but a mere listen to the Shurman tapes proves that each one of these themes was but an excuse for the guitarist to make forays into unexplored musical realms. This can easily be verified in the thirty minutes of intensely brilliant music, captured by Shurman that night at Theresa's as well as two days earlier at Pepper's Lounge, that saw the light partly on a memorial album put out by Chris Strachwitz in 1973, and more recently on another Arhoolie release. These recordings have an exceptionally crisp and clear tone considering the fact that they were taped on a portable machine with four cheap microphones, but Hooker's live music doesn't need to be judged by technical standards, its very essence and artistic content making up for what the recordings lack in quality. Of the four instrumental tracks released by Arhoolie, the first is particularly interesting because it gives a full idea of Earl's innovative genius. Hooker starts off with a regular statement of the "Dust My Broom" riff popularized by Elmore James that he then proceeds to analyze, dissect, permute, and transform into what seems like an endless run of improvisations. Never repeating himself as he uses alternatively his fingers or a straight pick, the wah-wah pedal, the steel slide, and the tone control of his instrument, Earl equals in imagination and creativity bebop greats like Clifford Brown, Charlie Parker, and Gene Ammons. Had he been drawn to the saxophone instead of the guitar, he no doubt would have become himself a legend in the jazz field. At any rate, the Shurman tapes confirm that Hooker only gave free rein to his talent in front of live audiences, making these rare recordings all the more precious.

In the audience at Pepper's that Wednesday night was producer Ed Michel, who insisted on catching Earl in a club setting on the occasion of a short visit to the Windy City. Michel and Hooker were bound to see more of each other within the following days. Clearly impressed by the extent of Hooker's genius, Michel had set up another series of Bluesway recording dates involving Hooker in California for the second half of September. This was the only opening left in Earl's busy timetable, since a tour of Europe organized by Chris Strachwitz was going to keep Earl away from the United States during all of October. Ed Michel conceived his next three sessions quite differently from the previous ones. During the summer he signed up vocalists Charles Brown and Jimmy Witherspoon as well as the world-famous team of Sonny Terry & Brownie McGhee. Since Brown and Witherspoon usually worked with pick-up units, Michel's idea was to bring together in the studio the most talented musicians he could find in order to provide his new recruits with exceptional sidemen.

Hooker, in spite of his reluctance to travel by plane, was looking forward to going back to Los Angeles for more studio work. He was particularly excited at the prospect of recording with Charles Brown, especially as he was partly responsible for the latter's comeback. Brown, originally a high school teacher from Texas with a degree in chemistry, made a highly successful career as a pianist and singer on the West Coast in the early postwar years. The mid-fifties brought about considerable changes on the R&B scene, and Brown's Nat King Cole–influenced style progressively grew out of fashion. With the exception of a minor hit record for the Cincinnati-based King company in 1961, Charles Brown was absent from the charts after 1952. As he drifted into oblivion, Brown quit music in order to start a furniture business in Ohio in the sixties, and it was not until 1968 and his return to northern California that he resumed his former occupation as an entertainer on a regular basis.

At the time of his extended stay in the San Francisco Bay area in the late spring, Hooker was both happy and surprised to discover that his early idol performed nightly to indifferent neighborhood crowds in Oakland's black bars. His first reaction was to get in touch with Ed Michel, who flew in from Los Angeles at Earl's instance, and a recording session for Bluesway was planned on the spot for the fall. "He was very excited about recording with Charles Brown," explained Dick Shurman, who escorted Hooker to Chicago's O'Hare airport right before the sessions. "He liked recording once he got started. For one thing it was easy money for him 'cause he was the kinda guy that could just go in and jam a whole album without any problem. When the album market caught up with him, he just recorded, bam! bam! bam! I think Hooker was the kinda guy that—'Why not?' that was his attitude. The one thing I remember talking about most was the session with Charles Brown, because almost every blues artist listens to Charles Brown and Johnny Moore and Oscar Moore.[20] Their influence on people is becoming recognized."

His second active recording spell for ABC-Bluesway started on a grim note for Hooker, who arrived in Los Angeles without a guitar; he had entrusted his instrument to a redcap at the Chicago airport but had never seen him again, and Michel had to find a replacement for the stolen guitar before the first session could start. When Hooker finally walked into the studio on Monday, September 15, he was carrying with him a fine Gibson Les Paul model. This first recording date featured singer Jimmy Witherspoon, but Charles Brown was there to highlight the event with his subtle piano playing. The rest of the band included Mel Brown, a mainstay on Bluesway sessions at the time who shared guitar chores with Hooker, and bassist Jimmy Bond, already present on B. B. Odom's Bluesway set. Art Hillery and Lavell Austin—respectively organist and drummer with the house band at the Parisian Room, a Los Angeles venue found at La Brea Avenue and Washington Boulevard—completed the outfit with their bandleader Red Holloway, a veteran tenor sax man whom Hooker knew from his days as a much sought-after session man in Chicago during the fifties. According to his usual pattern, Michel took this ephemeral unit to the Vault studios, where sound engineer Ed Fournier stood behind the soundboard while photographer Phil Melnick proceeded to take shots of the musicians for future promo material.

The songs taped that day were longer than was customary with blues sessions. "Pillar to Post," for instance, amounts to a full twelve minutes and forty-nine seconds—an inevitable outcome considering the loose, jam session–like atmosphere of the event and the number of leading talents who took turns to play lengthy solos. Hooker obviously felt at ease in this setting, and he was able to acknowledge more than ever before—with the exception of his performance behind B. B. Odom three months before—his debt to T-Bone Walker's swinging style, sprinkling all the while wah-wah and slide touches in his playing. The same could not be said of Mel Brown, who came up with boring and pointless solos in an attempt to outplay Hooker. Fortunately, Brown's guitar remained amazingly discreet on "You Can't Do a Thing When You're Drunk," by far the best number recorded that day, with its superb slide phrases and light shades of wah-wah, Charles Brown's sweet piano playing and Red Holloway's wailing sax.

Unsparing of his artists, Ed Michel brought Hooker, Holloway, Bond, and Mel Brown back to Vault the next day. For this second date, which hailed Charles Brown's comeback on record, drummer Ed Thigpen, just back from a tour with the Oscar Peterson Trio, took the seat left vacant by Lavell Austin. Midway into the session, a promising jazz bassist named Arthur "Joony" Booth took over the seat of Jimmy Bond, who had another recording engagement.

At Michel's instance, Charles Brown shared the spotlight on two tracks with a female club owner named Dottie Ivory, who spiced the proceedings with her soulful singing. The overall results were remarkable, although Brown later expressed the regret that more time was not spent on the careful production of this comeback session: "When Dottie Ivory and I went down to Los Angeles to make an album together, instead of taking time to get an arranger and really fixing it right—we jammed! Yet it was a good album but not what we could have done like others who have had arrangements. It makes a difference. . . . Earl Hooker was here then, as a matter of fact, he wanted to make a record with me."[21]

Even though he decided to cover his most popular records of the forties and early fifties, Brown went on to prove that his music could still hold its place in a modern context. In this respect, Hooker's support proved invaluable as the guitarist revitalized Brown's old hits: "New Merry Christmas Baby" with its soulful intro, and more especially "Drifting Blues" came off as new, thanks to Hooker's inspired slide work, although it certainly was no easy job for him to follow in the footsteps of Johnny Moore, the original guitarist on Brown's 1945 success.

Released shortly after Hooker's death under the title *Hunh!* (a reference to the hoarse grunt that chain gang workers uttered when using their hammers), Witherspoon's Bluesway album was greeted with varying comments. "Black blues at its high-power best played by people who know how,"[22] wrote Mike Leadbitter in *Blues Unlimited*, showing more enthusiasm than Bruce Iglauer in Chicago's *Living Blues*: "Hooker and Brown just get in each other's way and make the whole thing too busy. . . . They can't play together."[23] On the contrary, Charles Brown's *Legend!* set was unanimously acclaimed by critics, Leadbitter's reaction being representative of the comments published at the time: "The Legend, Charles Brown, is featured and the results are superb. The same musicians are used as for the famous Witherspoon *Hunh!* session and there is really some fine music behind Charles' bunged-up nose vocals and tinkling music. If you like Charles, you'll want this. . . . The throaty Dottie Ivory helps out with some vocals, but it is the long recreations like 'Black Night' and 'Drifting Blues' that make this a must for me."[24]

As record sales helped spread Earl's reputation after his death, his splendid contributions to Brown's LP in particular proved influential. So much spontaneity transpired from his work behind Brown that one may wonder whether Earl did not disregard his "dummy guitar" recording policy this time, to bequeath the world tangible evidence of his genius as the end was drawing near. At least one prominent Chicago guitarist didn't remain indifferent to this precious legacy, according to Dick Shurman: "In 1970 I was visiting Otis [Rush]. I took him down to a record store and we listened to a few albums and one of the ones that I turned him on to was that *Legend!* album by Charles Brown. That album has had more influence on Otis than any other record since. A lot of times when he plays a slow blues, he'll play with his fingers that slide part that Hooker plays on 'Drifting Blues' on that album, he loves to play that. Otis very seldom expresses appreciation of anything to anybody, but he did one time when he was in a sentimental mood. He really thanked me for turning him on to that album."

Hooker's last recording date took place at Vault on Wednesday, September 24. Turning to account the week that separated this final session from the Charles Brown event, Earl visited L.A.'s music stores and ended up purchasing a new guitar as a replacement for the one he had just lost. This time, the band featured behind Sonny Terry and Brownie McGhee included Ed Michel's favorite stand-up bassist Jimmy Bond, veteran jazz drummer David "Panama" Francis, as well as a fine keyboard player named Ray Johnson, brother of New Orleans stylist Plas Johnson—the sax player on the original "Pink Panther Theme." Following the current rock-age trend of rejuvenating the music of older icons, Michel deliberately chose to present the guitar-harmonica duet in an urban blues context. Judging from the resulting album, this was a questionable initiative. Not that anything was wrong with Terry's country-flavored harp playing and raw singing, McGhee's East Coast blues guitar patterns, Ray Johnson's spirited piano licks, or Hooker's adroit slide lines, but the mixing of these various ingredients sounds pointless because the musicians fail to adjust themselves to the situation. Michel himself was not satisfied with the outcome; he refused to release it with the Witherspoon and Brown sets, and it was not until four years later that ABC finally put it out under the title *I Couldn't Believe My Eyes*. No doubt this failure would have passed unnoticed by Earl Hooker fans if it hadn't been the guitarist's final studio appearance.

Goin' Down Slow

(1969–1970)

A t the end of his last Bluesway date, Hooker flew back to Chicago, where the last few days of September found him busy preparing for his forthcoming European tour. The event was placed under the responsibility of Arhoolie's Chris Strachwitz, who co-produced it with German promoters Horst Lippmann and Fritz Rau. Since this was Hooker's first trip overseas, a passport was needed, but getting one proved difficult, since no birth certificate had been filed with the relevant Mississippi authorities back in 1929. In order to establish his age and place of birth, Earl asked his mother and several relatives in the South, and appropriate affidavits were finally established. Besides administrative chores, Earl was busy packing his sharpest garments and flashiest suits, and he even found the time to decorate the new Univox guitar he had acquired in California with self-adhesive flowers and his name in big plastic type. After checking it along with his hefty double-neck Gibson at O'Hare airport, Earl boarded a plane to London, where his marathon tour of Europe with the American Folk Blues Festival was getting its start, a little over a week after the Sonny Terry & Brownie McGhee session in Los Angeles.

With the blues revival movement of the late fifties and early sixties, European audiences felt the urge to invite to their stages some of the blues performers whose music had only been available to them so far on rare records. Whereas tentative tours were set up here and there as early as 1949, the notion of package shows exclusively dedicated to blues music was conceived by German jazz critic Joachim-Ernst Berendt on the occasion of a blues party given in 1960 by Chicago promoter, bandleader, and drummer Jump Jackson. The idea was passed on to promoters Horst Lippmann and Fritz Rau of the German Jazz Federation, who rapidly set up from 1962 a yearly event labeled American Folk Blues Festival, or AFBF.

For many years the festival allowed many prominent blues artists to develop a strong following in the various western European countries that the AFBF visited extensively. At first, Lippmann and Rau's package deals consisted largely of so-called "country" blues singers, with a sprinkling of electric performers who sweetened their music lest it should hurt sensitive ears. With time, heavily amplified bluesmen were finally admitted on European stages, and Junior Wells, Buddy Guy, and Otis Rush, among others, introduced audiences to more modern Chicago sounds. By 1969, in spite of similar attempts made by other promoters, the AFBF remained the major annual rendezvous for a majority of European blues fans, but Lippmann and Rau, although they usually relied on the expert advice of Chicago bassist and producer Willie Dixon to select their roster, were starting to run out of ideas.

Wishing to revitalize their aging formula, Lippmann and Rau decided to co-produce the 1969 edition of the American Folk Blues Festival with an American promoter. An agreement was reached with Chris Strachwitz, who temporarily accepted the position of band manager in order to select the most qualified candidates. Strachwitz found himself confronted with a serious challenge, especially in the light of the harsh criticisms the two previous American Folk Blues Festivals had stirred up. An article titled "All Time Low," published in *Blues Unlimited* shortly after the passage in England of the 1967 festival, bears witness to the acid comments formulated then: "The 'modern blues' section of the American Folk Blues Festival must have really hit an all time low this year," a caustic and ironical Mike Leadbitter wrote, "and it is almost a re-

lief to know it couldn't possibly get any worse. . . . Horst Lippmann must go further than Chicago to find something new and raise the standard of his shows to
what they were. How about Katie Webster or Juke Boy Bonner. . . . Or if it must
be Chicago, what about Eddie Taylor, Earl Hooker or Magic Sam? . . . Fight for
the people you like."[1]

This desperate appeal visibly reached its target, for the policy that Strachwitz—himself a reader and occasional contributor to Blues Unlimited—decided
to carry out closely followed Leadbitter's recommendations. "Lippmann and
Rau have added a totally new element to this year's tour," read the official program of that year's American Folk Blues Festival, "an attempt to emphasize the
distinctive characteristics of blues in the various regions of America. They
want to document the different blues landscapes in America and the profiles
they have given their native artists."[2]

Strachwitz's task was made easier by the eclecticism of his own artist roster,
since the Arhoolie catalog presented a wide array of performers. In addition to
the amplified Chicago blues of Carey Bell, Earl Hooker, and Magic Sam (the
show's only non-Arhoolie artist, managed by Denny Bruce, who knew Strachwitz), his package included a quiet gravedigger by trade and occasional songster
from Virginia named John Jackson; one-man band Juke Boy Bonner and sev-
enty-year-old pianist "Whistlin'" Alex Moore, respectively from Houston and
Dallas; accordionist Clifton Chenier and brother Cleveland, an expert washboard specialist, noted ambassadors of the generally underestimated zydeco tradition of Louisiana; as for the show's backing unit, Magic Sam's bass player
Mack Thompson and the Cheniers' drummer, Robert St. Julien, combined
forces to provide their fellow bluesmen with driving support.

As was to be expected considering Strachwitz's taste and flair, this selection
was received extremely well throughout Europe by enthusiastic audiences
happy to note that the blues world didn't limit itself to the handful of wrinkled
men and women that Lippmann and Rau had clumsily overexposed on previous festivals, and that younger talents were there to perpetuate a living tradition.

After gathering all of his flock in Chicago, Chris Strachwitz brought everyone to England on Friday, October 3 for the tour's initial concert at London's
famed Royal Albert Hall. This first date was an essential one for three major
reasons. First, the show was to get into its stride on the occasion of this concert,

and more especially during the rehearsal that preceded it, since most of the performers had never shared the same stage before. Second, the recording of the album that Lippmann and Rau traditionally issued at the end of each festival to commemorate the event was to be done during that rehearsal. Last, the London show was essential because the leading European blues critics were British, and all of them would attend this only performance in England.

Fate had decided differently however, and this brilliant tour was kicked off in a most inauspicious manner, judging from the account of England's foremost blues writer, Paul Oliver. "The luck wasn't running for Horst Lippmann and Fritz Rau on October 3rd," Oliver reported at the time in Britain's *Jazz Monthly*, "when the seventh annual American Folk Blues Festival appeared in London. . . . There were the musicians, the engineers, the A-and-R men from Britain and Germany, the organisers and of course, the critics. But the amplification equipment was missing. . . . Tempers ran high, accusations filled the air, and the musicians gloomily sat in the auditorium or answered the questions of the blues researchers, who, with notepads at the ready, were having a field day—if they could get past the security guards at the Artist's entrance. So eventually the recording session was called off, and Dave Howells of CBS decided to record the concert live. If the instruments arrived. For though Clifton Chenier's electric accordion and brother Cleveland's specially made chest-vest washboard were seen on board the plane at Houston they didn't arrive in London. Earl Hooker had one guitar, but his twin-fingerboard, twelve string electric guitar didn't arrive either. . . .

"With all these disasters it was surprising that there was anyone who felt up to playing, but strangely, Horst Lippmann's explanation to a slightly restless audience, put over with no excuses, took them into his confidence. . . . Some critics apparently weren't too happy with the festival; for myself, I enjoyed it greatly and thought it one of the most musicianly (in the blues sense, I hasten to add) of any we have seen. The names weren't big but they were bluesmen without publicity gimmickry and that's what I, and a lot of other people, like about it. . . . Hitches then, rough in a few spots, but with the problems ironed out, a great show on the Continent I'm sure."[3]

This London concert was fully representative of the spicy performances the musicians gave throughout their tour. One-man band Juke Boy Bonner first opened fire—usually with a fast guitar boogie item—leaving the audience on their feet by the time fellow Texan Alex Moore took over to sing and whistle his old-time piano blues. Then on came the Chenier brothers, whose zydeco sounds, complete with strong rhythm and Creole French lyrics, brilliantly carried the show until intermission time. It did not take Magic Sam's personal brand of West Side blues long to command back the attention of the audience after a short break, thanks to his flowing emotional singing and lyrical playing, and the quiet and sincere acoustic guitar offerings of John Jackson were needed to cool off things a bit. Last on was Hooker, who had to give his best to stand out in such a crowd of fine performers. With the unfailing help of Carey Bell, he nevertheless succeeded in outplaying all in a flash, to the amazement of standing crowds who gaped at this eccentric guitarist who stole the show in his colorful attire with his nonpareil acrobatics, C&W instrumentals, and uncanny electronic devices.

"John Jackson's modest piece of showmanship," Paul Oliver wrote in the liner notes to the live album taped at the Albert Hall, "was followed by the flamboyant showmanship of the lean Earl Hooker resplendent in a purple pink suit, shirt ruffles and pink shoes. In Chicago they say that Earl Hooker is 'the best guitar-player in town' and he proceeded to prove it with his elegant flourishes, wah-wah pedal effects, playing his guitar with his teeth and even playing a country-and-western 'Steel Guitar Rag.' With Carey Bell, wailing on his harmonica, a great session came to a close, and Europe had once again been introduced to new talents in the blues by men who are for the most part, still 'prophets without honour' in their own country."[4]

Everywhere they played, from Oslo and Copenhagen to Hamburg, Frankfurt to Vienna and Brussels, Paris to Berlin, Munich to Geneva, Hooker and Carey Bell stunned audiences with their extroverted playing. Although the 1969 festival didn't last as long as preceding editions, in twenty concerts given in little more than three weeks Hooker convinced blues fans in England, Denmark, Norway, Sweden, Germany, Austria, Belgium, France, and Switzerland that he deserved his reputation as the greatest guitarist and showman in the trade, even though his act was not always to the liking of purists. While the Scandinavian Blues Association raved about Earl's October 11 and 12 performances in Gothenburg in *Jefferson* magazine, France's own *Soul Bag* published an interesting account of the concert given on Sunday, October 19 at Paris's famed Salle Pleyel: "Thanks to British Blues, many young listeners who are not afraid of furious sound effects and wah-wah guitar come to the AFBF. Of course, the best moments (Earl Hooker) were booed by a minority. . . . Earl Hooker, known at last, gave us a fine recital and an exemplary wah-wah guitar lesson. To those who don't like wah-wah, why do you accept bottleneck? Bottleneck may be a very basic gimmick, it still is a gimmick. . . . What we want is black American music of today, even if it must shock some of us . . . I'm glad if it does."[5]

Printed in the same issue of *Soul Bag* was a short interview of Hooker by discographer Kurt Mohr, in which Earl was asked to list his favorite musicians: these ranged from Paul "Guitar Red" Johnson to Matt Murphy, Wayne Bennett, Albert and B. B. King as well as keyboard player Ironing Board Sam— whose taste for weird instruments and unusual sounds excited the admiration of Earl. "Our meeting did not allow an in-depth interview," Mohr remembers. "Between backstage, the taxi ride, the hotel and the restaurant, we found enough time to chat, and although Hooker had a thousand stories to tell, we couldn't get into details. To the best of my recollection, Hooker was a radiant guy who greatly enjoyed his success, although his sickness obviously kept him in a constant state of exhaustion."

The warm reactions and laudatory write-ups Hooker got wherever he played in Europe shouldn't have surprised him. His currently available recordings, including his latest Blue Thumb release, whose catchy front cover was heavily advertised in the musical press at the time of his European tour, were pale and lifeless reflections of his explosive stage appearances, and even those aware of the man's reputation were taken aback by his proficiency. As strange as it may seem, Earl's tuberculosis had reached such a stage by then that it should have prevented him from performing at all, but it was just the opposite: it seemed to make him all the more eager to put all of his stamina into his art in an irrational attempt at defying his disease. What his body lost in life, his performances gained in force and sheer energy as he picked the guitar with his teeth and feet, played it behind his back or started bizarre ventriloquist-like conversations with his instrument, such as the one that may be heard on the live recording of his Royal Albert Hall concert:

> Hooker: Do you like those people out there?
> Guitar: I do.
> Hooker: Is they alright?
> Guitar: Yes they are.

Hooker: Is you glad to be in London tonight?
Guitar: Yes I am.
Hooker (surprised): Oh, you ain't glad to be in London!
Guitar (irritated): Yes I am!
Hooker: No, you ain't!
Guitar (angrily): Yes I am!!!
Hooker: Are you really?
Guitar: Yes I am.
Hooker: You like that little girl out there?
Guitar: Yes!
Hooker: Well, tell her that you like her. Say, "Hey, baby, I like you."
Guitar: Hey, baby, I like you!
Hooker (laughing): Oh, don't do that! How about whistlin' that girl one time?
Guitar: Wheeew, wheee!
Hooker: Say, "Hey, baby."
Guitar: Hey, baby!
Hooker: Everythin' gonna be alright?
Guitar: Yeah.
Hooker (getting into a tune): Alright. Let me hear you play some blues, now.

Due to the scarceness of blues concerts in most European countries at the time, radio and television coverage was extensive wherever the AFBF '69 artists performed. Hooker was particularly fond of such opportunities to display his talent, and his most sensational stage tricks were saved for television shows. His deep-rooted sense of entertainment was obvious on such occasions, as he gave the best of himself when he knew that the cameras were focused on him. To give but one example, the hilarious singing cowboy impersonation he made in front of an appreciative audience at a live television show in Germany con-firms the opinion of Earl's friend Kansas City Red, who once claimed that Hooker could have become an extraordinary comedian if he had put his mind to it. Strumming an acoustic guitar in a manner reminiscent of Roy Rogers, Earl first started singing an Ernest Tubb hit with a thick Texan drawl ("I'm a-walkin' the floor over you / I can't sleep a wiiiink, that is true, wahooow!") before he addressed the public in a similar way: "Yes, La'ies and Gen'men, this is Earl Hooker comin' to you from Houston, Texas, got all his mountain hill-billies with 'im. Wahooow! We gonna do a TV show t'night for ya, kind friends, an' I hope that you all a-like it, by Golly!"

Everywhere he played, Hooker found a way to stand out. If the October 25 Geneva concert that concluded the tour presented him in a regular blues set-

307   *Goin' Down Slow (1969–1970)*

ting, he insisted on showcasing his adequate piano technique in a short piece titled "My Own Piano Blues." Hooker's repertoire turned out to be rather varied, and his bag of songs was renewed almost nightly as a function of his mood. While he sang Lee Shot Williams's "Hello Baby" in Copenhagen, the live Albert Hall recording bears witness to Earl's convincing, if windless, renditions of Lowell Fulson's "Blue Shadows" and Jimmy Reed's "Baby What You Want Me to Do." As a rule, Robert Nighthawk's "Anna Lee" provided him with his most moving vocals. This was especially true of the version he sang at one of the two concerts he gave in Gothenburg. His emotion-laden wah-wah/slide playing and profoundly sad singing were so poignant, in fact, that it is difficult today, when listening to the tapes made then by dedicated fans, not to think that Hooker knew his career was reaching a decisive stage, particularly as he delivered the song's last verse with bloodcurdling somberness: "Anna Lee, this is my last time to cry, Anna Lee / Anna Lee, this is my last good-bye, Anna Lee / Well, now you say you gonna be mine, just hang around and see."

Regardless of his poor physical condition, and despite the exhausting working conditions the AFBF organizers imposed on the musicians—twenty concerts in twenty-three days in nine different countries!—Hooker tried to make the most of his stay in Europe. In addition to the long conversations he had with blues fans everywhere he performed, he tried to grasp everything he could see and hear. Days off were scarce, but he still managed to visit a large number of clothing and music stores in the course of his travels. His fee for the whole tour was nothing spectacular though, each artist receiving a weekly payment of five hundred dollars, out of which food and hotel rooms were to be taken, but by the time he reached Scandinavia less than a week after his arrival in London, he had bought a huge hollow-bodied Shaftsbury guitar that gave his playing a fuller and mellower tone, and he proudly wore an elegant black fur coat purchased somewhere along the way. For Earl, one of the highlights of this tour was his short stay in Switzerland, where he was treated like royalty by his friend Willy Leiser, who spent the tour's last day with him in Geneva. Together they made the rounds of local music dealers, listened to records, took pictures, and had a great time.

Hooker enjoyed the whole trip tremendously, but it wasn't free of minor hassles. Whereas his solid sense of humor and natural talent as a joke-teller proved invaluable during long bus rides, his jocular character was not to the liking of the irritable Clifton Chenier. This did not escape Earl's attention; in order to keep his fellow musicians laughing, he started teasing Chenier, making fun of his South Louisiana accent, exciting the anger of the touchy accordionist. At the same time, Chenier's creole French came in handy when the band reached French-speaking regions at the end of the trip. With the exception of the London date, the language barrier had plagued the daily existence of the musicians, who had a hard time ordering the food they liked in restaurants. When they arrived in Paris, Chenier acted as an interpreter, and they were able at last to decipher a menu and communicate with waiters. Disregarding his dislike of Earl, Chenier grumpily ordered his meal when the guitarist begged him to do so. Hooker's roadmates concur in saying that after Hooker was handed a plate of raw fish instead of the well-done steak he was expecting to get, he didn't mess with Chenier again until the end of the tour.

This journey overseas was a sort of apotheosis for Hooker, who regarded it, along with his recording trips to California, as the climax of his career. Earl was aware that he wasn't going to live much longer, but he knew on the strength of this tour that he had at last won the world's recognition, after twenty-five years of being considered a musicians' musician in black America. His pride, when he came back to Chicago in late October, showed in the enthusiastic accounts he never failed to give when he met friends or associates. At the same time, this trip was terribly demanding from a physical standpoint; even for someone as used to extensive traveling as Hooker was, the constant airplane and bus rides across the Old Continent proved tiresome.

Earl was so exhausted, in fact, that his friends noticed a severe deterioration of his health upon his return, even though he did his best to keep up a confident countenance, disclosing with exaggerated exuberance ambitious schemes for the future. "When he came back, he told me how it went," Earl's one-time booking-agent Herb Turner recalls. "He said that the acceptance there was good, and that it was a whole different scene from what he had ever saw before. He said that he was lookin' forward to the next trip when he came back this time. I was standin' out in front of my place when he came back and most times, he stuttered anyway, but he was really tied-tongued when he told me about it. He say, 'I-I-I-I w-w-wanna d-d-d-do it again.' He had a new van, and he told me that he was doin' pretty good, and he was gonna put his band back together, but after he came back he didn't live long, 'cause I remember when he came back, it was no longer the same Earl."

Despite an apparent abundance of plans, Hooker felt too weak to put a new outfit together and take to the road. Even though he made surprise club appearances around the city every now and then in November and early December, he spent more and more of his time resting at his mother's home. No longer able to hustle his own gigs on a regular basis, Earl even accepted gigs with old friends like Junior Wells. Junior was one of the rare artists with whom Earl had condescended to play earlier on in the year, much to the delight of Wells's booking agent Dick Waterman. Undaunted by Earl's refusal to team up with Junior on a permanent basis, Waterman entered into transactions with Hooker again in the fall with the idea of setting up a "Slider Festival" package that would present the blues' foremost slide guitarists and that would boast, in addition to Hooker, Mississippi stylists Son House, Fred McDowell, and Johnny Shines as well as Chicagoan J. B. Hutto. Appearing with a package show on a well-publicized tour of the United States appealed to Hooker, but if Waterman received Earl's consent, the guitarist did not live long enough for the project to materialize.

One of Hooker's very last Chicago club dates took place at a North Side location where both Buddy Guy and Junior Wells were hired with their respective bands, Earl guesting with Wells's outfit. "That was the last time that I talked to Hooker," Billy Boy Arnold, who was in the crowd that night, reports. "The place was jam packed, Lefty Dizz was playing guitar over Junior, and Junior had Earl Hooker playing too. And Hooker was very sick. That was right before he died. We talked about California, and he asked if I wanted to go to California. He could get me on a LP out in California. So I said, 'Okay, well, let me know,' and we talked for a while. He was very sick, but he didn't complain about it; I've never heard him talk about it. But he never did no touring because shortly after that he went back to the hospital. But I know one thing; Hooker wanted to live because he wanted to play. If there ever was a guy who wanted to live, I think it was Hooker."

In the judgment of those who knew him well, Hooker displayed courage and dignity until the end. With time his disease developed into an endless source of minor physical complications, but he constantly put on a smiling and unconcerned front although he obviously had to endure considerable pain. "In fact he could have taken a lot better care of himself," Dick Shurman states. "Everybody knows that, but he just wouldn't stop. [Keyboard player] Alberto [Gianquinto] told me once that Hooker had real bad hemorrhoids too; he said he went to the bandstand and just tucked his hemorrhoids in when he sat down and started to play, so he probably had a lot of other diseases, but he never complained about it to me. To me it was just the opposite, whenever I would ask him how he was feeling. Like I called him once, 'cause I had read in *Rolling Stone* that he was in the hospital, and he denied ever having been to the hospital. I think he liked to just sort of try to deal with it as best he could and not let it get him down, even though obviously it was having an effect besides what he could eat and drink. Like by the time I knew him he couldn't really sing anymore hardly and he played sitting down, and he had to give up his double-neck guitars 'cause they were too heavy, and everybody else was very concerned about him but he wasn't gonna complain in public about it, and he certainly wasn't going around crying about it."

The winter of 1969–1970 was an exceptionally cold and harsh one in Chicago. Hooker's general weakness was responsible for his hospitalization in December with a bad case of pneumonia that tied him to a hospital bed for almost three months. As the tuberculosis grew stronger than ever, heart trouble started developing. Adding to Hooker's distress, his mother's apartment at 4025 King Drive was burglarized in January. Among other things, the fur coat that Earl had bought in Europe was stolen, as Mrs. Hooker explained in a letter to Willy Leiser, dated February 13, 1970: "Mr Willie Leiser my dear friend . . . Earl got all of your letters, i hasnt had time to wright to anybody please dont thank hard of Earl because he has bind very low low sick—But he is getting better now thank to the good Lord for that i bind so busy seen after Earl— . . . i thank he will be home again very soon i hope. i am very well and my daughter is find dranking all of the wikey she can she still play music when she ant drunk . . . o yes listen some one broke in my house 17 of january took Earl pretty coat he bort over thair iv lost more thang—the police havn caught them yet—they tryid to steal all of his music i got home to quick they really was going to clean my ho[u]se out."

Mail from European friends made Earl's hospital sojourn look less grim. Even though he was still confined to bed in March, Mrs. Hooker, in reply to a get-well letter from Willie Leiser, bravely made plans for the future. "Mr Willie

Leiser my dear friend," Mrs. Hooker wrote on Sunday, March 9. "i got your s[w]eet letter and carried it to the hosptial to Earl, he was very glade to hear frome you . . . some day me and Earl will will make a record together and send it to you . . . —and dont bee sirprise at me sanging—smile—i thankt Earl will be out soon he dont now just when . . . Earl just smile when i read your letter to him and you ask me about my daughter she still liking the wiskey bottale—smile—with all of that talton she got—one of these days we try to record her on tape and send you one just to let you hear [her] sang." It was not until later in March that doctors finally let Hooker go home because he refused to rest and spent more time playing his guitar than lying down.

In those evil days, some consolation came with the excellent album reviews and concert write-ups that kept flowing in. The editors of *Blues Unlimited*, the leading publication of the genre, hardly put out an issue at the time without reviewing one of Hooker's albums or printing a laudatory concert report. The October 1969 issue included a positive point of view on his Blue Thumb set penned by Mike Leadbitter, who advised his readers to "get the Arhoolie [*Two Bugs and a Roach* LP] first, then this one," before he added: "This is a pleasant but not essential album."[6] In the same issue, a full-page ad boasting the fine picture of Earl featured on the sleeve of the Blue Thumb set appeared on the magazine's back cover.

In December a picture of Earl Hooker and Mack Thompson taken at London's Royal Albert Hall by Valerie Wilmer appeared on the front page of Britain's *Jazz Monthly*, and *Blues Unlimited* readers were treated to a two-page report on the 1969 American Folk Blues Festival, four of its performers, including Earl, sharing front-page honors. In his enthusiastic account of the London concert, Simon Napier thought the 1969 festival "very heartening after the 1968 debacle, as good as any since 1964 and potentially, the best of all time," while his description of Hooker's act sounded like a dithyramb: "He began with verve, picking the guitar with his teeth! He never looked back!! On 'Baby What You Want Me to Do' he found it necessary to talk with his axe, as if to convince us he's a boss guitarist—have no doubt he is; onstage he is quite remarkable, all over his instrument. Using a steel like never before he creates unique, remarkable music. Hooker is fast becoming the most recorded blues guitarist around and it is easy to see why. If his health stands up, he should be very big in a few months time."[7]

Readers learned more about Hooker as they went on, when they found an article titled "Bottleneck Blues," discussing the respective merits of three currently available slide guitar albums, including Earl's brand new Bluesway set. "His latest album, the fourth in little over six months has to be not only the best in toto as an album, but has to be the best blues album I've heard this year! . . . Earl is the first person to PLAY guitar with a wa-wa—and when he plays SLIDE with wa-wa, then hold onto your heads. Side 1 will have you all over the ceiling half-way through—honest! . . . EARL HOOKER IS A MOTHA!!!! . . . All the albums mentioned here are good, but the last-mentioned is the best and MUST be bought."[8]

Still, the most pleasant surprise of all came when *Blues Unlimited* chose to put on the cover of its February-March issue a picture of Earl taken at Moose Walker's Bluesway session, with the following caption: "Earl Hooker during his Bluesway recording session. Despite constant health problems Hooker in 1969 rose from obscurity to relative stardom."[9] In the same issue, Chris Strachwitz announced the forthcoming release of Earl's second Arhoolie set, but Hooker's presence was also noted in a sadder context, the picture illustrating Magic Sam's obituary showing Sam playing Hooker's guitar at the AFBF concert in Brussels.

By the time he left the hospital in March, Hooker was clearly conscious that his life had reached a decisive stage, and he finally resigned himself to stop fighting a losing battle against consumption. "He had been sick for so long that he wasn't afraid to die," says Billy Boy Arnold, and his statement was backed by the following story, collected from guitarist Louis Myers by Dick Shurman: "Louis told me that he knew that Hooker had made up his mind that he was gonna die the last time that Hooker got out of the hospital. Louis said that he and Moose got him out and they went to some greasy spoon in the Loop, and Hooker ordered a meal like spaghetti or something which they knew that he wasn't supposed to eat, and they inferred that when he was starting to eat like that that he had just given up, that he was ready to go."

The results of Earl's careless attitude were not long in coming. On Monday, April 6, Hooker entered the intensive care unit of Chicago's Municipal Turberculosis Sanitarium. The TB sanitarium, found in the northwestern part of town at 5601 North Pulaski Road—today a home for the elderly—was a large institution housing 1,500 patients. Although Earl had occasionally spent time at the sanitarium before, he felt very disappointed not to be sent to 1919 West Taylor, where he was well known, but his unruly conduct was responsible for his doctors' refusal to admit him at the State TB Hospital. "He ran out so much they wouldn't take him back in, to my understanding," Hooker's wife reports. "That's why he wound up in this different hospital. 'Cause the one on Taylor was a real nice hospital. The hospital he died in they said wasn't very much of a hospital. It was a run-down hospital."

Within a few days of his admission to the sanitarium, Hooker's condition deteriorated to such an extent that his mother refused to let anyone visit him, and only his closest friends were given the telephone number of his hospital room, as Dick Shurman recalls: "I was just gonna call him a few days before he died because I had a job for him if he wanted out near Seattle, but his mother told me that he was real sick, and she said, 'I'm not giving his number to many people,' but she said, 'I'll give it to you if you want to talk to him,' and I said, 'Well, if he's that sick, I'll just let him rest and I'll talk to him when he feels better,' and then he died."

During the few days that preceded his death, Hooker grew weaker as a heart condition developed. On Monday, April 20, two weeks after his arrival at the sanitarium, he called his mother to his bedside and told her that he was ready to go. "Earl is missing so much Willie i may get over it and i may not," Mrs. Hooker recounted the event with dignity in a letter sent to Willy Leiser three months later. "that day before he di[e]d he was talking about you and George Adin[s] how much he though of you and George you all was very nice to him he told me that heaven was a beautifull place to goe he told the family to gathring around the bed told all to beshore to look at him real good we wont neaver see him no more—mother you doe the best you can—that he was tird of suffring."

On the night that followed, Earl knew that he had but a few hours to live, and he gathered whatever little energy he still had in store to sneak out of the sanitarium in a desperate attempt to make it to his mother's third-floor apartment on the South Side, "borrowing" a car to cover the fifteen miles separating the hospital from his home. "Billy Boy [Arnold] said that right before he was gonna die, he decided that he wanted to die at home," Dick Shurman reports. "So he stole out of the hospital and stole one of the cars that belonged to somebody that worked at the hospital and drove down to his mother's house, but he was so weak when he got there that he couldn't make it up the steps, they lived on the top floor, and so they came from the hospital and figured that's where he went and found him at the bottom. They took him back to the hospital and didn't tell his mother until he was dead."

"Well, the last time he went into the hospital," Big Moose Walker confirms with a slightly different account, "he broke out and they caught him walkin' up the Expressway, goin' south. He was tryin' to make it home, that's the night he died. He got out of the hospital some kinda way. They picked him up on the Expressway, they probably warned the police and stuff that he was gone, on the radio, and he was on his way home. And they carried him back to the hospital and he died that night."

Regardless of where he was found, Hooker was hurriedly driven back to his room at the sanitarium, where he died around half past seven the following morning, Tuesday, April 21. "dear Willie Leiser," Earl's distressed mother wrote to her son's Swiss friend several days later, "this to let you now i lost my poor son Earl Hooker is dead i am a lonly mother with thought my son—please notifind all of his friend . . . i am sending you a program picture of his you keep this to rember him he talk about you all of the time doing his sickness. People bin very nice to me so pray for me that God will give me strength to cary on i did everything i could doe for my son Earl. . . . my hart is to full to say any thing ease to you . . . plase let all of the poeple [know] he is dead he di[e]d on Apr 21 1970 abou 745 am."

According to Dr. James R. Thompson, who performed the autopsy before he signed the death certificate, Earl died of "right myocardial insufficiency due to active, far advanced pulmonary tuberculosis." The medical data printed on Hooker's death certificate was the only accurate information to be found there, maybe with the exception of his social security number and current address. While his birth date was given as January 15, 1930, his wife's name, Bertha Nickerson, was erroneously printed Bertha "Nixon"—an understandable mistake as it took place under the administration of another "recording" artist, Richard Nixon.

Mrs. Hooker was notified at once of her son's death, but the blow was so hard that she kept it secret for a while, much to the displeasure of Earl's closest friends, who knew nothing about it until a couple of days later when she started making phone calls. Hooker had been expected to die any time for at least several months by those who knew him well, but the news of his death still came as a shock to them. "If I remember right, he was thirty-nine years old when he died, and you see how he looked. He looked like a old man seventy-some years old, but it was because of the TB he had. And they got him almost well two or three different times, and when he would get to that state, man, he would slip away from that hospital and get him a band and skip town. That was Earl Hooker," says pianist Eddie Boyd, whose reaction illustrates that of the Chicago community. "But he was a personality, one that was unforgettable. And I always did like him, and I was so sorry when I heard about his death. Having TB and treatin' himself like he did, I mean, there was nothing else to expect from him."

Earl's death was all the more traumatic when another prominent blues artist, pianist Otis Spann, died only days after Hooker. "Hooker died like this Tuesday and Spann died on Friday, three days apart, and then they were exactly the same age. Spann was dead before they had Earl's funeral. Three days apart, that's kinda shaky, you know," Big Moose Walker said with emotion as he reminisced about the event with Alligator Records' Bruce Iglauer, who had just moved to Illinois when Hooker and Spann died, and whose comments illustrate the state of shock the local blues scene was in: "I came here the first of '70. I didn't know Earl, but I went to see Spann in the hospital, and it was funny 'cause I remember when Earl died, I thought 'Earl's died instead of Spann, Spann's gonna live because Earl died in his place,' and then when Spann passed too, I just couldn't stand it."

Probably the most moving tribute paid by a fellow bluesman to both Hooker and Spann came from Memphis Slim. The fact that Slim resided in Paris, France, at the time clearly points to the universality of the grief that overcame the blues world then. Slim was currently working on an ambitious recording project called Blue Memphis Suite. When it was time for him to walk into the studio in early June, he decided to dedicate a slow blues to "Otis Spann and Earl Hooker," trying at the same time to draw the public's notice to their thankless trade: "So good bye Earl Hooker and Otis too / You will now get all the credit that you were always due / But I know everybody must pay their debt / So sad how quick your friends forget."

During the days that followed her son's death, Mrs. Hooker was busy making all the arrangements for the funeral with the ghetto's largest undertaker, the A. R. Leak Funeral Home, found at 7838 South Cottage Grove on the South Side. The over-possessiveness she had shown throughout her son's life became even more acute after his demise. In an attempt at reclaiming her Earl, she took care of the burial before Hooker's wife could arrive from Missouri. "She never did call me and tell me he was in the hospital," Bertha says bitterly. "In fact, I didn't even know he was in there until about two or three days before he died. One of the boys out of the band called me, but I can't think which one it was. It might have been Lee [Shot Williams], called me and axed me did I know Earl was up there in the hospital, and I said, 'No.' Then I just casually said, 'Well, I'll probably be up there in a little bit.' Then that Tuesday, his mother called and told me that he had passed like on that Tuesday mornin', and I got up there that Wednesday night, I went on the train by myself. When I got there, she had him all ready to be buried. She didn't ask me one question did I want him buried here or—she did the whole thing. She had already made arrangements. Everythin'! Everythin' was ready."

No doubt, Mrs. Hooker's need to exclude "strangers" from her sorrow made her act in a blunt manner, yet it may seem strange that Earl Hooker didn't see fit to keep in touch with his wife at the end. Bertha Nickerson explains the situation when she mentions the estrangement that progressively developed between her husband and herself due to Hooker's flightiness. "I hadn't saw him in maybe nine or ten months when he died," she sedately declares. "I think we was just about to get a divorce. It wasn't anythin' that he was doin', it wasn't me, but I was tired of that kinda life. In the long run I got tired. I just thought, 'Well, this is not a life for a marriage.' I didn't tell him I had made up my mind to that, but that's what my mind was makin' up to. Either slow down and stay home or I was gonna get a divorce, but he died before I could tell him that. Really, he didn't know it, but that's what I had on my mind because the marriage was too far apart. But we was still friends. We still kept in touch; he would call me. The last time I talked to him, I didn't have an idea that he was that sick. He never talked about death to me. He always was gonna do this and he was gonna do that. But he shoulda known, as sickly as he was, that he was gonna die if he didn't take care of himself."

Mrs. Hooker wanted to bury Earl in the best possible way, and she barely succeeded in gathering the total amount of funeral expenses, including embalming and the printing of the religious service obituary. In fact, the funeral director's bill of $1,519.50 might not have been paid but for the help of Hooker's friends, and more especially vocalist Andrew B. B. Odom, who set up a concert that week to raise some money. "I gave him a benefit at Pepper's Lounge at 503 East 43rd Street. Pepper's was still open then. I taken up quite a bit of money for him," Odom says, before he adds with bitterness: "And that's when I felt kinda let down, even though I wasn't lookin' for anythin'. But I feel like his mother should have gave me a microphone, or a picture or anythin' to remember him by, which I didn't get anythin'. Because his mother let his nephews and things come and just run through all of his stuff. He had a organ, horns, and everythin' else. She let his nephews and things come through and run through over all the bullshit."

The funeral took place on the following Saturday, April 25. The religious service was conducted by one of Earl's relatives on his mother's side, Reverend Edmond Blair Sr.—a prominent Chicago preacher with several recorded sermons to his credit. Blair's own son, Edmond Jr., played the organ prelude and two members of the church, Mrs. Daniels and Harry Reese, sang one solo each. At two o'clock in the afternoon, several hundred people gathered under the early spring sun in front of Reverend Blair's Omega Missionary Baptist Church at 4621 South State Street, across the street from the Robert Taylor projects, to pay Earl a last homage. Many members of the Hooker and Blair families present that day tried to comfort Mrs. Hooker and Earl's widow. "It was a nice day, a real nice day," Bertha, who felt somewhat lost in the crowd, recalls. "He had quite a few relatives at that funeral. It was some of 'em that I hadn't even met. It was some cousins, and he had a aunt, it was on his daddy's side, she lived in Indiana, but I didn't know too many peoples. I met some, just introduced to quite a few, but I never really knew 'em."

Next to the relatives came Hooker's closest friends, who acted as pallbearers at Mrs. Hooker's request. "His mother had him laid away first class, the best type of stuff," Billy Boy Arnold explains. "Me, Big Moose, Voice Odom, we carried the casket out to the car, I think Louis Myers was there too, I'm not sure. It was all musicians who carried the casket. A guy was here from ABC Records—Michel, he came from Los Angeles. He really liked Hooker. He was kinda very sad about it. I didn't go to the cemetery, me and Moose we were together, 'cause we went to the airport to take Michel."

"I felt close to Earl," Ed Michel recalls, "and went to his funeral. He was a fine fellow in every way and, for my money, was an amazing and profound player. Anyway, I was at Earl's funeral because he never failed to move me when he played and was a generally nice man." Besides Michel, who had flown all the way from California, several members of the musical press and a British film crew who happened to be in town attended Earl's funeral service. "The Omega Baptist Church at 46th and State Streets looks like so many other black churches in Chicago's South Side, New York's Harlem, or Los Angeles' Watts," the reporter hurriedly dispatched by *Rolling Stone* wrote in the illustrated one-page obituary the magazine published shortly afterward. "The preacher and the congregation are still wearing long robes and there is still the old call-and-response chanting and wailing when somebody dies. If you listen carefully, you can still hear the old, hopeless, country sadness in the singing. If you listen carefully, you can hear something that goes back beyond that. . . . At the Omega Baptist Church . . . Big Moose the piano player had come down from the LaSalle Towers hotel where he was staying temporarily. Little Blues Boy [Odom] was taking time off from his car wash job. A crew of British cameramen were there too. They'd been hanging around town, waiting for Otis Spann to die so they could film his funeral documentary. They'd decided to shoot Earl Hooker while they were waiting. 'It won't be long,' somebody said, 'before they all will be buyin' his records, and playin' his licks.'"[10]

If friends and relatives were many, they were outnumbered by the city's blues musicians. Those who were working out of town at the time—such as Buddy Guy or Carey Bell—sent their wives in their stead, but many others including Junior Wells, Mighty Joe Young, Little Mack Simmons, Detroit Junior, Koko and "Pops" Taylor, Lee Jackson, Willie Dixon, Lonnie Brooks, Lee Shot Williams, and Johnny Pepper were to be seen in the large crowd. "I was there," Junior Wells remembered with emotion. "I only did one thing, I went in, signed my name on the guest list, and walked back out. I didn't wanna know where he was buried. I didn't want to even look at him or anything." The only absentee of note was Hooker's close friend and former jail companion Kansas City Red, who later incurred the ire of Mrs. Hooker: "I didn't get a chance to make it to the funeral and she cursed me out. 'You could have been there, you know you and Hooker were the best of friends!' I said, 'That's right, Mrs. Hooker,' I said, 'but I was tied up, I just couldn't come.' I tried to but I couldn't go. You just don't leave your business, although I could have closed it up, but when you got that rent to pay and them bills to pay, you can't be closing up too fast."

The church was too small for the large number of people who attended the funeral, and several incidents arose in the confusion. At one point, Mrs. Hooker tried to get Hooker's friends to play but she met with the refusal of Johnny Big Moose Walker, who was hurt by her tactless attitude at the time of Earl's death and who was far too affected to grant her request: "I told her, 'No, not me.' I wouldn't play at the church. Bobby Davis, he had the drums, and she asked if the guys gonna play, I told her no. If I had been at the hospital when he died, his mother wouldn't let anyone see him, but if I had been at the hospital and *he* asked me to play, then I probably would have, but I just couldn't do it by his mother sayin' it."

This was not the most spectacular incident. In addition to Hooker's lawful spouse Bertha, the unexpected presence of several women who claimed to be Earl's wives caused a great commotion. Their claims were all the more convincing as several came with children who were the living image of Hooker, adding to his wife's distress. "Yes, there was a big mix-up about the women," Billy Boy Arnold remembers. "There was several women there with kids, you know, five or six women with children, one had two or three and one had one. All of the kids looked just like Hooker. His wife was there and these other women didn't wanna respect his wife, like when we were going to the cemetery, this one particular woman who's got a son and daughter by Hooker—he must have had those when he was very young, 'cause they were about eighteen at the time—well anyway at the funeral, she sits in the place where the wife's supposed to sit, right next to Hooker's mother, and Hooker's lawful married wife Bertha didn't like the idea. I was talkin' to her about it, I told her, I said, 'Listen, you know, I understand.' Moose was trying to keep her from starting a disturbance about it, and then when we got into the funeral parlor, this other woman jumps in the family car, so Hooker's lawful married wife was sorta like pushed into the background."

Bertha did feel deeply hurt by the rude way she was treated by her mother-in-law throughout the ceremony. Quite understandably, the presence at the funeral of children some of whom had been born during her marriage came as a shock, but the fact that her name was not even mentioned in the obituary crystallized her mortification. "His kids were there, I think most of 'em was there.

To my knowin'. From this woman, from that woman," Bertha remarks sharply. "That son of his looks like him. That older son, he looks like him. He had to be about fourteen, 'cause he was a big size boy then. But the rest of 'em were just children, I couldn't tell anythin' about 'em. The obituary stated that he had eight children.[11] That's why I said, 'I would have named a wife before I'd put those eight children.' But I wasn't listed in the obituary, I don't know why. I had a brother-in-law, he said, 'I'll just break that up, I know you don't want that on there,' he say, 'because you are the wife, and should have the last say.' I thought, 'Why have the last say over it now?' So after it was all like that, I didn't do one thing about it. Just went to the funeral, got situated and came home. I left all that stuff in Chicago with his mother. I didn't see a piece of his clothes, not anythin'. Not a guitar, not anythin'. She didn't offer to give me any and I didn't axe for any. I came home and I guess that's why we didn't keep in touch."

Things had quieted down by the time the procession arrived at Restvale Cemetery in Worth, a suburb situated southwest of the city at 115th Street and Laramie. Earl, joining a host of blues greats including Clarence "Pine Top" Smith, Magic Sam, Johnnie Jones, and Doctor Clayton, was put to rest in Section K, Lot 33, Grave 4, where a simple gravestone of moderate size with an engraved flowery cross reminds the world of the presence of EARL Z. HOOKER, 1929–1970, SON.

Hooker was home to mother at last.

Epilogue

A round the time of Earl Hooker's death, the blues went through some hard times. In the ghettos, young African Americans were drawn to the catchy social consciousness of soul music, while young Whites adhered to the pseudo-protest message of rock; in both cases, the public failed to see the debt these styles owed to the blues, and they discarded the blues. But for a handful of black ghetto club patrons and hard-core white fans, the blues might not have survived. Yet, thanks to a small number of publi- cations and dedicated record companies, blues amateurs were able to cling together. With time, as the blues slowly comforted its in- ternational audience, a handful of reissue labels put out rare recordings on compilation LPs—including Earl Hooker's Chief/Age sides.

The eighties brought about more changes, at various levels. Af- ter the political awareness of the sixties and the heedlessness of the following decade, the relative sense of collectiveness that pre- vailed so far gave way to the individualism so characteristic of the Reagan years. One of the consequences of this social interiorization was that the first-person language of the blues sounded relevant again: after years of hearing, "We're proud and strong," people could relate to someone who sang, "I feel down and out." Along with the advent of the compact disc, this phenomenon warranted the salvation of the blues, eventually leading to a boom in this market.

Possibly because he had been dead for over a decade, and certainly because he came short of becoming a star during his lifetime, Earl Hooker somehow missed the train of blues resurrection—possibly with the exception of the Japanese market, where he consistently had a faithful following, in spite of obvious linguistic and cultural problems (as a reader once said with much humor in a letter to *Blues Unlimited* magazine, "any language that transforms Earl Hooker into Earu Fooka has obviously got problems"[1]). In Hooker's own country, Chris Strachwitz didn't see fit to reissue two of the guitarist's three Arhoolie LPs in CD form until 1990, waiting eight more years before re-releasing Earl's third Arhoolie album, *Hooker and Steve*, along with four unissued sides. As for the Universal conglomerate, it took them until 1999 to dedicate a compilation tribute to Hooker (*Simply the Best*), with a mere sprinkling of Chess, Bluesway, and Blue Thumb sides.

In the specialized press, Hooker hasn't been deemed worthy of a serious portrait in years, even though hardly an issue of any of the leading magazines goes to print without Earl Hooker's name being mentioned by one or the other of his peers. His fellow musicians have been the only ones to keep the flame alive, actually, paying him the most fitting tribute by honoring his memory in their words and, most of all, through their music. Over the years, in spite of the indifference of the general public, Hooker's distinctive style has managed to survive in the playing of others. These include a limited number of students, namely the late Willie Kizart and Ike Turner, who were taught directly by Hooker in the late forties; this is also true of former associates like Son Seals, Luther "Guitar Junior" Johnson, Jimmy Johnson, and Jimmy Dawkins, who have pursued the tradition in Chicago. As for Hooker's strongest themes, including "Blue Guitar," "Will My Man Be Home Tonight," or "Universal Rock," they have now become part of the standard Chicago blues repertoire, inspiring spirited versions by the likes of Lacy Gibson, Eddy Clearwater, and Otis Rush—one most thorough assimilators of Hooker's playing, along with Billy Flynn. In 1992 Little Smokey Smothers probably paid the most moving homage to his late mentor when he recorded a "Tribute to Earl Hooker" in which both he and Flynn made eerie re-creations of Earl's style.

Many more players have been marked by Hooker's genius through his records, as was the case at the end of his life with representatives of the British blues boom, in bands like the Bluesbreakers or Led Zeppelin. To this day, Earl's influence will show in the constant borrowings from his music made by gui-tarists everywhere on the blues circuit—with the notable exception of New Orleans, where the Windy City tradition has never been much exposed, partly because the guitar has always been second in New Orleans to piano and horns.

Regardless of time, Earl's reputation doesn't seem to have waned in the blues milieu. Throughout the years, Buddy Guy (who claimed for a long time that he slept at night with one of Earl's slides), Junior Wells, Willie Dixon, Louis My-ers, and Wayne Bennett in Chicago; Albert Washington in Cincinnati; Little Milton and Albert King in Memphis; Guitar Shorty and Joe Louis Walker on the West Coast; Chicago Bob Nelson and Tinsley Ellis in Atlanta; Albert Collins and Lucky Peterson in Texas; and Ronnie Earl (who adopted his stage name as a tribute to Hooker at the instance of Muddy Waters) in New England all declared at one time or another that they considered Hooker the undisputed master of the electric guitar, confirming the following statement made by *Liv-ing Blues* cofounder Jim O'Neal in the fall of 1970: "He was the best blues gui-tarist in Chicago, maybe the best anywhere. Such was the reputation Earl Hooker earned amongst the most discriminating critics of all—the other musi-cians of the blues community."[2]

An alarming proportion of those who appear on the preceding list have dis-appeared in recent years, showing that the very survival of Earl Hooker's name and musical heritage is at stake. As the new century rolls in, we run the risk of losing much of what we could have learned about postwar blues life in the Chicago ghetto and on the chitlin' circuit. This may well be what the main contributors of *Living Blues* magazine feared when they put Earl Hooker's name on top of their list of "Postwar blues artists most deserving of wider recogni-tion" in the November/December 1999 issue of that publication.

Thirty years after Hooker's death, as a majority of blues lovers seem to be unaware of the everyday life of blues artists at a time when their music was still tightly related to ghetto reality, this account of Earl's life and deeds will hope-fully shed some light on the Chicago blues scene as a whole, putting it into proper perspective. If only for that, the present work will be meaningful.

Notes

INTRODUCTION

1. Jim Crockett, "B. B. King As Told to Jim Crockett—My 10 Favorite Guitarists," *Guitar Player* (March 1975): 23.

2. Charles Keil, *Urban Blues* (Chicago: University of Chicago Press, 1966), 20.

CHAPTER 1: THE EARLY YEARS (1929–1946)

1. Chris Albertson, *Bessie* (London: Barrie & Jenkins, 1972), 25.

2. Charles S. Johnson, *Shadow of the Plantation* (New Brunswick and London: Transaction Pub., 1996—originally published in 1934), 186–87.

3. Quoted in Stetson Kennedy, *Jim Crow Guide: The Way It Was* (Boca Raton: Florida Atlantic University Press, 1992), 135.

4. Lerone Bennett Jr., *Before the Mayflower: A History of Black America* (New York: Penguin, 1993), 358.

5. Quoted in Ira Berkow, *Maxwell Street: Survival in a Bazaar* (Garden City, N.Y.: Doubleday, 1977), 87.

6. According to Christine Hooker's birth certificate, she was the Hookers' second child. For the following years, the official records of the City of Chicago show that Mary Blair Hooker had no other children, which would tend to indicate that the other two children mentioned by Mrs. Hooker were stillborn. At any rate, all of Earl's friends only knew of his one sister, Christine.

7. Although it has usually been accepted that John Lee Hooker was born in 1917, he sometimes gave 1920 as his year of birth, and his daughter even suggested a 1913 birthdate.

8. George R. White, *Bo Diddley: Living Legend* (Chessington, Surrey: Castle Communications, 1995), 28.

9. Bill Greensmith, "Just Whaling," *Blues Unlimited* 122 (November/December 1976): 6.

10. Horace R. Cayton and St. Clair Drake, *Black Metropolis* (London: Jonathan Cape, 1946), 580.

11. Bill Dahl and Jim O'Neal, "Jimmy Johnson," *Living Blues* 47 (Summer 1980): 21.

12. Liner notes, *Earl Hooker/The Genius of Earl Hooker*, Cuca KS-3400 (1968); *Earl Hooker/Funk—Last of the Great Earl Hooker*, Blues on Blues LP 10002 (1970).

13. Helen Oakley Dance, *Stormy Monday: The T-Bone Walker Story* (Baton Rouge and London: Louisiana State University Press, 1987), 66–67.

14. Cayton and Drake, *Black Metropolis*, 204.

15. Mike Rowe, "I Was Really Dedicated," *Blues Unlimited* 126 (September/October 1977): 7.

CHAPTER 2: ON THE ROAD (1946–1953)

1. Pete Welding, "Ramblin' Johnny Shines," *Living Blues* 22 (July/August 1975): 27.

2. Bill Greensmith, "We Got a Song Called 'Rocket 88,'" *Blues Unlimited* 135/6 (July/September 1979): 15.

3. Charles E. Cobb Jr., "Traveling the Blues Highway," *National Geographic* (April 1999): 65.

4. Charles Dickens, *American Notes for General Circulation* (London: Penguin, 1985), 215–26.

5. Jim O'Neal, "Houston Stackhouse," *Living Blues* 17 (Summer 1974): 30.

6. Dick Shurman, liner notes, *Andrew Brown/Big Brown's Chicago Blues*, Black Magic LP 9001 (1982).

7. *Chicago Defender*, June 11, 1949.

8. O'Neal, "Houston Stackhouse," 31.

9. Jim O'Neal, "Joe Willie Wilkins," *Living Blues* 11 (Winter 1972/73): 15.

10. O'Neal, "Houston Stackhouse," 26.

11. Jim O'Neal, "Billy the Kid Emerson Interview," *Living Blues* 45/6 (Spring 1980): 29.

12. Cilla Huggins, "Ike Turner—In the Beginning," *Juke Blues* 37 (Spring 1997): 12.

13. Cary Baker, "Henry Stone Interview," *Shout* 80 (September 1980): 1–2.

14. Mike Leadbitter, "Mike's Blues," *Blues Unlimited* 102 (June 1973): 20.

CHAPTER 3: THE MEMPHIS SCENE (1953)

1. Jerry Hopkins, *Elvis* (London: Abacus, 1974), 46.

2. Chris Strachwitz, liner notes, *Earl Hooker/Two Bugs and a Roach*, Arhoolie LP 1044 (1968).

3. O'Neal, "Billy the Kid Emerson Interview," 37–38.

CHAPTER 4: THE CHICAGO COMPLEX (1953–1956)

1. "High and Lonesome," Jimmy Reed's first recording, was put on wax in Chicago in June 1953 with Earl Hooker's friend John Brim on guitar.

2. *Sic.* Actually Jacksonville, in northern Florida.

3. *The American Guide Series: Florida* (New York: Oxford University Press, 1947), 475.

4. Zora Neale Hurston, *Their Eyes Were Watching God: A Novel of Negro Life* (Philadelphia: J. B. Lippincott, 1937), 197.

5. Jim O'Neal, "Jackie Brenston," *Living Blues* 45/6 (Spring 1980): 19.

6. Jim O'Neal, "Bobby Bland! Backstage," *Living Blues* 4 (Winter 1970/1971): 17–18.

7. Johnny Otis, letter to Felix Steinmann, *Blues Unlimited* 68 (December 1969): 17.

8. Al Smith, liner notes, *Earl Hooker/Funk. The Last of the Great Earl Hooker*, Blues on Blues LP 10002 (1970).

9. Chinta Strausberg, "Gas Shut Off Reforms Called for after Death of Woman, 60," *Chicago Defender* (January 12, 1995).

CHAPTER 5: ZEB HOOKER (1956–1960)

1. Dick Shurman, "King of Postwar Blues Guitar—Earl Hooker," *Seattle Folklore Society Newsletter*, Vol. 1 #4 (June 15, 1970): 3.

2. Greensmith, "Just Whaling," 12–13.

3. Steve Cushing, "Odie Payne," *Living Blues* 96 (March/April 1991): 62.

4. Jim O'Neal, "Billy the Kid Emerson Interview," 38.

5. Amy and Jim O'Neal with Dick Shurman, "Otis Rush Interview," *Living Blues* 28 (July/August 1976): 24.

6. Jim O'Neal, "Lefty Bates," *Living Blues* 21 (May/June 1975): 34.

7. Jimmy Dawkins, "My Name Is Moose Walker," *Blues Unlimited* 92 (June 1972): 16–17.

8. Marcel Chauvard and Jacques Demêtre, "Voyage Au Pays Du Blues—V: Chicago," *Jazz Hot* 153 (April, 1960): 15–16, reprinted as *Voyage au pays du Blues—1959—Land of the Blues* (Paris: CLARB, 1994), 132–34.

9. Bez Turner, "Three Mexicans, a Hillbilly and a Polock," *Blues Unlimited* 141 (Autumn/Winter 1981): 7–8.

10. Jim O'Neal, "Cadillac Baby," *Living Blues* 6 (Autumn 1971): 26.

11. Ibid.

12. Ibid.

CHAPTER 6: THE LONDON YEARS (1960–1963)

1. Jim O'Neal, "Mel London Obituary," *Living Blues* 22 (July/August 1975): 21.

2. Neil Paterson, "Mel London," in *Nothing but the Blues*, edited by Mike Leadbitter (London: Hanover Books, 1971), 52.

3. O'Neal, op. cit.

4. At that time, Johnson was still using his real name, Jimmy Thompson. He didn't

start using the name "Jimmy Johnson" until the mid-sixties, when his younger brother Syl started a successful career under the name "Syl Johnson."

5. Jim O'Neal and Steve Wisner, "Obituaries—Earnest Johnson," *Living Blues* 55 (Winter 1982/1983): 39.

6. Lois Ulrey, "Junior Wells Interview," *Magic Blues* 4 (1992): 19.

7. O'Neal, "Jackie Brenston," 20.

CHAPTER 7: GUITARS, CARS, AND WOMEN

1. E. Franklin Frazier, *The Negro Family in the United States* (Chicago: University of Chicago Press, 1966), 32.

2. Shurman, "King of Postwar Blues Guitar—Earl Hooker," 3.

3. Jim O'Neal, "Junior Wells," *Living Blues* 119 (January/February 1995): 20.

CHAPTER 8: A MAN OF MANY STYLES

1. Strachwitz, liner notes, *Earl Hooker/Two Bugs and a Roach* LP.

2. O'Neal, "Review of Cuca LP KS-3400, Blue Thumb LP BTS-12, Bluesway LP BLS-6032, Arhoolie LP 1051," 32.

3. Donald E. Wilcock with Buddy Guy, *Damn Right I've Got the Blues* (San Francisco: Woodford Press, 1993), 34.

4. Strachwitz, op. cit.

5. Ibid.

6. Ibid.

7. "It's Gonna Work Out Fine"/"Won't You Forgive Me" (Sue 749), recorded in New York City in 1961, was a major R&B hit that summer.

8. "Hello Baby"/"I'm Trying" (Foxy 005) were recorded in Chicago with Mack Simmons and band in 1962.

9. Jimmy Dawkins, "I Was Born in the Swamps, Andrew 'Voice' Odom," *Blues Unlimited* 88 (January 1972): 14–15.

CHAPTER 9: CLUB GIGS AND ROAD TRIPS

1. Jim O'Neal, "Pepper's Lounge," *Living Blues* 5 (Summer 1971): 32.

2. Amy and Jim O'Neal, "Jimmy Reed Interview," *Living Blues* 21 (May/June 1975): 22.

3. Paul Oliver, *Conversation with the Blues* (London: Jazz Book Club, 1967), xiv.

4. Turner, "Three Mexicans, a Hillbilly and a Polock," 6.

5. Sebastian Danchin, "Little Bobby Neely—Spice Is What I Do," *Living Blues* 130 (November/December 1996): 41.

6. "I Do," (1965—ABC-Paramount 10629), and "In the Morning," (1968—ABC 11011), under the name of the Mighty Marvelows, to avoid confusion with the West Coast–based Marvelos.

7. Jimmy Dawkins and Keith Tillman, "Mr. Music Himself!" *Blues Unlimited* 59 (January 1969): 7–9.

8. Strachwitz, liner notes, *Earl Hooker/Two Bugs and a Roach* LP.

9. Shurman, "King of Postwar Blues Guitar—Earl Hooker," 6.

10. John Anthony Brisbin, "They'll Smell My Onions," *Living Blues* 112 (November/December 1993): 29.

11. Shurman, op. cit

12. Charles Sawyer, *The Arrival of B. B. King* (Garden City, N.Y.: Doubleday and Company Inc., 1980), 28.

CHAPTER 10: HOOKER AND CUCA (1964–1967)

1. Dawkins and Tillman, "Mr. Music Himself!" 7–9.

2. Bert Rosengarten, "An Interview with Fred Roulette and Skip Rose," in *Nothing but the Blues*, edited by Mike Leadbitter (London: Hanover Books, 1971), 110–15.

CHAPTER 11: TWO BUGS AND A ROACH (1967–1968)

1. Oliver, *Conversation with the Blues*, 114.

2. Dawkins, "I Was Born in the Swamps—Andrew 'Voice' Odom," 14.

3. Dawkins and Tillman, "Mr. Music Himself!" 7–9.

4. Ibid.

5. Jimmy Dawkins, letter to Keith Tillman, *Blues Unlimited* 57 (November 1968): 20.

6. *Chicago Daily News* (April 17, 1968): 1.

7. Mike Royko, *Boss: Richard J. Daley of Chicago* (New York: New American Library, 1971), 150.

8. Jimmy Dawkins, "Sonny Boy Was the Best," *Blues Unlimited* 64 (July 1969): 16.

9. Carey Bell, liner notes, *Carey Bell's Blues Harp*, Delmark LP DS-622 (1969).

10. Dawkins and Tillman, op. cit.

11. Tam Fiofori, "Elvin Bishop," *Guitar Player* (October 1969).

12. Strachwitz, liner notes, *Earl Hooker/Two Bugs and a Roach* LP.

13. Ibid.

14. Sebastian Danchin, liner notes, *Earl Hooker/Play Your Guitar, Mr. Hooker!*, Black Magic LP 9006 (1985).

15. The "Puppy Hound Blues"/"Ramblin' Woman" coupling by Johnny Big Moose Walker was released on The Blues 301 under the name Big Moose. Recorded in late 1967 with Louis Myers on bass and Freddie Roulette on lap steel guitar, it was the subject of many interrogations at the time by the contributors of the only blues publication of the time, *Blues Unlimited*, who thought it featured Earl Hooker's slide playing, and it took some time before Roulette was formally identified.

16. Willie Leiser, *I'm a Road Runner Baby* (Blues Unlimited publications, 1969), 11–13 and 16–18.

CHAPTER 12: NINETEEN SIXTY-NINE

1. Mike Leadbitter, "A Good Man Is Hard to Find," *Blues Unlimited* 50 (February 1968): 16 and *Blues Unlimited* 53 (May 1968): 3.

2. Mike Leadbitter, review of Arhoolie LP 1044, *Earl Hooker/Two Bugs and a*

331 *Notes*

Roach, *Blues Unlimited* 64 (July 1969): 28 and Harry Hussey, reviews of Cuca LP KS-3400, *The Genius of Earl Hooker*, and Arhoolie 45-521 *Earl Hooker—"Wah Wah Blues"/"You Don't Want Me," Blues Unlimited* 63 (June 1969): 21–22.

3. Pete Welding, liner notes, *Earl Hooker/Funk—Last of the Great Earl Hooker*, Antilles LP AN 7024 (1976).

4. Justine Picardie and Dorothy Wade, *Atlantic and the Godfathers of Rock and Roll*, (London: Fourth Estate, 1993), 48.

5. "Caught Pneumonia Every Winter," *Rolling Stone* (May 28, 1970).

6. Ibid.

7. Mike Leadbitter, review of Bluesway LP BLS-6038, *John Lee Hooker/If You Miss 'Im . . . I Got 'Im, Blues Unlimited* 79 (January 1971): 29.

8. Fred Stuckey, "John Lee Hooker," *Guitar Player* (March 1971).

9. Pete Lowry, "Bottleneck Blues," *Blues Unlimited* 68 (December 1969): 29.

10. Jackie Brenston, "Trouble up the Road," Sue 736 (1961).

11. Lightnin' Hopkins, "Have You Ever Seen a One-Eyed Woman Cry," 77 LP 12/1 (1959).

12. Langston Hughes, *The Big Sea* (New York: Knopf, 1940), 163.

13. Mike Leadbitter, review of Bluesway LP BLS-6055, *Andrew "Voice" Odom/Farther on Down the Road, Blues Unlimited* 103 (August/September 1973): 23.

14. Mike Leadbitter, review of Bluesway LP BLS-6036, *Johnny "Big Moose" Walker/Rambling Woman, Blues Unlimited* 79 (January 1971): 28.

15. Leadbitter, review of Arhoolie LP 1044, 28.

16. Jim O'Neal, review of Arhoolie LP 1051, *Earl Hooker/Hooker and Steve, Living Blues* 3 (Autumn 1970): 35, and Mike Leadbitter, review of Arhoolie LP 1051, *Earl Hooker/Hooker and Steve, Blues Unlimited* 75 (September 1970): 23.

17. Review of Arhoolie LP 1051, *Earl Hooker/Hooker and Steve, Billboard* (1970), reprinted in *Arhoolie Occasional* 1 (1971): 13.

18. Paul B. and Victoria Sheatsley, "Chicago Blues—Great Chicago Blues Festival of 1969," *Record Research* 101 (October 1969): 3.

19. Ibid.

20. Brown was the featured pianist and vocalist with Johnny Moore's Three Blazers in the forties, while brother Oscar Moore was the guitar player in the King Cole Trio.

21. Tom Mazzolini, "Living Blues Interview: Charles Brown," *Living Blues* 27 (May/June 1976): 25–27.

22. Mike Leadbitter, review of Bluesway LP BLS-6040, *Jimmy Witherspoon/Hunh!, Blues Unlimited* 75 (September 1970): 21.

23. Bruce Iglauer, review of Bluesway LP BLS-6040, *Jimmy Witherspoon/Hunh!, Living Blues* 2 (Summer 1970): 31.

24. Mike Leadbitter, review of Bluesway LP BLS-6039, *Charles Brown/Legend!, Blues Unlimited* 79 (January 1971): 28

CHAPTER 13: GOIN' DOWN SLOW (1969–1970)

1. Mike Leadbitter, "All Time Low," *Blues Unlimited* 48 (December 1967): 20.

2. Werner Burkhardt, "The Blues—No Passing Fancy," in *American Folk Blues Festival '69 Program*, (Frankfurt: Lippmann & Rau, 1969).

3. Paul Oliver, "The American Folk Blues Festival," *Jazz Monthly* 178 (December 1969): 24–25.

4. Paul Oliver, liner notes, *American Folk Blues Festival '69/Live! At Royal Albert Hall, October 3, 1969*, CBS LP 63912.

5. Jean Guerry, "American Folk Blues Festival—Impressions," *Soul Bag* 7 (November 1969): 2 [translated from the French by the author].

6. Mike Leadbitter, review of Blue Thumb BTS-12, *Earl Hooker/Sweet Black Angel*, *Blues Unlimited* 66 (October 1969): 27.

7. Simon Napier, "1969 Lippmann-Rau American Folk Blues Festival," *Blues Unlimited* 68 (December 1969): 4–5.

8. Pete Lowry, "Bottleneck Blues," 29.

9. *Blues Unlimited* 70 (February/March 1970): 3.

10. "Caught Pneumonia Every Winter," *Rolling Stone* (May 28, 1970).

11. Actually, the obituary only mentioned three children: Cathy, Waldine, and Andre Tampan.

EPILOGUE

1. Tim Barrett, letter to the editor, *Blues Unlimited* 116 (November/December 1975): 12.

2. Jim O'Neal, review of Cuca LP KS-3400 *The Genius of Earl Hooker*; Arhoolie LP 1044 *Earl Hooker/Two Bugs and a Roach*; Blue Thumb LP BTS-12 *Earl Hooker/Sweet Black Angel*; Bluesway LP BLS-6032 *Earl Hooker/Don't Have to Worry*; Arhoolie LP 1051 *Earl Hooker/Hooker and Steve*, *Living Blues* 3 (Autumn 1970): 32.

Selected Bibliography

INTERVIEWS CONDUCTED BY THE AUTHOR

Allen, Ricky————summer 1984 and spring 1993
Allison, Luther————winter 1979
Anderson, Bobby————summer 1978
Arnold, Billy Boy————summer 1978, autumn 1979, and summer 1984
Asbell, Paul————winter 1984
Bell, Carey————autumn 1979
Below, Fred————autumn 1978
Bland, Bobby "Blue"————spring 1988
Boyd, Eddie————autumn 1975, spring 1977, and autumn 1983
Brown, Charles————spring, 1992
Bruce, Denny————summer 1996
Campbell, Little Milton————summer 1979 and autumn 1982
Charles, Nick————spring 1979
Chenier, Clifton————summer 1984
Collins, Albert————winter 1983
Collins, Mel————summer 1978
Davis, "Blind" John————autumn 1978
Dawkins, Jimmy————winter 1984
DeKoster, Jim————spring 1980 and summer 1984
Demêtre, Jacques————winter 1979 and spring 1994
Dixon, Willie————summer 1976
Flowers, Lonnie————summer 1984
Furr, Arvel A.————summer 1984 and autumn 1992

335

Gibson, Lacy———spring 1979 and summer 1979
Guy, Buddy———autumn 1977
Hargraves, D. T. Jr.———summer 1984 and autumn 1986
Hooker, Earline———summer 1978
Hooker, John Lee———autumn 1979
Hooker, Mary———summer and autumn 1978 and winter 1979
Iglauer, Bruce———summer 1978 and autumn 1990
Johnson, Jimmy—autumn 1983
Johnson, Syl———autumn 1983
Jones, Carl———summer 1984
Jones, Casey———autumn 1978, summer 1979, and winter 1983
Kansas City Red———summer 1984
King, Riley "B. B."———autumn 1982 and autumn 1991
Kirchstein, Jim———autumn 1982, summer 1984, and winter 1999
Koester, Bob———summer 1978
Leiser, Willy———autumn 1977, autumn 1978, and spring 1980
Little, Bobby———autumn 1992
Memphis Slim———autumn 1975
Michel, Ed———summer and autumn 1982
Mohr, Kurt———spring 1981
Musselwhite, Charlie———summer 1978
Myers, Dave———autumn 1992
Myers, Jack———spring, 1984
Myers, Louis———summer 1984
Neely, Little Bobby———spring and summer 1993
Nickerson-Chism, Bertha———summer 1984 and summer 1993
Odom, Andrew "B. B."———autumn 1982
O'Neal, Jim———winter 1982, summer 1984, and winter 1997
Otis, Johnny———autumn 1982
Payne, Sonny———summer, 1984
Perkins, Joe Willie "Pinetop"———summer 1984
Peterson, Lucky———autumn, 1982
Phillips, Sam———summer, 1984
Reed, A. C.———autumn 1977, summer 1978, spring 1979, winter 1983, and autumn 1985
Scott, James, Jr.———summer 1978
Seals, Son———autumn 1977, summer 1978, and spring 1979
Shurman, Dick———summer 1978 to spring 1999
Smothers, Abe "Little Smokey"———spring 1993
Stidham, Arbee———summer 1984
Strachwitz, Chris———autumn 1983 and winter 1985
Taylor, Eddie———winter, 1979
Taylor, Koko———autumn 1993 and spring 1997
Taylor, Robert "Pops"———summer 1978
Thompson, James R———summer 1984
Turner, Herb———autumn 1978 and summer 1984
Walker, Joe Louis———spring 1993

Walker, Johnny "Big Moose"————summer 1976 and summer 1978
Wells, Junior————autumn 1977, summer and autumn 1978, spring and summer 1979, and winter 1983
Williams, Lee Shot————summer 1984
Witherspoon, Jimmy————autumn 1980

SELECTED BOOKS

Albert, George, and Frank Hoffmann. *The Cash Box Black Contemporary Singles Charts, 1960–1984*. Metuchen, New Jersey: Scarecrow Press, 1986.

Albertson, Chris. *Bessie*. London: Barrie & Jenkins, 1972.

American Folk Blues Festival '69 Program. Frankfurt: Lippmann & Rau, 1969.

The American Guide Series: Florida. New York: Oxford University Press, 1947.

Ames, Roy C., and Galen Gart. *Duke/Peacock Records*. Milford, New Hampshire: Big Nickel Publications, 1990.

Beale Street USA (Where the Blues Began). Bexhill-on-Sea: Blues Unlimited Publications, 1969.

Bennett, Lerone Jr. *Before the Mayflower: A History of Black America*. New York: Penguin, 1993.

Berkow, Ira. *Maxwell Street: Survival in a Bazaar*. Garden City, New York: Doubleday, 1977.

Bishop, Ian C. *The Gibson Guitar from 1950*. Shaftsbury: Musical News Services Ltd., 1977.

Bowman, Rob. *Soulsville U.S.A.: The Story of Stax Records*. New York: Schirmer Books, 1997.

Broonzy, William (as told to Yannick Bruynoghe). *Big Bill Blues*. Londres: Cassell, 1955.

Cayton, Horace R., and St. Clair Drake. *Black Metropolis*. London: Jonathan Cape, 1946.

Chauvard, Marcel, and Jacques Demêtre. *Voyage au Pays Du Blues: Land of the Blues*. Paris: CLARB, 1994.

Connor, Anthony, and Robert Neff. *Blues*. London: Latimer New Dimensions Ltd., 1976.

Cook, Bruce. *Listen to the Blues*. New York: Charles Scribner's Sons, 1973.

Dammann, George H. *Seventy Years of Buick*. Sarasota, Florida: Crestline Pub., 1973.

Danchin, Sebastian. *Blues Boy: The Life and Music of B. B. King*. Jackson: University of Mississippi Press, 1998.

Dickens, Charles. *American Notes for General Circulation*. London: Penguin, 1985.

Dixon, Robert M. W., John Godrich, and Howard Rye. *Blues & Gospel Records, 1890–1943*. Oxford: Clarendon Press, 1997.

Dixon, Willie, with Don Snowden. *I Am the Blues*. New York: Quartet Books, 1989.

Eagles, Brenda M., Mary L. Hart, and Lisa N. Howorth. *The Blues: A Bibliographical Guide*. New York: Garland, 1989.

Escott, Colin, and Martin Hawkins. *Good Rockin' Tonight: Sun Records and the Birth of Rock'n'roll*. New York: St. Martin's Press, 1992.

————. *Sun Records: The Discography*. Germany: Bear Family Pub., 1987.

Fancourt, Leslie, Mike Leadbitter, and Paul Pelletier. *Blues Records 1943–1970: The Bible of the Blues, Vol. 2 (L to Z)*. London: Record Information Services, 1994.

Farber, David. *Chicago '68*. Chicago: University of Chicago Press, 1988.

Ferris, William, and Charles Reagan Wilson, eds. *Encyclopedia of Southern Culture*. Chapel Hill: University Of North Carolina Press, 1989.

Forte, Dan, et al. *The Guitars*. New York: Quarto Marketing Ltd., 1984.

Frazier, E. Franklin. *The Negro Family in the United States*. Chicago: University of Chicago Press, 1966.

Gart, Galen, ed. *ARLD: The American Record Label Directory and Dating Guide, 1940–1959*. Milford, New Hampshire: Big Nickel Pub., 1989.

———. *The History of Rhythm and Blues, 1950, 1951, 1952, 1953, 1954, 1955, 1956, 1957, 1958*. Milford, New Hampshire: Big Nickel Pub., 1989 to 1997.

Gruber, J. Richard, ed. *Memphis 1948–1958*. Memphis Brooks Museum of Art, 1986.

Guralnick, Peter. *Feel Like Going Home*. New York and London: Omnibus, 1978.

———. *Lost Highway*. New York: Vintage, 1982.

Handy, William Christopher. *Father of the Blues*. New York: Macmillan, 1941.

Haralambos, Michael. *Right On: From Blues to Soul in Black America*. London: Eddison, 1974.

Harris, Sheldon. *Blues Who's Who*. New Rochelle: Arlington House Publishers, 1979.

Hopkins, Jerry. *Elvis*. London: Abacus, 1971.

Hughes, Langston. *The Big Sea*. New York: Knopf, 1940.

Hurston, Zora Neale. *Their Eyes Were Watching God: A Novel of Negro Life*. Philadelphia: J. B. Lippincott, 1937.

Johnson, Charles S. *Shadow of the Plantation*. New Brunswick: Transaction Pub., 1996 [1934].

Keil, Charles. *Urban Blues*. Chicago: University of Chicago Press, 1966.

Kennedy, Stetson. *Jim Crow Guide: The Way It Was*. Boca Raton: Florida: Atlantic University Press, 1992.

Leadbitter, Mike. *Delta Country Blues*. Bexhill-on-Sea: Blues Unlimited Publications, 1968.

Leadbitter, Mike, and Neil Slaven. *Blues Records 1943 to 1970: A Selective Discography Vol. 1 (A to K)*. London: Record Information Services, 1987.

Lee, George W. *Beale Street: Where the Blues Began*. New York: Robert O. Ballou, 1934.

Leiser, Willie. *I'm a Road Runner Baby*. Bexhill-on-Sea: Blues Unlimited Publications, 1969.

Lemann, Nicholas. *The Promised Land*. New York: Knopf, 1991.

Lerma, Dominique-René de. *Bibliography of Black Music, Vol. 2: Afro-American Idioms*. Westport: Greenwood, 1981.

Myers, Gary E. *Do You Hear That Beat: Wisconsin Pop/Rock in the 50's & 60's*. Downey, CA: Hummingbird Pub., 1994.

Oakley Dance, Helen. *Stormy Monday: The T-Bone Walker Story*. Baton Rouge: Louisiana State University Press, 1987.

Obrecht, Jas, ed. *Blues Guitar: The Men Who Made the Music*. San Francisco: GPI Books, 1990.

Oliver, Paul. *Conversation with the Blues*. London: Jazz Book Club, 1967.

———. *The Story of the Blues*. London: Barrie and Jenkins, 1969.

Otis, Johnny. *Upside Your Head! Rhythm and Blues on Central Avenue*. Hanover, New Hampshire: University Press Of New England, 1993.

Palmer, Robert. *Deep Blues*. New York: Viking Press, 1981.

Picardie, Justine, and Dorothy Wade. *Atlantic and the Godfathers of Rock and Roll*. London: Fourth Estate, 1993.

Pruter, Robert. *Chicago Soul*. Chicago: University of Illinois Press, 1991.

Rowe, Mike. *Chicago Breakdown*. London: Eddison, 1973.

Royko, Mike. *Boss: Richard J. Daley of Chicago*. New York: New American Library, 1971.

Salzman, Jack, David Lionel Smith, and Cornel West, eds. *Encyclopedia of African-American Culture and History*. New York: Macmillan, 1996.

Sawyer, Charles. *The Arrival of B. B. King*. Garden City, New York: Doubleday, 1980.

Shaw, Arnold. *Honkers and Shouters*. New York: Collier, 1978.

Southern, Eileen. *Biographical Dictionary of Afro-American and African Musicians*. Westport: Greenwood Press, 1982.

———. *The Music of Black Americans: A History*. New York: W. W. Norton, 1983.

Spear, Allen H. *Black Chicago: The Making of a Negro Ghetto 1890–1920*. Chicago: University of Chicago Press, 1967.

Tooze, Sandra B. *Muddy Waters: The Mojo Man*. Toronto: ECW Press, 1997.

Turner, Tina, with Kurt Loder. *I, Tina*. New York: William Morrow, 1986.

Weeks, Linton. *Clarksdale and Coahoma County*. Clarksdale: Carnegie Public Library, 1982.

Whitburn, Joel. *Top R&B Singles 1942–1995*. Menomonee Falls: Record Research, 1996.

White, George R. *Bo Diddley: Living Legend*. Chessington, Surrey: Castle Communications, 1995.

Wilcock, Donald E., with Buddy Guy. *Damn Right I've Got the Blues*. San Francisco: Woodford Press, 1993.

Wilmer, Valerie. *The Face of Black Music*. New York: Da Capo, 1976.

Wolff, Daniel, with S. R. Crain, Clifton White, and G. David Tenenbaum. *You Send Me: The Life and Times of Sam Cooke*. New York: William Morrow, 1995.

SELECTED ARTICLES AND ALBUM NOTES

"American Folk Blues Festival '69." *Jefferson* 8 (1969): 5–8.

Baker, Cary. "Henry Stone Interview." *Shout* 80 (September 1972): 1–2.

Barrett, Tim. "Letter to the Editor." *Blues Unlimited* 116 (November/December 1975): 12.

Baumgartner, Brian. "Eddie Snow." *Juke Blues* 42 (Autumn 1998): 15–19.

Bell, Carey. Liner notes to Delmark LP DS-622 *Carey Bell's Blues Harp*, 1969.

Blau, Ellen, and Dick Shurman. "Pee Wee Crayton—Part 2." *Living Blues* 57 (Autumn 1983): 6–10.

Brisbin, John Anthony. "They'll Smell My Onions." *Living Blues* 112 (November/December 1993): 22–31.

"Caught Pneumonia Every Winter." *Rolling Stone* (May 18, 1970).

Chauvard, Marcel, and Jacques Demêtre. "Voyage Au Pays du Blues—Parts 1 to 6." *Jazz Hot* 149 (December 1959) to 154 (May 1960).

Cobbs, Charles E. Jr. "Traveling the Blues Highway." *National Geographic* (April 1999): 42–69.

Crockett, Jim. "B. B. King As Told to Jim Crockett—My 10 Favorite Guitarists." *Guitar Player* (March 1975): 23.

Cushing, Steve, with Justin O'Brien. "Odie Payne." *Living Blues* 96 (March/April 1991): 52–63.

Dahl, Bill, and Jim O'Neal. "Jimmy Johnson." *Living Blues* 47 (Summer 1980): 15–22.

Danchin, Sebastian. "A. C. Reed." *Living Blues* 124 (November/December 1995): 12–25.

———. "Earl Hooker Disco." *Soul Bag* 103 (June/July 1985): 18–23.

———. "Earl Hooker Discography." *Blues Life* 29 (January 1985): 7–15.

———. "Lacy Gibson—First Born of the Seventh Son." *Soul Bag* 93 (February/March 1983): 5–8.

———. Liner notes to Black Magic LP 9006 *Earl Hooker/Play Your Guitar, Mr. Hooker!*, 1985.

———. "Little Bobby Neely—Spice Is What I Do." *Living Blues* 130 (November/December 1996): 34–46.

———. "Little Milton." *Soul Bag* 92 (December 1982/January 1983): 5–11.

———. "Sam Phillips: Recording the Blues." *Soul Bag* 105 (November/December 1985): 5–8.

Daniels, Bill. "Rockin' Records." *Whiskey Women And . . .* 10 (November 1982).

Dawkins, Jimmy. "I Was Born in the Swamps—Andrew Voice Odom." *Blues Unlimited* 88 (January 1972): 14–16.

———. Letter to Keith Tillman. *Blues Unlimited* 57 (November 1968): 20.

———. "My Name Is Moose Walker." *Blues Unlimited* 92 (June 1972): 16–17.

———. "Sonny Boy Was the Best." *Blues Unlimited* 64 (July 1969): 16–17.

Dawkins, Jimmy, and Keith Tillman. "Mr. Music Himself!" *Blues Unlimited* 59 (January 1969): 7–9.

Dutko, Mot. "Willie James Lyons Obituary." *Living Blues* 50 (Spring 1981): 44.

"Earl Hooker." *Living Blues* 2 (Summer 1970): 9.

"Earl Hooker, Otis Spann and Ishman Bracey." *Blues Unlimited* 73 (June 1970): 14.

Fiofori, Tam. "Elvin Bishop." *Guitar Player* (October 1969).

Foster, Mike. "Jimmie Bell." *Living Blues* 41 (November/December 1978): 12–17.

Gloger, Richard. "Life Full of Blues." *Polish Jazz* (1970).

Greensmith, Bill. "Below's the Name, Drummin's the Game." *Blues Unlimited* 131/2 (September /December 1978): 12–19.

———. "Carl Tate AKA Bob Star." *Blues Unlimited* 119 (May/June 1976): 4–9.

———. "Just Whaling." *Blues Unlimited* 122 (November/December 1976): 4–14.

———. "We Got a Song Called 'Rocket 88.'" *Blues Unlimited* 135/6 (July/September 1979): 14–19.

Greensmith, Bill, and Cilla Huggins. "Still Hanging Right On in There—Part 1 and Part 2." *Blues Unlimited* 140 (Spring 1981): 4–20 and *Blues Unlimited* 141 (Autumn/Winter 1981): 16–28.

Greensmith, Bill, and Sylvia Reeder. "M. C. Reeder's T-99 Club." *Blues Unlimited* 144 (Spring 1983): 19, 23.

Greensmith, Bill, and Mike Rowe. "I Was Really Dedicated." *Blues Unlimited* 128 (January/February 1978): 18–26.

Guerry, Jean. "American Folk Blues Festival—Impressions." *Soul Bag* 7 (November 1969): 2.

———. "Earl Hooker, la mort d'un espoir." *Soul Bag* 11 (July 1970): 23, 30.

"A Handful of Melons." *Sailor's Delight* 12a: 30–31.

Helland, Dave. "Luther Allison, Blues Guitar Boss." *Guitar Player* (March 1976): 14, 32.

Huggins, Cilla. "Ike Turner in the Beginning." *Juke Blues* 37 (Spring 1997): 8–14.

Hurst, Jack. "LP Gives Old Bluesman's Life New Spin." *Chicago Tribune* (September 19, 1982), Sections 6–7.

Hussey, Harry. Review of Arhoolie 45-521 "Wah-Wah Blues"/"Earl Hooker Blues." *Blues Unlimited* 63 (June 1969): 21.

———. Review of Cuca LP KS-3400 *The Genius of Earl Hooker*. *Blues Unlimited* 63 (June 1969): 22.

Iglauer, Bruce. Review of Bluesway LP BLS-6040 *Jimmy Witherspoon/Hunh! Living Blues* 2 (Summer 1970): 31.

Jung, Maureen. "Freddie Roulette—Zen of Lap-Steel Guitar." *Living Blues* 141 (September/October 1998): 30–35.

Leadbitter, Mike. "A Good Man Is Hard to Find." *Blues Unlimited* 50 (February 1968): 16 and *Blues Unlimited* 53 (May 1968): 3.

———. "All Time Low." *Blues Unlimited* 48 (December 1967): 20.

———. "Mike's Blues." *Blues Unlimited* 102 (June 1973): 20.

———. "P.S. Earl Hooker." *Blues Unlimited* 64 (July 1969): 17.

———. Review of Arhoolie LP 1044 *Earl Hooker/Two Bugs and a Roach*. *Blues Unlimited* 64 (July 1969): 28.

———. Review of Arhoolie LP 1051 *Earl Hooker/Hooker and Steve*. *Blues Unlimited* 75 (September 1970): 23.

———. Review of Blues on Blues LP 10002 *Earl Hooker/Funk—Last of the Great Earl Hooker*. *Blues Unlimited* 90 (April 1972): 27.

———. Review of Blue Thumb LP BTS-12 *Earl Hooker/Sweet Black Angel*. *Blues Unlimited* 66 (October 1969): 27.

———. Review of Bluesway LP BLS-6040 *Jimmy Witherspoon/Hunh!* *Blues Unlimited* 75 (September 1970): 21.

———. Review of Bluesway LP BLS-6036 *Johnny Big Moose Walker/Rambling Woman*. *Blues Unlimited* 79 (January 1971): 28.

———. Review of Bluesway LP BLS-6039 *Charles Brown/Legend!* *Blues Unlimited* 79 (January 1971): 28.

———. Review of Bluesway LP BLS-6038 *John Lee Hooker/If You Miss 'Im . . . I Got 'Im*. *Blues Unlimited* 79 (January 1971): 29.

———. Review of Bluesway LP BLS-6055 *Andrew Voice Odom/Farther On Down the Road*. *Blues Unlimited* 103 (August/September 1973): 23.

———. Review of Stateside LP SSL-10298 *Earl Hooker/Don't Have to Worry*. *Blues Unlimited* 74 (July 1970): 24.

Leiser, Willie. "Down in the Alley." *Blues Unlimited* 100 (April 1973): 29–34.

Lowry, Pete. "Bottleneck Blues." *Blues Unlimited* 68 (December 1969): 29.

Mazzolini, Tom. "Living Blues Interview: Charles Brown." *Living Blues* 27 (May/June 1976): 19–27.

Michel, Ed. "Lettres." *Jazz Magazine* 179 (June 1970): 14–15.

Mohr, Kurt. "Earl Hooker parle des guitaristes." *Soul Bag* 7 (November 1969): 11.

Moon, D. Thomas. "Dave Myers—Somebody Has to Live It First." *Living Blues* 142 (November/December 1998): 32–41.

Napier, Simon. "1969 Lippmann–Rau American Folk Blues Festival." *Blues Unlimited* 68 (December 1969): 4–5.

Nesmith, Chris, and Ken Woodmansee. "The Drummer Is the Key—Bobby Little." *Living Blues* 96 (March/April 1991): 36–41.

Oliver, Paul. "The American Folk Blues Festival." *Jazz Monthly* 178 (December 1969): 23–25.

———. Liner notes to CBS LP 63912 *American Folk Blues Festival '69/Live! At Royal Albert Hall.*

Olsson, Bengt. "Willie Cobbs." *Blues Unlimited* 73 (June 1970): 15–16.

O'Neal, Amy, and Jim O'Neal. "Jimmy Reed Interview." *Living Blues* 21 (May/June 1975): 16–40.

O'Neal, Amy, Jim O'Neal, and Dick Shurman. "Mighty Joe Young." *Living Blues* 28 (July/August 1976): 21, 24.

O'Neal, Jim. "Billy the Kid Emerson Interview." *Living Blues* 45/6 (Spring 1980): 25–48.

———. "Blues Esoterica." *Living Blues* 118 (December 1994): 128.

———. "Bobby Bland! Backstage." *Living Blues* 4 (Winter 1970–1971): 13–18.

———. "Cadillac Baby." *Living Blues* 6 (Autumn 1971): 23–29.

———. "Houston Stackhouse." *Living Blues* 17 (Summer 1974): 20–36.

———. "Jackie Brenston." *Living Blues* 45/6 (Spring 1980): 20.

———. "Joe Willie Wilkins." *Living Blues* 11 (Winter 1972–1973): 13–17.

———. "Junior Wells." *Living Blues* 119 (January/February 1995): 20.

———. "Lefty Bates." *Living Blues* 21 (May/June 1975): 34.

———. "Mel London Obituary." *Living Blues* 22 (July/August 1975):4, 21.

———. "Pepper's Lounge." *Living Blues* 5 (Summer 1971): 30–35.

———. Review of Cuca LP KS-3400 *The Genius of Earl Hooker*; Arhoolie LP 1044 *Earl Hooker/Two Bugs and a Roach*; Blue Thumb LP BTS-12 *Earl Hooker/Sweet Black Angel*; Bluesway LP BLS-6032 *Earl Hooker/Don't Have to Worry*; Arhoolie LP 1051 *Earl Hooker/Hooker and Steve*. *Living Blues* 3 (Autumn 1970): 32–35.

O'Neal, Jim, and Dick Shurman. "Otis Rush Interview." *Living Blues* 28 (July/August 1976): 10–28.

O'Neal, Jim, and Steve Wisner. "Obituaries—Earnest Johnson." *Living Blues* 55 (Winter 1982–1983): 39.

Otis, Johnny. "Letter to Felix Steinmann." *Blues Unlimited* 68 (December 1969): 17.

"Otis Spann and Earl Hooker." *Coda* (June 1970).

Paterson, Neil. "Mel London." In *Nothing but the Blues*, edited by Mike Leadbitter, 50–52. London: Hanover, 1971.

———. "Ricky Allen, 1964." In *Nothing but the Blues*, edited by Mike Leadbitter, 92. London: Hanover, 1971.

Rosengarten, Bert. "An Interview with Fred Roulette and Skip Rose." In *Nothing but the Blues*, edited by Mike Leadbitter, 110–15. London: Hanover, 1971.

Rowe, Mike. "Dee Dee's Shangrala Lounge—135 N. Sacramento." *Blues Unlimited* 41 (February 1967): 5–7.

———. "I Was Really Dedicated." *Blues Unlimited* 126 (September/October 1977): 4–7; and *Blues Unlimited* 127 (November/December 1977): 10–12.

Scott, Hammond. "Ironing Board Sam." *Living Blues* 23 (September/October 1975): 32–33.

Sheatsley, Paul B., and Victoria Sheatsley. "Chicago Blues: The Great Chicago Blues Festival of 1969." *Record Research* 101 (October 1969): 3.

Shurman, Dick. "Billy Boy Arnold's Story." In *Nothing but the Blues*, edited by Mike Leadbitter, 71–76. London: Hanover, 1971.

———. "Feel Like a Millionaire." *Blues Unlimited* 114 (July/August 1975): 16–17.

———. "Guitar Shorty—Blues on the Flip Side." *Living Blues* 95 (January/February 1991): 23–27.

———. "Jody Williams." *Living Blues* 16 (Spring 1974): 24–26.

———. "King of Postwar Blues Guitar, Earl Hooker." *Seattle Folklore Society Newsletter* 1, no. 4 (June 15, 1970): 2–7, 26–28.

———. Liner notes to Black Magic LP 9001 *Andrew Brown/Big Brown's Chicago Blues*, 1982.

Smith, Al. Liner notes to Blues on Blues LP 10002, *Earl Hooker/Funk—Last of the Great Earl Hooker*, 1970.

Strachwitz, Chris "Field Trip of Winter '68." *Blues Unlimited* 60 (March 1969): 18.

———. Liner notes to Arhoolie LP 1044 *Earl Hooker/Two Bugs and a Roach*, 1968.

Strausberg, Chinta. "Gas Shut Off Reforms Called for after Death of Woman, 60." *Chicago Defender* (January 12, 1995).

Stuckey, Fred. "John Lee Hooker." *Guitar Player* (March 1971).

Svacina, Fritz. "The Guitar Genius Earl Hooker." *Blues Life* 1, no. 9 (1980): 25–29.

Topping, Ray. "Henry Stone: The Rockin' and Chart Story." *Juke Blues* 33 (Summer 1995): 27.

Turner, Bez. "Three Mexicans, a Hillbilly and a Polock." *Blues Unlimited* 141 (Autumn/Winter 1981): 5–10.

Ulrey, Lois. "Junior Wells Interview." *Magic Blues* 4 (1992): 7–25.

Welding, Pete. Liner notes to Antilles LP AN-7024 *Earl Hooker/Funk—Last of the Great Earl Hooker*, 1976.

———. "Ramblin' Johnny Shines." *Living Blues* 22 (July/August 1975): 27.

Wisner, Steve. "Chicago Blues, Yesterday and Today, Mojo Buford." *Living Blues* 42 (January /February 1979): 22–26.

———. "Frank Thomas Jr." *Living Blues* 30 (November/December 1976): 7, 41.

———. "Smokey Smothers: Big Otis and Little Abe." *Living Blues* 37 (March/April 1978): 18–21.

———. "Sonny Rogers." *Living Blues* 42 (January/February 1979): 26–27.

———. "Sunnyland Charles and the Globetrotters." *Living Blues* 38 (May/June 1978): 27–30.

Discography

Johnny O'NEAL

Johnny O'Neal, v / Earl Hooker, g / Ed Wiley, ts -1 / Roosevelt Wardell, p / Robert Dixon, b / William Cochran, d.
Bradenton, Florida - Wednesday, November 26, 1952

K 9213	Woman -1	King unissued
K 9214	Johnny Feels the Blues	King 4599
K 9215	So Many Hard Times	King 4599
K 9216	A Whole Heap of Mama -1	King unissued

EARL HOOKER TRIO

Earl Hooker, g / Roosevelt Wardell, p / Robert Dixon, b / William Cochran, d.
Bradenton, Florida - Wednesday, November 26, 1952

K 9217	Shake 'Em Up	King LP 727
K 9218-1	Race Track	King 4600, LP 727
K 9219	Happy Blues	King LP 727
K 9220	Blue Guitar Blues	King 4600, LP 727

Note: King LP 727, John Lee HOOKER / Sings Blues, included the above four Earl Hooker titles. "Shake 'Em Up" and "Happy Blues," respectively mistitled "Poor Joe" and "Stomp Boogie," were unduly credited to John Lee Hooker, whereas "Race Track" and

"Blue Guitar Blues"—the latter track mistitled "Who's Been Jivin' You" on the record sleeve, although properly listed on the label—were credited to Earl Hooker on the label.

LITTLE SAM DAVIS

Little Sam Davis, hca-v / Earl Hooker, g / Tony (?), d.
Miami, Florida - Crystal Clear Studios - April, 1953

GR 15077-1	Goin' Home to Mother (Goin' Home Blues)	Rockin' 512
GR 15078-1	1958 Blues	Rockin' 512
GR 15079-1	She's So Good to Me	Rockin' 519, DeLuxe 6025
GR 15080-1	Goin' to New Orleans	Rockin' 519, DeLuxe 6025

EARL HOOKER

Earl Hooker, g-v -1 / Little Sam Davis, hca -1 / Tony (?), d / unk, v -2
Miami, Florida - Crystal Clear Studios - April, 1953

GR 15081-1	Ride Hooker Ride -2	Rockin' unissued, Hot CD 5502-2
GR 15082-1	Sweet Angel -1	Rockin' 513
GR 15083-1	Alley Corn	Rockin' unissued, Hot CD 5502-2
GR 15084-1	On the Hook	Rockin' 513
GR 15085-1	(Untitled) [Jammin']	Rockin' unissued, Hot CD 5502-2
GR 15086-1	After Hours	Rockin' unissued, Hot CD 5502-2

EARL HOOKER / BOYD GILMORE

Boyd Gilmore, g-v -1 / Earl Hooker, g / Ernest Lane, p / unk, b / poss. Willie Nix, d.
Memphis, Tennessee - Sun Studios - Wednesday, July 15, 1953

-	Jivin' Boogie [The Drive]	Sun unissued, Sun CD 29
-	Dynaflow Blues [Blue Guitar]	Sun unissued, Sun CD 29
-	Believe I'll Settle Down -1	Sun unissued, Sun Box 105
-	(Take 2)	Sun unissued, Sun CD 29
-	(Take 3)	Sun unissued
-	The Huckle-Buck	Sun unissued, Sun CD 29
-	Red River Variations	Sun unissued, Sun CD 29
-	Mexicali Hip Shake	Sun unissued, Sun CD 29

Earl HOOKER/Pinetop PERKINS

Earl Hooker, g-v -1 / Pinetop Perkins, p-v -2 / unk, b / Edward Lee "Shorty" Irvin, d /
back. vcl -1.
Memphis, Tennessee - Sun Studios - Monday, August 10, 1953

-		Going on Down the Line -1	Sun unissued, Arhoolie CD 324, Sun CD 29
-		Earl's Boogie Woogie [Razorback]	Sun unissued, Arhoolie CD 324, Sun CD 29
-		(Steel) Guitar Rag	Sun unissued, Arhoolie CD 324
-		Guitar Rag (alt. take)	Sun unissued, Sun CD 29
-		Pinetop's Boogie Woogie -2	Sun unissued, Sun CD 28
-		Pinetop's Boogie Woogie (alt. take)	Sun unissued, Sun CD 29

Note: Titles in bracket used on Sun CD 29. Actually none of these tracks were given titles at the time of recording. Titles granted later by compilers.

Earl HOOKER

Earl Hooker, g / p / b / d.
Chicago, Illinois - Chess Studios - c. August, 1956

8213	Frog Hop	Chess unissued
8214	Guitar Rumba	Chess unissued

Earl "Zeb" HOOKER

Earl Hooker, gtr / pno / poss. Willie Dixon, bs / dms.
Chicago, Illinois - Chess Studios - c. September, 1956

8252	Frog Hop	Argo 5265, LP 652
8253	Guitar Rumba	Argo 5265

The DELLS with Al Smith's Orchestra

Verne Allison, Charles Barksdale, Michael McGill, Marvin Junior, Johnny Funches, v /
Earl Hooker, g / Lefty Bates, g / Earl Washington, p / Al Smith, b / Al Duncan, d.
Chicago, Illinois - Universal Studios - Thursday, June 13, 1957

57-705	O-Bop She-Bop (Cubop Chebop)	VeeJay 251

Add Lucius Washington, ts / McKinley Easton, bs.

| 57-706 | Time Makes You Change | VeeJay 258 |

ARBEE STIDHAM - LEFTY BATES BAND

Arbee Stidham, v / Earl Hooker, g / Lefty Bates, g / Eddy "Sugar Man" Pennigar, ts / Tommy "Madman" Jones, bs / Al Smith, b / Fred Below, d.
Chicago, Illinois - Universal Studios - Friday, July 12, 1957

1634	Look Me Straight in the Eye	States 164
1635	I Stayed Away Too Long	States 164
1635-9	I Stayed Away Too Long (take 9)	States unissued, Pearl PL-17

THE EARLS

Vcl group / Earl Hooker, g / poss. same band as above.
Chicago, Illinois - Universal Studios - Friday, July 12, 1957

| 1636 | Meet Me After School | United/States unissued |
| 1637 | I Love You So | United/States unissued |

CHRISTINE "EARLINE" HOOKER

Christine "Earline" Hooker, v / Earl Hooker, g / p / d / back. v -1.
Chicago, Illinois - c. late fifties

-	Good Rockin' Tonight -1	United audition tape, unissued
-	I Love My Baby	United audition tape, unissued
-	I'm a Man	United audition tape, unissued

EARL HOOKER & HIS ROAD MASTERS

Earl Hooker, g-v / Johnny "Big Moose" Walker, p / Jack Myers, bs / Harold Tidwell, dms.
Chicago, Illinois - International Recording (IRC) - Early 1959

| 613 A | Do the Chickin (*sic*) | C.J. 613 |
| 613 B | Yea Yea | C.J. 613 |

LORENZO SMITH & HIS SWINGING CHANGES

Lorenzo Smith, ts / Earl Hooker, g / Johnny "Big Moose" Walker, org / b / d.

Chicago, Illinois - International Recording (IRC) - Early 1959

603 A	Moose on the Loose	C.J. 603
603 B	Blue Change	C.J. 603

EARL HOOKER WITH HAROLD TIDWELL

Harold Tidwell, v-d / Earl Hooker, g / poss. Lorenzo Smith, ts -1 / Tall Paul Hankins, p / Jack Myers, b.

Chicago, Illinois - International Recording (IRC) - Saturday, May 23, 1959

605 A	Senorita Juanita	C.J. 605
605 B	Sweet Soozie -1	C.J. 605

JUNIOR WELLS

Junior Wells, v / Earl Hooker, g / Dave Myers, g / Lafayette Leake, p / Willie Dixon, b-back. v -1 / Eugene Lounge, d / Mel London, back. v -1.
Chicago, Illinois - Universal Studios - c. late 1959

25-119	Little by Little (I'm Losing You) -1	Profile 4011, All Points 2000, Bright Star 146
25-120	Come On in This House	Profile 4011, All Points 2000, USA 790, Mel 1005

Note: Matrix numbers on All Points 2000 are respectively 432-38 and 432-37. Matrix number on Bright Star 146 is 1006, using title in bracket. Matrix number on Mel 1005 is M-4001, while wah-wah gtr and dms have been overdubbed.

BOBBY SAXTON

Bobby Saxton, v / Earl Hooker, g / Ernest Cotton, ts / Sax Mallard, bs / Tall Paul Hankins, p / Margo Gibson, b / Bobby Little, dms.
Chicago, Illinois - Hall Studios - Friday, January 15, 1960

106 A	Trying to Make a Living	Bea & Baby 106, Checker 947
107 A	Trying to Make a Living (Part 2)	Bea & Baby unissued

EARL HOOKER

Same as above session, except omit Saxton.
Chicago, Illinois - Hall Studios - Friday, January 15, 1960

106 B	Dynamite	Bea & Baby 106, Checker 947

Lillian OFFITT

Lillian Offitt, v / Earl Hooker, g / A. C. Reed, ts / Tall Paul Hankins, p / Earnest Johnson, b / Bobby Little or Harold Tidwell, d.
Chicago, Illinois - Universal Studios - Poss. Monday, February 1, 1960

| 25-123 | The Man Won't Work | Chief 7012 |
| 25-124 | Will My Man Be Home Tonight | Chief 7012 |

Lillian OFFITT

Lillian Offitt, v / Earl Hooker, g / A. C. Reed, ts / Tall Paul Hankins or Johnny "Big Moose" Walker, p / Earnest Johnson, b / Bobby Little or Harold Tidwell, d / Four Duchesses, back. v -1.
Chicago, Illinois - Universal Studios - Thursday, May 5, 1960

| 25-137 | Oh Mama | Chief 7015 |
| 25-138 | My Man Is a Lover -1 | Chief 7015 |

Junior WELLS / Earl HOOKER

Junior Wells, hca / Earl Hooker, g / A. C. Reed, ts / Tall Paul Hankins or Johnny "Big Moose" Walker, p / Earnest Johnson, b / Bobby Little or Harold Tidwell, d.
Chicago, Illinois - Universal Studios - Thursday, May 5, 1960

| 25-139 | Calling All Blues | Chief 7020 |

Note: Title originally released on Chief 7020 backed with Elmore James's "Knocking at Your Door," miscredited to James.

MAGIC SAM

Magic Sam, g / Earl Hooker, g / A. C. Reed, ts / Boyd Atkins, ts / Odell Campbell, bs / S.P. Leary, d / Four Duchesses, back. v.
Chicago, Illinois - Universal Studios - Thursday, May 5, 1960

| 25-141 | Square Dance Rock Pt. 1 | Chief 7017 |
| 25-142 | Square Dance Rock Pt. 2 | Chief 7017 |

Earl HOOKER

Harold Tidwell, d-v / Earl Hooker, g / Johnny "Big Moose" Walker, el-p / Earnest Johnson, b.
Chicago, Illinois - Universal Studios - Monday, August 8, 1960

| 25-144 | Swear to Tell the Truth | Age 29106 |

Junior WELLS / Earl HOOKER

Junior Wells, v / Earl Hooker, g / Johnny "Big Moose" Walker, org / Earnest Johnson, b / Harold Tidwell, d.
Chicago, Illinois - Universal Studios - Monday, August 8, 1960

25-145	Galloping Horses a Lazy Mule	Chief 7016, 7039

Earl HOOKER

Earl Hooker, g / Johnny "Big Moose" Walker, org / Earnest Johnson, b / Harold Tidwell, d.
Chicago, Illinois - Universal Studios - Monday, August 8, 1960

25-146	Blues in D Natural	Chief 7016, 7039, Mel-Lon 1001

Note: Mel-Lon 1001 gives matrix number as 27-163.

Junior WELLS - HOOKER & WELLS -1

Junior Wells, v except on -1, hca / Earl Hooker, g / Poss. Lacy Gibson, g -2 / Jarrett "Gerry" Gibson, ts / Donald "Hank" Hankins, bs / Johnny "Big Moose" Walker, p / Jack Myers, b / Fred Below, d / Mel London, back. v -3.
Chicago, Illinois - Universal Studios - Monday, October 17, 1960

25-157	Messin' with the Kid -2	Chief 7021, Mel 1005
25-158	You Sure Look Good to Me-3	Chief 7034

Same except Johnny Walker, org instead of pno.

25-159	So Tired	Chief 7037
25-160	Universal Rock -1	Chief 7021

Note: Mel 1005 gives matrix number as M-4000.

Betty EVERETT / Earl HOOKER Allstars

Betty Everett, v / Earl Hooker, g / Ike Perkins, g / Lafayette Leake, p / Bill Joseph, b / Harold Tidwell, d / back. v -1.
Chicago, Illinois - International Recording (IRC) - c. mid-1961

619 A	Happy I Long to Be -1	C.J. 619

351 *Discography*

BETTY EVERETT / IKE PERKINS ALLSTARS

Same - add Red Sims, ts.
Chicago, Illinois - International Recording (IRC) - c. mid-1961

| 619 B | Your Loving Arms | C.J. 619 |

EARL HOOKER

Earl Hooker, g / A. C. Reed, ts / Johnny "Big Moose" Walker, org / Lafayette Leake, p /
Earnest Johnson, b / Bobby Little, d.
Chicago, Illinois Universal Studios - Poss. Wednesday, May 3, 1961

| 26-205 | Blue Guitar | Age 29106 |

Note: "Blue Guitar," recorded first on the occasion of this session, was assigned a late
matrix number, as Mel London had not planned on its original release.

Add Austin (?), talking / Julian Beasley, as.

| 25-195 | Apache War Dance | Age 29101 |

Omit Austin, Beasley and Walker - add Jackie Brenston, bs.

| 25-196 | Rockin' with the Kid | Chief 7031 |

Beasley, as, replaces Brenston - Walker, org, replaces Leake.

| 25-197 | Rockin' Wild | Chief 7031 |

JUNIOR WELLS

Junior Wells, v / Earl Hooker, g / A. C. Reed, ts / Julian Beasley, as / Johnny "Big Moose"
Walker, org / Lafayette Leake, p / Earnest Johnson, b / Bobby Little, d.
Chicago, Illinois - Universal Studios - Poss. Wednesday, May 3, 1961

| 25-198 | I Could Cry | Chief 7038 |

Omit Beasley and Reed.

| 26-199 | I'm a Stranger | Chief 7030 |

Add Beasley and Reed.

| 26-200 | The Things I'd Do for You | Chief 7030 |

A. C. REED / EARL HOOKER & HIS BAND

A. C. Reed, v / Earl Hooker, g / Johnny "Big Moose" Walker, org / Lafayette Leake, p /
Earnest Johnson, b / Bobby Little, d.
Chicago, Illinois - Universal Studios - Poss. Wednesday, May 3, 1961

25-201	This Little Voice	Age 29101

RICKY ALLEN

Ricky Allen, v / Earl Hooker, g / A. C. Reed, ts / Julian Beasley, as -1 / Little Ray
Charles, org -2 / Lafayette Leake, p / Earnest Johnson, b / Bobby Little, d.
Chicago, Illinois - Universal Studios - Poss. Wednesday, May 3, 1961

26-203	You'd Better Be Sure -1	Age 29102
26-204	You Were My Teacher -2	Age 29102

Note: At this point, Mel London progressively replaced his 25-000 series with the
26-000 series. Yet things were done quite erratically, as the prefix numbers used for the
above session seem to indicate. This is confirmed by the fact that in the case of "I'm a
Stranger," "This Little Voice," and "You'd Better Be Sure," matrix numbers engraved in
vinyl (respectively 25-199, 26-201, and 26-202) do not correspond to the ones printed
on the label (respectively 26-199, 25-201, and 26-203).

MUDDY WATERS

Muddy Waters, v dubbed on "Blue Guitar" track.
Chicago, Illinois - Chess Studios - Wednesday, June 27, 1962

U 11711	You Shook Me	Chess 1827, LP 1544

Note: Flip of Chess 1827, "Muddy Waters Twist," as well as the remaining three titles
recorded along with it ("Going Home," "Down by the Deep Blue Sea," and "Tough
Times") were cut during the first weeks of 1962; contrary to what has usually been inferred by discographers, Earl Hooker was not the guitarist on these sides.

MUDDY WATERS

Muddy Waters, dubbed v / Instrumental track: Earl Hooker, g / A. C. Reed, ts / Jackie
Brenston, bs / Johnny "Big Moose" Walker, org / Earnest Johnson, b / Casey Jones, d /
dubbed percussion -1.
*Chicago, Illinois - Chess Studios - Inst. track: July, 1962 - Dubbing: Friday, October 12,
1962*

U 11836	You Need Love -1	Chess 1839

| U 11837 | Little Brown Bird | Chess 1839 |
| U 11838 | Black Angel | Chess unissued |

EARL HOOKER

Earl Hooker, g-v -1 / A. C. Reed, ts/ Jackie Brenston, bs / Johnny "Big Moose" Walker, org / Earnest Johnson, b / Bobby Little, d / back. v -1.
Chicago, Illinois - Chess Studios - Late July, early August, 1962

U 11786	Tanya	Checker 1025
U 11787	Put Your Shoes On Willie -1	Checker 1025
U 11788	Everything Will Work Out Fine	Chess unissued
U 11789	Sweet Brown Angel	Chess unissued

Johnny "Big Moose" Walker, p instead of org - add poss. The Earlettes, v.

| (?) | Oh Baby | Chess unissued, Chess CD RED 39 |

EARL HOOKER

Earl Hooker, g / Reggie Boyd, g / A. C. Reed, ts / Pinetop Perkins, p / Earnest Johnson, b / Casey Jones, d.
Chicago, Illinois - Universal Studios - 1962

| 26-121 | How Long Can This Go On | Age 29111 |

A. C. REED

A. C. Reed, v / Earl Hooker, g / Reggie Boyd, g / Earnest Johnson, b / Casey Jones, d / back. v.
Chicago, Illinois - Universal Studios - 1962

| 26-123 | Mean Cop | Age 29112 |

REGGIE "GUITAR" BOYD

Reggie Boyd, g / Earl Hooker, g / A. C. Reed, ts / Earnest Johnson, b / Casey Jones, d.
Chicago, Illinois - Universal Studios - 1962

| 26-124 | Nothing but Good | Age 29110 |

EARL HOOKER

Earl Hooker, g / Reggie Boyd, g / A. C. Reed, ts / Johnny "Big Moose" Walker, org / Earnest Johnson, b / Casey Jones, d.

Chicago, Illinois - Universal Studios - 1962

26-125   These Cotton Pickin' Blues   Age 29111

REGGIE "GUITAR" BOYD
Reggie Boyd, g / Earl Hooker, g / A. C. Reed, ts / Johnny "Big Moose" Walker, org /
Earnest Johnson, b / Casey Jones, d.
Chicago, Illinois - Universal Studios - 1962

26-126   Nothing but Poison   Age 29110

A. C. REED
A. C. Reed, v / Poss. Earl Hooker, g / Reggie Boyd, g / Johnny "Big Moose" Walker, p /
Earnest Johnson, b / Casey Jones, d.
Chicago, Illinois - Universal Studios - 1962

26-127   That Ain't Right   Age 29112

A. C. REED
A. C. Reed, v / Earl Hooker, g / Johnny "Big Moose" Walker, org / Earnest Johnson, b /
Bobby Little, d / The Earlettes, v.
Chicago, Illinois - Universal Studios - c. mid to late 1962

26-13?   Crying Blues   Age unissued, Charly
                                                             CRB 1135

Note: This track was issued as "Win the Dance" on some pressings of Age 29114, as well
as on Charly 1135.

BIG MOOSE & THE JAMS
Johnny "Big Moose" Walker, org / Earl Hooker, g / A. C. Reed, ts / Earnest Johnson, b /
Bobby Little, d.
Chicago, Illinois - Universal Studios - c. mid to late 1962

26-131   Off the Hook   Age 29113

EARL HOOKER & THE EARLETTES
Earl Hooker, g / A. C. Reed, ts / Johnny "Big Moose" Walker, p / Earnest Johnson, b /
Bobby Little, d / The Earlettes [Geraldine and (?) Taylor], v.
Chicago, Illinois - Universal Studios - c. mid to late 1962

26-132   That Man   Age 29114

BIG MOOSE & the Jams

Johnny "Big Moose" Walker, org / Earl Hooker, g / Earnest Johnson, b / Bobby Little, d.
Chicago, Illinois - Universal Studios - c. mid to late 1962

26-133	Bright Sounds	Age 29113

Note: Some Age 29113 45s give "Off the Hook" / "Bright Sounds" matrix numbers respectively as AG-9033 and AG-9032.

EARL HOOKER & the Earlettes

Earl Hooker, g / A. C. Reed, ts / Johnny "Big Moose" Walker, org / Earnest Johnson, b / Bobby Little, d / The Earlettes, v.
Chicago, Illinois - Universal Studios - c. mid to late 1962

26-134	Win the Dance	Age 29114

JACKIE BRENSTON with Earl HOOKER Band

Jackie Brenston, v / Earl Hooker, g / A. C. Reed, ts/ Little Ray Charles, org / Earnest Johnson, b / Bobby Little, d / Robbie Yates and the Elites, back. v -1.
Chicago, Illinois - Universal Studios - c. mid-1963

27-243	Want You to Rock Me	Mel-Lon 1000
27-244	Down in My Heart -1	Mel-Lon 1000

EARL HOOKER

Earl Hooker, g / A. C. Reed, ts / Jackie Brenston, bs / Little Ray Charles, org / Johnny "Big Moose" Walker, p / Earnest Johnson, b / Bobby Little, d.
Chicago, Illinois - Universal Studios - c. mid to late 1963

27-340	The Leading Brand	Mel-Lon 1001

RICKY ALLEN

Ricky Allen, v / Earl Hooker, g / A. C. Reed, ts / Jackie Brenston, bs / Sonny Lantz, org / Lafayette Leake, p / Earnest Johnson, b / Casey Jones, d / Eddie "Allen" Johnson, talking -1.
Chicago, Illinois - Universal Studios -c. February, 1964

100 503	Help Me Mama	Age 29125
100 504	The Big Fight -1	Age 29125

Earl HOOKER

Earl Hooker, g-v -1 / A. C. Reed, ts-v -2 / Richard (?), org / James Hamilton, b / Bobby Little, d.
Sauk City, Wisconsin - Cuca Studios - c. early to mid-1964

-	The Foxtrot	Cuca LP KS- 4100, Bluesway LP 6072
RK 5M 6767	Bertha	Cuca J-1194, LP KS-4100
RK 5M 6768	Walking the Floor (Over You)	(Same)
U5KM 3794	End of the Blues	Cuca J-6733, LP KS-4100
U5KM 3795	Dynamite	Cuca J-6733
-	Swear to Tell the Truth -1	Cuca unissued, Black Top CD 1093
-	Reconsider Baby -1	(Same)
-	She's Fine -2	(Same)

Note: Cuca J-1194 credited to "Earl Hooker & the Soul Twisters." Cuca J-6733 credited to "Earl Hooker & the Soul Thrillers." Matrix number order is irrelevant with Cuca sessions, since numbers were strictly assigned to titles issued on 45s at the time of release. Cuca LP was released under number KS-4100, even though KS-3400 appeared on the sleeve due to a misprint. KS-3400 had already been assigned to a Doc DeHaven LP.

Earl HOOKER

Earl Hooker, g-v -1 / Charles (?), as / unk, org / James Hamilton, b / Bobby Little, d.
Highland Park, Illinois - c. 1965

-	Chicken -1	Jim-Ko unissued
-	(?) -1	Jim-Ko unissued
-	(Untitled instrumental)	Jim-Ko unissued
-	(Untitled instrumental)	Jim-Ko unissued
-	(Untitled instrumental)	Jim-Ko unissued
-	(Untitled instrumental)	Jim-Ko unissued

LITTLE TOMMY & BOBBY LITTLE WITH Earl Hooker & His Soul Twisters

Little Tommy Isom, v / Bobby Little, v-d / Earl Hooker, g / Charles (?), as / unk, org / James Hamilton, b.
Highland Park, Illinois - c. 1965

S 4723	You Can't Hide	Jim-Ko
S 4724	Won't Be Down Long	Jim-Ko

EARL HOOKER

Earl Hooker, g-v -1 / Charles Lange, ts / unk, as / Johnny "Big Moose" Walker, org / unk, b / unk, d.
Chicago, Illinois - International Recording (IRC) - Thursday, April 29, 1965

643 A	Wild Moments	C.J. 643, Blue Flame LP 101
-	Wild Moments (2 alt. takes)	C.J. unissued
643 B	Chicken -1	C.J. 643
-	Chicken (instrumental) (2 alt. takes)	C.J. unissued

JIMMY LIGGINS, HIS GUITAR & ORCHESTRA

Jimmy Liggins, vcl, dubbed on a respliced version of "Wild Moments" (643 A).
Los Angeles - c. 1965

| - | The Last Round | Duplex 1002 |

EARL HOOKER & BAND

Unk, v / Earl Hooker, g / ts / bs / p / b / d.
Chicago, Illinois - International Recording (IRC) - c. mid-sixties

| - | I Can't Understand | C.J. unissued, Blue Flame BLP 103 |

EARL HOOKER

Earl Hooker, g / Freddy Roulette, steel g / g / org / b / d.
Sauk City, Wisconsin - Cuca Studios - c. mid-1966

-	Off the Hook	Cuca LP KS-4100, Bluesway LP 6072
-	Hold On . . . I'm Coming	(Same)
-	Two Bugs in a Rug	(Same)

Add Muddy Waters Jr., v

| - | Two Bugs and a Roach (short rehearsal) | Cuca unissued |
| - | Everything Gonna Be Alright | Cuca unissued, Black Top CD 1093 |

Unk, v / Earl Hooker, g / org / b / d.

| - | Stand by Me (In the Storm) (incomplete take) | Cuca unissued |

-	Same (2 false starts)	Cuca unissued
-	He Can Do	Cuca unissued
-	Didn't It Rain	Cuca unissued
-	He'll Understand and Say Well Done	Cuca unissued

EARL HOOKER

Unk, v except on -1 / Earl Hooker, g-talking -2 / org -3 / b / Bobby Little, d.
Unknown location - c. late 1966

-	Zombie -2/-3	Unissued
-	Hello Baby	Unissued, Black Top CD 1093
-	Monrovia	Unissued
-	Blue Greens & Beans -1/-3	Unissued

Note: Above four tracks, recorded as a demo tape by Earl and Band, were sent to Cuca Records owner Jim Kirchstein, who still holds them today.

EARL HOOKER

Frank "Crying Shame" Clark, v -1 / Earl Hooker, g / ts / org / b /Bobby Little, d.
Sauk City, Wisconsin - Cuca Studios - April, 1967

-	(organ instrumental)	Cuca unissued
-	Hooker Special	Cuca LP KS-4100
-	All Your Love	Cuca unissued, Black Top CD 1093
-	You Took All My Love -1	Cuca J-1445
-	The Misfit (Got to Keep Movin') -1	Cuca unissued, Black Top CD 1093
-	Something You Ate	Cuca LP KS-4100
-	Frosty	Cuca unissued, Black Top CD 1093

EARL HOOKER

Earl Hooker, g / Bobby Fields, ts / org / b / d.
Sauk City, Wisconsin- Cuca Studios - c. mid-1967

-	Dust My Broom	Cuca J-1445, LP KS-4100
-	Hot & Heavy	Cuca LP KS-4100
-	Hot & Heavy (alt. take)	Cuca unissued, Black Top CD 1093

	The Screwdriver	Cuca LP KS-4100
-	I Got You (I Feel Good)	Cuca unissued,
		Black Magic LP 9006
-	Blue Moon of Kentucky	Cuca unissued

EARL HOOKER

Earl Hooker, g / unk, g / Johnny "Big Moose" Walker, org / b / d.
Chicago, Illinois - Sound Studios - 1967

-	(Enough titles for an LP)	Globe / Mel Collins unissued

EARL HOOKER

Earl Hooker, g / poss. Abb Locke, ts -1 / Fred Roulette, steel g -2 / unk, org -2 / poss.
Odell Campbell, b / d.
Chicago, Illinois - Alex Club - Fall, 1968

-	Earl Hooker Blues -1	Black Top CD 1093
-	Dust My Broom -2	Black Top CD 1093

EARL HOOKER / TWO BUGS AND A ROACH

Earl Hooker, g-v -1 / Andrew "B. B. Jr." Odom, v -2 / Fred Roulette, steel g -3 / Carey
Bell, hca -4 / Pinetop Perkins, p-org / Gino Skaggs, b / Levi Warren, d.
Chicago, Illinois - Sound Studios - Tuesday, November 12, 1968

-	You Don't Want Me -1/-3	Arhoolie 45-521, LP 1044
-	New Sweet Black Angel -4	Arhoolie LP 1066
-	Earl Hooker Blues	(Same)
-	You Don't Love Me -2/-3	(Same)
-	Take Me Back to East St. Louis -2/-3 Arhoolie CD 468

Earl Hooker, g-v -1 / Andrew "B. B. Jr." Odom, v -2 / Carey Bell, hca -3 & v -4 / Fred
Roulette, steel g -5 / Louis Myers, hca -6 / Pinetop Perkins, p-org / Gino Skaggs, b /
Willie Williams, d.
Chicago, Illinois - Sound Studios - Thursday, November 14, 1968

-	Anna Lee -1/-5/-6	Arhoolie LP 1044
-	Two Bugs and a Roach -1/-2	(Same)
-	Love Ain't a Plaything -3/-	(Same)
-	Little Carey's Jump -3	Arhoolie CD 468
-	Wah Wah Blues	Arhoolie 45-521, LP 1044

Earl Hooker, g / Gino Skaggs, b / Levi Warren, d.
Chicago, Illinois - Sound Studios - Friday, November 15, 1968

-	Off the Hook	Arhoolie LP 1044

SLEEPY JOHN ESTES / ELECTRIC SLEEP

Sleepy John Estes, g-v / Jimmy Dawkins, g / Carey Bell, hca / Sunnyland Slim, p / Earl Hooker, b / Odie Payne, d.
Chicago, Illinois - Sound Studios - Tuesday, December 3, 1968

-	May West	Delmark LP DS 619
-	If the River Was Whiskey	(Same)
-	How to Sing These Blues	(Same)
-	Newport Blues	Delmark CD DD 619

Note: "If the River Was Whiskey" listed as "Diving Duck," and "Newport Blues" listed as "President Kennedy" on recording lead sheets. On "If the River Was Whiskey" and "How to Sing These Blues," basswork mistakenly credited to Joe Harper in Delmark DS 619 sleeve notes, whereas Harper actually appeared on "Sweet Little Flower," the bass part of which was unduly credited to Hooker in LP DS 619 sleeve notes.

EARL HOOKER

Earl Hooker, g / Paul Asbell, g / Jeff Carp, hca / Gino Skaggs, b / Roosevelt Shaw, d.
Chicago, Illinois - Pepper's Lounge - Thursday, May 1, 1969

-	Dust My Broom	Rarities LP 25
-	These Ole Cotton Pickin' Blues	Rarities LP 28
-	Chicken Shack	Rarities LP 25
-	Too Late	Rarities LP 25

Note: These various titles were recorded live by Dick Shurman, from whom they were bootlegged. Other titles credited to Hooker on Rarities LPs 25 and 28 actually involved guitarist-singer Bobby King. "Too Late" is a retitled version of "Universal Rock."

EARL HOOKER / FUNK. LAST OF THE GREAT EARL HOOKER

Earl Hooker, g-v -1 / Jeff Carp, hca-v -2 / Paul Asbell, g / Boots Hamilton, org / Gino Skaggs, b / Roosevelt Shaw, d.
Chicago, Illinois - Monday, May 5, 1969

-	Wa-Wa Blues - Part 1	Blues on Blues LP 10002
-	Wa-Wa Blues - Part 2 (Blues for Dancers)	Blues on Blues LP 10002, Red Lightnin' CD 092
-	Soul Cookin'	Blues on Blues LP 10002
-	Sweet Home Chicago -1	(Same)
-	Hooker Cooker	(Same)
-	Huckle Bug	(Same)
-	The Real Blues	(Same)
-	Ball Game on a Rainy Day -2	(Same)

Note: Title in bracket used on Red Lightnin' CD.

Earl HOOKER / Sweet Black Angel

Earl Hooker, g-v -1 / Ike Turner, p / poss. Jesse Knight, b / Ulysses "Soko" Richardson, d.
Los Angeles, California - May, 1969

-	Drivin' Wheel	Blue Thumb LP BTS 12
-	Shuffle	(Same)
-	Country & Western	(Same)
-	Sweet Home Chicago -1	(Same)

Add Little Mack Simmons, hca-talking -2 / ts -3 / tp -3 / tb -3.

8005-1	Boogie, Don't Blot -2	Blue Thumb BLU 45-103, LP BTS 12
8006	Funky Blues -3	(Same)
-	Catfish Blues	Blue Thumb LP BTS 12
-	Sweet Black Angel -3	(Same)
-	Cross Cut Saw -3	Blue Thumb LP BTS 12

Omit Simmons.

-	I Feel Good -3	Blue Thumb LP BTS 12

Note: "The Mood," included on Blue Thumb LP, features Ike Turner on guitar, not Earl Hooker.

John Lee HOOKER / If You Miss 'Im . . . I Got 'Im

John Lee Hooker, g-v / Earl Hooker, g / Jeff Carp, hca / Johnny "Big Moose" Walker, org / Gino Skaggs, b / Roosevelt Shaw, d.
Los Angeles, California - Vault Studios - Thursday, May 29, 1969

70028	If You Take Care of Me, I'll Take Care of You	Bluesway LP 6038
70029	Messin' 'round with the Blues	Bluesway unissued, MCAD-10760
70030	I Don't Care When You Go	Bluesway LP 6038
70031	Lonesome Mood	Bluesway LP 6038
70032 A	I Gotta Go to Vietnam	Bluesway unissued, MCAD-10760
70032 B	Baby, Be Strong (alt. take)	Bluesway LP 6038

Johnny "Big Moose" Walker, p instead of org.

70033	The Hookers (If You Miss 'Im... I Got 'Im)	(Same)

70034	I Wanna Be Your Puppy, Baby	(Same)
70036 A	Hold On Baby	Bluesway unissued, MCAD-10760
70036 B	Baby, I Love You (alt. take)	Bluesway LP 6038
70037	Walking the Floor over You	Bluesway unissued

Note: 70035 ("Bang Bang Bang Bang") and 70038 ("Have Mercy on My Soul") feature Paul Asbell on guitar, not Earl Hooker.

EARL HOOKER / DON'T HAVE TO WORRY

Earl Hooker, g-v -1 / Paul Asbell, g / Johnny "Big Moose" Walker, p / Gino Skaggs, b / Roosevelt Shaw, d.
Los Angeles, California - Vault Studios - Thursday, May 29, 1969

70039	New Look	Bluesway unissued
70040	Hookin'	Bluesway LP 6032
70041	Don't Have to Worry -1	(Same)

Johnny "Big Moose" Walker, org instead of p.

| 70042 | Universal Rock | (Same) |

Johnny "Big Moose" Walker, p-v - add Jeff Carp, hca.

| 70043 | Look over Yonder's Wall | (Same) |
| 70044 | Is You Ever Seen a One-Eyed Woman Cry? | (Same) |

Add Andrew "B. B. Jr." Odom, v / Johnny "Big Moose" Walker, org -2 - p -3.

70045	Moanin' and Groanin' -2	(Same)
70046	The Sky Is Crying -3	(Same)
70047	Come to Me Right Away, Baby -2	(Same)

Omit Carp and Odom.

| 70048 | You Got to Lose -1/-3 | (Same) |

Add Jeff Carp, hca.

| 70049 | Blue Guitar -3 | (Same) |
| 70050 | You Know It Ain't Right -3 | Bluesway unissued |

Andrew "Voice" Odom / Farther On Down the Road

Andrew Odom, v / Earl Hooker, g / Johnny "Big Moose" Walker, p -1 - org -2 /Jimmy Bond, b / Panama Francis, d.
Los Angeles, California - Vault Studios - Wednesday, June 4, 1969

70051	I Got the Feelin' -1	Bluesway LP 6055
70052	Take Me Back to East St. Louis -1	(same)
70053	Stormy Monday -2	(same)
70054	Feel So Good -2	(same)
70055	You Don't Love Me Yes I Know -2	Bluesway unissued
70056	It's My Own Fault -2	Bluesway LP 6055
70057	Don't Ever Leave Me All Alone -1	(same)
70058	You Don't Have to Go -1	Bluesway unissued
70059	Please Love Me -1	Bluesway LP 6055
70060	Long About Sunrise -1	(same)
70061	Farther Up the Road -1	(same)

Johnny "Big Moose" Walker / Rambling Woman

Johnny "Big Moose" Walker, org-v / Earl Hooker, g / Otis Hale, ts / Gino Skaggs, b / Paul Humphrey, d.
Los Angeles, California - Vault Studios - Monday, June 9, 1969

70062	Rambling Woman	Bluesway LP 6036
70063	Baby Talk	(same)

Johnny "Big Moose" Walker, p instead of org - no v on -1.

70064	Footrace	Bluesway LP BLS 6036
70065	Leave Me 'lone	(same)
70066	All My Love	Bluesway unissued
70067	Moose Huntin' -1	Bluesway LP BLS 6036
70068	The Sky Is Crying	(same)
70069	Chicken Shack	(same)
70070	Rock Me Momma	(same)
70071	She's Got a Good One	Bluesway unissued
70072	Moose Is on the Loose -1	Bluesway LP BLS 6036
70073	Would You Baby	(same)

Earl Hooker / Hooker and Steve

Earl Hooker, g-v -1 / Louis Myers, hca / Steve Miller, p / Gino Skaggs, b / Bobby Joe Johnson, d.
Berkeley, California - Sierra Sound Studios - Friday, July 18, 1969

-	The Moon Is Rising -1	Arhoolie LP 1051
-	The Hook	Arhoolie LP 1066
-	There Is a Man Down There	Arhoolie unissued

Miller, org instead of p.

| - | Conversion Blues -1 | Arhoolie LP 1051 |

Omit Louis Myers.

-	Earl's Blues	Arhoolie LP 1051
-	Guitar Rag	Arhoolie LP 1051
-	Hooker 'n' Steve	Arhoolie LP 1051

Same, except Skaggs, b-v.

| - | I'm Your Main Man | Arhoolie LP 1051 |

Miller, v replaces Skaggs.

| - | New Riviera | Arhoolie LP 1051 |
| - | Strung-Out Woman Blues | Arhoolie LP 1051 |

EARL HOOKER / HIS FIRST & LAST RECORDINGS

Earl Hooker, g / Eddie Taylor, g / Dave Myers, b / Arthur "Dogman" Jackson, d.
Chicago, Illinois - Pepper's Lounge - Wednesday, September 10, 1969

-	Improvisations on Dust My Broom	Arhoolie LP 1066
-	Improvisations on Frosty	Arhoolie LP 1066
-	Can't Hold Out Much Longer	Arhoolie CD 468

EARL HOOKER / THE MOON IS RISING

Earl Hooker, g / Dave Myers, b / Arthur "Dogman" Jackson, d.
Chicago, Illinois -Theresa's Lounge - Friday, September 12, 1969

| - | Swingin' at Theresa's | Arhoolie CD 468 |

JIMMY WITHERSPOON / HUNH! (BLUESWAY LP)/JIMMY'S BLUES (MCA LP)

Jimmy Witherspoon, v / Earl Hooker, g / Mel Brown, g / Red Holloway, ts / Art Hillery, org -1 / Charles Brown, p / Jimmy Bond, b / Lavell Austin, d.

Los Angeles, California - Vault Studios - Monday, September 15, 1969

70079	I Made a Lot of Mistakes	Bluesway LP 6040
70080	Parcel Post Blues	(same)
70081	Bug to Put'n Yo' Year -1	(same)
70082	Never Knew This Kind of Hurt Before	(same)
70083	Pillar to Post	(same)
70084	You Can't Do a Thing When You're Drunk	(same)
70085	Bags Under My Eyes	(same)

Charles BROWN / *Legend!*

Charles Brown, p-v/ Earl Hooker, g / Mel Brown, g / Red Holloway, ts / Jimmy Bond, b / Ed Thigpen, d / Dottie Ivory, v -1.
Los Angeles, California - Vault Studios - Tuesday, September 16, 1969

70086	Drifting Blues	Bluesway LP 6039
70087	New Merry Christmas Baby	(Same)
70088	Black Night	(Same)
70089	I Want to Go Home -1	(Same)

Arthur Booth, b, replaces Jimmy Bond.

70090	Rainy, Rainy Day	(Same)
70091	All Is Forgiven -1	(Same)

Same, except Charles Brown p only.

70092	The Combination	(Same)
70093	(?)	Bluesway unissued

Brownie McGHEE & Sonny TERRY / *I Couldn't Believe My Eyes*

Brownie McGhee, g-v / Earl Hooker, g / Sonny Terry, hca / Ray Johnson, p / Jimmy Bond, b / Panama Francis, d / George McGhee, Marsha Smith, Clark Kidder, back. v -1.
Los Angeles, California - Vault Studios - Wednesday, September 24, 1969

70094	Tell Me Why	Bluesway LP 6059, See for Miles CD 92
70095	Don't Wait for Me -1	(same)
70096	Brownie's New Blues	(same)
70097	Parcel Post Blues	(same)
70098	I Couldn't Believe My Eyes	(same)

Sonny Terry, hca-v / Brownie McGhee, g / Earl Hooker, g / Ray Johnson, p -tambourine -2 / Jimmy Bond, b / Panama Francis, d.

70099	When I Was Drinkin'	(same)
70100	My Baby's So Fine	(same)
70101	Poor Man Blues -2	(same)
70102	I'm in Love with You Baby	(same)

Same band, except Brownie McGhee, g-v / Sonny Terry, hca-v.

| 70103 | Black Cat Bone | (same) |
| 70104 | Beggin' You | Bluesway unissued |

Earl HOOKER

Earl Hooker, g-v -1 / Carey Bell, hca / Mack Thompson, b / Robert St. Julien, d.
London, England - Royal Albert Hall - Friday, October 3, 1969

| - | Blue Shadows Fall -1 | CBS LP 63912 |

Same, except Carey Bell, hca-b.

| - | Going Up and Down -1 | CBS LP 63912 |

Omit Bell.

| - | Walking the Floor over You / Steel Guitar Rag | CBS LP 52796 |

Carey BELL

Carey Bell, hca-v / Earl Hooker, g / Mack Thompson, b / Robert St. Julien, d.
London, England - Royal Albert Hall - Friday, October 3, 1969

| - | Medley: Rocking with Chromanica (sic) / I Feel Bad, Bad, Bad | CBS LP 63912O |

Index

Club names appear in **boldface.**

369

Delta. *See* Mississippi Delta
DeLuxe Records, 54
Demetre, Jacques, 114, 259
Dennis Simpson's Bar (Sarasota, Fla.), 50
DeSanto, Sugar Pie, 141
DeShay, James, 97
Detroit Embers, 248
Detroit Junior (Emery Williams), 319
Detroit, Mich., 6, 28, 33, 167
Dickens, Charles, 33
Diddley, Bo (Ellas McDaniel), 10–11, 87, 140, 157, 162
"Didn't It Rain," 231, 359
Dig Records. *See* Ultra Records
Dipsy Doodle (Osceola, Ark.), 94, 207
Distance's (Osceola, Ark.), 94
Dixie's Kitchen (Lawton, Okla.), 85
Dixon, Robert, 50, 345
Dixon, Willie, xii, 104, 119–20, 139, 260, 292, 302, 319, 325, 347, 349
Dizz, Lefty, 310
"Do Right Baby," 68, 282
"Do the Chickin," 112, 118, 348
"Do You Mean It," 67, 112, 169
Doggett, Bill, 139, 283, 294
"Doin' the Chicken." *See* "Chicken"
Domino Club (Chicago Heights, Ill.), 182
"Don't Ever Leave Me All Alone," 284, 294, 364
Don't Have to Worry, 363
"Don't Have to Worry," 68, 281–82, 363
Down Beat magazine, 289
"Down in My Heart," 144, 356
Drew, Miss., 30, 62
Drew, Patti, 226
Drew-Vells, 226
Drifters, 137
"Drifting Blues," 298–99, 366
Drive In (Sarasota, Fla.), 51
"Drive, The," 61, 346
"Drivin' Wheel," 276, 295, 362
Du Bois, W. E. B., 5
Duck Inn Lounge (Chicago, Ill.), 181
Dudlow. *See* Taylor, Robert "Dudlow"
"Duke of Earl," 109
Duke Records, 217, 229, 294
Duling, Vincent, 10–12, 20, 22, 83–84
Duncan, Adolph "Billy," 66, 219

Duncan, Al, 106–07, 347
Durham, Eddie, 12, 163
"Dust My Broom," 234, 255, 258–59, 261, 295, 359–61, 365
Dynaflow Club (St. Louis, Mo.), 98
"Dynamite," 117, 223, 225, 232, 258, 349, 357

Eagle's Park, Ill., 96
"Earl Hooker Blues," 256, 294, 360
Earl Park, Ind., 190–91
Earl, Ronnie, 325
Earlettes, 142, 178, 354–56
Earls, 108–09, 348
"Earl's Blues," 291, 365
"Earl's Boogie Woogie," 63, 347
East Chicago, Ind., 176
East St. Louis, Ill., 84, 96, 98, 104, 157, 175, 185, 205
Easton, McKinley, 107, 348
"Easy Go," 142
Eatmon, Narvel. *See* Cadillac Baby
Eddie Shaw's Place (Chicago, Ill.), 265
El Dorados, 106
Electric Dust Band, 193, 269, 287
Electric Mud, 257
Electric Sleep, 257, 361
Elektra Records, 274
Elites, 145, 356
Ellington, Duke, 111, 248
Ellis, Tinsley, 325
Emerson, Billy "The Kid," 50, 66, 101–02, 181
"End of the Blues," 222, 225, 232, 357
Estes, "Sleepy" John, 257, 361
Evans, David, xii
Evanston, Ill., 21, 230
Evansville, Ind., 186, 236, 250
Everett, Betty, 111, 133, 351–52
"Every Day I Have the Blues," 100
Every One a Pearl, 51
"Everything Gonna Be Alright," 231, 294, 358
"Everything Will Work Out Fine," 140, 354
Excello Records, 127–28
Exclusive Records, 140

"So Tired," 131, 351
"Something You Ate," 233, 359
Sonny Boy (Rice Miller impersonator), 72
Sonny Boy Williamson #2. *See* Miller, Rice
"Sorry About That," 258
Soul Bag magazine, xiii, 305–06
"Soul Cookin'," 272, 361
Soul Thrillers, 193, 225, 232, 357
Soul Twisters, 174, 193, 212, 214, 222, 224, 228, 230, 357
Sound studios (Chicago, Ill.), 235, 253, 255, 257
South Chicago, Ill., 70, 191
Spaniels, 106
Spann, Otis, 169, 268, 292, 316, 318
Spaulding, Henry, 33
Spirit of Memphis Quartet, 236
Spivey, Victoria, 238, 292
"Spring," 219–20
"Square Dance Rock," 130, 350
Stackhouse, Houston, 16, 26, 33, 38–39, 45–47, 168
Staple Singers, 107
State Line of Arkansas and Missouri. *See* **Club 61**
States Records, 83, 87, 107–09, 119, 271
Stax Records, 68, 217–18, 233
"Steel Guitar Rag," 64, 130, 305, 367
Stevenson, Arthur Lee. *See* Kansas City Red
Steve's Place. *See* **Roadhouse**
Stevie (drummer), 212
Stewart, Jim, 218
Sticks (Roadhouse owner), 183
Stidham, Arbee, 21–22, 78, 105, 107–09, 156–57, 159, 217–18, 271, 348
Stokes, Frank, 32
Stone, Henry, 52–54, 57, 142
"Stormy Monday," 284, 364
Strachwitz, Chris, 3, 65, 166, 168, 170, 252, 253, 255–56, 261, 264, 281, 289–91, 295–96, 301–03, 313, 324
"Strung–Out Woman Blues," 290, 365
Stuart, Fla., 50
Stuckey, Fred, 281
Sumlin, Hubert, 78, 277

Sun Records, 12, 57–66, 68, 69, 96, 105, 112, 252, 273–74, 291
Sunnyland Charles, 162
Sunnyland Slim (Albert Luandrew), 21, 22, 42, 70, 361
Sunset Lounge (Chicago Heights, Ill.), 44
Super Chef Lounge (Waterloo, Iowa), 195
Swan, Frank, 124, 143, 178
Swastika Records, 225
"Swear to Tell the Truth," 124, 130, 138, 169, 224, 286, 291, 350, 357
"Sweet Angel," 54–56, 346
Sweet Black Angel, 276, 362
"Sweet Black Angel," 275, 362
"Sweet Brown Angel," 140, 354
"Sweet Home Chicago," 272, 276, 361, 362
"Sweet Little Angel," 55
"Sweet Sixteen," 294
"Sweet Soozie," 113, 349
"Swingin' at Theresa's," 294, 365
Swinging Changes, 113, 348
Syd (Jive Club owner), 84
Sykes, Roosevelt, 107, 276

"Take Me Back to East St. Louis," 255, 360, 364
"Talkin' About Me," 285
Tampa, Fla., 50–51, 71, 243
Tampa Red (Hudson Woodbridge), 17, 55, 168, 254, 256, 264
Tampan, Andre, 333
Tampan, Cathy, 333
Tampan, Waldine, 333
"Tanya," 140, 179, 354
Tarpon Springs, Fla., 50
Taylor, Eddie, 281, 303, 365
Taylor, Koko, 292, 319
Taylor, Robert "Dudlow," 26–28, 45–46
Taylor, Robert "Pops," 319
Taylor, Roosevelt "Hound Dog," 7, 294
Taylor Sisters, 142–43, 178, 355. *See also* Earlettes
Taylor, Ted, 189
Taylor, Walter, 37
"TB Blues" (Jimmie Rodgers), 238